Gangster
Film
READER

Other Limelight Editions by the Same Authors
The Vampire Film
More Things Than Are Dreamt Of
What Ever Happened to Robert Aldrich?
Film Noir Reader
Film Noir Reader 2
Horror Film Reader
Film Noir Reader 3 (with Robert Porfirio)
Film Noir Reader 4

Other Books
David Lean and His Films
Film Noir: An Encyclopedic Reference to the American Style (with Elizabeth Ward)
The Noir Style
Film Noir (Taschen Film Series)
L.A. Noir: The City as Character
Roger Corman: Metaphysics on a Shoestring

Also by Alain Silver
The Samurai Film
The Film Director's Team (with Elizabeth Ward)
Raymond Chandler's Los Angeles (with Elizabeth Ward)

Also by James Ursini
The Life and Times of Preston Sturges, an American Dreamer
The Modern Amazons: Warrior Women On-Screen (with Dominique Mainon)

Gangster Film

READER

Edited by

Alain Silver and James Ursini

LIMELIGHT EDITIONS

Published in 2007 by Limelight Editions
512 Newark Pompton Turnpike
Pompton Plains, New Jersey 07444

Printed in the United States of America

Book design by Snow Creative Services

Library of Congress Cataloging-in-Publication Data is available upon request.

ISBN-10: 0-87910-332-9
ISBN-13: 978-0-87910-332-3

The editors are grateful for permission to reprint copyrighted material as detailed in the Acknowledgments.

www.limelighteditions.com

Contents

Part Three: Contemporary Views

Acknowledgments

As with our five previous anthologies most of the illustrations contained herein are from the editors' personal collections. Others were kindly loaned by David Chierichetti, Robert Porfirio, and Lee Sanders. Scene stills are reproduced courtesy of ABC Circle, AIP, Allied Artists, Columbia, Dreamworks SKG, HBO, MGM, Miramax, New Line, Office Kitano, Paramount, RKO, Rim Film, Selznick International, Sony Pictures, Toei, 20th Century-Fox, United Artists, Universal, and Warner Bros. Filmographic research was done at the AMPAS Library and on-line at the Internet Movie Database (imdb.com). Except as noted below all the articles are Copyright © 2006 by the individual authors and are printed here by permission.

"The Gangster as Tragic Hero" originally appeared in *The Partisan Review* (February 1948), copyright © Robert Warshow 1948, and is reprinted by permission of Peter Warshow.

"*Scarface*" originally appeared in *Howard Hawks* (Garden City, New York: Doubleday, 1968), copyright © Robin Wood 1968, and is reprinted by permission of the author.

"The Gangster Film" originally appeared in *The Gangster Film* (London: Zwemmer, 1970), copyright © John Baxter 1970, and is reprinted by permission of the author.

"Iconography of the Gangster Film" originally appeared in *Underworld USA* (New York: Viking, 1972), copyright © Colin McArthur 1972, and is reprinted by permission of the author.

"*Little Caesar* and Its Role in the Gangster Film Genre" originally appeared in the *Journal of Popular Film and Television*; vol. 1, no. 3 (Summer 1972) and was revised in *American Film Genres* (Chicago: Nelson Hall, 1985), copyright © Stuart Kaminsky 1972, and is reprinted by permission of the author.

"*Yakuza-eiga*: A Primer" originally appeared in *Film Comment*, vol. 10, no. 1 (January–February 1974), copyright © Paul Schrader 1974, and is reprinted by permission of the author.

"Big Funerals: The Hollywood Gangster, 1927–1933" originally appeared in *Film Comment*, vol. 13, no. 3 (May–June 1977), copyright © Andrew Sarris 1977, and is reprinted by permission of the author.

"Post-Code Gangster Movies" originally appeared in *Gangsters on the Screen* (New York: Franklin Watts, 1978), copyright © Frank Manchel 1979, and is reprinted by permission of the author.

"All in the Family, the *Godfather* Saga" originally appeared in *Crime Movies: From Griffith to the Godfather—and Beyond* (New York: Norton, 1980), copyright © Carlos Clarens 1980, and is reprinted by permission of W.W. Norton & Company, Inc.

"A Study in Ambiguity: *The Godfather* and the American Gangster Movie Tradition" originally appeared at http://www.crimeculture.com/Contents/Articles-Spring05/Godfather.html copyright © Geoff Fordham 2004, and is reprinted by permission of the author.

"De Palma's Postmodern *Scarface* and the Simulacrum of Class" is adapted from an original publication in *Criticism* (Winter 1993), copyright © Ronald Bogue 1993 & 2006, and is reprinted by permission of the author.

"Yoked Together by Violence: *Prizzi's Honor* as a Generic Hybrid" originally appeared in *Film Criticism*, vol. 22, no. 1 (Fall 1997), copyright © Tricia Welsch 1997, and is reprinted by permission of the author.

"Hits, Whacks, and Smokes: The Celluloid Gangster as Horror Icon" originally appeared in *Post Script: Essays in Film & the Humanities*, vol. 21, no. 3 (Summer 2002), copyright © Catherine Don Diego 2002, and is reprinted by permission of the author.

"Family Values and Feudal Codes: The Social Politics of America's 21st-Century Gangster" originally appeared in *Journal of Popular Culture*, vol. 37, no. 4 (May 2004), copyright © Ingrid Walker (Fields) 2004, and is reprinted by permission of the author and *Journal of Popular Culture*.

Portions of "The Gangster According to Aldrich" originally appeared in *Robert Aldrich: A Guide to References and Resources* (Boston: G. K. Hall), copyright © 1979, and "Robert Aldrich: A Critical Study," master's thesis, UCLA, copyright © 1973.

"Fukasaku and Scorsese: Yakuzas and Gangsters" originally appeared in the Web journal *Eiga* (http://es.geocities.com/eiga9/articulos/fukasakuandscorseseindex.html, July 11, 2003), copyright © Joaquín da Silva 2003, and is reprinted by permission of the author.

Gangster
Film
READER

The tommy gun as phallic substitute: Charles Bronson as the title character and Susan Cabot as his "moll" in Roger Corman's *Machine Gun Kelly* (1958).

Introduction

Alain Silver

> He is not responding spontaneously to given reality; he is responding to
> some thing, or word, or gesture, which automatically brings into play a
> previously installed suggestion.
>
> Aldous Huxley, "Knowledge and Understanding" (1956)

The history of any genre can be purely quantitative, and certainly schol-
arship based on statistics can offer insights. However, such a focus, or one
that is structural or cultural or from any perspective not primarily aesthetic,
can easily overlook the key concept in any film genre, which is, of course,
"film." There is no question that the gangster film in the United States in the
1930s coincided with very real and very sensational gangsterism at large in
American society. *Little Caesar* (1931), *The Public Enemy* (1931), and *Scarface*
(1932) borrowed liberally from the newspapers, magazines, and books of the
era.[1] With the release of just these three motion pictures in barely more than
a year's time, Hollywood quintessentially defined the genre. The characters,
the situations, and the icons from fast cars to fancy fedoras established the
catalogue of "things" that create the context Huxley cites, that defined the
genre expectations associated with the gangster film, and that remain in force
to this day.

Unquestionably there were also dramatic elements in the exploits of those
real gangsters and the G-men or other members of the law-enforcement community who strove to bring them to justice. The violent and dramatic deaths
of Dillinger and of Bonnie and Clyde were just that. What 1934 screenwriter
could have concocted a more spectacular Hollywood ending than the final
shooting of Lester Gillis, better known as Baby Face Nelson? After crashing
his disabled car, Gillis picked up his tommy gun and strode blasting away
toward two pursuing federal agents crouched behind their own vehicle. Before
they died, they shot Gillis seventeen times. In the epilogue, his partner and
wife drove Gillis in the agents' car to receive the last rites from a local priest.
Or consider the alternate versions of the apprehension of George "Machine
Gun" Kelly. As reenacted in *The FBI Story* (1959), when confronted by agents,
Kelly's reaction is the opposite of Gillis': he throws up his hands and shouts
"Don't shoot, G-men, don't shoot!" In the "real" version, a hung-over Kelly is

surprised at the front door, in the bedroom, or the bathroom by a Memphis police officer with a sawed-off shotgun; and if, in fact, armed FBI agents had been present they would have been subject to arrest themselves, as they were not licensed to carry until the following year.

Just one month after the FBI was allowed to carry weapons in May 1934, Hollywood handed a weapon to the Hays Office by permitting them actually to enforce the four-year-old Motion Picture Code.[2] The Code's preamble states that crimes:

> shall never be presented in such a way as to throw sympathy with the crime as against law and justice or to inspire others with a desire for imitation.

1. Murder
   a. The technique of murder must be presented in a way that will not inspire imitation.
   b. Brutal killings are not to be presented in detail.
   c. Revenge in modern times shall not be justified.

2. Methods of Crime should not be explicitly presented.
   a. Theft, robbery, safe-cracking, and dynamiting of trains, mines, buildings, etc., should not be detailed in method.
   b. Arson must subject to the same safeguards.
   c. The use of firearms should be restricted to the essentials.
   d. Methods of smuggling should not be presented.[3]

Under these conditions unfettered portrayals of the rise and fall of figures such as Rico in *Little Caesar*, Tom Powers in *The Public Enemy*, and Tony Camonte in *Scarface* were no longer possible in studio productions. The explicit and implicit violence and sexuality of the early gangster films was a successful combination for the studios. Although nothing in the pre-Code movies approached such sensationalist images as Bonnie and Clyde's bullet-riddled sedan or Dillinger on a morgue table, there was a clear equation of sex and violence and even a suggestion of the gangster as satyr that could not be revisited for decades.

The gangster as satyr: the infamous morgue shot of Dillinger appearing to be munificently endowed and another angle revealing that the first is a fabrication.

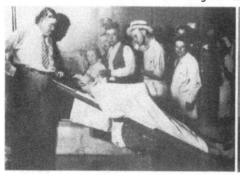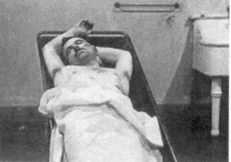

One can postulate that a pre-Code audience was somewhat divided in its view of movies such as *Little Caesar.* Clearly, even prior to enforcement of the stipulation that "the sympathy of the audience should never be thrown to the side of crime, wrongdoing, evil or sin,"[4] most moviegoers might not have empathized with the murderous Rico or a character who whistles a Donizetti aria while he ambushes and kills a man, the action that introduces Tony Camonte in *Scarface.* It is equally clear that shocking events sell not just newspapers but also movie tickets. "Public Enemy Number 1" John Dillinger was shot down outside a movie theater after witnessing the exploits of Clark Gable as the racketeer Blackie Gallagher in *Manhattan Melodrama.* For Depression-era audiences, whose suspicion and even resentment of establishment figures was likely, the avarice and attendant ruthlessness of such gangster characters could be interpreted at some level as a rebellion against the moneyed and powerful. "Populist" armed robbers such as Dillinger and Bonnie and Clyde had fans who actually cheered their deadly exploits, which they perceived as fighting back against those unseen powers responsible for the turmoil of the Depression.

The movie industry flourished as never before during the Depression with both escapist and non-escapist fare. Like the Western, the war movie, the horror film, or any other genre, the popularity of the gangster film has waxed and waned. Whether inhibited by enforcement of the Code or, as Thomas Doherty asserts in his study of pre-Code Hollywood, simply because the gangster film went into a natural decline, the end of the 1930s saw far fewer Rico and Camonte and Powers clones on U.S. screens.[5]

Commercial enterprises all, tabloids, newsreels, and books of the period freely conflated fact with fiction; but when movie gangsters die, it is pure drama. However enthralled the audience may be, no one mistakes the fiction for the world beyond the edges of the screen. Whether from a gritty, sensationalist gangster film or a musical with numbers staged by Busby Berkeley, many moviegoers trudged home after two hours of escape in the theater to cold-water flats with bare cupboards. Even as they included disclaimers or scenes of public outrage, the filmmakers of that—or any—era depended on middle- and lower-class audiences and benefited from any content that could be both escapist and proletarian.

The term gangster is purported to have originated in an Ohio newspaper in 1896 (the term gang, to mean a group of persons engaged in an ongoing enterprise, having evolved from its earliest, maritime association, cited as 1607 in the Oxford English Dictionary). As elaborated in several of the essays contained herein, the origins of the gangster film is still open to debate. Many would cite D. W. Griffith's 1912 short *Musketeers of Pig Alley*; but the gunmen on horseback riding across the New Jersey countryside in *The Great Train Robbery* (1903) were gangsters, too. As with our first *Film Noir Reader*, the purpose of this volume was not to define a film movement or genre—which is best left to the creators of the motion pictures—but to assemble a group of essays to give an introductory overview using both reprints of seminal articles and new essays.

Given that, where else could we begin but with Robert Warshow's celebrated piece, published nearly sixty years ago, examining the relationship between the audience and the gangster as a tragic urban figure. Explicitly or implicitly, Warshow's assertion that the gangster genre "has been a consistent and astonishingly complete presentation of the modern sense of tragedy" resonates through all the writing that follows. Part One continues chronologically with a selection from Robin Wood's study of Howard Hawks. Wood's unusual assertion that *Scarface* "belongs with the comedies" introduces his proposition that a gangster character's monstrous actions will not prevent him or her from retaining the audience's sympathy. According to John Baxter, in the introduction to his book-length study of the gangster film, even before it got ammo for its gun the Hays Office issued a specific memorandum proscribing its members from depicting the exploits of John Dillinger. Baxter surveys the evolution of the genre by comparing real mobsters and Hollywood's reprocessing of them. Two other long-out-of-print books are excerpted in Part One. Colin McArthur discusses the gangster figure within and without his own genre, as "the violence, suffering and *angst*" on the faces of the actors carried over into the thriller and film noir. Frank Manchel details how Hollywood altered its depiction of the gangster and phased out "old formulas," culminating with Bogart's depiction of "Mad Dog" Roy Earle in *High Sierra* in 1941. Stuart Kaminsky's essay focuses on *Little Caesar* as the seminal work in defining the gangster prototype. As he states, although *Little Caesar*

The earliest gangsters on film: *The Great Train Robbery* (top) and *Musketeers of Pig Alley.*

may not be the best example in terms of "the quality of the film . . . its contributions to the genre . . . are considerable." Noting that "few film historians have taken [George] Bancroft seriously as a prototype of the gangster hero," in addressing the period that inspired Warshow's perception of a "tragic hero" Andrew Sarris reaches back to the silent era and the hero's portrayal in von Sternberg's gangster pictures, as well as to other more obscure examples from 1927 to 1933 that differed from the sagas of Rico and Camonte and Powers. In the last book excerpt, Carlos Clarens explores the social, economic, and political context of the first movies in the *Godfather* saga. Finally, Part One also includes Paul Schrader's "primer" on *yakuza-eiga*, the Japanese version of the gangster film that flourished in the 1960s and continues to influence new generations of moviemakers around the world.

In Part Two, Case Studies, recent essays—most of them written for this volume—focus on individual films and/or filmmakers. Reynold Humphries analyzes in depth *The Gangster*, a compact and quirky movie with a title character who is anything but a prototype; Glenn Erickson does likewise with the better-known *White Heat*, the second of what he dubs "Cagney's two classic bookend star appearances in 1931 and 1949," wherein McArthur found Cagney's "physical dynamism [to be] interpreted as psychotic." Twenty years after Carlos Clarens, Geoff Fordham reconsiders *The Godfather* and the cycles of genre from a more distant perspective. In his reflection on the 1983 remake of *Scarface*, Ronald Bogue ranges from metanarrative to set dressing to discover why a postmodern Tony Camonte-*cum*-Montana wants you to "say hello to my little friend." Tricia Welsch examines *Prizzi's Honor* as "a canny hybrid" that uses narrative stratagems from screwball comedy. Constantine Verevis takes Scorsese's description of his second feature, *Mean Streets*, as "an anthropological study" and considers the director's later *GoodFellas* and *Casino*. James Ursini writes a coda to Schrader's primer on *yakuza-eiga* by examining Takeshi Kitano's recent work in that arena; and I search for an alternative to Warshow's tragic, urban figure in a reconsideration of Robert Aldrich's *The Grissom Gang*.

Part Three offers an even wider range of 21st-century perspectives on the genre with three reprinted essays from the last five years and five new pieces. Tony Williams chronicles, first, the British gangster film, whose history runs parallel to its better-known counterpart, and second, the more recent Hong Kong productions, which borrow from Japanese, American, and other cinemas to create "a more diverse genre and . . . distinctive brand" of Triad figures a world away from mafiosi or yakuza. Back in Hollywood, Sheri Biesen explains how American gangsters were reformed both literally and figuratively during World War II; and Dominique Mainon explores the literal and figurative roles of women in the crime genre. Seeking a different perspective, Catherine Don Diego finds synchronicity between the gangster and the horror genres. She describes how "creating a moral monster out of a criminal celebrity increases his ability to terrorize not just his victims, but society as a whole" and permits the gangster genre to cross over into horror. Ingrid Walker reflects on the state of cultural values in the 21st century and on an unlikely synthesis now creating codes for the fin-de-siècle gangster from gangsta rap and the samurai ethos. Finally, I look back at the themes and style of the gangster genre and film noir, at how the criminal figures of the gangster film penetrated to the heart of film noir and how the style and motifs used in the early examples of the genre came along for the ride.

Since our first reader a decade ago, the proliferation of DVD releases from studio archives has made the preeminent examples of just about any genre or movement available more or less on demand around the world. In the last two years our own reflections on the noir cycle have moved from the page to the audio track in commentaries for over a dozen releases by Fox and Warner Bros.[6] Part of the inspiration for this book was a result of my cursory participation in the Warner Bros. Gangster Collection. More than ever we can conclude this introduction with our usual admonishment that what comes first is watching the films themselves. So, to paraphrase the caveat from the introduction to *Film Noir Reader 2*, if the reader has not seen a key film such as *Little Caesar, The Public Enemy,* or *Scarface* (Hawks or De Palma), now would be a good time to pause, insert a bookmark, go to your local video outlet or add to your queue, and fill that gap.

Notes

1. The U.S. release dates were *Little Caesar,* January 9, 1931; *The Public Enemy,* April 23, 1931; and *Scarface,* March 31, 1932.

2. Named after Will H. Hays, a former postmaster general hired to preside over the Motion Pictures Producers and Distributors Association shortly after its formation in 1922, the Code Office promulgated a list of recommendations in 1927 and a formal, written Code in March 1930. The restrictions of the Code were easily ignored, however, until June 1934, with the establishment of the Production Code Administration and a requirement that all motion pictures produced by Association members obtain a certificate of approval prior to their release.

3. From "Particular Applications, I. Crimes Against the Law" in "A Code to Govern the Making of Talking, Synchronized and Silent Motion Pictures. Formulated and formally adopted by The Association of Motion Picture Producers, Inc. and The Motion Picture Producers and Distributors of America, Inc. in March 1930," ArtsReformation.com (February 1, 2000), at http://www.artsreforma-tion.com/a001/hays-code.html (accessed April 17, 2006). The opening titles for the pre-Code pictures are clearly influenced by the sentiments of the MPPDA code. *Scarface*'s opening has three title cards, which conclude: "Every incident in this motion picture is the reproduction of an actual occurrence, and the purpose of this picture is to demand of the government: 'What are you going to do about it?' The government is your government. What are _YOU_ going to do about it?"

4. Ibid., "Reasons Underlying the General Principles, I."

5. Thomas Doherty, *Pre-Code Hollywood: Sex, Immorality, and Insurrection in American Cinema, 1930–1934* (New York: Columbia University Press, 1999).

6. Cf. our commentaries on the gangster/noir DVD releases of *Kiss of Death, Street with No Name, Panic in the Streets, Out of the Past,* and *House of Bamboo,* as well as the other noir titles *The Dark Corner, Boomerang, The Lodger, Thieves' Highway, Call Northside 777, The Lady in the Lake, Murder, My Sweet,* and *Crossfire.*

PART
ONE

Seminal
Work

Edward G. Robinson as Cesare Enrico Bandello after the fall:
the urban gangster stripped of his pride.

The Gangster as Tragic Hero

(1948)

Robert Warshow

America, as a social and political organization, is committed to a cheerful view of life. It could not be otherwise. The sense of tragedy is a luxury of aristocratic societies, where the face of the individual is not conceived of as having a direct and legitimate political importance, being determined by a fixed and supra-political—that is, non-controversial—moral order or fate. Modern equalitarian societies, however, whether democratic or authoritarian in their political forms, always base themselves on the claim that they are making life happier; the avowed function of the modern state, at least in its ultimate terms, is not only to regulate social relations, but also to determine the quality and the possibilities of human life in general. Happiness thus becomes the chief political issue—in a sense, the only political issue—and for that reason it can never be treated as an issue at all. If an American or a Russian is unhappy, it implies a certain reprobation of his society, and therefore, by a logic of which we can all recognize the necessity, it becomes an obligation of citizenship to be cheerful; if the authorities find it necessary, the citizen may even be compelled to make a public display of his cheerfulness on important occasions, just as he may be conscripted into the army in time of war.

Naturally this civic responsibility rests most strongly upon the organs of mass culture. The individual citizen may still be permitted his private unhappiness so long as it does not take on political significance, the extent of this tolerance being determined by how large an area of private life the society can accommodate. But every production of mass culture is a public act and must conform with accepted notions of the public good. Nobody seriously questions the principle that it is the function of mass culture to maintain public morale, and certainly nobody in the mass audience objects to having his morale maintained.[1] At a time when the normal condition of the citizen is a state of anxiety, euphoria spreads over our culture like the broad smile of an idiot. In terms of attitudes towards life, there is very little difference between a "happy movie" like *Good News*, which ignores death and suffering, and a "sad" movie like *A Tree Grows in Brooklyn*, which uses death and suffering as incidents in the service of higher optimism.

11

But, whatever its effectiveness as a source of consolation and a means of pressure for maintaining "positive" social attitudes, this optimism is fundamentally satisfying to no one, not even to those who would be most disoriented without its support. Even within the area of mass culture, there always exists a current of opposition, seeking to express by whatever means are available to it that sense of desperation and inevitable failure which optimism itself helps to create. Most often, this opposition is confined to rudimentary or semi-literate forms: in mob politics and journalism, for example, or in certain kinds of religious enthusiasm. When it does enter the field of art, it is likely to be disguised or attenuated: in an unspecific form of expression like jazz, in the basically harmless nihilism of the Marx Brothers, in the continually reasserted strain of hopelessness that often seems to be the real meaning of soap opera. The gangster film is remarkable in that it fills the need for disguise (though not sufficiently to avoid arousing uneasiness) without requiring any serious distortion. From its beginning, it has been a consistent and astonishingly complete presentation of the modern sense of tragedy.[2]

In its initial character, the gangster film is simply one example of the movies' constant tendency to create fixed dramatic patterns that can be repeated indefinitely with a reasonable expectation of profit. One gangster film follows another as one musical or one Western follows another. But this rigidity is not necessarily opposed to the requirements of art. There have been very successful types of art in the past which developed such specific and detailed conventions as almost to make individual examples of the type interchangeable. This is true, for example, of Elizabethan revenge tragedy and Restoration comedy.

For such a type to be successful means that its conventions have imposed themselves upon the general consciousness and become the accepted vehicles of a particular set of attitudes and a particular aesthetic effect. One goes to any individual example of the type with very definite expectations, and originality is to be welcomed only in the degree that it intensifies the expected experience without fundamentally altering it. Moreover, the relationship between the conventions which go to make up such a type and the real experience of its audience or the real facts of whatever situation it pretends to describe is of only secondary importance and does not determine its aesthetic force. It is only in an ultimate sense that the type appeals to its audience's experience of reality; much more immediately, it appeals to previous experience of the type itself: it creates its own field of reference.

Thus the importance of the gangster film, and the nature and intensity of its emotional and aesthetic impact, cannot be measured in terms of the place of the gangster himself or the importance of the problem of crime in American life. Those European movie-goers who think there is a gangster on every corner in New York are certainly deceived, but defenders of the "positive" side of American culture are equally deceived if they think it relevant to point out that most Americans have never seen a gangster. What matters is that the experience of the gangster as an experience of art is universal to Americans. There is almost nothing we understand better or react to more

Rico (Edward G. Robinson), with his crony Otero (George Stone), knows that he may be brought down by his tragic flaw: "This is what I get for liking a guy too much."

readily or with quicker intelligence. The Western film, though it seems never to diminish in popularity, is for most of us no more than the folklore of the past, familiar and understandable only because it has been repeated so often. The gangster film comes much closer. In ways that we do not easily or willingly define, the gangster speaks for us, expressing that part of the American psyche which rejects the qualities and the demands of modern life, which rejects "Americanism" itself.

The gangster is the man of the city, with the city's language and knowledge, with its queer and dishonest skills and its terrible daring, carrying his life in his hands like a placard, like a club. For everyone else, there is at least the theoretical possibility of another world—in that happier American culture which the gangster denies, the city does not really exist; it is only a more crowded and more brightly lit country—but for the gangster there is only the city; he must inhabit it in order to personify it: not the real city, but that dangerous and sad city of the imagination which is so much more important, which is the modern world. And the gangster—though there are real gangsters—is also, and primarily, a creature of the imagination. The real city, one might say, produces only criminals; the imaginary city produces the gangster: he is what we want to be and what we are afraid we may become.

Thrown into the crowd without background or advantage, with only those ambiguous skills which the rest of us—the real people of the real city—can only pretend to have, the gangster is required to make his own way, to make his life and impose it on others. Usually, when we come upon him, he has already made his choice or the choice has already been made for him, it doesn't matter which: we are not permitted to ask whether at some point he could have chosen to be something else than what he is.

The gangster's activity is actually a form of rational enterprise, involving fairly definite goals and various techniques for achieving them. But this rationality is usually no more than a vague background: we know, perhaps, that the gangster sells liquor or that he operates a numbers racket; often we are not given even that much information. So his activity becomes a kind of pure criminality: he hurts people. Certainly our response to the gangster film is most consistently and most universally a response to sadism; we gain the double satisfaction of participating vicariously in the gangster's sadism and then seeing it turned against the gangster himself.

But on another level the quality of irrational brutality and the quality of rational enterprise become one. Since we do not see the rational and routine

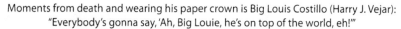

Moments from death and wearing his paper crown is Big Louis Costillo (Harry J. Vejar): "Everybody's gonna say, 'Ah, Big Louie, he's on top of the world, eh!'"

aspects of the gangster's behavior, the practice of brutality—the quality of unmixed criminality—becomes the totality of his career. At the same time, we are always conscious that the whole meaning of this career is a drive for success: the typical gangster film presents a steady upward progress followed by a very precipitate fall. Thus brutality itself becomes at once the means to success and the content of success—a success that is defined in its most general terms, not as accomplishment or specific gain, but simply as the unlimited possibility of aggression. (In the same way, film presentations of businessmen tend to make it appear that they achieve their success by talking on the telephone and holding conferences and that success *is* talking on the telephone and holding conferences.)

From this point of view, the initial contact between film and its audience is an agreed conception of human life: that man is a being with the possibilities of success or failure. This principle, too, belongs to the city; one must emerge from the crowd or else one is nothing. On that basis the necessity of the action is established, and it progresses by inalterable paths to the point where the gangster lies dead and the principle has been modified: there is really only one possibility—failure. The final meaning of the city is anonymity and death.

In the opening scene of *Scarface*, we are shown a successful man; we know he is successful because he has just given a party of opulent proportions and because he is called Big Louie. Through some monstrous lack of caution, he permits himself to be alone for a few moments. We understand from this immediately that he is about to be killed. No convention of the gangster film is more strongly established than this: it is dangerous to be alone. And yet the very conditions of success make it impossible not to be alone, for success is always the establishment of an *individual* pre-eminence that must be imposed on others, in whom it automatically arouses hatred; the successful man is an outlaw. The gangster's whole life is an effort to assert himself as an individual, to draw himself out of the crowd, and he always dies because he is an individual; the final bullet thrusts him back, makes him, after all, a failure. "Mother of God," says the dying Little Caesar, "is this the end of Rico?"—speaking of himself thus in the third person because what has been brought low is not the undifferentiated man, but the individual with a name, the gangster, the success; even to himself he is a creature of the imagination. (T. S. Eliot has pointed out that a number of Shakespeare's tragic heroes have this trick of looking at themselves dramatically; their true identity, the thing that is destroyed when they die, is something outside themselves—not a man, but a style of life, a kind of meaning.)

At bottom, the gangster is doomed because he is under the obligation to succeed, not because the means he employs are unlawful. In the deeper layers of the modern consciousness, all means are unlawful, every attempt to succeed is an act of aggression, leaving one alone and guilty and defenseless among enemies: one is punished for success. This is our intolerable dilemma: that failure is a kind of death and success is evil and dangerous, is—ultimately impossible. The effect of the gangster film is to embody this dilemma in the person of the gangster and resolve it by his death. The dilemma is resolved because it is his death, not ours. We are safe; for the moment, we can acquiesce in our failure, we can choose to fail.

Notes

1. In her testimony before the House Committee on Un-American Activities, Mrs. Leila Rogers said that the movie *None But the Lonely Heart* was un-American because it was gloomy. Like so much else that was said during the unhappy investigation of Hollywood, this statement was at once stupid and illuminating. One knew immediately what Mrs. Rogers was talking about; she had simply been insensitive enough to carry her philistinism to its conclusion.

2. Efforts have been made from time to time to bring the gangster film into line with the prevailing optimism and social constructiveness of our culture; *Kiss of Death* is a recent example. These efforts are usually unsuccessful; the reasons for their lack of success are interesting in themselves, but I shall not discuss them here.

"Prevailing optimism": landlady Mrs. Keller (Eda Heinemann) stands by as newly released convict Nick Bianco (Victor Mature) waits for a glimpse of his girlfriend Nettie.

Paul Muni as Tony "Scarface" Camonte.

Scarface

(*from* Howard Hawks, *1968)*

Robin Wood

It may seem perverse to approach the comedies via a gangster film of exceptional ferocity, almost the only Hawks film in which the protagonist dies. But
Scarface belongs with the comedies.

There are interesting parallels between *Scarface* and Godard's *Les
Carabiniers*. Though utterly different in style and method, both have leading
characters who consistently perform monstrous, violent actions which the
films never condone, yet who retain the audience's sympathy to the end, and
for similar reasons. Godard gives his Michelangelo the characteristics, not
only of a primitive, but of a young child, an innocent immune from moral
judgments because he has never developed moral awareness. Far from weak-
ening the statement of horror and despair, this intensifies it.

Tony Camonte (Paul Muni), the "hero" of *Scarface*, is always touching and
eventually pathetic, because he too is an innocent. Indeed, he captures and
keeps more of the spectator's affection than Michelangelo; this is surprising,
because Hawks allows us to see him killing sympathetic characters (Guino
Rinaldo), where Godard keeps the slaughter in *Les Carabiniers* strictly impersonal; but Hawks' method, though consistently objective, allows us much closer
to the characters than Godard's. There is one basic difference between the two
films: *Scarface* remains firmly within the conventions of naturalism whereas
Les Carabiniers refuses all such limitations (thereby discovering limitations of
its own). The difference is apparent in the "childlike" presentation of Tony
and Michelangelo (and even in their names). Tony's primitivism is entirely
credible naturalistically, where Michelangelo's infantilism is very stylized.

Tony is introduced as a squat shadow, evoking ape or Neanderthal. His
fascinated attraction to gaudy trappings (loud dressing gowns, ties, jewelry,
etc.) recalls the savage's fondness for beads. His attempts at elegance—large
acreage of handkerchief protruding from breast pocket, huge tie—are grotesque. With this goes his ignorance. When Poppy (Karen Morley) tells him
that jewelry on men is "effeminate" he is boyishly delighted, automatically
assuming a compliment. When she tells him his place is "kind of gaudy," his
reply is "Isn't it though? Glad you like it." When he rises to power as Johnny

Lovo's right-hand man, he wears a new shirt each day, sports an even fancier dressing-gown than Lovo's, boasts to Poppy of having several more suits, "all different colors," jumps up and down on the bed showing it to her, saying, "It's got inside springs. Bought it at an auction." His attempts at seduction show a childlike naiveté which eventually, touching Poppy, becomes an important factor in her capitulation. His infantile confusion of values—woman and dressing-gown placed on roughly the same level, half gaudy toys, half status symbols—anticipates interestingly Michelangelo's response to the *carabinier's* catalogue of the treasures of the world that he will bring back as loot.

This essential innocence is reflected in other characters. The fat Italian gangster Costillo, celebrating at a New Year's Eve party, paper-hatted amidst a debris of festoons among which is a discarded bra, boasts childishly of his prosperity (he is about to get shot), mentioning in the same breath the girl and the automobile that he can now afford. Guino Rinaldo (George Raft), when Cesca (Ann Dvorak) calls on him, is cutting out paper dolls; and it is he, the tough gangster, who is seduced by the sheltered Cesca. As Tony comes to kill Guino, Cesca is singing a comic song about a train-driver, complete with "poop-poop" noises. Tony's illiterate secretary has continual difficulty with telephones: he is afraid of them, and at one point wants to shoot one. Both here and in *Les Carabiniers* we are made to feel the frightening discrepancy between the achievements of civilization and the actual level of culture attained by the individuals who are its by-products.

Characteristically—though, considering the ostensible subject of *Scarface*, remarkably—there is little sense of social context. Members of normal society appear only as the merest background figures (waiters in the machine-gunned restaurant, nurses held up in the hospital where Meehan is finished off). Considered too simply, *Scarface* appears a dangerously immoral film. It opens with an explicitly moralizing foreword about "the intention of the producer" and halfway through there is an embarrassingly hammy scene (added by another director, apparently, as a safeguard against censorship) where a newspaper editor accused of sensationalism defends his position, arguing the need to expose outrages. But the film shows remarkably little society either to outrage or to defend. Hawks' naturalism is highly selective: he works by simply eliminating society. Hence in *Scarface* the ostensible subject, society threatened by gangsters, isn't really treated at all. We see almost nothing of the results of the outrages, bomb explosions, machine-gunning, in terms of human suffering. The police are uniformly unsympathetic. Hawks presents his gang wars as kids' games played with real bullets. A sardonic, macabre humor is seldom absent, and some of the outrages are treated as uninhibited farce: Gaffney's machine-gunning of the restaurant, with Tony's secretary struggling to cope with the telephone—an attempt continued, doggedly, throughout the attack, with boiling tea pouring out over his bottom through the bullet-holes in an urn. The film communicates, strongly, a sense of exhilaration: Hawks actually encourages us to share the gangsters' enjoyment of violence. If Tony has the innocence of a child or a savage, he also has the energy and vitality that goes with it.

Tony confronts his coin-flipping henchman Guino Rinaldo (George Raft).

Yet no one with a sensibility more developed than Tony Camonte's could find *Scarface* ultimately immoral. The attitude to Tony is complex. If we regard him sympathetically, we never feel that he is being glorified. His pitiful end is implicit throughout. He is funny and touching because he is an overgrown child, emotionally arrested at an early stage, with no sympathetic awareness of others and no self-awareness. He dies when he loses his essential innocence—when, in a very shadowy, disturbing way, he begins to see himself, and his armor of boyish self-confidence, like his steel shutters ("I got nobody. I'm all alone. My steel shutters don't work"), is no longer any protection.

How, then, does Hawks place this monstrous innocence and its effects? Why, if the killings are often exhilarating and farcical, are they also so disturbing? Hawks faced a difficult problem: how to discover images or references which could be incorporated unostentatiously within the naturalistic conventions? Instead of inviting judgment on the gangsters for subverting the social order, Hawks disturbs our response to the film's burnout with images and leitmotifs, very simple and traditional yet the more evocative because of it, with their accumulated associations. One thinks of the passage from Borges which Godard quotes at the start of *Les Carabiniers*: the writer returns increasingly to the "old metaphors" because they are enriched by past usage.

Scarface and his gang take out their last rival.

The image of the cross pervades the whole film. It is the first thing we see. Every killing is accompanied (often unobtrusively) by a cross, sometimes formed by patterns of light or shadow; the scar on Tony's face is a cross. In the scene of the St. Valentine's Day Massacre the camera moves down from seven crosses, the pattern in a wooden overhang, to show the seven victims. The majority of these are the multiplication-sign form of the cross: a straightforward sign for death, the crossing-out of a human being; but several take the traditional Christian shape. The pervasive image carries associative emotional overtones which contribute importantly to the effect of the killings. Individual instances carry their own overtones. Near the end of the film Tony, incestuously involved with Cesca without understanding the nature of his own feelings, kills Guino out of possessive jealousy; at the first meeting of Guino and Cesca, Guino is seen through a cross formed by the balcony edge and its support. The effect is very unobtrusive. Hawks never sacrifices the action of a scene to symbolism, but we are by that time sufficiently used to the association of the crosses with killings for it to carry an emotional charge. Lighting is of great importance in *Scarface:* in the scene where Gaffney (Boris Karloff) is shown the concrete results of the St. Valentine's Day Massacre, and he, among the most ruthless of the film's killers, is morally outraged, the accompanying cross is a radiant white. At another point the cross, Christian shape, is part of an undertaker's sign, shot from above so that it hangs over the body like a cross at a funeral. The associations give the killings a particular flavor of profanity.

For many of the killings in *Scarface* Hawks finds vivid epitomizing images. In the bowling alley Gaffney rolls a ball, the sound of gunfire tells us he has been killed, and then as the shot continues we watch the progress of the bowling ball until it knocks over all the ninepins. Gaffney will never know his throw was so successful. More than any face contorting and stomach-clutching, the shot conveys the finality of death, in a manner no less moving for being detached and indirect. Later, when Tony shoots Guino for touching Cesca (they are in fact married), Guino dies while the coin he has flipped is still in the air: its falling to the ground, after all the previous occasions on which he has infallibly caught it, conveys the fact of his death with great intensity. The death of Tony's secretary makes similar use of habitual behavior: he dies, mortally wounded by bullets through the door he has just closed, struggling to cope with the telephone that has defeated him throughout the film. But all the comic quality has gone, removed with the ill-fitting hat he automatically takes off as he staggers back from the door: his illiteracy, his unquestioning devotion to Tony, his funny clothes, his total childlike inadequacy in coping with his environment are no longer in the least funny, and we are left with a sense of terrible waste.

Other images and references in *Scarface* associate with the crosses. One in the historical data, the traditional associations of St. Valentine's Day giving the massacre an extra profanity, is neatly underlined by the killers' brutal talk about "bringing you a valentine." Earlier, Gaffney's attack on the restaurant was made under cover of a funeral procession, the machine gun hidden in the hearse. In two scenes flowers are used. Tony's men enter a hospital to finish off Meehan, survivor, though badly injured, of a previous attack. The intensity and terrible poetry of the scene are partly the product of its economy: no preliminaries, simply a brief sequence of shots of the gangsters, carrying bouquets, holding up terrified nurses in a corridor, opening a door beyond which is a heavily bandaged figure in a bed, with one leg strapped up, unable to move to cover, the leg support casting a cross-shaped shadow on the far wall. The figure is blasted with bullets, then a bouquet is flung in on the body as a parting cynicism. The scene (it is all over in a few seconds) epitomizes the disturbing power of the film. The tension and pace of direction and editing capture a sense of exhilaration: we respond to the uninhibited audacity of the gangsters, their freedom from all social and moral restraints, their ability to perform outrageous actions in the face of social institutions. At the same time the horror of the scene is overwhelming: only a Tony in the audience could find it *merely* exhilarating. As elsewhere in Hawks' work (*Monkey Business* offering the extremest instance), our yearnings for total irresponsibility are evoked to be chastised. Through the images of cross and flowers, the utter helplessness of the victim, the values appealed to are absolute rather than social; our horror derives from deeper sources than the violation of social stability.

The other scene centered on a flower is equally complex and disturbing. Guino Rinaldo brings Tony a rose as a token that he has killed a rival who ran a flower shop. Tony later in the scene gives it to Poppy, whom he is trying to seduce. The scene evokes the rose's traditional associations with love and beauty, tenderness and transience, and juxtaposes these with our knowledge of its actual *dramatic* significance.

Hawks, like Godard, uses the arts to suggest more developed values beyond the reach of the characters; though the examples in Hawks' film are again much simpler, and entirely integrated in the action. Tony's signature tune, whistled every time he kills (the sextet from Donizetti's *Lucia di Lammermoor*, "Chi me frena?" [What restrains me?]), gives his first appearance an almost surrealist quality: the squat ape-like shadow juxtaposed with the elegant phrases of Italian opera. His visit to the theater and his reactions to the play (*Rain*) anticipate *Les Carabiniers*' cinema scene. Tony does not, like Michelangelo, totally misunderstand the nature of the medium; but his attitude shows a similarly elementary contact. His dimly awakening sense of the existence of moral problems foreshadows his downfall: he is quite unable to grasp their nature, let alone cope with them. He tries to explain the play to his secretary, who prefers "shows with jokes": "This Sadie, she's a girl with a problem. . . . She's what you call disillusioned." He leaves the secretary to find out how the play ends while he goes to another killing that can't wait, and when he gets the garbled report, gives Sadie's solution (she "climbed back in the hay with the army") his delighted approval. His incomprehension of the issues (counterpointed with his further progress in bloodshed) beautifully defines the terrible innocence that permits him to kill and plunder, and which also allows him not to question his attachment to Cesca or his immediate, ferocious jealousy of any man who comes near her.

Tony admonishes his "wanton" sister (Ann Dvorak).

In the scenes of Tony's muddled self-realization and subsequent death the film's moral force becomes finally evident. Far from being a "moral" ending hastily tacked on in an attempt to make an immoral film respectable, it is as inevitable as the ending of *À Bout de Souffle*. Tony is strong only while he remains unaware. The shooting of Guino and Cesca's ensuing outcry are crucial. Tony loses control over her because he is losing control over himself. We see from his facial expression from his inability, now, to hold her, his dim, reluctant realization of what his real feelings for her are. When Tony's secretary dies struggling with the phone, it is Poppy on the other end. All Tony can find to say to her is a vague, confused, "I didn't know," which can refer simply to the dead secretary—Tony hadn't realized that he was hit—or to the realization of his own involvement with Cesca (which makes Poppy no longer of the slightest importance to him). The ambiguity prevents us from applying the words narrowly: they sum up Tony's whole appalling ignorance; after all the massacres, the audacities, the exhilaration, the success, they are all he can find to say for himself. After it, his reaction to Cesca's failure to kill him is "Why didn't you shoot?"—followed by a hysterical defiance of the encircling police which grotesquely parodies the exhilaration of the violence earlier in the film. His hysterical triumphant laughter coincides with Cesca's being struck by a bullet which ricochets off the much-vaunted steel shutter, symbol to Tony of his invulnerability, which he is holding open at that moment. The cross that has accompanied all Tony's killings is appropriately, though ironically, there for the death of his sister; after which his disintegration into blind panic as the gas bombs explode around him, the rising and overpowering clouds of gas providing the perfect visual expression for his bewildered state of mind, the protective innocence punctured stands as judgment on all his past.

The essential condemnation of Tony Camonte, like that of Michel Poiccard in *À Bout de Souffle*, whose anti-social behavior also conveys to the audience an irresistible exhilaration, is not imposed from any external moral standpoint (despite *Scarface*'s foreword to the effect that "justice always catches up with the

"Irresistible exhilaration": Jean-Paul Belmondo as the cheap grifter Poiccard in *À Bout de Souffle*.

criminal who must answer for his sins"), but is arrived at empirically in terms of the character's own development. Tony and Michel condemn themselves, ultimately, because their behavior is self-destructive, not only in the simple, literal sense that it gets them killed, but because it denies them fulfillment of their basic needs. Both directors have the courage to treat their characters' rejection of responsibility and rush toward self-destruction inwardly, with the implicit admission that they are dealing with universal traits and urges. A dangerous method (both films have been accused of immorality); but valid morality must be based on honesty.

The comparison with Godard reveals Hawks' strength and limitations. At first sight *Scarface* seems richer than *Les Carabiniers*. It works brilliantly on a popular narrative level, a dimension that Godard's film doesn't pretend to. Beyond this is the essential stability of Hawks' character and the traditional nature of his art: his successful films are pervaded by a robustness derived from stable values—loyalty, courage, endurance, mastery of self and environment—whereas the emotion underlying and characterizing *Les Carabiniers* is a terrible despair, arising from Godard's exposure to the complexities and confusions, the disintegration of accepted values, inherent in contemporary society. *Les Carabiniers* is a statement about the modern world of a kind Hawks nowhere attempts. This defines him as an artist; it doesn't invalidate him. Hawks takes the state of civilization for granted in a way that has become increasingly difficult for the modern artist, and he has been helped in this by the availability to him of cinematic traditions which manifest themselves in the genres, but his inability to make statements about modem society limits his work, affecting particularly certain of the comedies.

It is with the comedies that *Scarface* unquestionably belongs. It has almost nothing in common with the adventure films (besides the enclosed group); it has almost everything in common with the comedies. The overlapping and combining of farce and horror points ahead to *His Girl Friday*, Tony's destructive innocence to that of Lorelei Lee; in *Monkey Business*, the juxtapositions of ape, savages, and children are clearly related to the presentation of the gangsters in *Scarface*. Above all *Scarface* gives us the essential theme of Hawks' most characteristic comedies. If the adventure films place high value on the sense of responsibility, the comedies derive much of their tension and intensity from the fascination exerted by irresponsibility.

The Gangster Film

(1970)

John Baxter

"Ordinary people of your class," the killer Dancer says contemptuously in Don Siegel's *The Lineup*, "You don't understand the criminal's need for violence." The remark is typical of the modern gangster film. Like them, it implies that the rules of crime are different from those of ordinary society, and force on those who live by them a unique and rigorous ethic. "Crime is only a left-handed form of human endeavor," Louis Calhern says in *The Asphalt Jungle*, conveying in one sentence the code of these haunted people.

Characteristic too is the way in which Dancer's comment hints at social generalization. It is not only the criminal commenting on other criminals; it is the criminal commenting on society, and the forces that encouraged him to enter the half-world of crime. Few gangster films are free of the imputation that criminals are the creation of society rather than rebels against it. It is because this was often in the past true, and may still be, that the gangster film has become the province of men whose political and social views are unconventional.

Our ambiguous attitude to criminals, figures both of menace and glamour, has formed the basic gangster film character, the urban wolf. He is the product of his harsh environment, violent, laconic, and tough, but his involvement in crime seems a matter of chance rather than choice. An urban wolf can equally well be killer or detective, warden or prisoner. The ethics are similar, and all speak the same discursive language. When early gangster films took as their theme the conflict between boyhood friends who end up on opposite sides of the law, the writers, although always giving equal time to statements from both sides on the desirability of the alternatives, were usually forced by the subtlety of the distinction to settle the matter by violence.

Top left: Julian (Robert Keith) tries to reason with Dancer (Eli Wallach) as he menaces some "ordinary people" in *The Lineup*.

Bottom left: Dix (Sterling Hayden) stands by as Doc (Sam Jaffe) confers with Emmerich (Louis Calhern) about "a left-handed form of human endeavor" in *The Asphalt Jungle*.

True to the traditions of the entertainment film, the urban wolves, like Western heroes and the characters of science fiction and fantasy films, have strict and limited dimensions. They are almost always men in early middle age; only they have had the chance to live, and to cultivate the strict moral code which justifies their existence. (The real gangsters were usually young— Al Capone's golden period ended in 1929, when he was 34—but the cinema has never been sensitive to the truth in recording reality, as [a comparison of] real criminals and their screen incarnations show[s].)

A certain ironic humor and mordant philosophy are also common to both gangster and cop, each seeming able to express himself with wit and perception about his relative role in a way real men would find ludicrous. And they are united in their contempt for the amateur, the unprofessional, the "punks" interested only in profit, the "freaks" who kill for fun or terrorize without point. In *The Asphalt Jungle* this coincidence of attitude is intelligently underlined. Cop John McIntire early in the film orders his men to squeeze a witness of information by locking him up, frightening him some more. "Don't you know your job?" he snaps. And later, in an identical mood, gunman Sterling Hayden beats up a man who has tried to double-cross him, and snarls, "What kind of guy are you anyhow? Try to shake us down and don't have the guts to go through with it." For both, the rituals of professionalism seem more important than the formal necessities of crime and detection.

It is idle to generalize too much about gangster films, or any other field of cinema, so immense are the variations, particularly in Hollywood, where most genres have been crossed successfully. Gangsters have appeared in comedies, musicals, horror, and science fiction films, Shakespeare has been done as a gangster film, and there have been films about dogs reincarnated as private eyes and hardened killers moved to repent after hearing Billy Graham. But in general the best have been tied closely to the reality of crime, reflecting public interest in a particular criminal, robbery, or illegal activity. The history of the gangster film is in a sense the history of crime in the United States, and few of the best films have not taken some of their material from the reality of organized crime, which is a part of modern urban life.

Crime in America is an imported vice. No doubt it would have existed had the first waves of migration in the late 19th century not brought to the United States many of the underworld elements of European cities, but it would have been a lesser kind of crime, neither so ferocious nor so well organized as it was to become. With the migrants came representatives of the tightly organized street gangs of French and Italian cities, the violent political activists of Ireland and the Balkans, the blood-loyal mafiosi of Sicily. The influx laid the foundations of the fanatical and brutal criminal society of the twenties [1920s]. As Kenneth Allsop points out, "The gangster of the Prohibition era was almost invariably second-generation American; he was almost invariably a Sicilian, an Irishman, or a Jew." It was mainly from the sons of the 1880s immigrants that the underworld drew its most apt recruits.

Although the Mafia was in New York in the 1890s, its activities were limited by the meager sources of revenue. D. W. Griffith in *The Musketeers of Pig*

Alley (1912) showed how the street gangs of the time existed, ruling a few blocks, getting along on the proceeds of extortion and petty theft, a far cry from the profitable and well-organized activity of Italy, where in many communities the Mafia and local government were often indistinguishable. But the tempo of criminal life quickened in the period following the First World War, when soldiers, demobbed to unemployment, social unrest, and injustice, turned to civil disobedience, union agitation, and sometimes crime as a means of satisfying their taste for violence and their need for the necessities of life.

Into this potentially explosive situation the United States government in 1920 introduced prohibition of liquor, the nation's most disastrous social experiment. The European gangs found themselves with the ingredients of an illegal industry, bootlegging. Fattened by a rising market, already dissatisfied with a lax and cynical government, the public was not inclined to obey a puritan injunction to abstain, and welcomed as social institutions the illegal liquor merchant and secret bar. From among the unemployed ex-soldiers, the gangs drew men who had little respect for a government that had denied them social justice, a work force at once eager to advance and careless of whom they hurt in doing so. All over the United States, but particularly in Chicago, where geographical and social conditions favored the illegal liquor industry, the gangs fastened onto this new source of revenue and used it greedily to establish themselves.

With Prohibition, the legends of crime began. By the middle twenties, the public was becoming aware of certain individuals in the underworld who carried off their careers with flair, arrogance, and a style unusual in the characteristically anonymous world of crime. One was Arnold Rothstein, New York bootlegger, gambler, and racketeer, the original of Meyer Wolfsheim in F. Scott Fitzgerald's *The Great Gatsby* and Nathan Detroit in Damon Runyon's *Guys and Dolls* sketches, as well as of films like *Street of Chance* (1930), *The Big Bankroll* (1959), and a score of others. The stereotype of the brightly dressed, clever, and arrogant gang boss is derived directly from him.

The second figure who emerged as big news was Al Capone, the boy from Castel Amaro who, before he was 30, had taken over Chicago and the national bootlegging industry. Public interest in Capone, Rothstein, and people like them led to a string of autobiographical films, many based on actual figures. Most sought only to tell the story of a gangster's rise and fall, and were usually riotously amoral and violent until the last reel when, as a sop to the pious, he was shown shot down by the law. Ben Hecht's observation that "the forces of law and order did not advance on the villains with drawn guns but with their palms out like bellboys" was seldom observed in these phony fantasies of violence and sado-eroticism.

Rothstein was killed in 1928 and Capone jailed in 1931, but they left behind a legacy that would rack America for decades, and also provide Hollywood with the basis for its next cycle of crime films. Both men had realized that profit depended on organization and cooperation between gangs. Rothstein in New York and Capone in Chicago had put order above all, welding the dissident gangs into efficient mobs even if mass extermination was the only means whereby this could be achieved. After Rothstein's death, Capone called a meeting in New York of the major criminal powers and suggested the logical extension of this policy, a national syndicate to coordinate criminal activity. Although the plan was rejected by the mutually suspicious gangs, the meeting did lead to cooperative projects like the execution service later known as Murder Incorporated and the national illegal betting service that was to provide the gangs' main income after the repeal of Prohibition.

The gangs' new standing in national society was reflected in films that showed crime as a highly organized industry. Warner Bros., experts in entertaining the masses, had produced many of the biographical gangster films: *Little Caesar*, based on Capone, and *The Public Enemy*, based on Hymie Weiss, as well as many others. The first all-sound film, *The Lights of New York* (Bryan Foy, 1928), was also drawn from the genre that Warners recognized as a potential gold mine. A glance at the newspapers gave their writers dozens of plots, particularly when, after repeal, the gangs moved in on prostitution (*Marked Woman*), the cab business (*Taxi*), trucking, banking, politics. Often imitated by other studios but seldom anticipated, Warners pioneered the private detective film, the prison drama, and most of the sub-sections that make up the modern crime film.

While Hollywood explored the possibilities of organized crime, another phenomenon was catching public interest. This was the rise of the rural bandits, independent bank robbers, kidnappers, and petty thieves thrown up by the Depression who briefly ravaged the Midwest and South in 1933 and 1934. Racing across Oklahoma, Ohio, Kansas, Missouri, and Arkansas, they struck at isolated banks and filling stations in daring daylight raids, often shooting up buildings and people with submachine guns before roaring off in their stolen cars. Mostly small-town sports and embittered petty criminals, they traded on a corrupt and inefficient state police force to satisfy their simple needs, money, excitement, and fame.

With the possible exception of John Dillinger, these bandits—"Ma" Barker and her sons, Charles "Pretty Boy" Floyd, Bonnie Parker and Clyde Barrow, George "Machine Gun" Kelly, Lester Gillis ("Baby Face" Nelson), and the rest—stole only a tiny percentage of the money that Capone and his associates looted from the country. The gangs looked on them contemptuously as small-time thieves, thrill seekers, and freaks. Their notoriety stemmed solely from their value as news subjects, and the bloody childlike violence of their lives. Depression society, weary of corruption in government and apathy in business, welcomed the stories of banks held up and policemen baffled. It was not, after all, their money in the banks, and few public servants had proved themselves as corrupt and useless as the state police. Flattered by newspaper attention and their legendary status, the bandits responded, writing to the papers and the officers who hunted them, appearing casually in town to buy food, returning home to visit friends and family—gestures of their contempt for the impotent police force. This arrogance was their downfall. Left to compete solely with the state police, most of them would have lived for years, but their growing popularity encouraged the federal authorities to intervene. Given sweeping powers by Congress after the Lindbergh kidnapping, the FBI, with its biblically righteous leader, J. Edgar Hoover, swept down on the bandits, and within a few months in 1934 most were dead, pursued with icy determination across America by the G-men and shot down with dubious legality by men who knew they had nothing to lose. In 1933, at the height of the hunt, the Production Code authority issued an order that no film on Dillinger, or by implication any of the other bandits, should be made. No longer nourished by publicity, the legends died, not to be revived for another thirty years.

With the big crime rings, Hoover kept an uneasy truce. Even his power was unequal to that of the gangs, and to attack them would be to invite a costly battle that might eventually lead the FBI into the same disrepute as the state police. His neutralization of Capone in 1931 had merely been the end of a process begun by the gangs, who found Capone's rule galling. Beyond that, Hoover dared not go. Crime films, reflecting this agreement, became panegyrics to the fearless G-men, stories of prison, of racketeering on the city level with civic groups or alert police smashing the small gangs, or individual stories of crime and retribution peopled by private eyes and gentleman gang-

Bogart on the other side of the law portrays David Graham, inspired by prosecutor Thomas Dewey, confronting his key witness Mary Scrauber (Bette Davis) and her "taxi-dancing" friends.

sters who were already becoming figures of heroic mythopoetry, conveniently distant from the real facts of national graft and corruption.

The reality of war and of organized crime burst on the United States at roughly the same time. In the thirties, special investigator Thomas A. Dewey set about cleaning up New York, convicting Mafia leaders and deporting criminal heads. Continuing this work in 1939, other investigators found during a probe into crime in Brooklyn that "the big fix" extended far deeper than anybody had realized. A small-time killer named Abe Reles admitted that for years he had been a paid assassin for a criminal group that carried out executions for the nation's gangs, the group that became known as Murder Incorporated. His testimony uncovered evidence of gambling, prostitution, and union rackets covering the whole country, of corruption extending into government on all levels, into the state and federal police, into industry. The war [World War II] and America's growing involvement in it blunted the effect of these revelations and diverted Hollywood from making films based on them. It was not until 1946 that the first films on criminal corruption emerged, and when they did it was with a precision and power that nobody had expected. Many of them reflected the socialist/humanist views of men who had been attracted to Communism during the periods of Soviet reconstruction in the thirties and the wartime entente. Few of these productions were more fiery than the political parables of Warner Bros. in the early thirties, e.g., *Wild Boys of the Road*, but the Depression was gone and with it the memory of injustice and graft. In the post-war mood of relaxation, optimism, and nostalgia, the realism of *The Naked City, Brute Force, Force of Evil, Body and Soul*, and *Crossfire* forced social awareness and civic indignation once again on a careless public, and the world's filmgoers turned with new interest to Hollywood. Regretfully, the liberal spirit of the time was ephemeral, giving way abruptly to a more typical isolationism and xenophobia. The men whose talents had made these films great—Dassin, Dmytryk, Polonsky, Rossen, Trumbo, Garfield, Hayden—were first to suffer in the McCarthy witch hunts of the early fifties, and the spring of social comment that had welled briefly to the surface sank below once more, not to return for many years.

Despite the frankness of these socialist-oriented films, they had little effect on public opinion toward organized crime, now an invisible industry of immense influence and wealth. Since the forties, the small mobs had been quietly consolidating themselves into a loose confederation of independent area groups with the Italian/Jewish Mafia as informal link. In New York, a committee of Joe Adonis, Willy and Solly Moretti, Albert Anastasia, and Anthony "Tony Bender" Strollo met at Duke's Restaurant near Palisades Park through the war [World War II], planning strategy and maintaining Murder Incorporated and the Continental Press Service gambling machinery. The press ignored crime, but it was widely understood that a "combination" of top gangsters ran the rackets in America. Gordon Wiles' *The Gangster* (1947) was one of the first films to call it "the syndicate."

The word became the accepted one for organized crime in 1952, when Senator Estes Kefauver published the findings of the Senate Special

Realism: Spencer (John Hoyt) confronts the snitch Wilson (James O'Rear) in *Brute Force*.

Committee to Investigate Crime in Interstate Commerce, of which he was chairman from May 1950 to May 1951. "A nationwide crime syndicate does exist in the United States of America," he announced in a widely quoted report, and went on, "This nationwide syndicate is a loosely organized but cohesive coalition of autonomous crime 'locals' which work together for mutual profit. Behind the local mobs which make up the national crime syndicate is a shadowy criminal organisation known as the Mafia." Once again, as in 1939, the public was made aware that crime had become far more than a matter of movie stories.

The fifties spawned a rash of exposés that purported to tell the truth about graft in a number of cities. Some, like *The Phenix City Story*, were honest attempts to show how apathy led to corruption. Others—*Chicago Syndicate, New Orleans Uncensored, The City Is Dark/Crime Wave, Kansas City Confidential, Hoodlum Empire, The Case against Brooklyn*—settled for a trite formula in which a crusading cop or private citizen shows that behind the well-cut suit of some local dignitary is a gang boss with contacts in the Mafia or the mobs. Respecting the FBI's truce with big-time crime, these films confined themselves to corruption on a city level, limiting any reference to national organization to a veiled comment that the syndicate or "the Big Boy" was worried. Lacking filmmakers of social consciousness, the crime film degenerated into another aspect of the Hollywood experience, distinguishable from the cowboy and horror film only in the variety of its attitudes and realism of its settings.

Genres rise and fall, fertilizing the ground for new growth, and the gangster film today has been plowed back to nourish the James Bond cycle, with its suave super-crooks and elaborate gadgetry, or the smooth professionalism of "big caper" films like *Robbery* or *The Split*. Films about fantastic robberies, most of them inspired by real-life crimes like the Brinks armored car robbery or the Great Train Robbery in England, have become so common that the best of them—*Rififi, The Asphalt Jungle, The Big Caper*—are a sub-genre of their own, with special rules deriving more from the imagination of their writers than the realism of the news. As scenarist vies with scenarist to work out more elaborate plots, the underworld looks on, notebook ready, in case one comes up with a new wrinkle.

That the cinema should have become the criminal's university is particularly appropriate. For decades crime and film have had a close and mutually responsible relationship. Not only has the cinema played to crime by recording and glorifying its activities, but criminals have responded with interest to the pictures painted of them. Capone demanded that he be consulted over the script of *Scarface*, and actors from George Raft to Alain Delon have been unwilling to draw a line between their screen personae and real life. Films like *Yokel Boy* (1942), with Albert Dekker as a gangster invited to star in a film of his own life, and *The Hollywood Story* (1950), where Richard Conte solves a twenties murder while directing a film about it, are no more odd than *Broadway* (1942), starring George Raft as himself in a film that often looks and sounds like a thirties gangster romance. Both in the public eye, both dependent on the protection of their charisma to survive in an uncertain world, both doomed to short-lived careers, gangsters and actors seem too close for true separation.

Tied to the period that creates it, the gangster film has no more durability than the year from which it springs. For this reason today's crime films are thin. The poorest are rooted in nostalgia, pastel memoirs of forties detective dramas or thin parodies of a genre that in its time was brisk and relevant. Others, like *Madigan*, record without comment the commonplace brutality of the city streets and hope for some truth about our time to emerge from the grim catalogue. But in truth the gangster film seems gone for good, as the gangster is gone. With the trench coat replaced by the well-cut suit, the prison pallor by a Palm Springs tan, and guns by more subtle means of persuasion, he has passed beyond the area where cinema could say anything about him except that he once existed and gave rise to some of the American cinema's most powerful dramas.

The fifties gangster as cheap hood: Clem (John Larch) in *The Phenix City Story*.

Even as an innocent man behind bars in *Each Dawn I Die*, James Cagney radiates the "particular physical dynamism" of the gangster.

Iconography of the Gangster Film

(from Underworld USA, *1972)*

Colin McArthur

In *Little Caesar* (1930) a police lieutenant and two of his men visit a nightclub run by gangsters. All three wear large hats and heavy coats, are grim and sardonic, and stand in triangular formation, the lieutenant at the front, his two men flanking him in the rear. The audience knows immediately what to expect of them by their physical attributes, their dress, and their deportment. It knows, too, by the disposition of the figures, which is dominant, which subordinate. In *The Harder They Fall* (1956) a racketeer and two of his men go to a rendezvous in downtown New York. As they wait for the door of the building to be opened they take up the same formation as the figures in the earlier film, giving the same information to the audience by the same means. (The fact that they are, in the first case, policemen, and in the second case, racketeers, is an interesting ambiguity which will be examined later.) In *On the Waterfront* (1954) and *Tony Rome* (1967) there are carefully mounted scenes in which the central figure is walking down a dark and deserted street. In each case an automobile drives swiftly toward him, and the audience, drawing on accumulated experiences of the genre, realizes that it will be used as a murder weapon against the hero. Both these examples indicate the continuity over several decades of patterns of visual imagery, of recurrent objects and figures in dynamic relationship. These repeated patterns might be called the iconography of the genre, for they set it off visually from other types of film and are the means whereby primary definitions are made.

The recurrent patterns of imagery can be usefully divided into three categories: those surrounding the physical presence, attributes, and dress of the actors and the characters they play; those emanating from the milieux within which the characters operate; and those connected with the technology at the characters' disposal. Among Hollywood leading men, Edward G. Robinson and James Cagney dominate the gangster films of the thirties; Humphrey Bogart the thrillers and Richard Widmark the gangster films of the forties; and, though not in such a clear-cut way, Richard Conte has a good claim to this role in the gangster films of the fifties. In addition to these major icons of the genres, there are other players of the second rank such as George Bancroft, Barton MacLane, Joe Sawyer, Paul Kelly, Bob Steele, Ted de Corsia,

Charles McGraw, and Jack Lambert, to name only a few, who have become inseparably associated with the gangster film/thriller. The American cinema has traditionally achieved its effects with the utmost directness, and never more so than in the casting of gangster films and thrillers. Men such as Cagney, Robinson, and Bogart seem to gather within themselves the qualities of the genres they appear in so that the violence, suffering, and angst of the films are restated in their faces, physical presence, movement, and speech. By the curious alchemy of the cinema, each successive appearance in the genre further solidifies the actor's screen persona until he no longer plays a role but assimilates it to the collective entity made up of his own body and personality and his past screen roles. For instance, the beat-up face, tired eyes, and rasping voice by which we identify Humphrey Bogart are, in part, selections we have made from his roles as Sam Spade, Philip Marlowe, and others.

It is not only the actors playing the roles who recur, but the roles themselves. Genres become definable as such by repetition until fairly fixed conventions are established, and this is particularly apparent in the spectrum of characters in the gangster film/thriller: racketeers with brains who rise to the top, gangsters without who remain as hoods, gangsters' women, stool pigeons, cops and bent cops, crusading district attorneys and legal mouthpieces for the mobs, private eyes and heroes forced by circumstances to be such, nightclub owners and their sadistic strong-arm men; and the countless secondary figures on the fringes of this dark world, newspapermen, poolroom and gymnasium owners, news vendors, and so on. The interpretation of these roles may develop. For instance, James Cagney's particular physical dynamism was interpreted, in the gangster films of the thirties, as necessary ruthlessness in getting to the top, but in the gangster films he made in the post-war period, especially *White Heat* (1949) and *Kiss Tomorrow Goodbye* (1951), this physical dynamism was interpreted as psychotic. A touchstone of normality is usually present, often centered on the figure of the gangster's mother. This is apparent in the earliest examples of the genre such as *Little Caesar* (1930), *The Public Enemy* (1931), and *Scarface* (1932); it is present vestigially in *The Big Heat* (1954) and achieves almost pristine restatement in *The Brothers Rico* (1957).

But the figures in the gangster film/thriller proclaim themselves not only by their physical attributes and their roles but also by their dress. The peculiar squareness of their hatted and coated figures is an extension of their physical presence, a visual shorthand for their violent potential. Clothes have always been important in the gangster film, not only as carriers of iconographic meaning but also as objects which mark the gangster's increasing status. Scenes in tailors' shops are frequent (*The Public Enemy*; *Al Capone* [1959]), and both Rico (*Little Caesar*) and Tony Camonte (*Scarface*) invite comments on their clothes ("How do you like it? Expensive, huh?"). Alec Stiles, the gang leader in *The Street with No Name* (1948), tells a new member of his gang, "Buy yourself a closetful of clothes. I like my boys to look sharp." Characters in *Baby Face Nelson* (1957) ("Get rid of that gunny-sack") and *Murder, Inc.* (1951) ("Burn that tent you're wearing') are instructed to change their clothes as a mark of their rising status, and Tolly Devlin's ascent within the syndicate in

Tom Powers (Cagney) flanked by his crony Matt (Edward Woods) and "a touchstone
of normality," his mother (Beryl Mercer), in *The Public Enemy*.

Underworld USA (1960) is marked by syndicate boss Gela's comments on his
clothes.

Following *The Naked City* (1948), several gangster films and thrillers
appeared carrying the word "city" in their titles: *Dark City, Cry of the City, City
Across the River, While the City Sleeps, The Sleeping City, Captive City*, and so on.
Alongside these came other films featuring the word "street" in their titles:
The Street with No Name, Race Street, Side Street, Down Three Dark Streets, and
The Naked Street, not to mention *Where the Sidewalk Ends* and *The Asphalt Jungle*.
This development simply made explicit what had always been an important
element of the gangster film/thriller, the urban milieu. Robert Warshow, in
his essay "The Gangster as Tragic Hero," writes:

> The gangster is the man of the city, with the city's language and knowl-
> edge, with its queer and dishonest skills and its terrible daring, carrying
> his life in his hands like a placard, like a club . . . for the gangster there is
> only the city; he must inhabit it in order to personify it: not the real city,
> but that dangerous and sad city of the imagination which is so much more
> important, which is the modern world.

Thus the city milieu serves both as a background for the activities of the
gangster and the hero of the thriller and as a kind of expressionist extension
of the violence and brutality of their world. The sub-milieux of the gangster

film/thriller are, in fact, recurrent selections from real city locales: dark streets, dingy rooming-houses and office blocks, bars, nightclubs, penthouse apartments, precinct stations, and, especially in the thriller, luxurious mansions. These milieux, charged with the tension of the violence and mystery enacted within them, are most often seen at night, lit by feeble streetlights or more garish neon signs, such as the Cook's Tours sign "The World is Yours"

in *Scarface*, or the flickering signs which cast threatening shadows and half-disclose mysterious visitors in the offices of Sam Spade (*The Maltese Falcon*) and Philip Marlowe (*Farewell, My Lovely*). Fritz Lang, in his German film *Metropolis*, created a huge city embodying his expressionist fantasies. When he came to America he had no need to recreate his city; it already existed.

The gangster and the hero of the thriller, being modern men of the city, have at their disposal the city's complex technology, in particular the firearms, automobiles, and telephones which are recurrent images of the genre. It is fitting that the Western hero, moving balletically through his archaic world, should bear graceful weapons such as the Winchester rifle and the Colt pistol. The weaponry of the gangster film/thriller is much more squat and ugly: the police .38, which forms the title image of *Kiss of Death* and the opening image of *The Big Heat*; the Luger; the sawed-off shotgun; the submachine gun, which becomes an object of veneration in *Scarface* and *Machine Gun Kelly*. Andrew Sinclair, in his book *Prohibition: The Era of Excess*, describes the role of the automobile in the Prohibition/repeal debate:

> The armor-plated cars with windows of bullet-proof glass, the murders implicit in Hymie Weiss's phrase "to take for a ride," the sedans of tommy-gunners spraying the streets of gangland, all created a satanic mythology

A police .38 sits on the script for *Kiss of Death*.

of the automobile which bid fair to rival the demonism of the saloon. The car was an instrument of death in the hands of the crook and drunk, and prohibition was held to have spawned both of them.

The automobile is a major icon in the gangster film/thriller. It has a two-fold function in the gangster film: it is the means whereby the hero carries out his "work" (Tom and Eddie in *The Public Enemy*, waiting orders from Nails Nathan, stand beside their car like the crew of a Panzer about to go into action); and it becomes, like his clothes, the visible token of his success. Eventually it becomes the symbol of his unbridled aggressiveness, and it seems perfectly logical that the automobile should be used regularly as a lethal instrument in both thrillers and gangster films (see *The Dark Corner*, *Underworld USA*, *The Moving Target*, and others). So powerful a symbol has it become of the gangster's presence that characters may respond with fear to an automobile without seeing the men within it (see *Kiss of Death*, *The Garment Jungle*, *Assignment to Kill*, and others).

The telephone has, on occasion, been used as a murder weapon in the gangster film/thriller, and this, too, seems logical. The physical environment, an expressionist representation of the violent potential in the genres, becomes the instrument of violence. More often, however, telephones are used to intimidate the weak, as in the threatening calls to Mrs. Renato in *The Garment Jungle* and to Mrs. Bannion in *The Big Heat*.

It is, of course, an artificial exercise to discuss individual iconographic elements when they exist in dynamic relationship within the fabric of particular films. Now and then several iconographical elements combine in singular purity, and there are found the sequences most characteristic of the genres. For instance, the opening sequence of *The Harder They Fall*, showing several figures (Bogart, racketeers, and others) entering cars and hurtling through the empty New York streets to an early-morning rendezvous, evokes brilliantly the ugliness of the milieu and the ruthlessness of the racketeers before disclosing the squalid operation they are embarked upon. Again, the sequence in *Little Caesar* when Tony, the gang's driver, is shot down on the steps of the church by Rico from a speeding car, brings dynamically together several iconographical elements. The same elements are interestingly used in the French gangster film *Le Deuxième Souffle*, in which the trademark of the central figure is to shoot his victims inside a car which he himself drives. Perhaps the iconography of the gangster film is presented most strikingly (and, incidentally, the non-realistic quality of the genre most clearly exemplified) in the characteristic montage sequences of thirties gangster films where the outbreak of gang war is chronicled. The films at these points prise themselves free from their inhibiting narrative structures and present the pure imagery of aggression: speeding cars, screaming tires, figures blasting each other with revolvers and submachine guns. A frozen frame from such a sequence would look like a pop art poster representation of the essence of the gangster film.

But to define the gangster film/thriller solely by its iconography is to suggest that the genre is static and unchanging, that the gangster film of the thirties is indistinguishable from that of the fifties, or the forties thriller from its counterpart of the sixties. In fact, both thrillers and gangster films, especially the latter, are in constant flux, adding a new thematic dimension here, a new moral emphasis there.

Notes

1. There is within the gangster film a sub-genre, beginning with *Dillinger* (1945) and culminating in *Bonnie and Clyde* (1967), in which the action does not take place in the city, but in the small towns of the rural Midwest. Even within the gangster films of the thirties (*G-Men* [1935], for instance), the conventions allowed the city milieu to be forsaken for a final shoot-up at the gangsters' mountain hideout. Thrillers of the last decade have tended to move from the city to more exotic locales such as Florida and the California coast.

2. The menace of the automobile is not, of course, confined to the gangster film and thriller. Cars are used as blunt instruments in, for example, the black comedy *It's a Mad, Mad, Mad, Mad World*.

A violent man juxtaposed against a dark cityscape: rogue cop Mark Dixon (Dana Andrews) dumps the body of a murder suspect in *Where the Sidewalk Ends*.

The diminutive title figure and his henchmen.

Little Caesar and Its Role in the Gangster Film Genre

(1972)

Stuart M. Kaminsky

Little Caesar contains the first clear depiction of the elements which have defined the gangster film genre and have remained strongly evident in such films for over forty years. The genre elements (motifs, themes, and icons) in *Little Caesar* have evolved with the genre, but have remained persistently recognizable because they fill a public need.

The gangster films of the 1930s, of which *Little Caesar* was the first, were generally semiconscious attempts to deal with the Depression and the public's shaken confidence in American economics, politics, and myths of the self-made man. That was the first stage of the genre. In the 1940s, the next stage emerged carrying with it the elements of the first. The gangster became a conscience-stricken American, anxious to help his country, willing to put aside his ruthless quest "to be somebody" so that he could join in the battle against the common enemy (*All Through the Night, Hitler: Dead or Alive*). The Depression had ended and fear of the Axis had replaced fear of hunger.

After the war [World War II], the gangster or gangster figure returned as an object of psychological displacement, painful self-awareness, and uncertainty. Often the returning gangster could be seen in the character of Humphrey Bogart (*Dark Passage*) or Burt Lancaster (*I Walk Alone*). By the mid-1950s the film gangster had become less lost and disillusioned and more directed toward aggressive destruction of the society which had made him and the psychosexual problems with which he had to exist (*Machine Gun Kelly, Bonnie and Clyde*; in *The Dark Past* gangster William Holden is actually given psychotherapy by psychiatrist Lee J. Cobb, in whose house he has taken refuge).

The assessment of the genre elements in Le Roy's *Little Caesar*, the appearance of these elements in gangster films as they evolved, and the examination of the meaning of such elements are the goals of this article. As one of the first and possibly most elemental of the gangster films, *Little Caesar* was the grid on which the others which followed were placed. As Robert Warshow states, *Little Caesar* is archetypal. Other important elements of the gangster film were clearly evolved from Howard Hawks' *Scarface* (1932) and William Wellman's *The Public Enemy* (1931). Parenthetically, I believe *The Public Enemy* and *Scarface* are far better films than *Little Caesar*. However, I am concerned not with the quality of the film, but with its contributions to the genre, contributions which I believe are considerable.

Little Caesar refers ironically to "Caesar" Enrico Bandello (Edward G. Robinson). Initially, Rico's rise to power is an ironic parallel to the rise of a truly historic figure, an emperor, in more classical works of literature. Both *Macbeth* and *Julius Caesar*, for example, can be seen on one level as elevated gangster films. Indeed, *Macbeth* was used as the basis for a gangster film (*Joe Macbeth* [1956], directed by Ken Hughes and starring Paul Douglas). Shakespeare's Caesar is presented on a consciously grand scale of man's view of himself. Mervyn Le Roy's *Caesar* is on an intentionally reduced scale of a man's view of himself and his tragedy. Le Roy's film, in contrast to Shakespeare's play, was aimed at lower-class and solidly middle-class audiences and designed as a work of popular entertainment built on broad touchstones of vulgar behavior and images which would bring a response of social recognition in the viewer. Part of the irony of the situation in a gangster film is that the gangster feels that he is operating on a grand scale. The irony is pushed toward its limit when in John Huston's *Key Largo* (1948) Humphrey Bogart sarcastically says of Rocco (Edward G. Robinson in what is clearly an extension of Rico in *Little Caesar*) that he "was more than a king; he was an emperor." Johnny Rocco's pleased response is "That's right."

The tie-in to the irony of grand tragedy can be seen in the regal titles of the many gangster films which followed *Little Caesar* (*Queen of the Mob, King of the Underworld, King of the Roaring Twenties, The Rise and Fall of Legs Diamond*). To carry the ironic grandeur of the title to, perhaps, its most ambitious conclusion, we have the gangster as God and father in Francis Ford Coppola's *The Godfather.*

The use of the gangster's name as the title of the film, which appears to have originated with *Little Caesar*, is common in the genre and is also reminiscent of the practice of naming tragic plays for the central figure (*Al Capone*; *Baby Face Nelson*; *Mad Dog Coll*; *Machine Gun Kelly*; *Dillinger*; *Roger Touhy, Gangster*; *Bonnie and Clyde*). The frequency with which real gangsters are the subject, and title, of the films also tends to elevate the fictional gangster to a media-folk status. The most frequently used real gangster in the genre is Al Capone, who appears in picture after picture (sometimes with a slightly disguised pseudonym) complete with his icons: cigar, scar, fedora, topcoat, and big, black car. *Little Caesar* is based on Capone's life, as are, to name a few, *Scarface, Al Capone, Bullets or Ballots*, and *The St. Valentine's Day Massacre*. As the genre evolved, Capone became more of a folk symbol, a truly tragic figure surrounded by those who wish to kill him and take his empire (as, for example, is true of several of Shakespeare's royal gangster plays, including *Julius Caesar* and *Macbeth*). Certainly, the Capone figures in *Bullets or Ballots, The Big Combo*, and *The Brotherhood* take on such a dimension.

The "little" of the title is also central to an understanding of the gangster genre. It is ironic in *Little Caesar* because it points out the contrast between the tragic figure's aspirations and the possibilities of the situation. As Flaherty, the cop, says of Rico, "The conceit of that guy." If Rico is a Caesar, he is indeed a little one, little in the possibility of his conquest and little in size. The two central gangster figures of the 1930s, Robinson and James Cagney, are extremely short. Consciously or unconsciously this emphasized the affinity between the cocky gangster and the "little" man in the audience who identified with the gangster

"The most frequently used real gangster in the genre": "Scarface" Al Capone.

on the screen and was, at the same time, told to shun him.

Robinson and Cagney are, in the gangster films from 1930–31 (*Little Caesar* and *The Public Enemy*) to 1948 (*White Heat* and *Key Largo*), quick to attack people bigger than they are with their fists, even if they have to kick them in the shin (Robinson in *Bullets or Ballots*) to get them low and land a punch. The size of such protagonists is, of course, an added ironic overtone considering their aspirations. It is also an identification image of great power. The small gangster automatically gains our sympathy. We know part of his problem and tend to react by thinking: if that little guy on the screen can push his way to the top, why can't I . . . at least for the duration of the cathartic experience of seeing the movie. In *Our Movie Made Children*, published in 1933, a number of teenage slum children were interviewed about their identification with Rico. According to the book, a great many boys, instead of denying Rico, identified with him, especially in that they, too, were small. The book goes so far as to state that the identification was so strong in several cases that the boy adopted the name Rico and wound up shot or in jail attempting to duplicate the film gangster's acts.

George Raft, who soon joined Robinson and Cagney as a gangster hero, was also short. Paul Muni (Scarface) was of average height. As the genre evolved and the heroes became more seriously considered as worthwhile figures with which to identify, Humphrey Bogart emerged as the primary gangster figure. Whenever a director or producer has chosen to reassert the irony and consciously reduce identification with the gangster, he has gone back to the small actor (Mickey Rooney in *Baby Face Nelson*, Alan Ladd in *This Gun for Hire*, Peter Falk in *Murder, Inc.*, John Cassavetes in *Machine Gun McCann*, Al Pacino in *The Godfather*).

Time and Fate

Little Caesar opens with the robbery of a gas station. The instant the film begins, Rico is committing a major crime. There is no turning back for him after the first few seconds. His fate is sealed by moral conviction of the audience and the code of the 1930s (the criminal must be punished for his crimes). Many gangster films begin with such an irrevocable act, usually a murder in the course of a robbery (*White Heat, The Grissom Gang*). The viewer is warned that once a first step has been taken one's fate is sealed; there is no turning back. This idea of not being able to turn back is carried through in another genre motif.

"Once in the gang . . . ," Joe Massara (Douglas Fairbanks, Jr.) begins, and trails off, "You know the rest. I've never seen the guy who got away from it." The gangster's fate is decided. He can no more evade the gang, break away from it, than Oedipus could have avoided the wrath of gods. Later, in *Little Caesar*, Joe echoes his early statement, saying, "Can't a guy ever quit?" Finally, Olga (Glenda Farrell) tells Joe he must go to the police, that the world is not large enough to escape from Rico and the gang. "Where do we run to?" she asks. "There's no place to hide." This attempt, always futile, to hide, escape

"The small actor": hit man Raven (Alan Ladd, right) is dwarfed by his employer, Willard Gates (Laird Cregar), in *This Gun for Hire.*

the gang and one's destiny, is repeated constantly in gangster films (*Tight Spot, The Enforcer, The Brothers Rico, Kiss of Death*).

In the scene immediately following the initial robbery in *Little Caesar*, Rico and Joe are in a diner. Rico turns back the diner clock to establish an alibi. Joe admires him for being smart: "Got to hand it to you, Rico. The old bean's working all the time." We do not see the alibi called into question in the film, but the screenplay carries the scene through to a confrontation with the police in which Rico's faith in his turned-back clock does save him. The visual attempt to arrest time is a generic warning in the gangster film. Time, for a gangster, goes quickly. His chances of reaching old age in a film are almost nonexistent and he knows it. His life is lived at a rapid, precarious pace, not the cautious one-step of the viewer. For this reason, the criminal tries to live as much as possible, to hold back time while he is doing so. Coppola plays on this in *The Godfather* in showing that Sonny (James Caan), the overtly emotional man of action who reminds us of the film gangsters of the 1930s, is, like Rico (and Tony in *Scarface* and Tom in *The Public Enemy*), gunned down at an early age. Brando, who shows little public emotion and displays great caution, manages to survive for an, ironically, natural death.

Closely allied to the holding back of time is the gangster's reliance on specific timing, being at a particular location at a specific time. The gangster must control time, as Rico does with the diner clock, or it may elude him and send this world crashing down. Practically, timing is important because if things are not done quickly and precisely, the police will arrive. The element of control of time is also evident. In *Little Caesar*, Rico insists that the Bronze Peacock robbery take place at midnight on New Year's Eve. It does and precisely at that moment Rico murders the crime commissioner. In *Bullets or Ballots*, Robinson sets 10 P.M. as the time he will deliver marked money to the bosses. Even though he is mortally wounded, he keeps the appointment. Again, Robinson in *Key Largo* checks his watch and insists on the phone that Ziggy (Marc Lawrence) keep their appointment on time or "the deal's off." In Don Siegel's *The Lineup*, Dancer (Eli Wallach) has to deliver heroin to The Man at a precise moment. To miss it is to die for his failure.

To the Big City

Another motif of the genre established in *Little Caesar* is closely tied to the concept of the self-made man in American popular fiction since Revolutionary days. We first meet Rico and Joe in a small town (not the case in W. R. Burnett's novel) and find that Rico wants to go to the big city, "East," and make something of himself like "Diamond" Peter Montana, about whom he has just read in a newspaper.

Rico leaves rural America, the last vestige of frontier echoes, to make his way in the new American frontier, the big industrial urban complex. It is the exact reversal of the other primary American film genre, the Western, in which we find that the hero has frequently come from the East to escape the constrictions of the urban scene, the new American (*The Virginian* is the classic example, but the moral carries over as recently as *Something Big,* in which Dean Martin is an easterner trying to avoid the need to return to the city).

The advantage of going to the big city for the gangster is that he knows, from fiction about the American dream, that it is the place of opportunity in which an enterprising young man with nothing but nerve, drive, and loyalty for sale can get ahead whether he comes from rural America (Rooney in *Baby Face Nelson,* Shelley Winters and sons in *Bloody Mama,* Bogart in *High Sierra,* Scott Wilson in *The Grissom Gang*), another country (the fictional Capone in all the Capone films, Henry Silva in *Johnny Cool,* Robinson in *Key Largo,* Marlon Brando in *The Godfather*), or the alienated slums of the city itself from which the audience is often not more than a generation removed (Cagney in *The Public Enemy,* Bogart in *Dead End,* John Davis Chandler in *Mad Dog Coll,* Clark Gable in *Manhattan Melodrama*).

Gangsters and Dancers

A minor but interesting motif in gangster films emerges in the diner scene in *Little Caesar.* Joe is a dancer, wants to dance professionally. At one point in the film, we actually see him dance on the stage of the Bronze Peacock. Both Cagney and Raft were professional dancers before becoming movie gangsters, and they continued to dance in films, sometimes tying the skill to the gangster film directly (Cagney in *Battling Hoofer* and Raft in *Bolero*). The motif of the gangster and dance also emerges in *The George Raft Story* and *The Rise and Fall of Legs Diamond.*

The dancer as criminal allows the genre to include a nervous, graceful sense of movement, hyper-vitality. It is used specifically for this purpose, for example, in *The Lineup,* in which Dancer (Eli Wallach) moves intentionally like a dancer as he goes through his series of brutal murders. This vitality of motion is important to the American sense of affirmation, dynamism, and spontaneous expression. Few moments are as clearly expressive of this in American films as that in which Cagney (in *The Public Enemy*) actually breaks into a dance step on the street after meeting Jean Harlow.

The dancer as criminal also ties in to the musical genre of the 1930s. In films from *The Gold Diggers* of 1933 through *Ziegfeld Girl* (1941), the dancer, usually female (perhaps, as a parenthetical note, the dance musical gave females of the 1930s a protagonist with which to identify in much the way gangster films of the same period gave males ambiguous figures with which to identify), rises ruthlessly to the top over competitors "who don't have it any more." The dancer's rise, like the gangster's, is often halted just when success is within her reach. It is snatched suddenly from the hands of the dancer and gangster and, vicariously, from the audience because the rules of the game of "getting ahead" have somehow been violated. There is an interesting ambivalence in both gangster films and dance films on this point. The self-made man is expected to move ahead ruthlessly, accept power, and be dynamic, but this lauded behavior is contrary to the dominant Protestant ethic. Society worships ruthless ambition, but insists that we love our neighbor. The gangster or dancer, by deserting the limbo existence between these clashing concepts, is writing his own doom. We both root for the gangster and are guiltily gratified when he is gunned down.

Sex and the Gangster

The dancer as criminal also invites a kind of simple-minded aspersion on his masculinity in generic terms. Rico calls Joe a "sissy." "Dancin's all right for a sideline," says Rico, "but it ain't a man's game." However, Rico clearly protests too much. Rico's attachment to Joe, and to a great extent Joe's to Rico, can be seen most clearly in terms of latent homosexuality. Rico works hard to keep Joe from going back to Olga. Without knowing how much he is revealing, Rico says, after he cannot shoot Joe, "This is what I get for liking a guy too much." The subdued sexual flaw can also be seen, as Robin Wood points

Dancer disposes of "The Man" (Vaughn Taylor) with a high leg kick to his wheelchair in *The Lineup*.

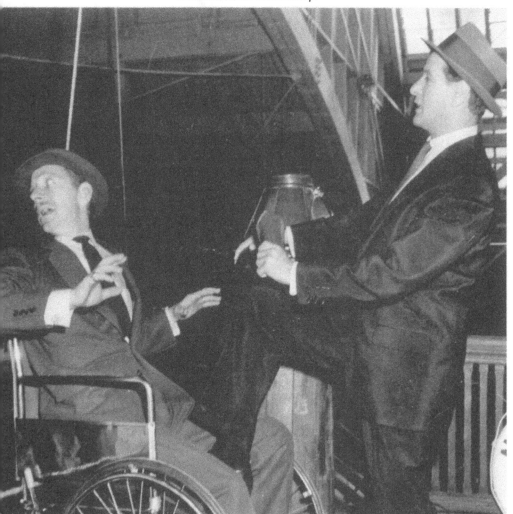

out, in Tony's (*Scarface*) covert incestual feelings for his sister. Oedipal over-tones are evident in such gangster films as *Machine Gun Kelly*, *Baby Face Nelson*, *Gun Crazy*, *Bloody Mama*, and *The Grissom Gang*. These sexual flaws or under-currents accomplish two things. First, they render the gangster somewhat impure in conventional social/moral terms, but it is an impurity which may well touch the repressed sexual guilt of the viewers, who are both identifying with and condemning the gangster. Second, the sexual nuance of depravity elevates the tragic elements of the genre, for such problems are not normally associated with the anti-social figure in drama, but with the lofty tragic figure (for example, in the Oedipal relationship in *Hamlet* or the overt statements of incest in *Jane Shore* or *The Castle of Otranto*).

Women and Acquisitions

Women do have an important function for the gangster, but it is not a sexual one. Women are, as Warshow points out, acquisitions for the gangster. Conscious interest in sex is not within the gangster. He is an ascetic. Rico does not drink, and we seldom see a Capone figure actively interested in women as sexual objects. Women and liquor are to be displayed but not trusted. They can both betray the gangster. In *Little Caesar*, Rico, in his speech at his testimonial banquet, says: "The liquor is good. I don't drink it myself. . . . Good to see you gents with your molls." In *Key Largo*, Rocco calls Gay (Claire Trevor) out of a dark room to display her proudly to Ziggy, his old gangster friend. Rocco then dismisses her and gets down to business. The pure gang-ster disdains women as sex objects. "Women . . . dancin'. . . . where do they get you?" says Rico with a sneer. One reason we know James Caan will make a poor "Don" early in *The Godfather* is his interest in sex, his overt passions contrasted with the control over his sexual urges of Al Pacino, who emerges as the properly controlled "Don" to whom Brando passes his mantle.

Women are rewards, proof of success, like the stick pin and the ring Rico admires on Peter Montana and the $1,500 painting he looks at in awe in the Big Boy's home. Women, jewels, paintings, big houses, flashy cars, tuxedos, cigars, are all evidence that the gangster has "made it" in his business, in American society. He engages, quite simply, in a parody of conspicuous con-sumption.

Getting Up in the World

Getting ahead is the gangster's single goal. No matter how high up he gets, the gangster always wants to get higher until he has gone so high that he is sure to fall (rather like Chaplin as Hitler on the rising barber chair in *The Great Dictator*). Rico keeps talking about how Sam Vettori, Diamond Pete, and even the Big Boy "can't take it." In *Key Largo* Bogart says he knows what Rocco wants even though Rocco can't articulate it. "He wants more," says Bogart. Rocco beams and says, "That's right. I want more." "And will you ever have enough?" says Bogart. "No," responds Rocco seriously, "I never have."

The higher the gangster gets, the more dangerous is his position, not unlike the situation of an aggressive young man in a corporate structure, but the gangster can't turn back. "You're getting up in the world, aren't you, Rico?" says Flaherty the cop at the banquet. Rico smiles. Later, Rico preens himself in his first tuxedo before a mirror as he gets ready to meet the Big Boy. Otero (George E. Stone) says with admiration, "You're getting up in the world, Rico." Rico nods.

Getting up in the world is tied to the idea of aspiration and social success. The gang, in gangster films, is very often an efficient business, a corporation.

The Gang as Business

The gang is a business in the genre, but a very special kind of business created in American fiction and in Hollywood. The gang's corporate structure, like the depiction of the life of the gangster himself, is not that of the real gangster and it is not relevant to the genre or the needs that it meets that it be "real," whatever real might be. When Roger Corman states at the beginning of *The St. Valentine's Day Massacre* that "this is what really happened" he is making a joke and yet being quite serious at the same time, for Corman's film, like the genre since *Little Caesar*, is not an attempt at re-creation of reality, but a creation of a legend which can be used for a thematic purpose. To draw an example from a related genre which also deals with the establishment of legend, I direct you to the response of the newspaper editor in John Ford's *The Man Who Shot Liberty Valance*. Given the truth about the death of Valance, he prefers to ignore it and print the legend, which is more meaningful to the public and has already been accepted by them as reality. The gangster genre itself is, possibly, more a part of the meaningful life in America than the real gangster, has more to do with shaping our views of society than real criminal activity, and has more to do with our behavior than any contact with criminals through the news media.

Specifically, the business milieu of the gangster film reflects our view of American business enterprise in general even if we happen to be part of a business structure which does not conform to this view. In no film is this more evident than in *The Godfather*, in which Brando, and later Pacino, repeatedly refer to their activities as business, a family business supporting many employees for whom they are responsible.

In the gangster film, the gang is often a loose feudal system with individual warlords held in tow by one strong regent who reports to a mysterious boss or bosses. The bosses remain above the gang, anonymous, aloof, and in control. When the bosses are revealed we find they are "upper class," affluent, influential, wealthy. They may be idle rich (Sidney Blackmer in *Little Caesar*), bankers and government officials (*Bullets or Ballots*), or apparently respectable middle-class businessman (Jack Elam in *Baby Face Nelson* and Fred Clark in *White Heat*). It is these upper- and middle-class bosses, hiding behind a gang leader of courage, whom we are taught to hate in the gangster films. They, in the midst of the Depression we know exists in the films of the

"This is what really happened": Roger Corman's reenactment of the St. Valentine's Day massacre in his film of the same name.

1930s but seldom see, are accumulating wealth, taking what there is of available money, wearing tuxedos, and living off the labor of ambitious gangsters who have risen from the working classes. We see the gangster take the risks, hold the small gang boss in line, protect his position, exact tribute from the workers who don't have enough for themselves, and, finally, inevitably, fall only to be replaced by another like him, while the bosses continue protected. The pattern recurs from *Little Caesar* in which the Big Boy is neither caught nor punished and can be seen, strikingly, in the quasi-gangster film *On the Waterfront*, with Lee J. Cobb as the ambitious gangster–union leader who fronts for the bosses.

In contrast to the upper-class manipulators, the social chairmen of the board of crime, are the workers, the on-the-line gangsters. Between these extremes are the tragic figures of the genre, the Ricos, members of the minority trying to get ahead. The attainable epitome for such men is to replace the man who reports to the bosses, to replace a man who, like him, has also risen from his class. More recently, in films like *The St. Valentine's Day Massacre* and *The Godfather* we see the ironic twist, the immigrant gangsters as bosses, controlling destinies and dividing spoils at a businesslike meeting of the board.

In the early gangster films, the gang itself is often composed of first- or second-generation immigrants, like the people who made up much of the movie audience of the 1930s. In *Little Caesar* the gang members are clearly Italian. They meet at Palermo's and have names like Bandello, Masara, Passa, and Otero. Arnie Lorch doesn't have a particularly Italian name, but he and his assistant have the only Italian accents in the film (outside of "yellow" Tony's mother). Often, when protest did not rise too loudly over the years, gang members have been Italian (*Little Caesar, Scarface, The Brothers Rico, The Brotherhood, The Godfather*), but they can be Irish (*The Public Enemy, The Roaring Twenties*), rural whites (*Pretty Boy Floyd, Bloody Mama, Bonnie and Clyde, The Grissom Gang*), or Jewish (*Murder, Inc., King of the Roaring Twenties*, or Nails Nathan in *The Public Enemy*). Black gangs, it might well be added, although they existed in life from the 1910s on, did not appear in an American film until the 1970s (*Dirty Harry, Cotton Comes to Harlem, Shaft*). Hollywood clearly felt that black aspirations were not such that they had to include them in the genre as a mainstream element, and the black moviegoer did not see fit to protest his not being depicted as a criminal.

Law Abiders and Middle Americans

The social forces against which the gang fought in the 1930s and which have carried into the present were invariably represented by people with middle American names. The crime commissioner Rico kills is Alvin McLure. In *Bullets or Ballots* Bogart kills the wealthy crusading publisher named Bryant. Even within the gang structure the upper-middle-class echelons are usually manned by middle Americans like Pete Montana.

The middle management and upper levels of the criminal structure are solidly American, as are the forces of "good" which battle gangsters. Whether law-abiding or not, there is a level above which the lower class cannot rise, a point at which the American dream draws the line. Rico's downfall is partly a matter of his aspiring too high, to a level of society and business filled by more "solid" Americans. The result in an audience viewing a gangster film, especially in the 1930s if they were members of the working class, may well have been to feel that there was something to be despised in a system in which they cannot get ahead as they had been led to believe. At the same time, however, they may have been reinforced in their belief that this is the way things are and will inevitably remain.

Surroundings and Ceremonies

The gangster's very aspirations and their manifestations are parodies of American business as the American public had been conditioned through films to accept it. The middle-class gangster boss has a comfortable or even plush office (Sam Vettori and Arnie Lorch in *Little Caesar*) in which he conducts his business, although one finds it difficult to determine why the gangsters need offices other than to display them. The offices are often precarious places which have to be heavily guarded to protect the always-threatened gangster from those who would take his place.

The gangster's office is often in a nightclub or bar (*Little Caesar, I Walk Alone, Bullets or Ballots, The Grissom Gang, King of the Roaring Twenties*), which ties the gangster in with entertainment, a colorful way of life, an exciting but slightly unsavory social endeavor which both attracts and frightens the viewer (like the movies, perhaps?). The tie-in becomes explicit in *The Godfather* with the Corleone family moving into the movie business and Las Vegas nightclubs.

A funeral is frequently held in which the central gangster bids a fond, expensive farewell to the man he has replaced or a rival gang leader he has eliminated. The gangster sends the biggest wreath and there is often a joke made by him or the members of his gang about how deeply touched the boss is. This foreshadows the death of the boss himself, while mocking the sacred image of the funeral, and contrasts with the central figure's downfall and ignoble death (Rico behind the billboard, Cagney in *The Public Enemy* mummified and dropped through his front door, Muni in the bullet-riddled room in *Scarface*, Rooney coughing blood in the graveyard as he dies in *Baby Face Nelson*). James Caan's death and the funeral parlor sequence in *The Godfather* are grim reminders of the tradition and clearly identify Caan as having been

"The middle-class gangster boss has a comfortable or even plush office": a confrontation between icons Bogart and Cagney in *The Roaring Twenties*.

part of it. In a sense, the ignoble death of the gangster involves us more than the death which resulted in the grand funeral. In most of the films this becomes a comment on a society which falsely mourns those it has discarded or, to paraphrase Howard Hawks, those who have shown by their death that "they aren't good enough."

Another frequent ceremony in the gangster genre is the banquet which is often held as a testimonial for the gangster when he has "made it." There is always a parodic element to such a banquet, a mocking of the businessman's testimonial for service (*Little Caesar, The St. Valentine's Day Massacre, Some Like It Hot*, the wedding feast at the beginning of *The Godfather*). "Loyalty and friendship" are printed on the banner behind Rico at his banquet, a banquet in which he is given a stolen watch. Rico has displayed neither loyalty nor friendship and he can expect neither. Business is not a matter of loyalty and friendship. He who displays such traits is certainly doomed in the gangster film and, by extension, perhaps in life. This is intentionally reversed in *The Godfather*, as are so many of the *Little Caesar* archetypes. The loyal gang members, Robert Duvall and Richard Castellani, survive and are rewarded while all who have betrayed the Corleones are executed.

The church is often seen in gangster films, but only briefly. The church is a place on whose steps the gangster dies. The church is a place of irrelevance and ineffectuality in life and the society of the genre. Nowhere is this more intentionally evident than in *The Godfather* in the sequence in which we cut quickly between the church at which Pacino is serving as godfather for his sister's baby to the violent murders Pacino has arranged to have take place while he establishes his alibi. It is only in death that a film gangster finds himself concerned about God, and even his arrival at the church is less a matter of choice than chance (Tony's death in *Little Caesar*, Cagney's death in *The Roaring Twenties*, Weiss' death in *The St. Valentine's Day Massacre*).

The Gangster's Decline and Fall

The downfall of the gangster comes rapidly after he has briefly reached the apex or, ironically, almost reached it. The downfall is often one of position and not just death. Rico is reduced to poverty (as is Cagney in *The Roaring Twenties* and Raft in *If I Had a Million*), emphasizing what happens to those of the lower classes who dare challenge society on its own terms. Rico's downfall, one should note, does not take place in Burnett's novel, only in the film. The downfall is complete so that the audience can pull away at the end, realize that we are not like Rico, that we are not so foolish as to aspire beyond our known limits. It is questionable whether the downfall of the gangster worked to this end as it was clearly intended to do. According to Warshow, we identify with the central figure, immerse ourselves in his anti-social behavior, but are purged of our guilt for this by drawing away from him as he falls. It is difficult, however, to pull away so quickly. The fall is so sudden, and the memory of the gangster's rise and vitality are still so vivid. Thus, when Cagney staggers in the rain in *The Public Enemy* after attacking the rival gang alone and being shot, he says, "I ain't so tough." We are certainly supposed to agree with him, but it is difficult for he has been admirably tough. We do not feel that he is worthless. So, too, Rico's dying words are supposed to be pathetic and his fate deserved. "Mother of Mercy," says Rico. "Is this the end of Rico?" We are supposed to marvel at Rico's turning to God after all he has done and to remark on his vanity for thinking of himself in the third person, as someone above the normal traffic of existence.

The problem is, and it is part of the ambivalence of the genre which both admires and rejects the gangster, that before his death Rico has gone down in a blaze of glory, has once more challenged society even though he couldn't win. Death is the result for the gangster, but ambivalence is our reaction to his existence and demise. This ambivalence exists with irony in *The Godfather*, in which it is not the gangster's demise that causes our unease, but his survival and success.

A balletic demise: Tom Powers watches as his pal Matt's body gyrates under the impact of machine-gun bullets in *The Public Enemy*.

Weapons and Style

It is interesting to contrast the use of weapons in gangster films and Westerns. "Shoot first and argue afterwards," says Rico. Muni says approximately the same thing in *Scarface*. For the gangster, the gun is a means to an end, not an object or style. There is no fast draw, no moment of decision. You get as close as possible with as big a gun as possible and shoot your enemy as full of lead as you can. It is best if the man you are shooting is unarmed. The gun, like a typewriter, Dictaphone, or telephone, is a tool of business and not an object through which the gangster can express himself. It is an extension of his matter-of-fact character, the only skill he knows and the one on which he must build his career. Of his gun, Rico says, "That's all I got between me and them, between me and the whole world."

The Public

For all the lip service given to "the public and its protection" in gangster films, it is remarkable how little of the public is actually seen. The reason seems clearly in keeping with the genre as established as early as *Little Caesar*. The public, the ordinary man, is in the background of gangster film, seldom stepping out to be identified, seldom harmed, detached, often admiring the

"Shoot first and argue afterwards": Rico narrowly avoids his comeuppance by machine-gun ambush in *Little Caesar*.

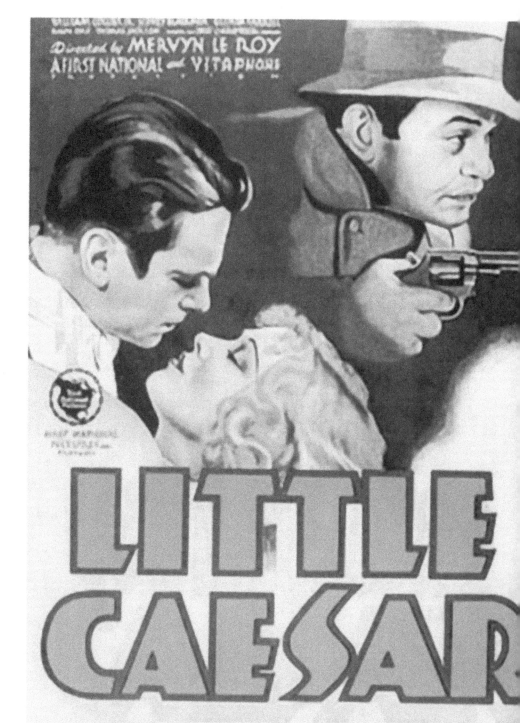

gangster (newsboys and manicurists always smile sincerely and say "Come again" to them). The public is not really relevant. In the gangster film, we view the working out of a myth, a genre which can be repeated with variations dependent upon the sociopolitical milieu of the time and country. The myth does not deal with the effect of crime on real people. It is concerned with the persona of the gangster and the qualities in him and our society with which we identify and against which we react.

The elements of the genre, the motifs with which we have been dealing, can be controlled and explored to make an aesthetic statement. Defining the genre as it emerged from *Little Caesar* helps us appreciate films which draw upon the tradition. An understanding of the generic roots of a film like *The Godfather* or *The St. Valentine's Day Massacre* helps us appreciate the deeper irony played upon by the filmmaker.

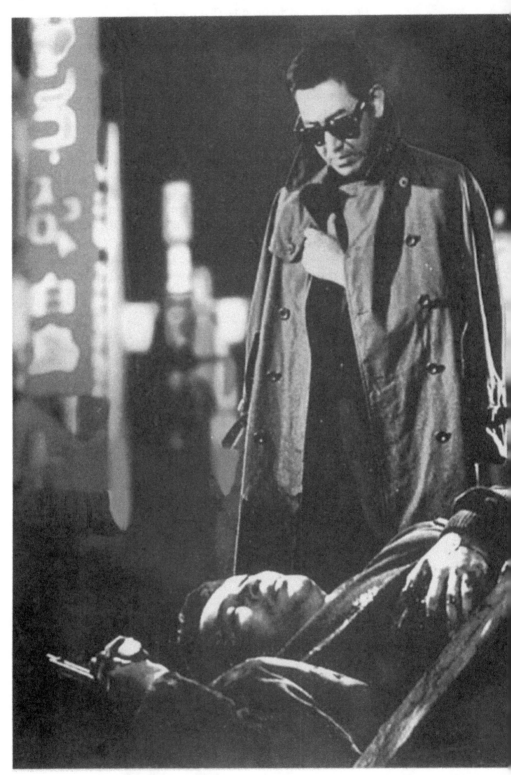

Gunji (Koji Tsuruta) stands over a victim in *Sympathy for the Underdog*.

Yakuza-eiga: A Primer

(1974)

Paul Schrader

"We're outlaws, but we're humane."

The Japanese gangster film (the *yakuza-eiga*) is, as a yakuza would say, a lone wolf in the clan of gangster films.[1] The *yakuza-eiga* bears little resemblance to its American or European counterparts. The rules formulated by Robert Warshow for the seminal American gangster films do not apply to the Japanese gangster film; neither do the more recent definitions of the American and French film noir. The yakuza film does not reflect the dilemma of social mobility seen in the thirties gangster films, nor does it reflect the despair of the post-war film noir.

The Japanese gangster film aims for a higher purpose than its Western counterparts: it seems to codify a positive, workable morality. In American terms, it is more like a Western than a gangster film. Like the Western, the *yakuza-eiga* chooses timelessness over relevance, myth over realism; it seeks not social commentary, but moral truth. Although the average yakuza film is technically inferior to an American or European gangster film, it has achieved a nobility denied its counterparts—a nobility normally reserved for the Western.

History

"Yakuza" literally means "gambler" or "good-for-nothing,"[2] but has come to mean "gangster" or "mobster" and refers to the 125,000 or so very real gangsters in the Japanese underworld today. The *yakuza-eiga* is a youngster in the community of film genres. The first yakuza films appeared less than a decade ago, and it is only in the last few years that the *yakuza-eiga* has assumed the preeminent position in the Japanese film industry. Approximately one hundred gangster films are now made each year in Japan and, along with sex comedies, constitute the backbone of Japan's declining film industry.

The *yakuza-eiga* did not originate, as did the American gangster film, out of a desire to capture today's headlines, but instead evolved from an older genre, the samurai film—an evolution by chance rather than design. Before

1964 all Japanese sword films were *jidai-geki*, period films. The government had banished the samurai and banned the long sword in 1868, and there were no films set in the post-1868 period in which the protagonists used long swords. By legal definition, the swordsman was an outlaw; no filmmaker wished to assign the simon-pure samurai code of *giri-ninjo* ("duty-humanity") to an outlaw; and without *giri-ninjo* there could be no protagonist. Samurai films of the fifties often featured pale-faced, wholesome young samurai who defeated whole clans of yakuza, but there was always a clear distinction made between the code of the samurai and the code of the yakuza. There could also be realistic portrayals of yakuza—Toshiro Mifune played a small-time gangster in Kurosawa's *Drunken Angel* (1948)—but, deprived of the samurai code, these portrayals had neither epic nor heroic dimensions.

In the early sixties the rigid demarcation between the ancient samurai and the modern yakuza began to dissolve. The samurai films were declining in popularity and the studios sought ways to update them for the new audiences. As with every important development in *yakuza-eiga*, Toei studios took the lead. The transition from *jidai-geki* to *yakuza-eiga* can first be seen in the *Jirocho* series, produced by Toei from 1962 to 1964.

This series, which starred Koji Tsurata as Jirocho and was directed by Masahiro Makino, has been called a *chonmage yakuza-eiga*. (The *chonmage* is the topknot hairstyle of the samurai.) Toei continued the *Jirocho* series *jidai-geki*, but the *Jirocho* films are period films primarily in their costumes; in character and conflict they foreshadow the first phase of the *yakuza-eiga*.

The first authentic yakuza film was *Bakuto* (*Gambler*), directed in July 1964 by Shingehiro Ozawa and starring Koji Tsurata. Ozawa had been directing period films for Toei since 1954, but after the success of *Bakuto* he devoted himself exclusively to writing and directing yakuza films. Toei itself made only three pure yakuza films in 1964, but they were so well received that by 1965 Toei was in almost full-scale *yakuza-eiga* production.

The initial phase of *yakuza-eiga* lasted from approximately 1964 to 1967. This was a period of low budgets and fast shooting schedules. Toei explored the new market, developed new stars, and evolved the paraphernalia and ritual of the new genre. It soon became clear that audiences preferred *yakuza-eiga* to period films, and one by one the older, established directors were transferred to the new genre: Ozawa and Makino in 1964, Tai Kato and Tomu Uchida in 1965. Koji Tsurata was the major star of this first period, but he was soon joined by the other two stars of Toei's yakuza triumvirate: Ken Takakura and Junko Fuji.

The new genre was legitimized primarily by two films. *Abashiri Bangaichi* (*Abashiri Prison*), directed in April 1965 by Teruo Ishii and starring Ken Takakura, was the first great yakuza commercial hit. The Abashiri prison story was so successful that Takakura has remade it eighteen times to date. (When a Japanese film is successful, [the studio] doesn't rerelease it, it remakes it.) Although it was of marginal artistic value, *Abashiri Prison* clearly demonstrated that yakuza films had a far greater potential audience than anyone had imagined.

Poster for *Bakuto* (*Gambler*), starring Koji Tsurata.

Yukyo Ippiki: Seiki No Yatape, directed in January 1966 by Tai Kato and starring Kinnosuke Nakamura, was the first yakuza artistic success. Later that year Kosaku Yamashita directed the stunning *Kyodai Jinji (Family Obligations)*, also the first of a series, and the new genre not only had its stars but its two best directors.

In its second period, from 1968 to 1971, the *yakuza-eiga* enjoyed the blessings of large(r) budgets and mass audiences. It was now an authentic genre. Toei made twenty-six yakuza films in 1969 and considers it their peak year for profits. Yakuza films now used exterior locations (sparingly) and had a classier look. Yamashita's *Bakuchiuchi: Socho Tobako (Gambling House: Presidential Gambling)*, considered the "masterpiece" of the genre, was released in 1968. Tomu Uchida, one of Japan's oldest and most respected directors, filmed one of the best yakuza films, *Jinsei Gekijo: Hishakaku to Kiratsune (Theater of Life: Hishakaku and Kiratsune)*.

It was during this period that the other studios realized they could no longer afford to ignore Toei's lucrative "B" genre and got into the act themselves. Toho, Shochiku, Nikkatsu, and the now defunct Daiei Studios all sank money into yakuza productions. Shochiku's three-hour version of *Jinsei Gekijo (Theater of Life)* directed by Kato in 1971 is certainly the most expensive and ambitious yakuza film thus far produced. It is also one of the best.

At the moment the *yakuza-eiga* is again in a period of transition, moving uncertainly toward its third phase. Production remains high (Toei made thirty gangster films in 1972), but audiences' tastes are fluctuating. The enormous success of *The Godfather* in Japan caused the Toei brass, again leading the way, to finance more "documentary-style" yakuza films. In these documentary-style films the setting of yakuza conflicts was updated from the "classical" period (1915–35) to contemporary times. Whereas the classical-style yakuza films were open morality tales, the newer documentary-style films featured a far more dubious morality. This transition has caused an uproar at Toei, and Koji Tsurata, the genre's oldest and most respected star, has publicly stated that the new documentary-style films "have no *kokoro*" (heart). (In *Bakuto Kirikomitai [Gambler's Counterattack* (1971)], for example, Tsurata was forced to shoot a corrupt policeman in the back, an unforgivable breach of code for a samurai-esque yakuza—not only in the back, but with a gun rather than a sword!) Toei is currently making both the classical and documentary-style yakuza films, and it is uncertain which will dominate the third phase of *yakuza-eiga*.

Part of *yakuza-eiga*'s current dilemma stems from the fact that it is making the transition from a "B" to an "A" genre. Yakuza films have always been made with low budgets and short shooting schedules. (Even today a "big" budget yakuza film costs $300,000 and has a three-week shooting schedule.) For the most part the genre has been critically ignored in Japan—although such esteemed writers as Yukio Mishima, Ryuho Saito, and Tadao Sato have come to its defense—and is virtually unknown in the West. The prestigious Japanese directors, though often unemployed, have refused to work within the yakuza conventions (although Shinoda's first film, *Pale Flower*, was a yakuza variant). But now yakuza has come into respectability. Its stars are the greatest in Japan; its films the most popular. Ken Takakura will soon star with Robert Mitchum in a large-budget yakuza film to be directed by Sydney Pollack and financed by Warner Bros.[3] The Japanese gangster film is no longer a "B" genre. As greater demands are made of it, the traditional *yakuza-eiga* film will respond by either rising to maturity or slipping into self-parody.

Themes

The *yakuza-eiga* has two primary themes: duty (*giri*) and humanity (*ninjo*). That the genre has two themes, *giri* and *ninjo*, rather than one, *giri-ninjo*, is more than a semantic distinction. It helps explain not only how the *yakuza-eiga* came into existence, but also why it continues to thrive.

The samurai film, of course, had only one theme: *giri-ninjo*; the Siamese-twin themes of duty and humanity were so interlocked as to be indistinguishable from each other. For the samurai, duty was humanity, and vice versa. But this single theme proved to be financially limiting in a contemporary setting. The high-flown code of *giri-ninjo* could not be applied to a modern gangster, who, by the very fact that he carried a long sword, was an outlaw and therefore violated the duty expected of him as a member of the state. Ergo: there could be no yakuza heroes.

This inhibiting syndrome was unraveled by some unsung Toei executive who divided that single word in two, transforming a single concept into an oxymoron. *Giri-ninjo* became *giri* and *ninjo*; duty-humanity became duty or humanity, thus sidestepping the samura/yakuza dichotomy. It was now possible for a gangster to have duty without humanity, humanity without duty, or any combination thereof. Under certain circumstances, the yakuza could be both honorable and criminal.

"The yakuza world—where duty is more important and humanity hangs in the balance," proclaims a yakuza movie poster—a statement which would have never applied to a samurai film. The oxymoronic yakuza theme of *giri-ninjo* is the subject of Tadao Sato's lengthy essay "Reflex of Loyalty," perhaps the best article written to date on *yakuza-eiga*. Sato explains, then laments the bifurcation of the traditional concept of *giri-ninjo*; he sees the *yakuza-eiga* as having created a new situational morality where duty can be "more important" than humanity—thus opening many new doors to old forms of fascism. This explains the infatuation of both the new Left (the Zenkyoto student radicals) and the new Right (Mishima's Self-Defense Force) with *yakuza-eiga*. Student radicals have been known to spend hours watching yakuza films in preparation for a clash with the police; similarly, ultra-Right novelist Yukio Mishima interviewed Koji Tsurata and wrote lengthy articles in praise of *yakuza-eiga*. Both Left and Right can draw great spiritual sustenance from a genre which allows one individual to forego his duty if humanity must be served, and another to forego humanity for the sake of duty. In Yamashita's *Kyodai Jinji* the following words are sung as Tsurata goes into battle: "I may be a fool. But maybe a fool is needed to awaken the people." What grander sentiments could any radical ask for?

The yakuza morality of *giri-ninjo* may seem potentially fascistic to Sato, but to Americans, accustomed to the open fascism of films like *The Godfather* and *Dirty Harry*, yakuza movies seem clearly humanitarian. The conflict between duty and humanity is always a complex one; and humanity, even when it is rejected, is given a far richer examination than in American gangster films, where it seems to have been dismissed even before the projector starts.

The yakuza protagonist is stripped of the moral security of the samurai. The total war he wages against his enemies is less important than the moral conflict he must fight on the battleground of his own conscience. Invariably, the *yakuza-eiga* protagonist is a man (or woman) of high moral principles trapped in a web of circumstances which compromise him. He attempts to pursue both duty and humanity but finds them drawing increasingly apart. In the end he must choose between duty and humanity, a decision that can only be made in a bath of blood.

A typical Toei yakuza film—there's no use mentioning specific titles since most of Toei's three hundred or so yakuza films have the same plot structure—opens with the release of the hero from prison. He has gone to prison to spare his clan a police investigation, but, upon his return, finds the clan has fallen under the control of an evil *oyabun* (godfather). True to his duty, he nonetheless rejoins the clan and attempts to exert a moral influence from within. He soon finds he has little influence and is himself being requested to commit deeds totally alien to his personal morality. Still he doesn't flinch from his duty. Even in service to an openly vile *oyabun*, the yakuza hero will suffer intense physical pain, reject the love of a woman, see helpless persons oppressed, and, in some cases, kill a decent and good man.

But as the yakuza pursues his duty, his world becomes more openly schizoid. On one side, duty and its incumbent virtues are assembled; on the other stand humanity and its virtues. With the forces of duty stand such virtues as obedience to the *oyabun*, obligation to the clan (or *kyodai jinji*, literally, "family obligations"), humility, stoicism, and willingness to die for duty. On the other bank stand humanity and its virtues: social consciousness, sympathy for the oppressed, love for wife, sweetheart, friends, and relatives, humility, stoicism, and willingness to die for humanity. Whether he chooses duty or humanity, the yakuza hero's attitude will be the same. He will be humble, stoical, prepared to die.

For the first seventy-five or so minutes, the yakuza film carefully builds this web of duties and humanitarian obligations. These forces are in continual conflict; they permeate every conversation and action. Lines like "We yakuza obey our code no matter what happens" are counterbalanced by statements that "evil has no code." In *Chizome No Karajishi* (*Blood-Stained Courage* [Toei, 1967]) an *oyabun* states, "We're outlaws, but we're humane," then ten minutes later says, "A friend is a friend, and a job is a job."

Trapped in this schizoid world, the moral yakuza has little to look forward to, "There are only two roads for a yakuza," a minor character says in *Hishakaku To Kiratsune*, "prison and death." Before he goes on his march to the final fight in the *Abashiri Bangaichi* series, Ken Takakura sings, "I'm off to kill the enemy / My sword in my hands / And when it's over / It's back to Abashiri Prison again."

The moral dilemma is invariable solved by blood. At some point the *oyabun* does a deed so reprehensible that duty can no longer be served and humanity demands his death. All moral struggle falls from the hero's shoulders as he takes his long sword in hand and marches toward the evil *oyabun*'s house where he will kill or be killed. He is suddenly free to punish evil and kill his *oyabun*. The ancient samurai would kill himself before killing his evil master; the contemporary yakuza, however, because *ninjo* has been split off from *giri*, is free to forsake duty and kill his master. In this prolonged ten-minute slaughter which follows, the evil *oyabun* always dies, whereas the yakuza does in some cases and survives to start anew in others. The contrast with the samurai film is complete: the samurai forsakes duty and dies, the yakuza forsakes duty and lives. This is the post-war ethic overlaid on the grid of the samurai film.

These themes are presented in their richest form in *Socho Tobaku*, a film which Mishima called a masterpiece and whi ch Sato has written about at length. Made by Toei in 1968, *Socho Tobaku (Presidential Gambling)* was directed by Kosaku Yamashita and written by Kazuo Kasahara. Technically, it is not much better than most *yakuza-eiga*; thematically, it is the most complex and introspective of all the yakuza films.

Nakai (Koji Tsurata) and Matsuda (Tomisaburo Wakayama) are blood brothers and high-ranking yakuza in the Tenryu syndicate. The aging beneficent *oyabun* dies and Nakai, out of humility, refuses the successorship. Semba, an outside business-oriented *oyabun*, prevails upon the clan leadership to pass over Matsuda and give the *oyabun*-ship to an unwitting puppet. Nakai, the personification of duty, accepts the injustice and attempts to serve the new leadership in the best manner possible. In contrast, Matsuda, the unbounded force of humanity, vows to fight the new leadership at every turn. First Matsuda is reprimanded, then demoted, then finally ostracized. Nakai defends Matsuda publicly on every occasion but privately attempts to get Matsuda to submit to the new *oyabun*. In a long, shattering scene set in a cemetery, Nakai, in the midst of a downpour, breaks the blood-bond cup with Matsuda. "Nothing," Nakai tells him, "is more important than loyalty."

Matsuda prepares to attack the clan from without while Nakai vainly tries to reform it from within. Matsuda kills the puppet *oyabun*, and Semba's forces take over the syndicate. Nakai is then accused by Semba of protecting the murderer, his former blood brother, Matsuda. True to his *oyabun*, Nakai searches out Matsuda and kills him wordlessly. He then returns and prepares to kill Semba. "Where is your loyalty?" Semba cries. "Loyalty?" Nakai answers. "What do I know about loyalty? I'm just a common criminal." He vengefully kills Semba and is captured by the police and led away to prison

Poster from the Abashiri Bangaichi series in which "Ken Takakura sings, 'I'm off to kill the enemy / My sword in my hands / And when it's over / It's back to Abashiri Prison again.'"

where, the narrator, tells us, he will spend his life as a murderer "beyond rehabilitation."

Socho Tobaku is the richest and most complex *yakuza-eiga* made to date; it is also the darkest and most pessimistic. Both duty and humanity end in death; no middle road is offered. It is the only yakuza film I've seen that does not even give the audience the standard cathartic closing fight scene.

Films like *Socho Tobaku* do not seem, at least to my Western mind, to open up the new possibilities of fascism Sato suggests. Films like *The Godfather* openly promote the fascist gangster-family community; *yakuza-eiga* struggle against it. *Socho Tobaku* rams home several fundamental themes—themes which lead to individual despair rather than groupthink militance: (1) the traditional Japanese values of duty and humanity have come unjoined and polarized by contemporary society (i.e., "the center does not hold"); (2) an unrestrained amount of either duty or humanity leads to death; [and] (3) a noble man can survive if he continually maintains the proper balance of duty and humanity, but his life will be full of loneliness, suffering, and despair.

Genre Conventions

Yakuza-eiga is probably the most restricted genre yet devised. Only a limited number of things can happen in a yakuza film. The characters, conflicts, resolutions, and themes are preset by genre conventions. To be sure, the whole notion of genre is one of predictability, but yakuza films may carry it even further than necessary. It is not unusual to find four or five films virtually indistinguishable in stars, script, and direction.

Japanese gangster films draw upon a catalogue of genre paraphernalia far more extensive than anything in their Western counterparts. Yakuza films are litanies of private argot, subtle body language, obscure codes, elaborate rites, iconographic costumes and tattoos. An entire film may consist of nothing more than a series of set-pieces. An uninitiated viewer may see huge chunks of film pass before his eyes without every having the slightest idea of their significance.

Because *yakuza-eiga* is such a young genre, it is still possible to describe its circumference—to speak of a "typical" yakuza plot or character. The controversial documentary-style *yakuza-eiga* of recent years are the first open dissenters from what has been a remarkable orthodox genre. The American gangster film, on the other hand, has undergone dozens of schisms and separatist movements.

The average *yakuza-eiga* screenwriter's job is more one of organization than free imagination. Given the basic storyline the screenwriter is free to determine several things: the setting and time, the type of industry over which the clans are contesting, the shadings of the relationships, and the sequence of the various genre set-pieces.

There are twenty or so basic yakuza set-pieces. All of these scenes do not occur in every yakuza film, but every yakuza films will have six to ten of them. Working from a hypothetical master list, a screenwriter can select a sequence of these scenes and assemble them like beads on a rosary. When he has strung enough beads to fill an hour and a half of screen time, the rosary is finished. A hypothetical master list of *yakuza-eiga* set-pieces would be certain to contain these scenes:

1. The protagonist comes out of prison.
2. The evil *oyabun* plots the takeover of the clan.
3. The evil *oyabun's* henchmen, all huffing and puffing, bully local merchants or workmen.
4. The gambling scene. Apart from their protection rackets, yakuza clans make their money from gambling rooms. In the gambling scene colorful flower cards are spread across a white table. These scenes end in a minor unresolved confrontation.
5. Yakuza introduction scene. A yakuza introduces himself to a fellow gangster in a special ceremony. Putting his right hand on his right knee, he extends his left hand, palm upturned, and states his name, place of birth, and clan affiliations. These ritual introductions can go on for several minutes.
6. The revealing of the tattoo. Most yakuza wear a full upper-body tattoo. The dramatic revealing of this tattoo reveals the bearer's profession and is an invitation to fight. The workmanship and motif of the tattoo (dragons, peonies, etc.) serve to define even further the personality of the wearer.
7. The blood brother ritual. Small porcelain cups are exchanged in an elaborate ritual. If, at a later point, this cup is broken willfully, the formal blood brothers are now mortal enemies.
8. Low comedy scenes with workers and townspeople.
9. The disclosure scene. The hero, geisha, or best friend reveals a tortured episode from the past which serves to further tighten the web of duties and obligations.
10. The finger cutting. To atone for a great offense or injustice a yakuza is sometimes required to cut off his left little finger and present it to the one he has offended. The protagonist will sometimes do this to atone for the mistake of his evil *oyabun* or an errant follower.
11. The evil *oyabun* dupes the honorable *oyabun* into accepting a dubious liaison. The protagonist respectfully registers his protest.
12. Deathbed scene. The good *oyabun* or some other honorable person slain by heavies offers a variety of deathbed platitudes to his weeping family and friends.
13. Duel scene. Two honorable yakuza protagonists are forced to fight each other out of duty to the *oyabuns*.
14. The redeeming of the geisha. Sometimes the protagonist will purchase the geisha he loves outright (borrowing money from enemies if necessary).

Poster for *Ikasama Bakuchi* from the *Bakuchi Uchi* series.

Sometimes he will offer his life as a stake in a gambling contest for her life. In either case, their love will never be consummated.

15. Cemetery scene. The hero visits the grave of his dead *oyabun* (wife, father) before seeking revenge.

16. The entreaty. The geisha or lover entreats the protagonist not to seek his revenge, but he does not heed her pleas.

17. The final march. The protagonist and his one or two closest friends walk down darkened empty streets toward the enemy compound. The movie's theme song, usually sung by the protagonist, plays as they walk.

18. The final battle. A tour-de-force fight scene where all the accumulated obligations are expiated in a grand finale of bloodletting.

It is not difficult to be a standard *yakuza-eiga* screenwriter. If one has read two good books and doesn't fear ghosts (in H. L. Mencken's phrase) and knows the genre elements, he can assemble a shootable yakuza script. The only requirement is that he be able to work fast.

I have described the restrictions imposed upon a yakuza story line in the most unflattering way possible because one should have no illusions about the "creative freedom" possible within a genre format. *Yakuza-eiga* are production-line films. Scripts are conceived by committee and assigned to directors by rotation. Stars like Tsurata and Takakura appear in ten to fifteen films a year. Every two weeks a yakuza film plops off the Toei assembly line, ready or not.

Genres are not free flights of the imagination. The art of the genre occurs within the strictures. Only when one understands that icons are supposed to be two-dimensional does the study of their shape and form become interesting. Similarly, it is only after one understands—and appreciates—the genre conventions of *yakuza-eiga* that the study of its themes and styles becomes enlightening. The beauty and the power of Kasahara's *Socho Tobaku* script stems from the fact that it works within the genre, not against it.

The purpose of genre conventions is first of all functional; each has an assembly-line task to perform. The function of a yakuza plot is to create a web of duties and humanitarian obligations. The function of yakuza characterization is to create characters susceptible to the demands of those obligations. The function of the set-pieces is to put flash and filigree into the film so that it will not drag while the web of duties and obligations is being woven.

Stylistics

I wish I could say *yakuza-eiga* has clearly established its own film style, but it hasn't. For the most part the style of yakuza films is a function of the budget. Long static takes, flat backdrops, and interior sets are favored not because they are ideally suited to the story or theme, but because they are ideally suited to a low budget. Directors, cinematographers, and set designers are not given the time or money to plan their scenes properly. A director, if has any talent or artistic ambition at all, must save his resources for one or two tour-de-force scenes and let the rest of the film slip past. Most everyone else literally "walks through" a picture, completing the shooting in two weeks, the editing in one, and moving on to the next picture.

Among the more talented directors, cinematographers, and designers, one can see the stirrings of a unique *yakuza-eiga* style. The more yakuza budgets are increased, the clearer this style will become. Yakuza films contain various inchoate stylistic elements which—given time, money, and care—will develop into a major genre style. To the extent this style exists I would call it (for want of a better term) Japanese expressionist.

Japanese expressionism is keyed to drama and individual moments. It is the visual equivalent of the Revealing of the Tattoo, the Gambling Scene, or the Final Fight. Mad erratic splashes of color are favored; the film will unexpectedly cut to a sold deep blue or red backdrop. These abrupt transitions will often be accompanied by Morricone-esque gongs and clangings. As Tsurata walks off in the final shot of Uchida's *Hisakaku To Kiratsune* (a perfect example of a film where a major director concentrates only on certain moments), a burst of bright red smoke suddenly appears from nowhere and fills the background.

Action directors like Yamashita and Kato have developed unique tracking patterns which, unlike Ophuls', are not for fluidity but are full of false energy and excitement. Like the color schemes, these tracking patterns serve to hype the dramatic moments.

Personalities: Stars

The studio star system is still very much intact in Japan. A star is contracted to a single studio. In return, he works continually and is carefully built up to a position of national prominence. The star's name is advertised above that of the film. It is not uncommon for a film to be advertised as so-and-so's "new series." Toei Studios is the MGM of the yakuza star system, controlling the three major genre stars: Ken Takakura, Koji Tsurata, and Junko Fuji. (For the purposes of this article I have concentrated most of my attention on Toei, the pioneer of yakuza films and still the largest and most methodical producer of *yakuza-eiga*.)

Ken Takakura, born in 1930, has the rugged lean features of Paul Newman or Steve McQueen and is the number one star in the Orient today. (It is a measure of the neglect accorded to *yakuza-eiga* in the West that neither Takakura nor any of the other personalities mentioned in this section appears in the only English-language index to Japanese film.) He has made over two hundred films since he joined Toei in 1956. Although he originally appeared in samurai films and domestic comedies, he is now solely a yakuza star. His most popular (and still continuing) *yakuza-eiga* series are *Abashiri Bangaichi* (*Abashiri Prison*), *Nihon Kyokakuden* (*Japanese Chivalry*), and *Showa Zankyoden*. "Star" is the best word to describe Takakura; he has a magical sense of presence,

Ken Takakura as the archetypal yakuza.

an ability to control the frame around him by poise, gesture, and expression. Unlike most Japanese actors, Takakura is a master of understatement. He is most effective when he is silent, bowing, nodding, reacting; he speaks reticently and with great authority. Three books have been published about him in Japan, and he has achieved cult status. He represents everything that is old, strong, and virtuous in Japan, and stands as a symbol against Westernization and compromise. As such he is revered by the student radicals, the far right, and the Westernized but guilt-ridden sections of the middle class.

Koji Tsurata, born in 1924, was the first *yakuza-eiga* star. He pioneered the personality of the yakuza hero. His portrayals of tormented conscience-torn gangsters helped make the crucial transition from the pure samurai heroes of the fifties to the compromised yakuza heroes of the sixties. Tsurata made his first film for Toei in 1953 and remains one of the foremost stars of the genre today. (Some of my Japanese friends report that the number one spot may be shifting back to him.) His most popular series is the *Bakuto* series, also called *Bakuchi Uchi*. During the Second World War Tsurata was a kamikaze pilot whose mission was thwarted by the timely end of the war. Like Takakura, he understates his acting and presents an unimpeachable image of duty and honor. If Takakura is similar to Newman and McQueen, then Tsurata resembles those older, more seasoned stars like Mitchum, Wayne, and Holden.

Junko Fuji is (or was) the third of Toei's triumvirate, the genre's leading female star and a screen presence quite unlike any other in the world. In her most famous series, *Hibotan Bakuto* (*The Red Peony Gambler*), she plays Oryu, the Red Peony, a young woman who is forced to avenge her father's death. Unable to find a man brave and skilled enough to seek her revenge, she must repeatedly take on the man's duty. Because she takes on the man's role, she receives a great amount of abuse from villainous types, all of which she accepts with total graciousness and femininity. There is one chilling moment in *Hibotan Bakuto: Jinji Toshimasu (The Red Peony Gambler: To Side with Duty* [1971]) where a geisha says to Oryu, "The Red Peony? I had expected a more manlike woman," and Oryu replies softly, "Never mind. I am a man." Because she has accepted the man's role she is unable to accept a lover of her own (just as the male yakuza heroes are unable to live happily ever after); she must content herself with telling other women that "a woman is happiest when she gives herself to a lover." Therefore, at the end of the film, when she is allowed to wreak her revenge upon the villains, it comes with a singular vengeance. Taking long sword in hand, she ruthlessly decimates her enemies, stabbing the evil

Junko Fuji as the female gambler Red Peony.

oyabun repeatedly even after he is dead. Western cinema has no equivalent for a gracious, polite woman who, given the proper circumstances, can exact violent physical revenge upon the men who oppress her without ever losing her sense of femininity. Unfortunately—and I'll make no comment on this—Fuji Junko retired two years ago at the age of 28 and at the height of her popularity to get married.

Hideki Takahashi is the only non-Toei star to achieve major *yakuza-eiga* star status. He is a young Steve McQueen type of great promise. He seems less sensitive than Takakura but has more physical force. He formerly worked for Shochiku and Nikkatsu studios but is now a free agent. One of his best performances is in Kato's epic *Jinsei Gekijo* (Shochiku, 1971).

Directors

Tai Kato, 56 years old, is the genre's leading director and considered by many to be the top commercial director in Japan. He is a free agent although he works primarily for Toei and Shochiku. He began directing in 1951 and has made thirty-seven films to date. In his films one can see the clearest examples of a Japanese expressionist style. Kato seems to have evolved from a Delmer Daves to a Sergio Leone phase without ever experiencing the interim John Ford period; portions of *Jinsei Gekijo* (Shochiku, 1971) are very reminiscent of the best of Sergio Leone. His best films are *Kutsukake Tokijiro: Yukyo Ippiki* (Toei, 1966), *Meiji Kyokakuden: Sandaime Shumei* (Toei, 1965), and *Hibotan Bakuto: Hanafuda Shobu* (Toei, 1969).

Kosaku Yamashita is 43 years old and is considered the best of the new directors. (All Japanese directors undergo a lengthy studio apprenticeship before they are allowed to direct.) He has only worked for Toei Studios, for which he began in 1960 and has directed forty-seven films to date. He was the first director to demonstrate that *yakuza-eiga* could be more than an exploitation genre, the first to construct individual tour-de-force scenes and to give more attention to the genre themes. Although his style is not as flashy and immediately identifiable as Kato's, his characters seems richer and more thought out. His staging on an exterior fight scene in *Kyodai Jinji* is the best I've seen in any yakuza film, and even in his most mediocre work there is at least once scene which shows his flair and finesse. Yamashita represents the best of Toei Studios, and Toei executives quite proudly call him "pure Toei." His best films are *Seki No Yatappe* (1963), *Kyodai Jinji* (1966), and *Bakuchiuchi: Socho Tobaku* (1968).

Other directors are less interesting. Toei considers its three top directors to be Yamashita, Shingehiro Ozawa, and Masahiro Makino.

Shingehiro Ozawa, 50 years old, began for Toei in 1954 and has directed eighty films. He began as a screenwriter and remains to this day a consistently inventive writer and mediocre director.

Masahiro Makino, son of famous Japanese film pioneer Shozo Makino, is Toei's second workhorse. He began directing in 1951 and has made over sixty films. He directed Koji Tsurata's *Jirocho* series in the early sixties. His status as competent director and son of a famous film pioneer makes him the rough equivalent of our Hank Williams, Jr.

Norifumi Suzuki is a better-than-average director whose fame rests primarily on the fact that he is Junko Fuji's uncle and launched her on her highly successful *Hibotan* series. His best film is *Hibotan Bakuto: Issuku Ippan*.

Kinji Fukasaku is another young better-than-average stable director for Toei. He is best known for his fine sense of color, and currently directs documentary-style *yakuza-eiga*.

Tomu Uchida, the old director of the legendary Japanese film *Earth* (*Tsuchi* [Nikkatsu, 1939]), directed several *yakuza-eiga* for Toei before he died in 1970 at the age of 71. His 1968 version of Shiro Ozaki's novel *Jinsei Gekijo* (subtitled *Hishakaku to Kiratsune*) is particularly interesting.

Poster for *Tekkaba Retsuden* from the *Hibotan Bakuto* series.

Screenwriters

Kazuo Kasahara, Koji Takada, and Tatsuo Nogami are considered Toei's top three screenwriters. Ozawa should also be added even though he also works as a director, and also Suzuki for his scripting of the *Hibotan* series (the best *yakuza-eiga* series, taken as a single unit).

Producer

Kouji Shundo is an ex-yakuza who became general producer of Toei and is largely responsible for that studio's preeminence in the *yakuza-eiga*. He supervises the careers of Takakura and Tsurata, and produces all of Toei's top yakuza films.

The important thing to remember about strict genre forms like *yakuza-eiga* is that these films are not necessarily individual works of art, but instead variations on a complex tacit social metaphor, a secret agreement between the artists and the audiences of a certain period. When massive social forces are in flux, rigid genre forms often arise to help individuals make the transition. Americans created the Western to help codify a morality of the frontier; they created the gangster film to cope with the new social forces of the city. If the original social metaphor is valid, the resulting genre will long outlive the individual artists who created it—it may even outlive the times which evolved it. In the present personality-oriented culture, rigid genre forms are the closest thing we have to a popular "art without names."

When a new genre comes into being, one immediately suspects that its causes run far deeper than the imagination of a few astute artists and businessmen. The whole social fabric of a culture has been torn, and a new metaphor has arisen to help mend it.

The social structure of Japan has in fact been severely disrupted in recent years. Westernization, the rapid rise of Japanese capitalism, and the emergence of Japan as an economic superpower have further challenged those tattered traditional Japanese virtues which were able to survive the war [World War II], MacArthur, and the occupation. The *yakuza-eiga* is a popular social contract between the artists and audiences of Japan to reevaluate and restructure these traditional virtues. The samurai film was no longer serving its intermediary function; new characters, themes, and conventions had to be created. Just as early-20th-century Americans needed the Western, contemporary Japanese need a genre which can serve as a moral battleground—a genre on which the traditional virtues of duty and humanity can fights to the death.

Notes

1. This article is of necessity a "primer" on *yakuza-eiga*. My research was limited by both film resources and factual information. Toei Studios maintains a theater in Los Angeles (the Linda Lea, the only Toei theater in the continental

United States [editors' note: no longer in operation]), and I was able to see approximately fifty *yakuza-eiga* there. (Like Japanese theaters, the Linda Lea changes its bill three times a week.) In addition, my brother Leonard and several friends in Japan, Joyce Kruithof and Heigo Hosaya, were able to furnish factual information and interview Toei executives. In the United States Nobuyo Tsuchida and Haruji Nakamura assisted me by translating various materials.

2. [Editors' note: Actually "ya-ku-za" is literally "8-9-3," from the worst hand in certain card games which the feudal gangs of gamblers (*bakuto*) staged for their patrons.]

Thunderbolt: "Few film historians have taken Bancroft [seated right] seriously as a prototype of the gangster hero."

Big Funerals:
The Hollywood Gangster, 1927–1933

(1977)

Andrew Sarris

When the late Robert Warshow published his epochal essay on "The Gangster as Tragic Hero" in the 1948 *Partisan Review*, he referred explicitly to only two movies: *Little Caesar* (1930) and *Scarface* (1932). Yet, we can trace the urban criminal on the screen from D. W. Griffith's *The Musketeers of Pig Alley* in 1912 to the present day. One of Buster Keaton's funniest short films, *The High Sign* (1920), finds Buster struggling to survive in a Mafia-infested metropolis in which every fruit peddler is a potential "hit" man in the old slapstick tradition. But these virtually omnipresent "crooks" and criminals are not what Warshow had in mind when he wrote his essay. Instead, he dealt with a genre which consists of less than a dozen movies, beginning with *Underworld* in 1927 and ending with *Scarface* in 1932.

The textbook titles in the standard film histories have not varied too much over the years—*Little Caesar, The Public Enemy, Quick Millions, City Streets*. One might add *Dragnet, The Racket, Alibi, Thunderbolt, Broadway, Doorway to Hell, Corsair, The Secret Six*, and *Blood Money*; but one is already stretching the genre beyond its original conception and romantic hero. The gangster as a type survives long after he disappears as a tragic figure. But he merely lurks in the background of urban life. In the murder mystery, for example, he is often suspect, but no more so than the butler in the manor house–type murder mystery. More often, he represents a lower order of being, in contradistinction to the morally marginal hero who teeters between good and evil as he strives for money, sex, and power. Indeed, most urban melodramas are concerned with the hero's tightrope act between legality and morality, between cutting corners and turning them irrevocably.

Crooks and criminals go back very far and down very deep in all cultures: Cain as sinner rather than criminal because murder violated God's law before there were any laws drawn up by men, *The Thief of Bagdad*, MacHeath in *The Beggar's Opera* and later in *The Threepenny Opera*, Fagin, Bill Sikes, Raskolnikov, Smerdyakov, the denizens of François Villon's Paris, the pirates, outlaws, highwaymen, and cutthroats of song and story. There is also the Robin

Hood legend, with its explicit indictment of a corrupt and unjust society. The movie gangster drew from time to time on all these prior cultural sources. *Scarface*, for example, was conceived as a conscious fusion of Al Capone and the Borgias. The Elizabethan and Jacobean revenge melodramas, and even Shakespeare's royal gangster sagas, had bequeathed a bloody tradition to the moviemakers. When John Barrymore delivered the "Now is the winter of my discontent" soliloquy from *Richard III* in the Warner Brothers *Show of Shows*, he prefaced his rendition with the remark that Richard had been a more murderous creature than Al Capone.

The gangster movie was thus born full grown out of the union of mythology and sociology, literature and journalism. It is fitting that Ben Hecht should have been the scenarist for both Josef von Sternberg's *Underworld* and Howard Hawks' *Scarface*, perhaps the beginning and the end of the notion of "the gangster as tragic hero." Hecht had been a newspaperman in Chicago before he became a novelist, dramatist, and scenarist. He and Charles MacArthur collaborated on *The Front Page*, which, while not primarily concerned with gangsters, did suggest an atmosphere of corruption and venality in which lawlessness could flourish with impunity.

A minor gangster character in *The Front Page* is kidded about his loan shark activities. This was a very knowing touching since gangster movies never dealt with loan-sharking as an activity of gangsters. Extortion, yes, loan-sharking, no. Extortion as the taking of money from people involves a straight persecutor-victim relationship between the gangster and the honest citizen. By contrast, loan-sharking involves the complicity of the victim in his own victimization and comes perilously close to putting the gangster into the banking business. Similarly, the treatment of gambling in gangster movies was generally tolerant and sympathetic, particularly when the gambling hall was bathed in a glossy aura of luxury and glamour. Again, gambling required the complicity of honest citizens, and was therefore not as reprehensible as other criminal activities in which the honest victim was absolutely guiltless.

Even in the treatment of bootlegging the emphasis was not on victimless crime, particularly in the omnipresent speakeasies, but on violence related either to the struggle for power between rival gangs, or to armed robberies of presumably honest merchants. Both Little Caesar and Scarface are finally gunned down by the police more as murderers than as gangsters. It would never do either dramatically or morally for movies to imitate reality by showing an Al Capone type sent to prison for tax evasion, as, indeed, Al Capone was in anticlimactic real life. Most crime reporters were well aware that Capone could not have flourished as he did if the entire Chicago police force and municipal government had not been on the take. Yet on the screen the overall honesty of the police force was postulated as one of the civic verities. Little Caesar had his detective-avenger nemesis in the Lieutenant Tom Flaherty of Thomas Jackson, and Scarface in the grim-faced Guarino of C. Henry Gordon. The censors, even in the early thirties, set a limit to the degree of society's complicity in crime. Nonetheless, when the gangster reigned supreme in his own genre, the forces of law and order were reduced to a Greek chorus of furies, howling over the hubris of hoods. The law always had the last laugh, but only after all the fun had been squeezed out of the subject for the audience.

From the moment that George Bancroft comes lurching out of a jewelry store robbery in *Underworld*, the criminal looms larger than life on the screen. Josef von Sternberg's crime trilogy—*Underworld, Dragnet, Thunderbolt*—crossed the divide between silent pictures and sound pictures. Yet few film historians have taken Bancroft seriously as a prototype of the gangster hero. In Sternberg's stylized world, crime is a projection of sexual potency. The women—Evelyn Brent in *Underworld* and *Dragnet*, Fay Wray in *Thunderbolt*—are the ultimate goals of criminal activity, rather than the fringe benefits to which they are reduced in subsequent mobster sagas. As activators rather than accessories, Brent and Wray tend to feminize a brutish genre. Sternberg's underworld is a hellish cauldron of desire for dames smothered in feathers and furs. There will be dames and molls in post-Sternbergian gangster films, but they will never again seem so crucial to criminal existence. Also, Sternberg's slow tempo, dream-like decor, and romantic psychology tended to subvert the complicated intrigues of his scenarios. There was little or no feeling of a world above and beyond the underworld. One felt no laws or morals in Sternberg's world, only codes of honor. And as it turned out, Bancroft's blustering superman was a law unto himself, walking to the electric chair (in *Underworld* and *Thunderbolt*) with a metaphysical majesty comparable to the descent into hell of Molière's Don Juan.

Bancroft had been preceded in movie crime by Lon Chaney earlier in the twenties [1920s], but Chaney was more the crook than the criminal in that he was not blessed with Bancroft's bravado, but afflicted instead with self-pity for his physical and spiritual deformities. It follows that whereas Bancroft was a personality performer with buoyantly bulging cheeks and playfully popping eyes, Chaney was a make-up artist who delighted in his deceptions. Bancroft was also more the gangster than Chaney in that the Sternbergian

The "big funeral" in *Little Caesar*.

felon seemed to participate in some semblance of a shadow government, whereas the Chaney wrongdoer was an eccentric freelancer on the edge of certifiable lunacy.

If Edward G. Robinson's Little Caesar obliterated the public's memory of Bancroft and Chaney as underworld figures, it was because there was more fact and less fantasy in his very thinly veiled characterization of Al Capone. W. R. Burnett's novel and Francis Faragoh's screenplay pick up Robinson's Cesare Enrico Bandello early in his career before he becomes that regal Rico—Little Caesar. The scenario thus unfolds as a depraved version of the American Dream. The opening shots of Rico and his sidekick Joe Massara (Douglas Fairbanks, Jr.) staging a holdup evoke laughter in seventies audiences at the irrepressible villainy of the abrupt action. There is not time to interpret the influence of the environment. But whereas Bancroft comes hurtling out at the audience at the beginning of *Underworld*, Robinson goes scurrying in like a furtive rat. The audience hears the bang-bang inside and laughs, but Rico himself is yet to emerge as a full-blown personality. Mervyn LeRoy's camera tends to stay at a middle distance as Rico does his megalomaniacal routines, thus giving the viewer a double perspective on the character. As big as Rico may think he is, he never floods the screen with the florid presence of Bancroft's Bull Weed in *Underworld*. Bancroft was of course a much larger man than Robinson, but there was no effort made to trick up Robinson's size à la Alan Ladd in the forties, and there was not head-shot introspection attributed to this out-and-out punk.

Consequently, Robinson's portrayal of Little Caesar contains the seeds of its own parody. The oh-yeah tough-guy mannerisms are essentially comic rather than romantic. It was as if Robinson had done Capone once and for all. Henceforth, his roles tended to be more shaded, more civilized, more sympathetic, until 1948 in *Key Largo*, in which he lapses back into self-parody as an updated Little Caesar. Most film historians have ranked LeRoy's *Little Caesar* a poor third to both Howard Hawks' *Scarface* and William Wellman's *The Public Enemy*. This judgment is justified for the most part, but it might be said in defense of *Little Caesar* that it came out several months before *The Public Enemy*, and more than a year before *Scarface*. In the early years of sound, a few months made an enormous difference in the smoothness and slickness of the production values, particularly in the realm of sound. *Little Caesar* opened in New York near the end of 1930, and already the sound of gunfire had attained a more persuasively percussive timbre than in Sternberg's 1929 *Thunderbolt*, in which the boom-boom sounded terribly tinny. 1931 and 1932 were therefore years of rapid stylistic adaptation, contrary to the prevailing wisdom of some vintage film histories that the sound film only came into its own in 1935 with *The Informer*. LeRoy himself displayed a considerable advance from the stultifyingly static camera set-ups and haphazardly neutral compositions of *Little Caesar* with the more dynamic devices of *Five-Star Final* in 1931 and *I Am a Fugitive from a Chain Gang* in 1932.

The frog-faced Robinson was the least sexual of all the gangster leads, and, perhaps as a consequence, the plot of *Little Caesar* takes a peculiar turn when Rico proclaims that he is jealous of his pal's girlfriend (Glenda Farrell). The fact that the pal (Douglas Fairbanks, Jr.) is much more attractive than Rico gives the buddy-buddy romance an extra twist. One genre historian has suggested an outright homosexual attraction at work, but the plot is complicated even further by the banal determination of the pal to "go straight." When the showdown comes, Rico is unable to gun down his friend, and thus loses face with his mob. The viewer may interpret Rico's fatal restraint as the redeeming flaw of an evil man, or as the proof of his hitherto suppressed passion for his pal. All is forgiven when Robinson asks aloud, "Mother of Mercy . . . is this the end of Rico?" (Thirty years later, James Cagney rendered that line as an impromptu homage to Robinson in Billy Wilder's *One, Two, Three*.)

Whereas *Little Caesar* is locked into a series of tableaux, *The Public Enemy* roams more freely in time and space to provide an urban ambience for its gangster characters. James Cagney's Tom Powers and Eddie Woods' Matt Doyle are followed from delinquent childhood on pre-Prohibition city streets, where beer buckets are prominently featured, to their bloody fate as gangsters of the Prohibition era. John Grierson and other socially conscious critics of the time hailed *The Public Enemy* for suggesting the evolution of criminals within a specific environment. Nonetheless, *The Public Enemy* has many of the same structural problems as *Little Caesar*, and at one point the camera takes the point of view of a rival gang as they lie in wait for the Cagney-Woods duo.

Fortunately, there are so many high points in Cagney's kinetic performance that the entire picture is carried along at a rollicking pace. The humor is richer, funnier, and more plentiful in *The Public Enemy* than in *Little Caesar*. Among the most memorable set-pieces: Cagney pushing the grapefruit in Mae Clark's kisser; Cagney and Woods getting a court order so that they can

"Cagney pushing the grapefruit in Mae Clark's kisser" in *The Public Enemy*.

shoot a horse responsible for the fatal fall of their beloved boss (that the horse is shot offscreen only adds to the merriment); Cagney being seduced by an affectingly awkward Jean Harlow to the strains of "I Surrender, Dear" on the radio; Cagney scooting around a corner with a balletic grace to avoid a hail of machine-gun bullets.

The longueurs in *The Public Enemy* derive mainly from nagging family scenes in which an uptight brother (Donald Cook) and an upright mother (Beryl Mercer) provide a moralistic contrast to the depredations of the Cagney character. Cagney developed very early in his career a mama's-boy complex in his roles in the midst of all his womanizing. This complex was to resurface most spectacularly in *White Heat* in 1949. Yet, Cagney was the foremost gangster womanizer in this era—if one excepts Clark Gable's magnetic malignancy in *A Free Soul* and *Night Nurse*, both movies oriented to their female stars (Norma Shearer, Barbara Stanwyck). Gable's brief career as a gangster ended appropriately in the electric chair of *Manhattan Melodrama* (1934), not only the movie Dillinger saw the night he was shot down by Purvis, but also the movie mentioned prominently in *Gravity's Rainbow* by Thomas Pynchon, who described William Powell—the district attorney who sends best friend Gable to the hot seat—as a "chinless bastard." In his way, Pynchon may have registered a delayed reaction to the great change that took place in Hollywood

Tom's first meeting with Gwen (Jean Harlow) in *The Public Enemy.*

in the mid-thirties. The execution of Gable as gangster may have served as a ritual murder of the entire genre.

Certainly, the pressure was being felt by the time of *Scarface*, as evidenced by a clumsily inserted scene in which a pack of civic reformers preaches directly to the camera in a clear breach of Howard Hawks' very rigorous consistency of visual narrative viewpoint. But the censors were up in arms over what they felt were incitements to crime in the glorification of gangsters on the screen. In their very useful reference work, *The Great Gangster Pictures*, James Robert Parish and Michael R. Pitts seem to take the pious protestations of the good guys in gangster pictures at face value. They also fail to make a distinction between the anarchic era in gangster pictures, ending, more or less, with *Scarface* in 1932, and the authoritarian era, beginning, more or less, with *G-Men* in 1935.

But *Scarface* itself is nothing if not devious as it traces the rise and fall of Paul Muni's cross-scarred Tony Camonte, another Capone approximation. If we postulate *Little Caesar, The Public Enemy*, and *Scarface* as the great gangster trilogy of the early thirties, we find the Muni character resembles the Robinson character in being introduced under an evil star without any environmental explanation or family connection. Camonte's first entrance is almost mystical in the shadowy style of German expressionism as he comes insistently upon his victim in a fatefully sustained camera movement by which the focus is fixed entirely on the fate of the victim. Yet, once the first murder is consummated, Hawks shifts to a more lucid, more humorous treatment of the adventures of his gangster protagonist. The women (Karen Morley, Ann Dvorak) are far more subtly depicted than the women in *The Public Enemy*. Indeed, Karen Morley's sophisticated sensuality and eye-gleaming perversity takes *Scarface* all the way back to the Sternbergian sirens of *Underworld* and *Thunderbolt*. Ann Dvorak's Cesca Camonte introduces more than an intimation of incest to the proceedings as she boldly confronts her brother's kinky possessiveness. The Robinson-Fairbanks relationship in *Little Caesar* finds its parallel in the Muni-Raft relationship in *Scarface*. Indeed, Raft was in real life somewhat comparable to the Fairbanks character as a dancer with ties to the mob.

In *Scarface*, however, there is no hesitation in pulling the trigger on one's best friend. The violence has been ritualized into an imperative. For Hawks and his scenarists, character is violence. And when Camonte comically mispronounces "habeas corpus" as "hocus pocus" he not only encourages lynch law, but encourages it also against immigrant types who misuse the language as they break the law. *Scarface*, like all gangster movies, thus stirred up anti-urban bigotries, which Warshow never took sufficiently into account in his essay. Even to celebrate sinful pleasures of the city was to stir up a storm of rural Puritanism. In many ways, *Scarface* was not so much innovative in and of itself, as it was a masterly summation of the entire genre. By 1932, the Chicago of *The Front Page* and *Little Caesar* had become a cliché. In *Scarface* the social context is thus stripped down to its most expressive elements. One does not have to establish the premises of power-seeking any longer; they are

"Sophisticated sensuality and eye-gleaming perversity": Karen Morley as Poppy with Paul Muni as Tony.

built into the genre. The need for exposition is gone. Scarface is consequently streamlined, but also offensive to the law-abiding. An era ends, and the censors exploit the customary lethargy of movie distributors to make sure that it never returns either with new films of the gangster as hero, or with revivals of old.

In the process many gangster films are completely forgotten. Only in the sixties and seventies are they brought back into view. Among these a select few deserve to be revived and remembered for their own distinctive idiosyncrasies. Archie Mayo's *Doorway to Hell* (1930) was released even before *Little Caesar*, but it never became part of movie mythology. Lew Ayres incarnated mobster Louis Ricarno more in a sensitive baby-faced manner than in the brutal, swaggering style of Robinson, Cagney, and Muni. With Cagney playing Ricarno's sidekick, *Doorway to Hell* would seem in retrospect to have been fatally miscast, with the anguished Ayres as its lead. Nonetheless the scene in which Ricarno returns to the tenements where he grew up is far more detailed psychologically and sociologically than any comparable scene in *Public Enemy*. Adapted from a Rowland Brown short story ("A Handful of Clouds") by George Rosener, *Doorway to Hell* may have been too disenchanting a descent into the underworld for the general public. The film seems to lament the loss of innocence and trust without any compensation from the pleasures of criminal power. It may be Rowland Brown's influence on the project that makes it seem like a commentary on American life in general.

Brown is one of the mysterious figures of early talkies, with a lingering reputation as the stormy-petrel Peckinpah of his period. Kevin Brownlow has insisted that Brown had more of a flair for publicity than actual talent. Nonetheless, the films he did manage to direct—*Quick Millions*, *Hell's Highway*, and *Blood Money*—display a very original though erratic imagination. Grierson was profoundly impressed by *Quick Millions* as the kind of gangster movie in which crime serves as a metaphor for capitalism, or, in the words of Louis Calhern's shyster lawyer in *The Asphalt Jungle*, crime as merely the left hand of human endeavor.

That *Quick Millions* is not as well known as the three official classics of the genre can be attributed to several factors: the relative inaccessibility of early Fox films as opposed to early Warner films, the miscasting in retrospect of Spencer Tracy (like Lew Ayres) as a gangster lead, and Brown's curiously elliptical rendering of the action so that the movie turns out to be more pugnacious than violent. Brown clearly lacked Hawks' dynamic flair for storytelling and Wellman's eye for gritty detail, but *Quick Millions* is unique for its time in suggesting the affinity between racketeering and big business. There was also in Brown's vision of life a grown-up awareness of the nuances of the class struggle. "The society swells really have big weddings," one gangster tells another, "But we have big funerals." This last line of the film also serves as

"Sternbergian siren" Evelyn Brent in *Underworld*.

Tracy's requiem. He has been murdered by the mob for letting his lech for a high-society dame (Marguerite Churchill) jeopardize their delicate relationship with the establishment.

Hell's Highway (1932) was a far-fetched prison movie that seemed to have been influenced by the Russian cinema in the matter of defiant groupings of the convicts as if they were posing for revolutionary posters. But, again, Brown's narrative style seems remote and elliptical, as if he knows what everything means before he begins, and cannot be bothered to make his continuity plausible.

Blood Money (1933) is another matter entirely. George Bancroft is near the end of his tether as a character lead. Here he plays a bail bondsman, dangling on the edge of criminality without ever losing his legal footing. The dames steal the show, however, with Judith Anderson's compliant, low-cut-gowned nightclub hostess and Frances Dee's wild-eyed nymphomaniac giving Hollywood one last fling with grown-up sensuality before the age of Shirley Temple officially began.

Roland West's dilettantish contributions to the genre—*Alibi, Bat Whispers, Corsair*—were richer in a menacing atmosphere of tricks and stratagems than in the psychology and sociology of gangsterdom. West's self-financed efforts were filmed at night and reveal a leisurely cultivation of a pictorial style. Chester Morris, a much-neglected and underrated performer from this period, was the center of each of these films as either a hammy villain (*Alibi, Bat Whispers*) or a handsome hero (*Corsair*). The opening scene of *Corsair* is as overtly anti-capitalistic as one could wish. Chester Morris plays a young stockbroker who, proclaiming his disgust at peddling worthless stock to unsuspecting little old ladies, decides to get into the relatively honest work of rum-running. A very complicated intrigue then ensues in which gravel-voiced, cigar-chomping deadpan Ned Sparks gives the performance of his life as a doomed double agent.

Less impressive is Rouben Mamoulian's much overrated objet d'art *City Streets*, in which Gary Cooper and Sylvia Sidney enact a turgid drama of frame-ups and escapes. Cooper, as a rural slowpoke type, is the most miscast gangster in the genre's entire history. The film has been hailed, however, as a textbook example of creative montage, composition, and symbolic expression in the early sound era. The narrative, unfortunately, functions in fits and starts, and the final denouement is so wildly improbable that it seems to belong in a musical. Still, the fact the Cooper character becomes a gangster, and yet escapes unscathed, gives the film a heady quality of casual amorality, which the censors will tolerate only a year or two more.

All in all, the period between 1927 and 1933 was a marvelously uninhibited, and yet oddly unappreciated one. It is in this period that Hollywood's rangingly raunchy unconscious was allowed to hang out in the name of sordid realism. Most movies were mediocre, as always, but even in their mediocrity, they breathed a demotic, demonic fire. It is no accident that the era of *Little Caesar, The Public Enemy*, and *Scarface* was the era also of *Frankenstein, Dracula,*

Tarzan, King Kong. Robinson, Cagney, Muni each die like monsters: Robinson like a writhing reptile, Cagney like a falling mummy, Muni like a contorted creation of mad science. For a time the id reigned supreme, and anarchic rebellion was implied everywhere. The most powerful prison movie of all time remains *The Big House* of 1930, a movie in which Wallace Berry and Chester Morris wage such a powerful revolt that army tanks have to be called in the yard to quell the uprising. The censors would never allow such massive violence in the screen's penal system ever again. What is curious is that the intellectuals never rose to the defense of this defiant cinema until it was much too late. After 1935 it would be decades before Hollywood could recapture the lustful license it accepted as a matter of course in 1929.

Bogart as older and old-school gangster Roy Earle in *High Sierra*.

Post-Code Gangster Movies

(*from* Gangsters on the Screen, *1978)*

Frank Manchel

J. Edgar Hoover may seem an unlikely person to credit with starting a new gangster film cycle in 1935. As director of the Federal Bureau of Investigation, he naturally hated movies that glamorized gangsters. Yet his actions in the thirties triggered a return to fast-action crime films.

Ever since taking over the Bureau in 1924, Hoover fought to improve the agency's image. That was no easy job. His agents couldn't carry guns or make arrests. Besides, organized crime was too large for his undermanned squads to fight. Then came the public uproar over the Lindbergh case, and Congress passed in 1932 a law making kidnapping a federal crime. This gave the federal agents power to act effectively in their war against gangsters. Hoover seized the moment to publicize how the Bureau was society's major safeguard against crime. It wasn't true, particularly since the Treasury Department had been the major force in sending Al Capone to jail in 1931 for tax evasion. But Hoover devised a brilliant scheme. Through his contacts in the mass media, he published a Public Enemy list of the nation's "most desperate" criminals. The list came out at the time the FBI was set to capture these gangsters. Hoover's brilliance lay in turning small-time, midwestern hoodlums like Alvin "Old Creepy" Karpis, "Pretty Boy" Floyd, Bonnie Parker, Clyde Barrow, "Ma" Barker, "Machine Gun" Kelly, and John Dillinger into national problems. Unable to fight organized crime's giant army, Hoover went after smaller hoods and made it seem big stuff.

"Machine Gun" Kelly illustrates the Public Enemy game the FBI played. Kelly was a small-time bootlegger who often bragged, "No copper would ever take me alive." His showoff ways fooled few people. They knew he was stupid, easygoing, and drank too much. His image changed, however, when he married Cleo Shannon. She wanted a headline gangster for a husband. So Cleo bought him a machine gun, nagged George into robbing some banks, and insisted that he kidnap a millionaire oilman. Kelly's fear and incompetence almost wrecked the ransom arrangements. Soon after the victim's release, a Tennessee policeman burst into Kelly's hideout and captured the meek outlaw. Hoover, however, made sure that Americans believed this "public menace" was pursued and captured by the FBI. Newspapers reported the terrified gangster as yelling, "Don't shoot, G-Men!"

Warner Bros. decided to cash in on Hoover's commitment to improving the public image of the FBI. They saw it as a way around the studio's censorship battles over gangster films. If you made the crusading lawman the hero, you could still emphasize fast-paced, violent action. In 1935, the studio experimented with William Keighley's *G-Men*. The sly melodrama dealt with a slum kid who is sent to law school by a friendly gangster. When a college friend is later killed trying to arrest a hoodlum, the young lawyer joins the FBI, seeking revenge for the murder. Using his former underworld contacts, he discovers his benefactor's role in the crime and kills him in a shoot-out. He then decides to quit the Bureau but changes his mind when another gang kidnaps his girlfriend. He rescues her and wins the Department's respect.

By using Cagney as the reformed crusader, Warner Bros. successfully merged the old and new gangster formulas. The public saw their popular star doing what he had always done, only now on the side of justice. Furthermore, censors couldn't complain. More important, gangster films had new ingredients. Old-time villains with slum backgrounds were replaced by new front-page mobsters, native born and residing in rural areas. Instead of the standard bootlegging stories, audiences got bank robbers, kidnappings, and interstate manhunts.

Cagney takes a turn as a government agent in *G-Men*.

The Petrified Forest, directed by Archie Mayo in 1936, gave Warners its next major gangster film. Though mainly a photographed stage play, its theme of brute force versus intellectualism proved popular with audiences. The story dealt with a mixed group of people held captive in an isolated service station by the vicious Duke Mantee and his gang escaping from the law. Despite the talky script, the dialogue produced some memorable observations about gangsters. Upon meeting Mantee, the hero (Leslie Howard), a penniless intellectual with a death wish, raises his glass and declares, "You're the last great apostle of rugged individualism." Another character argues that Mantee isn't a gangster. "Gangsters are foreigners, he's an American." Elsewhere Mantee himself summarizes a gangster's story, "I've spent most of my time since I grew up in jail . . . and it looks like I'll spend the rest of my life dead."

Still, the best part of *The Petrified Forest* is Humphrey Bogart as the brutal Mantee. Tough, cynical, menacing, the rugged actor offered a sharp contrast to the by now familiar swaggering, optimistic screen gangsters. Bogart moved slowly about the set wearing a two-day beard, his body visibly slumped over, suggesting an apelike mentality that threatened mankind. The Mantee role (originally slated for Edward G. Robinson but gotten for Bogart by Leslie Howard) saved Bogart's film career. Having done ten bad movies prior to *The Petrified Forest*, he seemed unsuited for Hollywood. This film proved to be the turning point. Bogart remained typecast over the next few years as a sneering, heartless gangster who dies in the end and became a fixed member of Warners' immortal murderers' row, which includes James Cagney, Paul Muni, Edward G. Robinson, and George Raft.

The same year saw Robinson switch to the right side of the law in *Bullets or Ballots*. Based loosely on Manhattan detective Johnny Broderick's exploits, Seton I. Miller's screenplay dealt with the special powers granted crusading policemen. William Keighley's taut direction deglamorized racket life and made crime busters the heroic figures. Robinson played a tough cop who fakes his dismissal in order to join Bogart's mob and then destroy it. The role appealed to Robinson, who explained in an interview, "It was a hard part. I had to play it differently from those gangster roles, play it down, make it quieter. . . . Even so, in that scene where I had to convince the audience as well as the gang that I was turning racketeer, I could see a trace of Little Caesar again." Bogart's role, on the other hand, played both on his Mantee image and the real-life Dutch Schultz. The actor now became typecast as an unrepentant, calculating, and double-crossing mobster.

This cycle of gangster films brought back Hollywood's attacks on the social conditions that breed criminals. Signaling the return was director William Wyler's 1937 screen adaptation of Sidney Kingsley's Broadway hit *Dead End*. The United Artists film pictured the conflicting lifestyles in New York City's East River district, where luxury and poverty existed side by side. Six young boys, headed for trouble, meet the notorious "Baby Face" Martin (Bogart), who revisits the old neighborhood to see his mother (Marjorie Main) and take up with his old girlfriend (Claire Trevor). A poor but talented architect (Joel McCrea) and a sister of one of the boys (Sylvia Sidney) join forces

Only four years before playing the grizzled Roy Earle, Bogart portrayed "Baby Face" Martin in *Dead End* (with Claire Trevor as Francey).

to oppose the gangster's influence on the Dead End kids. Although forced by the Motion Picture Code to downplay violence and eliminate vulgarity, screenwriter Lillian Hellman successfully captured the play's powerful message about poverty, ignorance, and neglect. One unforgettable scene had the gangster's mother slapping him in the face and growling, "You dog, you dirty yellow dog, you! You ain't no son of mine!" His bitter response: "I killed a guy for looking at me the way you are now." Another famous exchange occurs when the mobster discovers that his old girlfriend is a prostitute. Horrified, he barks, "Why didn't you starve?" Her quick reply is, "Why didn't you?" Most popular with audiences of the day was the realistic acting of the Dead End kids themselves. Brought to Hollywood from their roles in the original stage play, the youngsters went on to become movie fixtures for the next two decades.

Angels with Dirty Faces (1938) further advanced the argument that criminals are made, not born. The cliché-ridden story of two boyhood chums, one a gangster (Cagney) and the other a priest (Pat O'Brien), took a hard look at rat-infested tenements, hoodlum influence on neighborhood slum kids, and ineffectual settlement-house programs. At one point, Father Connolly grudgingly admits to Rocky Sullivan, "Whatever I teach them, you show me up. You show them the easiest way." Admitting that crime appears profitable and gangster behavior seems heroic, the dedicated priest pleads with the soon-to-be-executed gangster to destroy the Dead End kids' worship of Rocky. "You've been a hero to them in life, and if you go to the chair without a quiver, you'll be a hero to them in death. I want them to despise your memory. They've got to be ashamed of you." The film's climax has the gangster screaming that he doesn't want to die, but Michael Curtiz directs the scene with such subtlety that no one ever knows whether Rocky died a coward or hero. Aided considerably by performers like Cagney, O'Brien, the Dead End kids, Bogart, and Ann Sheridan, *Angels with Dirty Faces* emerged as the best gangster film of the late thirties.

The golden age of gangster films faded by the end of the decade. One reason was that producers just burned out the formula. No matter how hard-boiled Bogart might be in a film like *Racket Busters* (1938), you knew he was a loser. The same predictability hurt Raoul Walsh's *The Roaring Twenties* (1939). Audiences were bored by the old familiar Prohibition stories. Not even humorous attempts like *A Slight Case of Murder* (1938), which turned Robinson's Little Caesar role into broad comedy, revived sagging box-office profits. Another reason the public lost interest was the tie existing between the gangster movies and "headline news." By 1938, the famous public enemies were dead or behind bars. Tough-minded crime busters like Thomas E. Dewey had finished their sensational investigations, and a false sense of confidence swept the nation. Gangsters no longer seemed a threat to society. The danger now came from foreign agents, and studios like Warner Bros. began shifting the crime conventions to espionage films like *Confessions of a Nazi Spy* (1939).

About the only formula profiting from gangster types in the late thirties was the serial. Here again newspapers provided the inspiration. Many comic-strip heroes such as Dick Tracy, Captain Marvel, and Superman fitted ideally into the weekly chapter format. The standard plot featured a dangerous gang pitted against the forces of justice. Typical was Republic's *Dick Tracy Returns* (1938), in which the master lawman joins the ranks of federal agents through fifteen episodes to destroy the notorious Pa Stark gang.

Hollywood thus had two choices in 1939: either forget about gangster films or find another way to make use of the once-popular violent material. America learned shocking facts about war and organized crime in the forties. It discovered that President Roosevelt's attack on big-city bosses, with their corrupt and graft-ridden administrations, fostered the growth of the syndicate. Gangsters fleeing the "big heat" in New York, Pennsylvania, Illinois, Ohio, and Massachusetts set up new crime operations in Florida, Arizona,

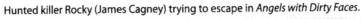

Hunted killer Rocky (James Cagney) trying to escape in *Angels with Dirty Faces*.

and California. Until early 1940, the public believed that gangbusters like Hoover and Dewey had broken the back of organized crime. Major mobsters like Luciano were in jail, while others were being deported monthly.

Then came the sensational probe by assistant district attorney Burton Turkus into Brooklyn crime. A two-bit murderer named Abe "Kid Twist" Reles confessed he belonged to an elite group that killed by contract. Victims were selected by gangs across the country and then OK'd by national criminals like Lepke, Benjamin "Bugsy" Siegel, and Albert Anastasia. As the case against "Murder Inc." unfolded, Turkus revealed the vast criminal network covering the nation, corrupting government on all levels, state and federal law enforcement bodies, and labor and management groups. The syndicate's power thrived on the revelations. Since Murder Inc. included old-fashioned killers like Lepke, their conviction and execution eliminated outmoded gangsters. The gangland killing of the "canary" Reles, who was thrown out of a heavily guarded police hotel window, let the public know that no one was safe when the syndicate was after you. The fact that Siegel and Anastasia escaped criminal prosecution proved the syndicate's power.

Bogart slaps some sense into the "young twerps" portrayed by Arthur Kennedy and Alan Curtis (on the floor) as Marie (Ida Lupino) looks on in *High Sierra*.

The forties also saw a major change in gangster films. Crimes became more terrifying, the characters more dishonest and double-dealing. Announcing the end of the old formulas in 1941 was director Raoul Walsh's *High Sierra*. Scripted by John Huston and W. R. Burnett, the nostalgic plot was Hollywood's way of saying goodbye to a folk hero of the Depression. Sprung from jail by a fatally ill gangland pal, Roy "Mad Dog" Earle discovers that organized crime as he knew it is no more. His friend tells him that screwballs have taken over: "Young twerps, soda jerkers and jitterbugs. . . . Yep, all the A-1 guys are gone. Dead or in Alcatraz. . . ." Committed to doing the ill-fated bank robbery, Earle finds himself confused and alone in the modern criminal setting. "Sometimes," he observes, "I feel I don't know what it's all about any more." The robbery itself reveals that the gangster's new associates are inexperienced, cowardly, and disloyal. Accepting his tragic destiny, the Dillinger-like Earle chooses to make his last stand high in the mountains, symbolic of his isolation from the world around him.

High Sierra not only put aside old formulas, but also ended Bogart's days as a "minor" gangster figure next to Cagney and Robinson. Their refusal to play the Earle role—they didn't want a part George Raft had turned down—

Bogart as "cynical, tough private eye Sam Spade" watches with Brigid O'Shaughnessy (Mary Astor) as co-conspirator Joel Cairo (Peter Lorre) is hauled off by the cops.

provided Bogart with one of his best acting jobs. Even more significant, *High Sierra* promoted him to star status.

Later that same year Bogart ushered in a new era for gangster movies with *The Maltese Falcon*. Cast as the cynical, tough private eye Sam Spade, he turned Warner Bros.' third version of the Dashiell Hammett novel into a film masterpiece. The story, brilliantly scripted and filmed by John Huston in his directorial debut, studied what happens when a San Francisco detective agrees to help a beautiful but murderous lady gain possession of a legendary jeweled statuette. Cinematographer Arthur Edeson established the perfect tone and mood for evil characters to do their worst. Huston's faithful adaptation of the novel's dialogue realistically presented a world where good and bad people are almost indistinguishable. Bogart, for example, appears to put money before honor. He tells the lying Brigid O'Shaughnessy (Mary Astor), "We didn't believe your story, we believed your money." Only at the film's conclusion does he try to state his real values. "If your partner is killed," Bogart explains to the murderess, "you're supposed to do something about it."

"Power and its resultant status are to be passed on from father to son, if the son proves worthy": Marlon Brando as the elderly Don Vito Corleone and Al Pacino as his son Michael.

All in the Family: The *Godfather* Saga

(from Crime Movies, *1980)*

Carlos Clarens

For all the curiosity the Mafia arouses in the layman, *The Black Hand* and *Pay or Die* adopted an external, legalistic viewpoint and an attitude tinged with outrage. *The Godfather* reversed the viewpoint, looking from inside the underworld out into a hopelessly corrupt society from which tradition, loyalty, honor, and respect for one's elders had almost totally vanished. This daring dramatic device would ruinously have failed had the outside, straight world been allowed to intrude. Two of the most debatable propositions about the criminal world were carried to a claustrophobic extreme; namely, that there is a code of honor among thieves, and that this perfectly self-contained (and self-sustaining) world rarely touches the man in the street. There was a frightening, memorable scene in Walsh's *The Roaring Twenties* in which an elderly couple was caught in the crossfire between rival gangs at a restaurant. There were virtually no bystanders in *The Godfather*, and none of those who were included retained any innocence.

The Godfather might be reviewing the Renaissance through the eyes of the Medici, a perspective similar to that adopted by the Italian director Luchino Visconti in *The Damned* (1969), wherein he showed the rise of Nazism through the eyes of the (fictionalized) Krupp family. In fact, there is more of Visconti in *The Godfather* than of any of the above-mentioned directors. Coppola's Don Corleone appeared at times as a kindred soul to Visconti's Sicilian prince in *The Leopard*, both icons of an order about to pass. Visconti's original choice for his princely hero was Laurence Olivier; so was Coppola's for the godfather. For a role demanding a charisma beyond that of most actors, George C. Scott was also considered, but Marlon Brando, Puzo's first choice, was the final choice. Olivier would have undoubtedly brought to the part his own thin-lipped, ascetic alertness as well as some of the papal authority that is apparent in photos of a genuine godfather such as Carlo Gambino; he would have been chilling in the role. Brando, affecting a wheezy delivery and using more makeup than any major star since Paul Muni, mellowed the Don into a patriarch in autumn.

For visual style, Coppola and his cameraman, Gordon Willis, relied mostly on one lingering, controlling image, that of hushed ceremonials among men in darkened rooms. The lowered Venetian blinds that established the mood in film noir by casting stripes of psychological guilt across the screen now suffused interiors with amber, old-masterly light. In the opening shot, the mood was already confessional, and the godlike character of Don Vito Corleone was boldly established. Holding audience and granting favors on his daughter's wedding day, Don Corleone listens to an outraged father demand death for the attackers of his daughter who have been set free because of family influence or the sheer laxity of the law. "That would not be fair, my friend, your daughter is alive," is the sober reply, as if the godfather were restoring a rapport between deed and retribution long lost in the byways and intricacies of the legal system, and dispensing an eye-for-an-eye justice in direct contact with the plaintiff.

In *The Godfather*, when Don Corleone took on his main adversary from the straight world, a Hollywood producer patently inspired by Harry Cohn, and when his younger son and heir, Michael (Al Pacino), clashed with a U.S. senator in *Part II*, these opponents were depicted as racist, uncouth, venal, and, more significant, as sexual perverts. ("Infamia!" mutters Don Corleone upon learning that Jack Woltz, the producer [John Marley], keeps a child star in his palatial home for sexual purposes; the WASP senator plays heavy sado-masochistic games with prostitutes.) Their proclivities clearly offend

"Brando, affecting a wheezy delivery and using more makeup than any major star since Paul Muni, mellowed the Don into a patriarch in autumn."

the Corleones, abstemious family men, more than does their pride. The producer and the senator appear guilty of crimes against nature, next to which the Corleones are merely granting justice without resorting to the law, or at worst transacting business in an unorthodox way. The manner in which the guilty are humbled, in blood-soaked beds, seems somewhat scriptural, as if the godfather were omniscient as well as all-powerful. This power and its resultant status are to be passed on from father to son, if the son proves worthy.

Michael prepares to kill the men who threaten his father, Police Capt. McCluskey (Sterling Hayden) and rival mobster Virgil "the Turk" Sillozzo (Al Lettieri).

The Godfather is also about the transition from the archaic, relatively honor-bound order of Don Corleone to the more pragmatic and less scrupulous regime of his younger son, who would develop the family business into an impersonal national corporation. When first introduced, Michael is an unlikely candidate to head a prominent Mafia family in the eastern United States; a college student and a war veteran, Michael seems on his return to civilian life uncommitted to the family business. Soon enough, an attempt is made on Don Corleone's life, and Michael is claimed by the imperatives of honor and of his own Sicilian blood to take revenge on his father's enemies. When Michael kills for the first time, the act takes on an aspect of ritual blood-spilling: the training and planning, the breathtaking gravity with which Michael dispatches the two men at a restaurant table, the deadly calm that follows the shooting as Michael unhurriedly leaves the scene, abandoning his gun (which cannot be traced: an enchanted weapon)—each has its own initiatory justification.

As the new Don, Michael expands the family's sphere of influence to the gambling casinos of the West. *The Godfather* concludes with the death of Don Corleone and the ensuing bloodbath, a fictional counterpart of the Banana War of the late forties, which will consolidate Michael's power within the Mafia. The old Don's death, of a heart attack while playing with Michael's son in a sun-drenched orchard, serves for an effective improvisation: Don Corleone has fashioned a grotesque denture from an orange peel in order to play the bogeyman for his grandchild, and the little boy struggles with the same ambivalence experienced by the audience—the scary suggestion that a monster lurks after all behind the benign grandfather figure.

Part II provided the addenda and corrigenda to a subject treated a bit too hurriedly in *The Godfather*. The making of the first film was marked by dissension between the producer, Al Ruddy, and Coppola, who went on to produce the sequel himself, combining leftover material from Puzo's novel with an updating of the plot that took the Corleone family into the late fifties. By then Michael had moved the seat of power to Lake Tahoe in California and had planned an alliance with the Jewish branch of the mob, as represented by Hyman Roth (Lee Strasberg), that would result in profits undreamed of by Don Corleone. Patterned after the notorious Meyer Lansky, best publicized of the Jewish gangsters in the syndicate, Roth delivers Lansky's by now legendary boast: "We're bigger than U.S. Steel." The wily, avuncular Roth lacks the warmer traits of his Italian contemporary, and, compared to Don Corleone's, Roth's family life is drab and there is no visible issue, only a few hulking bodyguards prowling around his modest Miami house. Munching a sandwich in front of his TV set, Roth reminisces: "I've loved baseball since Arnold Rothstein fixed the World Series in 1919." Poor Rothstein, dead for more than forty years, was the only real gangster mentioned by name in all of *The Godfather.*

Part II pursued the parallel between crime and big business into the imperialistic fifties, transporting Michael and Roth to Havana and seating them at the table of dictator Fulgencio Batista, next to the ITT representatives, to take part in the despoiling of the island. Although it is obvious that Michael, deep inside, finds the operation distasteful—he is equally ill at ease at the live sex shows patronized by American tourists—he backs out of the deal, not because of any moral qualm, but because his Harvard Business School instinct tells

"The wily, avuncular Roth lacks the warmer traits of his Italian contemporary":
Lee Strasberg as Roth.

him that the Batista regime is about to collapse; mafioso flair scoops even the *New York Times*. Stateside, another climactic purge is launched to liquidate Roth and his supporters, among them Michael's weak, older brother. The success of the purge leaves Michael at the top, sharing the desolate fate of those who gain the world but lose their immortal soul, or so Coppola would have us believe.

Mario Puzo's novel was on the *New York Times* best-seller list sixty-seven weeks. Paramount picked up the film rights for a paltry $50,000 before publication: the recent failure of *The Brotherhood* seemed to sour any prospects for a successful Mafia movie. *The Godfather* surprised even its makers by becoming the most profitable film up to its time: in December 1977, *Variety* listed rentals of $86 million. The sequel came in at $29 million. Both pictures were later combined with one hour of discarded footage to make a nine-hour television film aired on four successive evenings in November 1977, for which rights the National Broadcasting Corporation paid $12 million. Billed as "the complete novel for television" and preceding each chapter with the most absurd disclaimer ever—"does not represent any ethnic group. . .fictional account of a small group of criminals"—the series failed to capture the vast nationwide audience that had made *Roots* a television event earlier that year. Along with the millions of viewers who had flocked to the theaters only a few years before, something had been lost in transition.

Back then, apart from the film's intrinsic quality, a chain of events had conditioned audiences to accept *The Godfather* as the long-awaited, final word on organized crime. Paramount had carefully orchestrated press releases during production. There had been warnings and threats from Italian civil-rights groups and, reputedly, from the Mafia as well. *Time* reported that the producer's car had been riddled with machine-gun fire, although the fact was never authenticated. It did prove, however, that publicity agents still functioned the same old way, like lower-echelon Mafiosi—the filmed-under-threat routine had worked wonders back in the days of *Doorway to Hell*. Interviews during production and at the time of release stressed authenticity above all. Robert Evans, then a top Paramount executive and a Coppola supporter, justified his director in a *Time* interview. "He knew the way these men ate their food, kissed each other, talked. He knew the grit!" Anyone with a family connection, however remote or fictional, seems to have been consulted, or appeased, or in some cases hired. Despite opposition from the production staff, a Las Vegas master of ceremonies, Carlo Russo, landed a meaty minor role as Carlo Rizzi, Don Corleone's treacherous son-in-law. He got the part on the strength of his friendship with Anthony Columbo, who was Joseph Colombo's son and vice-president of the Italian-American Civil Rights League.

The elder Colombo contributed his share of headlines during the production, some of them in tragic opposition to his platform. In June 1971, at an Italian-American Unity Day rally in New York, he was shot in the head by a black gunman named Jerome A. Johnson, who had allegedly been hired by a rival New York family headed by Joseph Gallo. Johnson was then shot by Colombo's bodyguards. (At first, it seemed unlikely that a black assassin would do the job for a Mafia family; but that one indeed had only proved that eligibility rules had been relaxed in the sixties in order to admit blacks and Puerto Ricans.) Colombo died in 1978 without ever recovering from the wounds inflicted by Johnson. In April 1972, when *The Godfather* had been playing for only a few weeks, Gallo was shot dead while celebrating his 43rd birthday at Umberto's Clam House in Little Italy. It was soon afterward made public that an underground war had been raging between the Colombo and Gallo families.

The Mafia was very much alive, despite Colombo's campaign to pronounce it dead and gone with a generation of Italian and Sicilian immigrants. *The Godfather* could be read as a roman à clef, and it was considered hip to detect the fictionalized portraits of Harry Cohn, Frank Sinatra, Meyer Lansky, and Bugsy Siegel. Puzo had done his homework thoroughly. The Corleones were made up of a composite of various Mafia families and set into a historical context. Puzo used some real names, including Maranzano and Lucchese. As he candidly admitted later in *The Godfather Papers*, he had done a job that even met with the approval and respect of those concerned, a fact corroborated by Gay Talese in *Honor Thy Father*, a detailed chronicle of the Bonanno family.

Puzo supplied the Corleones with fairly mythological dimensions, but Coppola was to go even further in the same direction. The director adopted as key scenes in both films that classic moment in mythological fiction in which the hero, under the influence of the past, confronts his fate and accepts it, as if the future had suddenly been revealed to him. Michael's first kill in *The Godfather* and Vito's in *Part II* did not carry the same significance in Puzo's novel, where they were presented as stages in the development of the characters.

NBC's high hopes for a second *Roots* were not so absurd, for in its way *The Godfather* undertook a similar exploration in time, striving to set up a continuity between the old and the new worlds. In the spring of 1978, the four-part television film *Holocaust* almost matched the success of *Roots*. Both series dealt with the trials and tragedies of racial persecution, concluding with statements of achievement and hope. But *The Godfather* traced a downward graph within a mere two generations. The final effect was far from elating, as the romance of immigration hardened into a power play behind closed shutters, the mystic freemasonry of crime deteriorated into utilitarian carnage. The films contrasted a romantic past—bucolic, primitive Sicily; Little Italy through a patina of affection—to the harsh and somber present. Rearranging the events in chronological order, the TV version exposed this strategy a little too starkly, gambling on the cumulative effect of the dynastic novel, an effect that, in this case, turned out to be depressingly negative.

The Godfather, especially *Part II*, has undergone close scrutiny (in *Jump Cut* magazine, for one) along critical lines that constitute a politicization of Robert Warshow's famous dictum that the gangster embodies a denial of capitalist society. And Coppola, at least ex post facto, encouraged this reading of *The Godfather* by admitting to a metaphorical critique of the American system.

It was a metaphor, however, that Coppola could only activate at the expense of genre, that could only function by leaving narrative gaps which, were they filled, would compromise the dominant premise of the Mafia as a self-supporting, self-regulating, alternative society.

Where does the Corleone family income come from? There was some talk of power and influence, of the family "owning" judges and politicians, but not one word about such bread-and-butter activities as prostitution, hijacking, loan sharking, or the numbers racket. At times Coppola went soft on his characters in a way Puzo never did. The godfather refused to get involved in the drug market because of vague moral principle—"Drugs will destroy us" was the Don's one failed prophecy—while Puzo simply presented the deal as a shaky investment that the shrewd Don turned down. Sonny Corleone (James Caan) was not portrayed as the feared family executioner he was in the novel but as a lusty, boyish ladykiller.

The almost total suppression of the godfather's criminal dimension removed his main social characteristic from the film. The murders, extortion, and exploitation of others which originally inscribed the character in the underworld were transmuted into retaliatory action, correction of power abuse, business transactions of a more ethical nature than seemed customary among mobsters. The intimidation of potential victims—the godfather's famous offer that cannot be refused—was carried out on behalf of the deserving and the deprived, whether to obtain a Hollywood contract for a favorite godson of certified talent or to obtain a stay of eviction from a miserly landlord.

Diane Keaton as Kay, "a Yankee princess" who "had no place in the cinematic saga of the Corleones."

Another sleight of hand concerned the role of Kay (Diane Keaton), Michael Corleone's girlfriend, later his second wife. A Yankee princess, Kay might have functioned (as she did in the novel) as a representative of the non-Italian, non-criminal world she left behind to marry into the Corleone family. But her role gave Coppola the worst trouble, since to admit the honest outside world would have imperiled his airtight universe. Consequently, Kay was made to act unduly stupid, asking questions that no sensible mafioso wife had the right to ask her man (the answers being more than obvious); and once this tiresome tactic made her presence expendable, there was the unexpected revelation that she had willingly aborted Michael's third child. This was truly the unkindest blow to the character, since abortion, in the eyes of the Catholic church, is sin, and Kay thus joined the unnatural company of the pedophile producer and the sadistic senator. When Michael slammed the door in her face, his action had all the force of justifiable rejection, and audiences were bound to accept and even applaud it. Kay had no place in the cinematic saga of the Corleones.

At the height of the war between the families, Don Corleone delivers a short but precise line: "This war stops now." During the period in which *The Godfather* was made and released—that of the Vietnam War—this sort of pacifist slogan in the mouth of a ruthless and powerful man had the force of an exorcism and henceforth identified him as the righteous man whose moral superiority transcended all legality. In the final analysis, Don Corleone is the upholder of natural law, God's law, separating good from evil. By intent, religious ceremony was used repeatedly to counterpoint some of the most violent deeds of the Corleones: the preparations for a massacre are intercut with the christening of Michael's firstborn; a procession is in progress as the young Vito stalks his first victim across the roofs of Little Italy. Rather than implicating the church in the underworld, as the Marxist observer might have it, these parallels serve to turn the violence into a sacrament. To reinforce the impression of justified, sacramental violence, some vaguely biblical references were scattered throughout: the "kiss of death" with which Michael casts off his treacherous brother (John Cazale), and some visionary lines, such as "Whoever comes to you with the Barzini meeting, he's a traitor," or "Before I get to my hotel I'll be assassinated," which sounded like parodies of parables.

Toward the end of *Part II*, fiction became historically certifiable, and the film was thereby led into implications it could not handle. Following the Cuban revolution and his falling-out with Hyman Roth, Michael says, "If history has taught us anything it's that you can kill anyone." Considering the failed attempts on the lives of Roosevelt, Churchill, Hitler, at the film's own milieu, Frank Costello, all of these evidence to the contrary, the line can only strike the viewer as an intimation of things to come: the suspected underworld participation in the Kennedy assassination or the documented involvement of the syndicate in the CIA plots against Fidel Castro, in which John Rosselli, once of Hollywood and Bioff and Browne notoriety, acted as middleman. The line worked on the viewer all right—Michael proved his point by having Roth assassinated in full view of the FBI by a kamikaze gunman—but by then it was too late for the film to avail itself of a fresh set of implications. Having spent close to seven hours of screen time to establish a seemingly valid parallel between criminal and corporate behavior, *The Godfather* still could not sound the alarm on crime.

"We had been sure of the square audience," wrote Mario Puzo with a certain surprise at what Coppola had wrought from his novel, "and now it looked as if we were going to *get* the hip avant-garde too." To *Rolling Stone*, the godfather seemed an omniscient figure capable of taking on Con Edison single-handed, a displacement of authority away from the establishment.

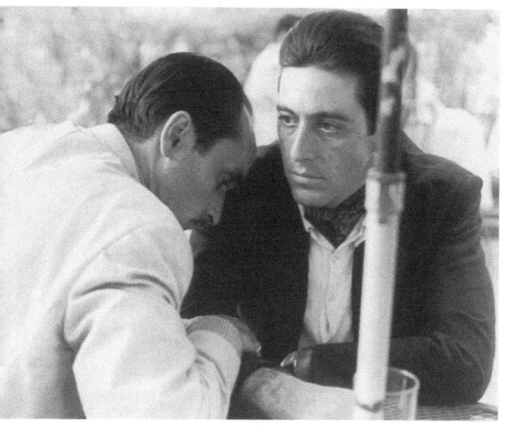

Michael casts off his treacherous brother Fredo (John Cazale) in *Godfather II.*

What if the films also endorsed a paternalistic, repressive, sexist sub-society that conservatives all over would recognize, identify with, and tip their hard hats to? Later in the seventies, the godfather seems more castrating than charismatic—a figure of the Nixonian era rather than a man for all political seasons—because ensuing events have left the film's cool, knowledgeable, guiltless stance behind.

Thus, a movie for détente. In 1972, the year of the first *Godfather* and also the year of Watergate and the Republican Convention in Miami (during which Norman Mailer appropriated the title "Godfather" for Richard Nixon), concerns like the perfectibility of society and the regeneration of the criminal seemed to belong forever to the twenties and thirties [1920s and 1930s]. Over such issues the film extended the soothing acquiescence that, left to themselves, criminals would leave society unmolested except to dispute the powerful for a slice of the power. Rarely has there been a film so much of a piece with its discourse, so untempered by distance or irony. Could *The Godfather* have pleaded less openly for peaceful coexistence with the underworld or seemed less accepting of things as they are and still have become in its time the most successful film ever?

PART
TWO

Case
Studies

Karty (John Ireland) tries to talk Shubunka (Barry Sullivan) into backing
one of his get-rich-quick ideas.

A Gangster Unlike the Others: Gordon Wiles' *The Gangster*

Reynold Humphries

The title of this study is a translation of the French title given to Gordon Wiles'
1947 film *The Gangster* when it was shown on television in a sub-titled version.
It sums up accurately the character of the gangster of the title, although we
shall see later that he is not unique in what he represents in the film. Since *The
Gangster* (1947) is not among the best known films of the genre, I shall offer a
summary of the plot before making any further comments.

The gangster of the title is one Shubunka (Barry Sullivan) who runs a
protection racket in a seaside town on the East Coast, not far from New York
City. Arrogant and paranoid, he is more obsessed with his girlfriend Nancy
(Belita) who is in show business in a modest way than he is with the racket,
the day-to-day running of which he leaves to employees presumably versed in
strong-arm tactics, several of whom we glimpse, and then only briefly, toward
the end of the film. However, he does have an associate, Jammey (Akim
Tamiroff), who owns and runs an ice-cream parlor and on whom Shubunka
counts to see things run smoothly.

Jammey becomes the focus of the attention of a crime syndicate anxious
to move in and take over, making Shubunka's racket part of its own widen-
ing circle of influence. Faced with Jammey's refusal to betray Shubunka and
the man's lack of interest in big-time money and power, Cornell (Sheldon
Leonard), the leader of the new syndicate, starts buying out Shubunka's
employees until only Jammey is left. Cornell now counts on him to convince
Shubunka to give in; Cornell wants to avoid trouble in an effort not to compromise the racket and to ensure continued anonymity. Jammey, however, is
being asked for help by one Karty (John Ireland) who owes his wife's brothers money as a result of losing his bets on horses and who spends his time
bemoaning his lot in Jammey's ice-cream parlor. When Jammey is confronted
by the desperate Karty at the precise moment when he is counting his takings,
his refusal to lend Karty money leads Karty to knocking him down and killing him. As Cornell had warned Shubunka that he would kill him if anything
should happen to Jammey, the gangster goes into hiding. Abandoned by
everyone, he confronts Cornell's men in the street and is shot down. The film
ends with an off-screen narrator telling of how the police rounded up Cornell

and his men and how the weekend visitors to the seaside town feel sorry that Jammey cannot take advantage of the return of the good weather.

This synopsis sketches the film's events as they can be isolated within the script, but it gives little idea of the latter's subtleties, nor of the themes that can be teased out from these events and of the ways the various characters relate to them. Certainly it hardly justifies our considering Shubunka as "a gangster unlike the others." However, once we begin to ascertain how the film's main theme—the function of money within carefully delineated male–female relations on the one hand, and as an inherent part of male rivalry on the other hand—is represented in the more general relations between all the characters, then Shubunka's particular status starts to become more apparent.

Three couples appear in the film: Shubunka and Nancy, Karty and his wife, and Jammey and his wife (present in discussions only, she never appears). In each case the relationship turns on money, albeit in very different ways, with different attitudes on view. Thus Jammey believes his wife squanders his money on doctors and accuses Shubunka of squandering his on a "showgirl," while a desperate Mrs. Karty pleads with her pathetic husband to stop gambling, to come home, and to settle things with her brothers, whom he robbed while in their employ as an accountant. Although Jammey's relation to his wife is quite different from Shubunka's to Nancy, and both relationships differ sharply from that between Karty and his wife, I shall argue that these real differences hide something far more fundamental which, as we shall see, returns insistently throughout the film and finds its key expression in the confrontation between Shubunka and Cornell's syndicate.

Jammey is a modest, small-town, and small-time entrepreneur approaching the age of retirement who has succeeded in making a living as the owner of an ice-cream parlor employing a waiter Shorty (Harry Morgan) and a cashier Dorothy (Joan Lorring). Although Jammey is in the pay of Shubunka, *The Gangster* is unclear as to the precise financial arrangement between the two men, apart from the fact that Jammey has Shubunka's complete trust and makes it a point of honor to respect this.[1] It is clear that Jammey is in no way rich, but he is proud of his little business and, crucially, something of a miser. Thus at the outset he has difficulty with the notion that his wife should spend ("squander") his money on her health, which is an irrational attitude unless we interpret it as part of the Protestant capitalist work ethic that sees a man's savings as his and his alone, to the point of making everyone subservient to him, including his wife. Jammey has worked for his money; therefore only he can say what is to be done with it. Significantly, Mrs. Karty's three brothers adopt an identical attitude toward Karty whom they beat up because he has taken ("squandered") their hard-earned profits and put them to trivial use. The question, however, is: to what extent is Karty really different from the brothers-in-law, Jammey, and Shubunka?

For a start, we can say that Jammey, quite unconsciously, looks upon his wife as one of his employees, or, to put in another way: he considers she owes him everything and that her everyday, material existence depends on his good will. In other words: she should not abuse his generosity. He has worked hard to succeed and refuses to see that money go up in smoke. This is exactly the attitude adopted by Mrs. Karty's brothers: they make it perfectly clear to Karty as they work him over that they have risen in society through hard work and refuse to let a failure like him compromise their success. The film's sophistication here lies in the fact that two radically different situations—Jammey's wife at least has the right to expect her husband to look after her health, whereas Karty has no right to expect his brothers-in-law to stand by and watch the money he has embezzled thrown down the drain—can be seen as conveying the same ideological stance: money is sacrosanct and the person with money owes his success to himself and to himself alone. For Jammey and the brothers, they have succeeded in becoming owners of their own businesses thanks to the spirit of free enterprise threatened by someone—one's wife, one's brother-in-law—who fails to understand the true value of money. In short, Mrs. Jammey and Karty are irresponsible.

This is precisely the point Jammey is really making when he criticizes Shubunka for throwing his money around on Nancy. Superficially, this would seem to be surprising: as it is his own money Shubunka is spending, why worry about it? He has a right to spend it as he wishes. This notion of deriving pleasure from wealth enters into conflict, however, with the ideology that money must be used to make more money, must be invested or saved for the right moment. Shubunka is not therefore behaving like a "good capitalist," an implicit criticism being leveled at him by Jammey that will have dire consequences in what is to follow, unsuspected, of course, by both men: by Jammey because he is the unconscious product of an ideology that remains hidden to him; and by Shubunka because, for reasons we shall see presently, he has failed to grasp the meaning of Cornell's syndicate and to understand that one world has ceased to exist and that another world is taking shape before his resolutely blind gaze.

I stated earlier that there were three couples in the film, but in fact there are four, the last being Shorty and Olga, the owner of a corset shop whom he attempts to woo. The relationship soon breaks up, and the reason for the split will help explain the relationship between each man and his money, on the one hand, and the subordination of people to money, on the other. Shorty exudes sexual arrogance and considers himself God's gift to women. When an encounter falls through, he accuses Olga of standing him up, to which she replies by letter to the effect that he has misjudged her cruelly. Obviously delighted, he sits down in the ice-cream parlor to write her a reply. This occurs in a scene that involves Karty, his wife, Jammey, and Shubunka and ends with all the characters "united" in one shot. Karty is seated on the left, looking at his wife, who, in utter despair, has collapsed over a table in the foreground. Shubunka and Jammey are seated on the right, in the background, after a conversation in which Jammey admits his wife has been ill for fifteen years but that the doctors can't find what's wrong with her. He now talks of her with tenderness, trying to explain to the icy Shubunka, who's just sitting there, how important it is "to have someone near and dear to you," how only his wife listens to him. Either Jammey has had a change of heart about her, or else he can maintain two contradictory views on the same person. It would perhaps be more accurate to say that Jammey needs both his wife and his money and has difficulty in reconciling them.

Wiles creates visual and spatial parallels between Karty and his wife not talking to each other and Jammey talking to Shubunka, between Mrs. Karty seated in a state of collapse in the foreground and Shorty standing in the background after penning a reply to Olga. The opposition between Mrs. Karty and Shorty (he feels elated) is clear, for Olga will soon discover that Shorty is on the make, the implication for the spectator being that his generosity toward her must be followed by a gesture on her part, one of a clearly sexual nature. It is therefore revealing that this scene in the ice-cream parlor is followed abruptly, with no attempt at creating the usual spatio-temporal link to explain such a break, by a scene where Shubunka is standing over Nancy's bed watching her sleeping. When she wakes up, he says he's brought her a present. As we know he is forever showering her with gifts, I propose we interpret this as a manifestation, in an inverted form, of the fact that Shorty sees himself as God's gift to women, both men in fact considering they have certain rights due to their male status, a status overdetermined in Shubunka's case by his wealth. For him, Nancy is very much one of his possessions because of his generosity, just as Olga is meant to behave as Shorty's possession because of an invitation to dinner.

Thus the fetishization of money goes hand in hand with the commodification of people which, in Shubunka's case, expresses itself via his paranoid behavior toward Nancy. However, *The Gangster* does not fall into the usual Hollywood trap of portraying this as an individual pathology; Shubunka's sickness has precise social roots and connotations. Early in the film he tells her that he'd like to walk with her along Fifth Avenue, to which she replies that she can't go with him because her sister's baby is sick and she has to go to Queens to help out. Shubunka actually goes to the length of following her and increasingly large close-ups of his face stress his paranoia over her movements. And it would seem he is right: she meets up with a man in a café. However, he turns out not only to be her agent but to be accompanied by his fiancée, hardly conducive to an illicit assignation. Nancy wants to get ahead in show business but is so afraid of Shubunka's possessiveness that she feels constrained to lie.

What befalls Nancy at the end of the film shows just how completely *The Gangster* is able to articulate the individual and the social by showing what happens, in the last instance, when money speaks louder than anything else. If her agent in no way has designs on her sexually, he does transform her into a mere commodity by turning out to be part of Cornell's syndicate: art is also subject to corporate financial interests and Nancy must simultaneously abandon Shubunka and submit to the new corporate law. If the film has been careful to show that Shubunka behaves shoddily toward her, it also shows the negative consequences when the ideology of success is uppermost at an early stage in a person's life. Shubunka states at one point how he remembers, when young, seeing a man and a woman kissing on a balcony on Park Avenue. This juxtaposition of love (or simply sex) and money returns to haunt him: hence his desire, referred to above, to walk Nancy along Park Avenue. It is as if placing her in a context of luxury will lead her to fall into his arms or his bed. The irony for Shubunka lies in the fact that she has succumbed to his charms but wants love, not luxury and gifts. Shubunka is incapable of making the essential distinction between the two and hence assumes she will stay with him through thick and thin if he only keeps on offering her presents. Her accepting Beaumont's offer of a career at the end is thus less a betrayal than a form of freedom in her eyes, but it is a gesture that leads her to being even less free under the control of the syndicate than she ever was with Shubunka. Like him, Nancy has fallen victim to (the ideology of) success. I shall return to this in my concluding remarks.

Nancy (Belita), an unknowing "victim to (the ideology of) success," talks to Shubunka as she changes costumes between shows.

Only Dorothy, the cashier in Jammey's ice-cream parlor, has fully understood the true nature of an exchange economy. Unconsciously, Shubunka considers that offering Nancy gifts means that she must offer her body in return, a view akin to that of Shorty toward Olga. Thus Dorothy refuses all form of gifts from Shubunka, tells him how she despises him, and refuses to owe him anything. Significantly, she lives in very modest circumstances with her father: she has no other source of income than her obviously modest salary. Through the character of Dorothy and the ethical choices she makes, *The Gangster* is attacking the whole system of living on credit. Yet it is to her that Shubunka, now a wanted man on the run from Cornell, turns for help, which she refuses: he must pay for his sins. Here Shubunka makes a remark that, from the standpoint of the film, is absolutely correct and indicates that *The Gangster* refuses a simple good = evil equation in favor of analysis. He replies to Dorothy that his only sin is that he wasn't mean and rotten enough. In other words: he's preferable to Cornell and the syndicate. And on this score the film comes down on Shubunka's side.

Just who is Shubunka and how did he evolve to become what he is at the opening of the film? At one point, both worried over the threat posed by Cornell and incensed at Nancy's criticisms, he points out that he started working at the age of 6, was in the pay of gangsters by the age of 9 and a bootlegger when he was 14. I would suggest that we are entitled to draw two conclusions from this, given Shubunka's current attitude as a gangster at the head of a system based on racketeering: he is from a working-class background; and that he believes firmly and rigidly in the ideology of the "self-made man." This, I shall argue, is crucial for his downfall and for the tentative political reading it is possible to make of *The Gangster.*

Early in the film Shubunka-as-narrator remarks: "I made good, my conscience never bothered me." Although we would be justified in seeing the second part of this statement as a case of disavowal—if his conscience has never bothered him, why evoke it at all?—we would be wise to take him at his face value when he talks of making good. In which case, Shubunka is convinced that he has got to the top by working hard and that he owes this success to himself alone. There is a most revealing parallel here with the attitude of Mrs. Karty's brothers who alternate striking the wretched Karty and making comments such as "We work for our money, we're not white collar." This remark can surely be read both as an indication of the men's working-class origins and of a certain *ressentiment* toward those in a position to work in a profession more socially acceptable than one involving manual labor. *Ressentiment* can therefore function as a veil drawn over the real social relations prevailing, a way for the subject to mask his alienation and blame it on others without having to reflect on the precise economic and political forces at work. Ideology at work in its "purest" form.

Three scenes in particular enable us to grasp the nature of the film's criticism of post-war economic and social conditions. Two of the scenes involve Shubunka, the third Cornell. In the first of the two scenes with Shubunka, he is spending the day on the beach with Nancy when two of Cornell's hoodlums

Shubunka looms menacingly over the cashier Dorothy (Joan Lorring) as he tries to explain his behavior.

come with a warning from Cornell: Shubunka is through. His reaction is, to put it mildly, surprising: "Let's talk this over, man to man." Which is precisely what he manages to do in the second scene where he goes to see Cornell in his offices and makes the following remark: "What right have you to take it [the racket I've built up] from me?" However, does Shubunka's formula "man to man" correspond to what we are being shown? He sounds rather like a petulant child being deprived of a toy by his father, which partakes of his narcissism and his belief that he is at the center of a world which he created and where everyone is in his debt. In that case, Cornell represents very much the reality principle, but it is a reality of a most sinister kind.

Before attempting to elucidate its nature, let us turn to the third scene mentioned, quite the most fascinating in the movie, where Wiles and the screenwriter, Daniel Fuchs, make things crystal clear for us.[2] Jammey is "invited" to lunch by Cornell. The scene takes place in a booth in a plush restaurant, with poor Jammey seated between Cornell's two hoods (one played by the ever-reliable Charles McGraw) and Cornell sitting opposite, preparing a salad with loving care while talking to Jammey. It is essential that this scene precede the two we have just mentioned, for the audience will thus be in a position to attribute to the two later scenes all the weight they are meant to carry. In the scene in the restaurant Cornell is dressed very much like a businessman, as he is when Shubunka visits him in his office. We can read the scene as an ironic early example of that more recent phenomenon "the businessman's lunch."

The film clearly means this to be taken seriously, just as Shubunka is meant to take seriously the threats issued by Cornell via his hoodlums. It is clear that, for Cornell, Shubunka simply no longer exists; Jammey alone interests him as he has all the information Cornell needs about those collecting money for Shubunka. Individualism is obsolete for Cornell: the only thing that counts is corporate business where mutual economic interests—those of gangsters on the one hand, those of bankers on the other—come together—or "merge." Cornell's intended takeover of Shubunka's business is clearly presented in the discussion between the two men in Cornell's offices as a simple case of a capitalist merger.

Two contemporary film noir will help us elucidate what is at stake in *The Gangster: Out of the Past* (Jacques Tourneur, 1947) and *I Walk Alone* (Byron Haskin, 1948). In the former, Kirk Douglas is very much the astute and ruthless businessman gangster, hiring a lawyer, appropriately named Eels, to cook his books for him so that, unlike other citizens, he won't have to pay taxes. And Robert Mitchum, as a private eye, even visits, uninvited, the offices of the Douglas character in a scene where his encounter with Douglas' thugs on the stairs echoes the shot where Shubunka is frisked by Cornell's men prior to gaining access to him. *I Walk Alone*, however, sets up parallels of a far more eloquent nature: even the film's title applies to Shubunka. In the later film

"Very much the astute and ruthless businessman": Kathie Moffat (Jane Greer) stands by as Whit Sterling (Kirk Douglas, center) speaks with Jeff Bailey (Robert Mitchum, right) in the Tahoe cabin.

Burt Lancaster returns to civilian life after a long stretch in prison where he took the rap alone, while his partner in crime (Kirk Douglas again) continued to work the rackets. However, as Lancaster finds out, literally to his cost, times have changed. He has been going on the assumption that he only has to ask Douglas to split the profits down the middle for the latter to agree and give Lancaster his share. Not a bit of it. Douglas has his accountant (a corporate version of Karty, played by Wendell Corey) explain the situation to the bewildered Lancaster. There is no longer one racket, but a business divided up into several spheres of interest in such a way that no one particular sphere can be sold off without the agreement of those who have put money into the other branches of the business, i.e. banks. In other words, Douglas is a sort of chairman of the board and cannot share on a 50-50 basis with his former partner an enterprise that bears no relation whatsoever to the one Lancaster created with Douglas at the time of Prohibition.

The parallels with *The Gangster* are striking, with Lancaster taking over the role of Shubunka, Douglas that of Cornell. What is crucial, however, is the question of the period under discussion in both films, carefully provided in both cases: Prohibition and World War II. As far as the latter is concerned, *I Walk Alone* is quite explicit: the Lancaster character was imprisoned before the war and released after it was over. Significantly Shubunka makes no reference to this momentous event. This is precisely the point: why should he? For Shubunka, things are just as they were before the war; for him it was the end of Prohibition that changed the nature of gangsterism, not the particular economic and political climate of the post-war era. What is really at stake has been shown to us by a striking use of editing in the course of the sequence where Cornell is grilling Jammey in the restaurant. We see Cornell cutting with both delicacy and delectation into a large steak, a shot which fades out to a shot of gulls feeding on the beach. This both introduces the later scene on the beach where Shubunka's idyll with Nancy is rudely interrupted by Cornell's hoodlums and makes a neat comment on the situation. Shubunka is, as it were, in the place of the steak, and what we are seeing is Cornell "carving up" his empire. But Shubunka is also surely in the place of the gulls too, feeding as he does off others via the strong-arm tactics of the racketeer. *The Gangster* is less concerned with telling us that Cornell is even worse than Shubunka than with hinting at what this new corporate order is.

Let us leave aside for the moment the fact that Shubunka is a gangster, i.e. a criminal, and turn to what he represents ideologically: he is the small entrepreneur who has made good, a species we find represented by Carl Denham in *King Kong* (Schoedsack and Cooper, 1933) and Max Renn in *Videodrome* (David Cronenberg, 1982),[3] to take just two examples as far removed from each other in their spatio-temporal settings and concerns as they both are from *The Gangster*. If Renn's is "the story of the classical struggle between a small businessman and entrepreneur and a great faceless corporation,"[4] then Denham and Shubunka are simply variations on a theme. Behind Denham (and very much a part of the film's political unconscious) is the capitalism of the Crash of 1929 and the subsequent Depression, whereas Shubunka's espousal of illegality is, to quote Emmerich in *The Asphalt Jungle* (John Huston, 1950), just "a left-handed form of human endeavor."[5] I quote Jameson again:

> So we have here a fairly explicit economic reading of the text as a narrative about business and competition, and it is worth measuring the distance between this overt and explicit commercial content. . .and that deepest allegorical impulse of all, which insists on grasping this feature as an articulated nightmare vision of how we as individuals feel within the new multinational world system.[6]

What is surely exceptional about *The Gangster*, especially in the light of Jameson's remarks, is that Wiles and Fuchs had already proposed that "articulated nightmare vision" as early as 1947, showing an uncanny—if not necessarily conscious—grasp of the post-war thrust to impose a consensus around the need for the hegemony of American capitalism and the cultural manifestations of "the American way." In my article referred to in note 5 I had the pleasure of using Jonathan Munby's path-breaking study of the gangster film, a section of which, devoted to *Force of Evil*, concerns "the corporation as racket."[7] What is decisive and incisive about Munby's work is already clear from the title of the chapter in which this section appears: "Screening Crime the Liberal Consensus Way." *The Gangster* is one of a number of gangster movies featuring "the problems of old-styled 'ethical' gangsters failing to adjust to the new order."[8] This "new order" is not simply that of modern, increasingly global capitalism but also that of Hollywood under the aegis of Eric Johnston, formerly of the American Chamber of Commerce and now in charge of imposing harmony against dissidence, the idyllic post-war way as opposed to the negative New Deal way, and the classless white society as opposed to the "nightmare of class conflict" represented by the Hollywood Left, the Cultural Front of the 1930s and the titanic struggles against racism and fascism throughout the 1930s.[9] Thus, if Shubunka's attitude corresponds to that of those on the Left who refused to see the writing on the wall in 1947 or who, having deciphered the script, decided to go through to the bitter end rather than compromise their convictions, then Cornell IS the new order, hiding behind faceless men who pull the economic and political strings, like those behind Douglas in *I Walk Alone*.

In what I can only call an "uncanny" echo of the Fredric Jameson text already quoted, Munby refers, in the piece quoted in note 7, to "the faceless organization" that has ousted such gangsters as Shubunka. Whether a coincidence or a singularly appropriate instance of the Lacanian thesis of the subject as effect of the signifier, this formula (which is obviously meant literally by both theorists inasmuch as it designates those behind the scenes who never show their faces in public) is also a most pertinent comment on an element of *The Gangster* which has always intrigued me and whose possible significance, until I started writing this article, had always appeared enigmatic. The element in question opens the film (it is the very first shot) and occurs for a second time later. It is a painting hanging on the wall in an apartment. It turns out to be that of Shubunka who is lying on his bed, staring into space and not at the painting. The zoom out from a close-up gives pride of place to the gaze of the spectator, as will also be the case with the second appearance of the painting. It represents four figures, of which the two on the right are wearing hoods. It would seem that this painting, which is anything but explicit, represents two executioners and their future victims.

It is used a second time in a scene that immediately follows the one where Shubunka, suspecting Nancy of infidelity, finds her in the company of her agent Beaumont. When the others leave, Shubunka is left alone and Wiles cuts to a big close-up which insists on the character's continued suspicions, despite the assurances he has received from Nancy and the presence of Beaumont's fiancée. This close-up is transformed by a rapid fade into a close-up of one of the two "executioners" in the painting. Thus Shubunka "becomes" the character in the painting. I would suggest the use of the painting, and its juxtaposition the second time with a scene highlighting Shubunka's paranoia, indicates the character's dual status in the movie: from the role of "executioner" he moves to that of "victim." At the same time we can see a form of condensation in the Freudian sense and an example of inversion at work. Shubunka is both executioner (at the beginning) and the victim duly executed at the end, both the person who runs the show and a man who is blind to what is going on around him. The inversion occurs by representing "the faceless corporation" or "organization" mentioned by Jameson and Munby as the hooded victims in the painting. Thus the painting symbolizes both Shubunka's view of himself (a view that is more imaginary than symbolic) and the fate that is to be visited upon him as the plot slowly but inexorably unfolds. The fact that Shubunka is absent from his apartment when we are shown the painting for the second time merely stresses how irrelevant he is in the throes of becoming. The decisions are being taken in his absence.

The Gangster is, in many ways, a remarkable little film. The word "little" is not to be taken as pejorative but as a description of the film. Quite short (just over eighty minutes), it is a "B" feature produced by the King Brothers, who also produced *Gun Crazy*, an even more remarkable achievement on which Gordon Wiles acted as production designer.[10] Wiles shows considerable talent at making the most of a modest budget, although his achievement here does not quite match that of Lewis in *Gun Crazy*, or that of Edgar G. Ulmer on that "Poverty Row" production *Detour* (1945). A careful look at *The Gangster* shows Wiles exploiting the lack of spacious settings and numerous walk-on roles to stress the notion of characters in general and Shubunka in particular being cornered, literally hemmed in. The scene on the beach where two of Cornell's hoodlums interrupt the idyll between Shubunka and Nancy and the restaurant scene where Jammey is squeezed in between two other strong-arm men of Cornell's are striking instances of Wiles turning an apparent handicap into a virtue by creating an atmosphere perfectly in keeping with the film's themes and concerns.

What is most remarkable about the film, however, is its uncanny prescience: it mirrors, in a variety of ways, the forces at work to change U.S. society after 1945, to impose what Munby calls "the liberal consensus."

Shubunka continues to define himself in relation to the 1920s and 1930s, whereas Cornell's attitude suggests that this past is now simply irrelevant in the era of dawning corporate capitalism. *The Gangster* is not therefore trying to glorify Shubunka who is in no way represented positively or heroically. Rather, its thrust is to suggest, via certain details, that any reference to the past is doomed to destruction in the new post-war world; and that citizens must be led or forced to adapt. As I shall try to show through a couple of examples, *The Gangster* is both a film of its time and ahead of its time.

Let us return, to conclude, to Nancy and Jammey in an attempt to tease out the issues the film is addressing. As I have pointed out, Nancy chooses her career rather than Shubunka, which is fair enough. Unfortunately for her, Beaumont her agent is a cog in the wheel of the syndicate represented by Cornell, so Nancy's understandable desire to make something of her talents as a singer is immediately subordinated to the economic dictates of corporate capitalism. This situation bears a certain resemblance to the behavior of stars like Bogart who at first supported the Committee for the First Amendment created after the HUAC hearings of October 1947 in order to defend Hollywood and the freedom of speech and thought, then capitulated to the demands of Jack Warner and made the sort of anti-Communist statement to the press soon to be required of those who had once harbored beliefs in a more collective and now proscribed form of democracy. I do not wish to draw a precise parallel between the real-life event and the fictional one, but simply to point out that Nancy's apparent desire for freedom is in fact a new and more subtle form of submission and that *The Gangster* is furnishing us here with a nice example of the notion that "every work of art contains within it past, present, and future struggles over culture and power."[11]

Now let us consider the following remark:

> For Americans to accept the new world of 1950s consumerism, they had to make a break with the past. The Depression years had helped generate fears about instalment buying and excessive materialism. . . . Depression era and wartime scarcities of consumer goods had led workers to internalize discipline and frugality. . . . Government policies after the war encouraged an atomized acquisitive consumerism at odds with the lessons of the past.[12]

Lipsitz goes on to discuss the relationship between television and the advertising industry, notably the attempts by a "motivational specialist" to address "customers who had only recently acquired the means to spend freely and who might harbor a lingering conservatism about spending based on their previous experiences."[13] I see this as an accurate summary of aspects of the behavior and values of Jammey, who accepts unquestioningly the public's need to consume but cannot conceive of himself in like terms. There is a tension at the heart of the way Jammey relates to the new society, of which he is suspicious in the light of past experience. He refuses to switch sides even when threatened and is shown to be a frightened man with principles, surely a rare bird in film noir and gangster movies. It is perhaps of interest to note in *The*

Big Sleep that Marlowe admires Harry Jones for choosing death over betrayal of the woman he loves, a choice fast becoming eccentric, even obsolete, but one which appeals to the "old-fashioned" Marlowe. The fact that *The Gangster* concludes with the information that the police have rounded up Cornell and his men is perhaps an indication that resistance to the new corporate way was possible. The events of the coming years, however, showed what the cost of that resistance was to be.

Notes

1. Jammey clearly oversees for Shubunka the collecting of protection money.

2. In his review of the film in *Film Noir: An Encyclopedic Reference to the Noir Style* (Alain Silver and Elizabeth Ward, Overlook Press, 1979), Blake Lucas suggests that Dalton Trumbo may have had a hand in the script. Unfortunately, he cites no evidence for this and Trumbo makes no reference to the film in the volume of his letters entitled *Additional Dialogue: Letters of Dalton Trumbo, 1942–1962*, ed. Helen Manfull (New York: M. Evans, 1970). Nor does Peter Hanson even evoke the film in his study *Dalton Trumbo: Hollywood Rebel* (Jefferson, NC: McFarland, 2001). We know that Trumbo had an anonymous hand in such key examples of post-war *noir* as *Gun Crazy* (Joseph H. Lewis, 1949) and *The Prowler* (Joseph Losey, 1950), but I fail to see why he should always be brought into the discussion whenever a film shows unmistakable signs of intellectual and political ambition at odds with the climate of the time, as *The Gangster* undoubtedly does.

3. The theme of Denham as capitalist entrepreneur is worked out systematically in *The Son of Kong* (Ernest B. Schoedsack, 1933). I analyze the character and his implications in detail in Humphries, *The Hollywood Horror Film, 1931–1941: Madness in a Social Landscape* (Metuchen, NJ: Scarecrow Press, 2006).

4. Fredric Jameson, *The Geopolitical Aesthetic: Cinema and Space in the World System* (Bloomington: Indiana University Press, 1992), 26.

5. See Reynold Humphries, "The Politics of Crime and the Crime of Politics: Post-War *Noir*, the Liberal Consensus and the Hollywood Left," in *Film Noir Reader 4*, ed. Alain Silver and James Ursini (Pompton Plains, NJ: Limelight, 2004), 227–45. Certain remarks made in this earlier study have served as the basis for the current article.

6. Jameson, *Geopolitical Aesthetic*, 26.

7. Jonathan Munby, *Public Enemies, Public Heroes: Screening the Gangster from Little Caesar to Touch of Evil* (Chicago: University of Chicago Press, 1999), 126–33. See also Reynold Humphries, "When Crime Does Pay: Abraham Polonsky's *Force of Evil* (1948)," *Q/W/E/R/T/Y*, University of Pau, France, October 2001, pp. 205–10.

8. *Public Enemies, Public Heroes*, 130, n. 17.

9. The "nightmare of class conflict" is Johnston's expression, and it is taken up for critical analysis in Lary May, *The Big Tomorrow: Hollywood and the Politics of the American Way* (Chicago: University of Chicago Press, 2000), esp. 175–213. On the Cultural Front, see Michael Denning, *The Cultural Front* (London: Verso, 1997).

10. Wiles fulfilled the same function on *The Underworld Story* (Cy Endfield, 1950). I have no other information pertaining to his career.

11. George Lipsitz, *Time Passages: Collective Memory and American Popular Culture* (Minneapolis: University of Minnesota Press, 1990), 68. Lipsitz is discussing here the work of Mikhail Bakhtin.

12. Ibid., 44–45.

13. Ibid., 47.

"Made it, Ma, top of the world!"

White Heat: I Am Cody Jarrett, Destroyer of Worlds

Glenn Erickson

Raoul Walsh's *White Heat* has served as a frequent focus for critical discussion on film noir, as it shows the influence of that style on established gangster conventions. But it is also a "last call" for the classic gangster picture, recapitulating many of the genre's strongest themes while pointing the way to the future. This violent tale of an outlaw bandit battling the modernized forces of the law closes the door on previous waves of gangster films, as if acknowledging that the world had outgrown the notion of the hoodlum character as defined twenty years earlier.

The manic Cody Jarrett is both a criminal anachronism and the face of the future. Old-style gangland ambition has been displaced by psychological mania. His love for his gray-haired but equally murderous "Ma" is far greater than his attraction for his blonde gun moll. And his expertise at armed robbery cannot keep up with a new system of law enforcement wielding technological resources beyond his understanding. Bursting with the anxieties of the modern era, Jarrett is nothing less than Al Capone with an atomic bomb inside his head.

White Heat may be the first modern action thriller, as its structure and content prefigure today's ultra-violent escapist entertainments, with their multiple climaxes and heightened brutality. *White Heat* expresses a highly unstable world in which familiar gangster themes rush toward a literally explosive climax. The racketeer with a gun has mutated into an Oedipal madman who would gladly blow up the entire world to serve as his funeral pyre.

When *White Heat* first appeared, only a few French film critics were beginning to synthesize the concept that American crime films could be part of a genre with significance beyond the Saturday matinee. And few would have thought that Cody Jarrett stood at a crossroads between fantastic figures such as Fantomas and Dr. Mabuse and later super-criminals like Dr. No and Auric Goldfinger. Many contemporary reviewers of *White Heat* had their hands full just coming to grips with its unrelenting violence:

> [*White Heat* is] an unending procession of what is probably the most gruesome aggregation of brutalities ever presented on the motion picture screen under the guise of entertainment.[1]

... an exhibition of human depravity balanced only by [director Raoul] Walsh's high pitch, an "agitato" score and Cagney's mocking grin.[2]

Raoul Walsh's *White Heat* hit American screens in September 1949 like a blast from an open furnace. Cultural watchdogs warning of a rising tide of film violence had plenty to complain about. In terms of individual acts of brutality, *White Heat* was by far the most violent crime film ever. In the very first scene three men are shot in cold blood and another's face is gruesomely scalded by a blast of steam. The final cops-and-robbers battle has more onscreen fatalities than did many war films of the time, and Cody Jarrett's demise comes in a grandiose conflagration comparable to a nuclear detonation.

Bosley Crowther of the *New York Times* was quick to call *White Heat* "unhealthy stimulation (for the) weak and young," revisiting the popular notion that any movie less wholesome than Andy Hardy fare would poison the youth of America. The alleged corruption of youth by sadistic comics and movies was a frequent sticking point of church groups and conservative pundits, who were still quoting the notorious old-lady-down-the-staircase killing in Henry Hathaway's *Kiss of Death* as a marker for the end of Western civilization. Crowther did his duty by watching *White Heat* a second time in a matinee packed with excited kids, and noted their enthusiastic approval of the ruthless criminal Cody Jarrett. After one particularly satisfying act of sadism, Crowther heard a potential juvenile delinquent shout out an admiring, "Bee-yoo-tee-ful!"[3]

The high-powered Warner Bros. release came with a built-in shield to deflect the usual attack strategies: admiration for "Jimmy" Cagney, still strongly associated with *Yankee Doodle Dandy*, shifted criticism away from the corruption of youth. For every negative review expressing concern for the health of American youth, there was a notice like the one from the *L.A. Citizen-News*, which happily acknowledged an "old style James Cagney, back in (an) old-style gangster-prison picture, with new-style trimmings." The *Los Angeles Examiner* praised the film's thrills, calling it "loaded with sex, double crossing, violent death and absolutely agonizing suspense." Mainstream audiences clearly relished the heightened realism and brutality with which robber Cody Jarrett plied his trade, and *White Heat* became a box-office winner.

The Production Code had weakened considerably during the 1940s, but changes made to *White Heat* during production suggest that it was shaped and influenced by the same outside forces that had affected the gangster film since its inception. Understanding *White Heat*'s relationship to its genre requires a look back at the transformation of the gangster film, from hardboiled realism to FBI-sanctioned law-and-order fantasy.

The development of the American gangster film goes hand in hand with the industry's adoption of codes of self-censorship. The gangster genre changed greatly between James Cagney's two classic bookend star appearances in

1931 and 1949, as Hollywood did its best to comply with the repressive Production Code.

The well-documented furor over the initial three or four core popular titles (*Little Caesar, The Public Enemy, Scarface*) helped to usher in a stricter adherence to the Production Code, as the industry adopted self-regulation to avoid outright government censorship. Production of gangster fare was halted by Code provisos specifically banning any scenario deemed to glorify criminality. As if to pacify the reformers, the major studios developed pictures with strong law-and-order themes. The result was a spate of reactionary pictures expressing a yearning for extremist solutions to social problems.

Cecil B. DeMille's disturbing ode to vigilantism, *This Day and Age* (1933), swings the moral pendulum directly toward fascism. Outraged small-town college students combat Charles Bickford's venal racketeer by forming into a vigilante lynching party. They torture a confession from Bickford by suspending him over a pit of rats. MGM's *Beast of the City* (1932) invents a police chief (Walter Huston) unwilling to compromise with racketeers. When left with no further options, he provokes a final showdown, a bloodbath far more violent than the "immoral" gangster films the movie was clearly intended to counter. Huston's elected vigilante police chief would soon become a fantasy president in MGM's *Gabriel over the White House*, solving America's domestic and foreign problems by dismissing his corrupt party cronies and ruling in a virtual dictatorship. One of the president's most pressing concerns is how to handle an Al Capone–like racketeer; he suspends the Bill of Rights with martial law and orders the army to seize and execute the gangland leaders. The political extremism of these reactionary films can be traced directly to the perceived threat of the gangster as glorified by Hollywood.

A second big change in the gangster film reflected the unofficial influence of the FBI on what kinds of criminal subject matter could be shown on the screen. Having already submitted to voluntary censorship by church groups and moral monitors, the industry was an easy target for J. Edgar Hoover's publicity war on crime. The direct result of this campaign is well known—the 1935 epic *G-Men* simply moved James Cagney to the other side of the law, making him a cocky but true-blue defender of the nation.[4] The public still got their fill of crime-busting bloodshed, with the telling difference that *G-Men's* hoodlums were reduced in stature to deserving targets to be mowed down by heroic government agents. Encouraged to think of crime in terms of rural Dillingers and Machine Gun Kellys, the public was reassured that J. Edgar was on the job. No mention was made of the threat to America represented by crime organized on a much larger scale. Nationwide syndicates were consolidating their power base in the big cities, corrupting more government officials than ever.

MGM did its part in the Hoover anti-crime campaign through its popular *Crime Does Not Pay* series of two-reel featurettes, mini-dramas claimed to be straight from law enforcement files. Many episodes provided useful warnings about common con-game scams and other swindles, but the series' overall tone redefined crime and criminals according to FBI needs. Avoiding the notion that American crime could be organized on a vast scale or routinely involve political corruption, *Crime Does Not Pay* instead insisted that crime was the exclusive domain of aberrant individuals separate from decent society. The greatest threat to America was that young Johnny might shoplift for fun, fall in with the wrong crowd, and become part of this unholy underworld. The hidden point of the fantasy was to justify the need for a bigger anti-crime bureaucracy with expanded legal powers.

World War II put the film gangster into a relative dormancy, and in the darker noir crime thrillers that emerged afterwards, it became more difficult to distinguish between desperate criminals and disenchanted everymen. Shady gangsterlike characters were no longer restricted within genre boundaries. One subplot in the social-issue drama *The Best Years of Our Lives* presents *White Heat*'s Steve Cochran as a returned GI having no trouble "getting back into the swing of things" as he dresses up like a conventional hood to escort his date out for a big night . . . right from under her husband's nose. *White Heat*'s Virginia Mayo plays the unfaithful war bride—one can almost see the two of them leaving the William Wyler film to join up with Cody Jarrett's gang.

After World War II the rigid Production Code began to soften. The King Brothers' 1945 *Dillinger*, a minor film in every other aspect, used a famous criminal's real name, albeit eleven years after the bank robber's death. Its success did not launch a rebirth of gangster heroes, probably because they seemed tame after the experience of the war. There was no longer room in the urban crime scene for a fresh-faced red-hot like Enrico Bandello to move in and take over. The fix was in, as was discovered by Burt Lancaster's Frankie Madison in the prescient *I Walk Alone* (1947). The 1930s bootlegger Madison emerges from a long jail sentence, having missed out on fifteen years of history. When he steps up to rejoin his previous partnership he finds that everything is changed. The rackets have erected a veneer of legitimacy organized along corporate lines, and there is no way he can reclaim his piece of the pie. The noir trend was slow to acknowledge the existence of widespread organized crime, but it characterized crime as a murky underworld of conspiracy and altered appearances. Ordinary business enterprises served as fronts for criminal activity, and a town's finest citizens might be revealed as corrupt murderers (as in *The Strange Love of Martha Ivers* [1946]).

The most dramatic difference in post-war films was the heightened level of violence, which at first glance made it seem as if the Production Code no longer existed. By 1948 film noir had opened up new frontiers in screen wrongdoing. Lovers shoot each other in the stomach in *Double Indemnity*. Helpless men are pushed out of windows (*The Dark Corner*) and forced to drink poison (*The Big Sleep*). A hit man perfumes his bullets in *Railroaded* and convicts use blowtorches to force one of their own into a steam press in *Brute Force*. As for the FBI's taboo on rural bandits, the Bureau is now far too busy rooting out agents of the new Cold War menace, the new political public enemies. A number of noir pictures have even made visual centerpieces out of extended crime sequences, technically violating the Code proviso that criminal acts not be shown in a step-by-step, how-to manner.

White Heat's initial impression is that of a return to the pell-mell action and frantic pace of classic gangster films, setting a new record for violence and sadism. Cagney's electrifying Cody Jarrett does everything screen gangsters were forbidden to do for fifteen years.

The genre trends outlined above do not fully account for the gangster films of James Cagney made in the previous fifteen years. Although his career as the premiere screen criminal was exceptional in every way, censor influence determined the shape of each of his gangster appearances.

Cagney remains firmly associated with gangsters despite the fact that he only occasionally played one; many of his early characters were semi-crooked taxi drivers and con men, nervy New Yorkers with cocky attitudes. After his controversial Tom Powers in *The Public Enemy*, Cagney's Rocky Sullivan in *Angels with Dirty Faces* and Eddie Bartlett in *The Roaring Twenties* were greatly compromised to satisfy the moral guidelines erected by the Production Code.

The Public Enemy presents the hoodlum Tom Powers as a natural product of a squalid environment. As he rises in the rackets, Powers is betrayed by earlier role models and eventually becomes a cold-blooded killer. Although Powers loves his mother and eventually sees the folly of his profession, *The Public Enemy* remains resolutely unsentimental and ends with an image worthy of a horror film. It should have been obvious that no rational punk would see Tom Powers' gruesome demise as endorsing a life of crime. Yet the reformers demanding an end to gangster fare argued that impressionable minds would only remember Powers' earlier high life as a mobster, drinking champagne with Jean Harlow.

Cagney didn't return to the role of a bona fide gangster until 1938's *Angels with Dirty Faces*, a slickly conceived vehicle contrived to put Cagney's "whaddaya hear, whaddaya say?" banter up against the wisecracks of the Dead End Kids, an ensemble of young punk actors from Sam Goldwyn's 1937 *Dead End*.

Warners' script was clearly reverse engineered to retool a gangster story as a morally uplifting lesson for youth. *Angels with Dirty Faces* redirects its every objectionable aspect to serve a fake but emotionally effective melodrama. Rocky Sullivan's lifestyle is repeatedly criticized. His crimes all take place offscreen. When cornered by the police he resists just long enough to provide a trailer with some tough-guy action.

In a brilliantly evasive scriptwriting maneuver, Rocky purposely reverses his negative influence on his delinquent disciples by turning "yellow" during his execution in the electric chair. By disillusioning the Dead End Kids as to the nobility of crime, Rocky fulfills a debt to his best friend, a priest (Pat O'Brien), who has suggested the stunt. It's not difficult to imagine church censors clucking in approval at Rocky's Christian sacrifice, "dying yellow" to save the souls of his impressionable flock. As in *The Public Enemy*, ultimate responsibility for Sullivan's ill-spent life is assigned to his slum upbringing; O'Brien's priest offers a prayer to the little boy who got into trouble.

After announcing that he was through with gangster roles, Cagney bounced right back as Eddie Bartlett in 1939's *The Roaring Twenties*, a nostalgic ode to the Prohibition era directed by *White Heat*'s Raoul Walsh. Writer Mark Hellinger organizes the film around a newsreel narration format, prefiguring the docu-noirs and even, to some extent, *Citizen Kane*. A newsreel voice lectures the audience on the impact of the 1919 Volstead Act, indicating that the subject was no longer familiar to 1939 audiences. Eddie Bartlett is an honest taxi driver seduced into bootlegging by hard times; the real villains are other, more ruthless mobsters. Eddie stays true to his basically noble character even as he dooms himself to the gangster's traditional death in the gutter.

The preachy documentary tone is most likely what allowed *The Roaring Twenties* to find a production seal when other gangster stories were strongly discouraged. The presence of James Cagney surely helped as well. Warners could point to the symbolism of *The Roaring Twenties'* final scene when asking for special dispensation. After all, Eddie Bartlett's demise occurs on the steps of a church, tracing an arc up and down the steps before he collapses in death. Is that not the gesture of a sinner seeking absolution?

James Cagney's box office success masked his recurring dissatisfaction with Warner Bros. He broke away from the studio after *Yankee Doodle Dandy* and attempted a series of independent productions with his brother William. The once ubiquitous actor made only four pictures in seven years, one of them for 20th Century Fox. *White Heat* was Cagney's first picture under a new and lucrative Warners contract, which came about only after other Warners executives overruled Jack Warner's personal objection. As with Edward G. Robinson in the previous year's *Key Largo*, Cagney's comeback vehicle would be a tough gangster saga to make his previous outings look like kiddie fare, one last "A" picture battle against the forces of law and order. What better way to restart his career than to return to the kind of role that had made him a star?

In extensive notes by Patrick McGilligan appended to the published screenplay,[5] we learn that *White Heat* began as a much different movie, and that its development hewed closely to the "FBI glamorization" model as applied to *G-Men* and the *Crime Does Not Pay* series of short subjects. Virginia Kellogg wrote the original story, a heroic tale of Treasury agents assigned to capture a desperate criminal. Kellogg's title *White Heat* originally referred to the pressure put on the crooks by the tireless T-Men.

Kellogg's outlaw "Blackie Flynn" pulls off a crime modeled after a 1922 Denver Mint robbery that netted $200,000 and resulted in the murder of a guard. We learn just enough about Blackie to know that he loves his brother. Flynn eventually goes crazy when the brother is killed; rather than be captured, he chooses to throw himself through a high window.

McGilligan's overview of the *White Heat* production process came from his 1981 interviews with the prolific screenwriters Ivan Goff and Ben Roberts, who first teamed as wartime propaganda writers. They inherited two treatments from Virginia Kellogg but proceeded with a major rewrite.

When James Cagney joined the project, the new writers' first mission was to alter Kellogg's tale to feature Blackie Flynn as the central figure. They renamed him Arthur Cody Jarrett and expanded his scenes. At the same time, they carefully altered Jarrett's particulars to remove any qualities that would encourage audience sympathy. The final touches to the character, the ones that enlarge Jarrett's personality to fantastic proportions, are not in the final script and appear to be the doing of Raoul Walsh and Cagney himself.

Goff and Roberts started by replacing the Cagney character's beloved brother with a criminal mother, modeled after Ma Barker but with only one son. The historical Ma Barker (real name: Arizona Clark) was the matriarch of a group of bandits that committed robberies and kidnappings between 1931 and 1935. She was shot dead by the FBI, which encouraged tales that she was the head of the gang and had incestuous relations with her sons.

With the Ma Barker association implying a depraved family background, Goff and Roberts position Jarrett as unworthy of liberal audience sympathy. The apologetic "bad environment" and "victim of society" themes of *The Public Enemy* are carefully avoided. Cody has fond memories of his Ma but says that his father died "raving in a nuthouse." This deviant upbringing deprives Cody of the romantic, "Robin Hood" origin sometimes attributed to legendary rural bandits like Pretty Boy Floyd.

The effort taken to deglamorize the gangster character is accompanied by major script changes to sanitize the film's T-Men heroes. McGilligan reports that Goff and Roberts' early drafts spent more time with the T-Men and detailed their flaws as well as their dedication. Virginia Kellogg had written Treasury agent Phillip Evans as a nervous and worn-out public servant nearing retirement age. Job fatigue accounts for his being beaten to the draw by Cody at the motor court.

Stoic he-man John Archer plays Evans in the finished film. The original fatigued federal cop has become a tireless crusader existing only to dog the heels of criminal scum. Evans barks out his dialogue in clipped declarations of absolute fact, mirroring Jack Webb's just-the-facts patter in the then brand-new *Dragnet* radio show. The energetic Evans is nowhere near retirement age; Cody Jarrett bests him in a gun duel only through the use of a sneaky trick.

Field agent Hank Fallon began as a womanizing playboy and a devil-may-care man of action, similar to the later James Bond. When he goes undercover as Vic Pardo to become Cody's criminal apprentice, Fallon is assigned a fake "Mrs. Pardo," a curvaceous female treasury agent named Margaret Baxter. Margaret visits Fallon in prison and carries messages back to Evans. Early drafts implied that the two agents are carrying on an affair.

By the final script, Fallon's skirt chasing is reduced to a few smiles and raised eyebrows. As deftly played by Edmond O'Brien, Hank is more happy-go-lucky than daredevil, and his prison visits with Margaret (Fern Eggen) are mild parodies of domesticity. They chat about divorce while arranging for Cody's police-monitored prison breakout.

Evans and Fallon's main mission is to arrest "The Trader," an international currency smuggler considered a serious menace to the U.S. economy. The original scripts introduce the Trader much earlier and the agents worry more about his capture. The final script makes the Trader into little more than Cody's fence. On the film's soundtrack, "Trader" sounds rather close to "Traitor." When coupled with the mention that the stolen currency is being laundered outside the country, that observation suggests a vague association with Communist subversion. Are the Reds trying to undermine America's monetary system?

On the script page, Ivan Goff and Ben Roberts' rebalancing of character emphasis puts *White Heat* firmly on the side of the federal agents. They are resolute defenders of the law, as incorruptible as angels with flaming swords and as uncomplicated as the two-fisted heroes of Republic serials. Fallon is an undercover genius and Evans a bureaucratic automaton. They have to be nearly infallible if they're going to get their hands on the resourceful and elusive Cody Jarrett.

Jarrett transcends earlier definitions of gangster villainy. Goff and Roberts presented James Cagney with a crazy character to play, a mass of contradictions. Cody is an experienced master thief with a pathological hatred of police. He sees his life as a never-ending battle against the system, and his sense of vengeance borders on the maniacal. His only true loyalty is to his "Ma" (Margaret Wycherly), the one person he places above his own survival.

According to McGilligan, Cagney contributed heavily to key aspects of the Cody Jarrett character, exaggerating scenes that are much more subdued in the script. Goff and Roberts repeatedly have Jarrett become depressed and withdrawn in extreme situations, script directions that Cagney and Raoul Walsh ignore. Two scenes reportedly improvised by Cagney on the set clarify Jarrett's personal loyalties. Cody sits on his mother's lap and exchanges endearments with her as she soothes him. The moment has inspired numerous suggestions of an Oedipal relationship, but the simple juxtaposition of vicious killer and Mama's boy is an inspiration in itself.

In the second scene, the faithless Verna (Virginia Mayo) stands on a chair to admire her new fur coat in a mirror. She mocks Cody's relationship with his Ma, saying that the old woman went shopping to get "her

Cody Jarrett upends the "faithless" Verna (Virginia Mayo).

boy" some strawberries. Jarrett was supposed to simply give Verna a dirty look, but he instead kicks over the chair, dumping Verna onto a sofa. This leaves no doubt as to where the two women stand in Cody's affections.

Cody's most alarming new character trait is a violent mental illness that resembles epilepsy but takes the form of searing migraine attacks. One seizure episode cuts to a series of steel shop tools pounding and grinding away—Cody describes the sensation of the seizure as "like having a red-hot buzz saw inside my head." The "white heat" of the title is thus shifted from describing the T-Men to expressing the film's grotesque violence: not only scalding steam, but psychic torture generated by Cody's own brain.

Cody blacks out during these attacks, a weakness he can't hide from his gang. They think he's a criminal genius but are also terrified of his violent rages. Ambitious gang member Big Ed (Steve Cochran) concludes that Jarrett is plain nuts and ought to be locked away.

Neither Cody nor his Ma offers any explanation for the seizures, but a visitor to the set, journalist Ezra Goodman,[6] quotes Cagney as describing Jarrett as a "diseased psychopathic killer," suggesting that the mental seizures are perhaps meant to be a side-effect of syphilis. Another Cagney improvisation firmly links Cody's attacks to his relationship with his Ma. Cody is informed of Ma's death in the famous scene in the middle of a crowded prison cafeteria. The script indicates that he's supposed to collapse in grief and simply be carried away sobbing. Cagney asked to do another interpretation and played the scene as a raving maniac, stumbling down the lunchroom table and attacking the guards as they try to intercept him. McGilligan reports that the hundreds of extras playing inmates didn't expect Cagney's volcanic outburst and were honestly shocked.

Cody Jarrett, "a raving maniac, stumbling down the lunchroom table and attacking the guards as they try to intercept him."

The script pointedly derails potential audience sympathy for Cody's mental problems, this time through T-Man Philip Evans' smugly self-serving diagnosis. In a speech comparable to Simon Oakland's lecture in *Psycho*, Evans explains that as a child, Cody pretended to have headaches to avoid work and monopolize Ma's attention: "Eventually, the feigned headaches became real." This prejudiced value judgment characterizes mental illness in general as a fraud invented by "soft" liberals. Evans deprives Cody of an excuse and warns us not to show pity—it's his own darn fault.

White Heat gives Cody Jarrett yet another fatal flaw, his ignorance of modern crime-busting technology. Throughout the film Cody remains unaware of the scientific tools arrayed against him. The Treasury agents wield communication and detection devices developed in wartime, gadgets that only ten years before would have been science fiction fantasies: spectrum analysis of dust and dirt, precise fingerprinting, improved data retrieval, tag team surveillance tracking, homing devices, and radio beam triangulation. Undercover agent Hank Fallon is able to construct a radio-signal "oscillator" right under Cody's nose, using Verna's ailing bedside radio. This "007"-styled gadgetry was also a part of Goff and Roberts' writing contribution. Their early drafts stipulated that the Cody Jarrett character be brought down in total darkness by a sharpshooter using a "snooperscope," an infrared riflescope.

"'007'-styled gadgetry": the control room where radio signals are triangulated.

The finished *White Heat*, therefore, carefully sets up an old-fashioned conflict heavily favoring the side of Law and Order, as in *G-Men*. Unlike the then prevailing fashion for moral ambiguity with compromised heroes and complex villains, the film as finished is a clearly delineated battle between the forces of Good and Evil—America's high-tech federal police force versus thieves and murderers led by a psychotic, depraved madman.

The obvious irony is that *White Heat*'s vigilant T-Men pale beside the incandescent appeal of Cody Jarrett, who grows more attractive with every new outrage. Audiences were fascinated by Jarrett's violent excesses. He commits cold-blooded murder as if it were a household chore. Having hidden the untrustworthy Roy Parker (Paul Guilfoyle) in the trunk of a car, Cody executes him as a callous afterthought. We never see Parker and only hear his muffled voice asking for a little air. Cody responds by firing his pistol through the trunk lid while snacking on a chicken leg.

These sadistic images surely had an impact on the young. In Peter Medak's 1991 docudrama *Let Him Have It*, a teenaged gang of English Spivs marches past a large poster of *White Heat*; the hoodlums model themselves after ruthless movie criminals. We can imagine young toughs in the audience grinning at Cody Jarrett's sadistic rejoinders:

Roy Parker: You wouldn't kill me in cold blood, would ya?

Cody: No, I'll let ya warm up a little.

Cody: I told you to keep away from that radio. If that battery's dead, it'll have company.

White Heat may be 1949's apex of violent screen excess. Its high production values and the charismatic presence of James Cagney definitely make a criminal life seem an exciting way to go out in a blaze of violent glory.

If *The Roaring Twenties* was a recap of the Prohibition bootlegger circa 1939, *White Heat* is a veritable catalogue of gangster movie lore, unearthed and reinterpreted after ten years of dormancy. In spirit, Cody Jarrett is little changed from the rural bandits of the depths of the Depression years. The storyline of *White Heat* breaks down into a series of densely plotted episodes, most corresponding to a major theme in classic gangster pictures. The average 1930s gangster film might address only one or two of the following content categories; *White Heat* features a constant barrage of gangster iconography.

The picture opens with a major train robbery already in progress, ignoring traditional expository introductions of characters and motivations. A major heist serves as the finale as well. This realignment around action set-pieces strongly prefigures thrillers of the 1960s and 1970s.

There is treachery within Cody's gang. The ambitious Big Ed connives with Cody's unfaithful moll Verna to take over at the first opportunity. The insolent Big Ed must wait until Cody is behind bars to make his move—the rest of the gang is far too intimidated. Cody is well aware of the situation: "You know something Verna, if I turned my back long enough for Big Ed to put a hole in it, there'd be a hole in it."

White Heat uses its updated gun moll character Verna (Virginia Mayo) as comic relief, playing against Jean Harlow's sleek platinum goddess in *The Public Enemy*. Verna makes a display of crass and unladylike behavior. She snores in close-up, blubbers like a baby for the benefit of the T-Men and spits out her chewing gum only when getting ready to kiss Cody. She's unfaithful, untrustworthy, and treacherous—too snooty to cook, eager to encourage Cody to steal all the loot, and quick to turn against him when the heist goes sour.

Ma Jarrett is Cody's only real soul mate. Her beady eyes glint gleefully at hearing her boy's latest crooked schemes. Vowing to "do right" by Cody when he's behind bars, Ma comes off as kind of a hillbilly wildcat, Al Capp's Mammy Yokum as criminal zealot.

The precise crime-busting tactics of the Treasury agents are presented with a confidence that borders on parody, from Special Agent Philip Evans' clipped speech to the Agency's ability to field teams of specialists anywhere at a moment's notice. This theme was already well established in semi-docu noir films and with adjustments would dominate crime films of the fifties, emphasizing the expertise and dedication of law enforcement officers.

In keeping with its semi-documentary style, *White Heat* uses real place names. Although probably filmed in Burbank, the script places the automobile pursuit of Ma Jarrett at the corner of Beverly and Alvarado, just west of downtown Los Angeles. Jarrett's chemical tanker truck is detected heading west on the Old Highway from San Bernardino (no freeways yet), stopping in Colton. It is tracked right through the center of the city, heading south on Figueroa Avenue to the refineries of El Segundo and Long Beach. This part of the film plays like a time machine back to L.A. in 1949.

A strong gangster theme in the pre-Code years focused on crooked attorneys routinely helping notorious criminals avoid prosecution through legal loopholes (*Crime without Passion, The Mouthpiece*). To avoid a capital charge in the train holdup, Cody pulls off an impressive legal dodge by turning himself in for a lesser crime in another state—a robbery he preplanned for just such an eventuality. But direct legal aid is never depicted—the script refuses to implicate the legal system in Cody's schemes.

White Heat's second act encapsulates the entire prison subgenre, complete with a "Big House" code of honor. The prison has regimented work and eating routines, trusties, and stoolies; one of Cody's cellmates (G. Pat Collins) is a lip-reader who can receive silent messages sent between cells.

The prison episode introduces the classic theme of the undercover agent. Posing as a small-time crook named Vic Pardo, Edmond O'Brien's Hank Fallon penetrates Cody's confidence, ingratiating himself by assisting during one of Cody's traumatic seizures. After Ma is killed, Fallon becomes Cody's key partner and emotional crutch. Despite his dramatic undercover mission, Fallon is nowhere near as charismatic as Cody. He comes off as a Judas-like betrayer, not a daring secret agent.

Writers Goff and Roberts take advantage of the opportunity to stage an elaborate prison bust-out. Cody feigns a mental collapse to effect a transfer to the lower-security medical wing, where an armed escape is easier. The script pauses to belittle a progressive psychologist, who lamely states that "hunger is such a hopeful sign" when Jarrett suddenly decides he wants to eat. A few moments later Cody is clubbing guards and using the chief medic as a hostage.

Fallon's undercover plans go horribly awry when he's forced to accompany Cody's gang of escapees as they run wild through the countryside. To avoid the obvious conclusion that T-Man incompetence has set loose a deadly crime wave, Goff and Roberts take care to show that Cody's only victims are fellow inmates like Roy Parker.

Big Ed and Verna hide out in a cabin in the San Bernardino Mountains, which later becomes the staging area for Cody Jarrett's final heist. The woodsy locale is vaguely reminiscent of the "Little Bohemia" retreat used by the Dillinger gang and famously pictured in *G-Men* and John Milius' 1973 *Dillinger*.

Undercover agent Hank Fallon (Edmond O'Brien) gets close to Cody in prison.

The finale's elaborate raid on a chemical plant is initiated with an allusion to the Greek story of the Trojan Horse, a plan praised by The Trader, an educated crook with an appreciation of the Classics. Cody explains the ploy to his gang in street-jargon monologue that parodies Homer: "Way back there was a whole army tryin' to knock off a place called Troy, and gettin' nowhere fast. Couldn't even put a dent in the walls."

The first part of the heist proceeds as planned, with Cody hidden in the empty chemical tanker and smuggled into striking position within the refinery gates. Up until this point *White Heat* has been a progressive but familiar series of variations on classic gangster themes, but when the tension escalates the film leaps to a new level beyond genre limits.

A small army of Treasury agents, policemen, and highway patrolmen flood into the chemical plant. The maneuver is as impressive as D-Day, reminding us that the majority of the police are experienced ex-soldiers far removed from outdated images of the friendly public servant walking a beat. The dynamic angles of cops swarming among the pipes and power grids create a vision of a newly militarized nation. The stakes have been sharply raised. This is war, a fight for survival. A wave of American firepower rushes like antibodies to repel the societal cancer represented by Cody Jarrett.[7]

The setting for the finale has been transferred to a new and futuristic landscape. Old-style gangsters were traditionally trapped in run-down warehouses or shot down in the gutter. Cody Jarrett's last stand takes place in an elaborate complex of steel pipes and tanks more suited to a science-fiction film. The industrial maze sometimes resembles an abstract painting or a printed circuit board. Shotgun blasts and machine-gun bullets fly amid millions of gallons of potentially poisonous or explosive chemicals. [8]

The horde of police may have cornered the gang, but Hank Fallon's betrayal is the catalyst that pushes its leader over the line of sanity. Fallon levels a riot gun at Cody, who responds with contemptuous laughter: "A copper! How about that! And his name is Fallon! And we went for it! *I* went for it! Treated him like a kid brother!"

Jarrett is so unfazed that Fallon is for a moment unsure who has the drop on whom—he looks down to make sure he really has a gun in his hands. With Hank Fallon unmasked and every available lawman closing in, Cody Jarrett does exactly what everyone's been afraid of—he goes completely off his rocker. *White Heat* becomes deranged as well, its rising arc of violence keeping pace with Cody's mania. In response to Evans' demand for surrender, a blast from Cody's shotgun tears big chunks out of the insulation on an array of pipes, a graphic effect unequaled until 1969's *The Wild Bunch*: "Here's my answer, you dirty. . . ."

Cody's gun drops several lawmen in their tracks. The showdown is bigger than the cornering of a single criminal. Cody is the most dangerous man alive, and his resistance is spectacular. He sends two hapless cohorts directly into a hail of machine-gun fire to check an exit route. Reaching the top of an enormous chemical storage tank, Cody shoots another of his gang in the back.

When the T-Men finally get a clean shot, Cody refuses to die, even after being hit by Fallon's high-powered rifle bullets. Poetically speaking, Cody's madness has granted him the supernatural powers his gang feared—he's bigger than life. His demise is certainly scaled larger than that of any ordinary mortal—he dies in defiance, his arms outstretched like some kind of gangster anti-Christ. Echoing the prominent sign from the conclusion of *Little Caesar* ("Cook's Tours: The World is Yours"), Cody's final cry is, "Made it, Ma, Top of the World!" The apocalyptic finale bathes the screen in boiling explosions, a fiery funeral for a superhuman villain of the atomic age.

There is one more aspect to *White Heat* that connects it to cultural trends larger and wider than the gangster genre. Although there's nothing overtly fantastic about *White Heat*, its grandiose finale and Cody Jarrett's equally explosive personality place it at a crossroads in the development of pulp terror in the 20th century, a trend that repeatedly envisions quasi-superhuman characters.

Cody Jarrett's bigger-than-life villainy makes him a key link in the chain between Fritz Lang's "Age of Terror" *Dr. Mabuse* crime films of the 1920s and the freewheeling action thrillers of the second half of the century. We've established that *White Heat* raised the violence and jeopardy of the gangster film. The real inheritor of the heightened action thrills introduced in *White Heat* is the super-spy world of Ian Fleming's agent 007, much of which transplants gangster and film noir iconography into simplified fantasies about Cold War politics. Just as Cody Jarrett exhibits some aspects of a comic-book super-villain, James Bond is confronted by Cold War bogeymen interpreted through older pulp forms. Sinister crime lord Ernst Blofeld is a watered-down version of Dr. Mabuse. The cartoonish Dr. No combines the racist pulp villain Fu Manchu with Chairman Mao.

The James Bond film series was preceded by Ian Fleming's popular books, some of which appear to have been directly inspired by earlier gangster thrillers and noir films. Fleming's 1957 novel and the 1963 film *From Russia with Love* have a passage on the Orient Express that seems a direct transposition of the situation in Richard Fleischer's 1952 crime thriller *The Narrow Margin*. James Bond takes the Orient Express knowing that assassins plan to kill him; a friendly conductor tries to help but a hired assassin boards the train in disguise. Bond and the assassin fight to the death in a cramped compartment. In Fleischer's film noir, policeman Charles McGraw faces a pointedly similar predicament on a swift express train. He can't tell who the killers are and has difficulty sending out messages, even with the help of a friendly conductor. A key assassin boards the train to finish him off, and one of the action highlights is a brutal fight in a cramped washroom.

White Heat looks to have been the source inspiration for the conclusion of another of Ian Fleming's James Bond fantasies, the 1959 novel *Goldfinger*. As the prisoner of super-criminal Auric Goldfinger, James Bond is forced to go along on the big raid on Fort Knox. He leaves a message in the men's room of a chartered airplane, hoping that it will be forwarded to the police. Miraculously, the message gets through, and Goldfinger's heist is interrupted by a horde of army troops.

The Fort Knox passage's similarity to *White Heat*'s final heist is too exact to be coincidental. The desperate Hank Fallon is also forced to accompany a master criminal on a major heist. He uses the mirror of a filling station men's room as a message board in an equally desperate attempt to contact the police, which thankfully pays off. Just as Cody's raid is bearing fruit, an army of police close in.

The film version of *Goldfinger* has Bond use an electronic "homing device" to report his whereabouts to his backup team; it became a famous 007 gadget. *White Heat* invented this concept through the radio-triangulation "oscillator" device that Fallon cobbles from an ordinary radio.

These connections between James Bond and *White Heat* indicate much more than the influence of one school of filmmaking on succeeding entertainments. Just as Fleming drew from the screen thrillers he admired, gangster epics and noir films owe a huge debt to earlier forms, especially the sophisticated crime and espionage thrillers of Fritz Lang. Lang's conception of technologically advanced masterminds committing crimes and stealing state secrets probably had as big an influence on authentic intelligence organizations as his prophetic *Woman in the Moon* had on later space flight research. *White Heat* is a powerful offshoot of the gangster genre, and also a key link in a chain that reaches backward from 007 and *Mission Impossible*, through Fritz Lang to Feuillade's *Fantomas* and Norbert Jacques' *Dr. Mabuse, der Spieler*. There is a continuity of themes in pulp thrillers, most of which share two qualities: a villain with an anti-social ambition and a tendency toward megalomania, and advanced technology. *White Heat* elevates the generic gangster figure into this new category.

If we accept Cody Jarrett as one in a series of 20th-century pulp super-villains, he becomes a pivotal figure, the last classic movie gangster who also inaugurates the genre into the atomic age. Molded by censors and emerging

Donald Pleasance as "sinister crime lord Ernst Blofeld . . . a watered-down version of Dr. Mabuse," in *You Only Live Twice*.

from post-war psychological traumas, Cagney's mother-worshipping fanatic represents man at his most irresponsible, the Frankenstein that the police, the church, and government must suppress and deny.

Standing alone and defiant atop millions of gallons of explosive chemicals, Jarrett is a deranged monster willing to unleash destruction on a grandiose scale; he's all of society's fears of chaos personified. Modern culture persists in conceiving of the world's ills, whether criminal conspiracies or political conflicts, as face-offs between Good and Evil as simplistic as the heroes and villains of our action entertainments. In the years since *White Heat* the world has witnessed super-criminal acts of war that dwarf the fantasies of violent action thrillers. Cody Jarrett is the shape of demonized villains to come.

Rudolf Klein-Rogge as the title character in *Dr. Mabuse, Der Spieler.*

Notes

1. Anon., *Cue* magazine, September 3, 1949.

2. Philip K. Scheuer, *Los Angeles Times* (no date).

3. Bosley Crowther, *New York Times* (no date).

4. Carlos Clarens, *Crime Movies: An Illustrated Guide* (New York: W. W. Norton, 1980). Clarens points out that there was no official supervisory FBI link with G-Men.

5. Screenplay, *White Heat*, introduced and edited by Patrick McGilligan, Wisconsin/WB Screenplay series (Madison: University of Wisconsin Press, 1984).

6. *New York Times*, June 12, 1949 (the words "diseased psychopathic killer" appear in another review, suggesting that they may have come pre-written in a press handout.)

7. The urge to polish the image of the T-Man Philip Evans altered the ending as well. According to Patrick McGilligan, in the script Velma's offer to negotiate Cody's surrender isn't turned down flat (Evans: "No deal!"). But before she can talk to Cody, she's killed by one of his wild shotgun blasts.

8. A similar oil refinery was utilized as the futuristic setting for an almost identically filmed machine gun battle between striking workers and faceless guards possessed by invaders from outer space in Val Guest's superior English science fiction film *Quatermass 2* (a.k.a. *Enemy from Space*, 1957). Mirroring *White Heat*'s use of a colossal "Hortonsphere" storage tank, *Quatermass 2* uses a similar domed tank looming on the horizon to symbolize a frightening future.

AMES
CAGNEY
VIRGINIA
MAYO
WHITE HEAT
Edmond O'BRIEN
RAOUL WALSH

"Barbara confronts a grotesque mutation of her previous life."

The Gangster According to Aldrich

Alain Silver

Superficially, Robert Aldrich's *The Grissom Gang* (1971) is a gangster film. Presuming that gangster films require gangster protagonists, *The Grissom Gang* is only half that. Robert Aldrich made no pure "gangster film," and other than *Kiss Me Deadly* (1955) and *The Garment Jungle* (1957), he made no other pictures in which gangsters figure at all. What distinguishes *The Grissom Gang* from the typical genre piece is its uneasy mixture of offhanded violence and ill-fated romanticism. Slim Grissom's murder of his cohort Eddie Hagen is arguably the most purely violent of any scene in Aldrich's films, a canon Andrew Sarris claimed was "notable for its violence even in genres that subsist on violence."[1] The truth of Sarris' generalization in *American Cinema* notwithstanding, the reason the simpleminded Slim stabs Eddie so savagely and repeatedly is for love. On the one hand, Slim resembles Aldrich's deadliest psychopath, Maggot from *The Dirty Dozen* (1967). On the other, there is no character in any Aldrich film whose devotion to a woman is more powerful and uninhibited. Part of this, of course, has to do with the kind of male characters Aldrich chose to portray.

Aldrich's declared strategy when first approaching any subject or genre was to stand it on its head, and the generic range of his work as a producer and director is considerable, from Westerns and war movies to Hollywood melodramas and film noir. Aldrich's other characters who suffer for love, such as Callahan in *World for Ransom* (1954) or Gaines in *Hustle* (1975), are also involved in twisted relationships. In fact, Callahan's devotion to the bisexual manipulator Frennessey and Gaines' long-term affair with a high-priced prostitute are, in their own ways, as perverse as Slim's. Slim mawkishly resembles the bumbling thugs Max and Sugar, whom Mike Hammer handles so easily in *Kiss Me Deadly*. There are no Tony Camontes or Ricos in *The Grissom Gang*, no ambitious immigrants with sartorial pretense, no one remotely as smooth as Carl Evello, whose Beverly Hills mansion Hammer visits and for whom the thuggish Max and Sugar do the heavy lifting. These Grissom gangsters are just a bunch of dumb, violent white trash dressed in coveralls and toting tommy guns.

In *The Garment Jungle* Artie Ravidge is a cheap, strong-arm guy whose white teeth flashing between pockmarked cheeks personify the low-rent

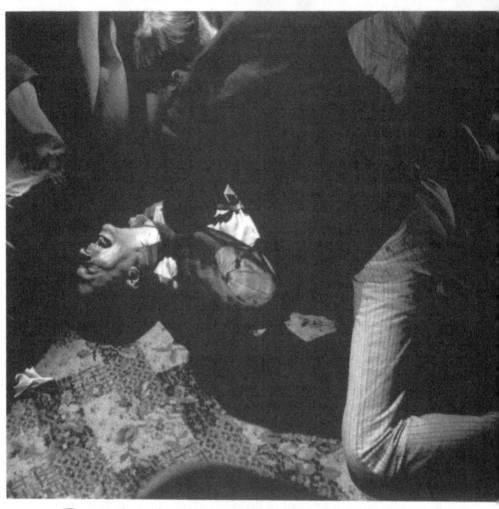

"The reason the simpleminded Slim stabs Eddie so savagely and repeatedly is for love."

urban gangster. This clichéd, quasi-satirical characterization satisfies audience expectations. Ravidge's habit of keeping people at a distance with the tip of a burning cigarette is a quirk typical of an Aldrich character, typical as well of how Aldrich deconstructs a genre portrayal. On the one hand, by turning an everyday item into a menacing object, Ravidge demonstrates a cruel ingenuity of the sort shared with classic gangster types. On the other, it is also the effete gesture of a cheap hood, a parody of true menace.

The conflicting forces at work in the crime narrative of *The Garment Jungle* are embodied by a variety of stylistic devices, including Aldrich's favorite metaphor for sub-surface chaos, the ceiling fan. As Ravidge's henchmen close in on a union official, the low angle medium shot reveals a network of twisting shadows thrown by such a fan on all the surrounding walls. As the distracting play of light and the severe angles inject instability into the frame, Ravidge's unpredictable violence does the same on a narrative level. The image of the black elevator shaft, down which an innocent man is pitched to his death at the film's beginning, hangs over *The Garment Jungle* and evokes the ever present threat of annihilation with shuddering simplicity.

The final sequence in which Ravidge is physically defeated by Alan Mitchell, the son of a corrupt garment manufacturer, does nothing to remedy the social problem that sustains gangsters of his sort. This is explicitly established in the epilogue, as Mitchell takes over for his father and is quickly subsumed by the undertow of business demands. The film ends sardonically on a shot of a Roxton Fashions telephone operator as she mechanically switches lines and informs callers that "Mr. Mitchell is busy," just like all the people, seen and unseen, who looked the other way in the gangster films of the early 1930s. Less than ten years after Robert Warshow asserted that "the importance of the gangster film, and the nature and intensity of its emotional and aesthetic impact, cannot be measured in terms of the place of the gangster himself or the importance of the problem of crime in American life," Aldrich's narratives in *Kiss Me Deadly*, *The Garment Jungle*—and other genres ranging from the Western to war film—repeatedly suggested that there are no heroes, tragic or otherwise.

The Grissom Gang is set in the 1930s and, like the prototypical gangster films of that era, is about unsophisticated criminal activity: kidnapping, murder, and assorted lesser felonies. Ma Grissom's motley group of miscreants does constitute a gang. But Ma herself is as much a caricature as a character, a machine-gun-wielding variant of the mother figure in *White Heat*. But while *White Heat*'s Cody Jarrett fully participates in the lineage of gangster portrayals going back to *The Public Enemy* and Tom Powers' normal devotion to his law-abiding mother in that film, no element of the relationship between Slim and Ma is touching or selfless. Slim is, after all, Ma's enforcer, the one whom even his fellow gang members fear, the loose cannon that keeps Ma in control. "Slim's a good boy," Ma asserts, "always does what his mother tells him." Ma's print dresses, grimy aprons, and unkempt hair suggest the female half of *American Gothic* gone psycho. The twang in her voice when she warns Barbara Blandish that "we ain't the kind of people who fool around—get it, dearie?" makes her all the more menacing. Ma's demise, with her cackling like a demented Lucy Ricardo as the police close in and her tommy gun jams, is closer to Captain Cooney's two-stepping in a hail of bullets in *Attack!* than to the grisly gang-related deaths in *Kiss Me Deadly* or *The Garment Jungle*. In fact, most of the criminals in *The Grissom Gang* verge on parody, from Joey Fay's pudgy Woppy to Ralph Waite's hayseed Mace to Tony Musante's Eddie with his slicked-back hair and white-toothed grin. They are full-color, 1970s versions of the gangster movie stereotypes from the 1930s. Compare, for example, the contemporary gangster-noir *The Outfit* (1973). The gangster figures in that film "act like they own the world," and yet a single determined individual is able to resist and overcome them. As in *Point Blank* (1967), an earlier adaptation of the Parker novels of Donald Westlake (writing as Richard Stark), or *Charley Varrick* (1973), whose title character is "the last of the independents," the smugness of the syndicate bosses is the decadent weakness that permits determined individuals to resist them. Although the same attitude underlies more recent period pictures such as *The Untouchables* (1987) or *Road to Perdition* (2002), the "historic" view of mobsters is that accountancy is

"Ma [Irene Dailey] herself is as much a caricature as a character, a machine-gun-wielding variant of the mother figure in *White Heat*."

their Achilles heel. In the later picture, in particular, adapted from a graphic novel, the 1930s is now rendered with a somber pictorialism that romanticizes the era. The hit-man Sullivan, portrayed by Tom Hanks, becomes the ethical center of the narrative, an ironic position for a hired killer. At their core all these pictures contemplate mob decadence in a way that permits their protagonists to murder at will with a combination of earnestness and savagery that is far different from Slim Grissom's or Bonnie and Clyde's.

There are other expressions of a far more sardonic undertone in *The Grissom Gang*, mostly in the music, full of banjos and up-tempo chase cues, so that the careening period cars recall the Keystone cops as much as *Little Caesar* or *Public Enemy*. There are also the black-and-white freeze frames in the title sequence that simulate still photographs and are part homage to and part parody of a similar montage of stills in *Bonnie and Clyde*. And much as in *Bonnie and Clyde*, many of the incidents in *The Grissom Gang* are part of a deconstruction of the traditional Hollywood gangster. Like the reenactment of the killing of the real Bonnie and Clyde at the end of Arthur Penn's film, the destruction of all the Grissom gang except Slim is effected in a series of scenes in which the title characters are riddled with bullets. The detail adds a layer, a savage satire: Ma's "death dance" as she gyrates wildly from the gunshots; the art deco panels of the boudoir shattering to reveal armor plate beneath; the colored light that keeps flashing as Woppy expires. Slim learns of the massacre through a radio report in which the scene is jokingly described as "more bullets flying around than ticks on a cow's back."

The slow-witted Slim Grissom is clearly a child of his unwholesome environment. When he and his gang take Barbara from her original abductors, Slim behaves as if his mother were watching. "Like Ma says," Slim notes approvingly to Eddie, who has just pumped a man full of lead, "they's real punks." Slim has no compunctions about anyone's violent behavior, least of all his own. After killing a man he grins, sticks out his tongue, and wipes his knife blade on his victim's lapels. For Slim, only the sweaty, traumatized Barbara in her soiled, satiny evening gown, a disheveled vision of loveliness, merits a second glance or a second thought.

The most significant music cue which opens and closes *The Grissom Gang* is Rudy Vallee singing "I Can't Give You Anything But Love, Baby." For Slim, at the picture's beginning, romantic love is an unlikely prospect. So while the others see dollar signs over the Blandish girl's head, Slim sees a halo. The transformation of his captive from angel to sex slave is a hesitant one for Slim, partly because he is unfamiliar with the process, partly because his childlike outlook makes no necessary distinction between the two. What is unusual in the film's narrative is the transformation of Barbara Blandish. To her Slim is the most repellent of the gang, a "cretinous half-wit" or a "creepy-crawly slimy slug." His very naiveté makes him all the more repugnant.

Since Slim knows he is her sole protector, Barbara's behavior is puzzling to him. When he complains to Ma that "she's saying bad things," Barbara gets beaten but starts guzzling more gin. "Ladies ain't supposed to drink," Slim tells her, "not hard liquor." When she realizes that the gang means to collect

"A somber pictorialism that romanticizes the era": the sinister prelude to the rain-drenched tommy-gun attack in *Road to Perdition* recalling Tom Powers' assault in *The Public Enemy*.

the ransom and kill her, Barbara knows that Slim is her only hope for survival, and she actually seduces him. The early scenes with Slim and Barbara are in the dingy upstairs room where she is kept. Shot with little fill light so that dark wedges cut across walls and floors, Aldrich also uses over-the-shoulder shots and travels in from medium close to close to constrict the frame even more and to externalize Barbara's sense of being caged. After their first sexual interlude, Barbara looks at herself in a clouded mirror and Slims comes up behind her. Surrounded by Slim and his reflection and facing the empty liquor bottles arrayed on the dressing table before her, Barbara confronts a grotesque mutation of her previous life. It is in this context, as Slim professes his love, that the emotional transference between them begins.

Ultimately, after the gang buys a nightclub with the ransom money, Slim takes her to a secret love nest. It is a kaleidoscopic maze of primary colors and diamond shapes complete with a "gold leaf flush toilet" and a kitchen. "I don't cook" is all Barbara can think to say. Although Slim does seem to become smarter as the narrative progresses, his understanding of how things are is always instinctive rather than intellectual. For Barbara, the wealthy sophisticate, the reverse is true. The brutalization she endures is part of the transference in which she comes to understand the insights of someone like Slim.

Slim's devotion is mirrored in Anna Borg, a nightclub singer and the girlfriend of one of the original kidnappers killed by the Grissoms who takes up with Eddie Hagen. When Fenner, the private detective hired by Barbara's father to pay the ransom and find his daughter, tricks Anna, she realizes that Eddie killed "her Franky." When she pulls a gun, Eddie shoots her first and notes with disgust, "Dumb, Anna, you were really dumb." It is this scorn of Eddie's, the smart guy and pseudo-sophisticate, both for Anna and for Slim that mirrors Barbara's feelings at the film's beginning. It is only after Eddie attempts to rape her and Slim violently intervenes that Barbara grasps the nature of the primal emotion which drives people like Anna and Slim. Barbara screams and shudders with each thrust of Slim's knife into Eddie. After this mock orgasm, it remains only for Barbara to reciprocate the love of her valiant defender, Slim, to complete the transference.

As the police close in on her and Slim hiding in a barn, Barbara does reciprocate that love. Although it may only be with a nod of her head when Slim asks her if she would really care if he died, Barbara's affirmation both liberates and condemns her. Slim dies a grisly Grissom death in a hail of bullets. Barbara's father vilifies her for crying over Slim's body; and the press crowds around. As with Zarkan at the end of Aldrich's Hollywood film *The Legend of Lylah Clare* (1968), Barbara's own personality has been subsumed into the idealized Slim whom she helped to create. Like Zarkan, she is lost without that object. Over a freeze frame of her despairing glance backward as Fenner drives her away, Rudy Vallee croons on the soundtrack.

Barbara (Kim Darby) is vilified by her father (Wesley Addy) for crying over the dead Slim (Scott Wilson).

As with the hoboes and train men in Aldrich's *The Emperor of the North Pole* (1973), the milieu and period of *The Grissom Gang* color their characterization as outsiders. Barbara and her father are the only ostensibly normal persons in the film, but their rupture at the conclusion is indicative of the existential vagaries of Aldrich's worldview. Fenner, the private detective who is a bridge between the world of the Grissoms and that of Mr. Blandish, is a shadowy, alienated figure from the first. His social situation and the dialogue with the police chief suggest a dark past, but it is never revealed. He is at his most animated when playing a role, posing as a theatrical agent to extract information from Anna Borg. He wears dark suits that allow him to blend into the shadowy background and is often photographed with sharp sidelight. The staging of his conversation with Mr. Blandish in the nightclub love nest after the police raid uses matching close-ups in which a silhouette of each restricts the other's screen space, as if expressing the narrowness of their respective outlooks. Fenner is the only one who seems to understand Barbara's pain at Slim's death.

Like Rico in *Little Caesar* and Tony Camonte in *Scarface*, Slim is cut down by police bullets; but his death has a subjective connotation in that the audience identifies with Barbara and participates in her emotional anguish. Although the same could be said of the grisly demise of Tom Powers in *The Public Enemy*, whose body is discovered by his brother while his mother is upstairs making up his bed, the "romantic" relationship between Slim and Barbara colors the audience's identification differently. In Aldrich's subversive mise-en-scène, the distinction, or lack thereof, between hero and anti-hero is always in play. Just as the smug, self-centered "hero" of *Kiss Me Deadly*, Mike Hammer, is an anti-Galahad, Slim Grissom is something of an anti-gangster. The big dreams of Rico and Camonte lead them down a path of violence and destruction. As Warshow suggests, "The real city produces only criminals; the imaginary city produces the gangster: he is what we want to be and what we are afraid we may become." Certainly Slim Grissom does nothing to validate Warshow's observation that "the gangster is the man of the city," nor does he bear the tragic burden that Warshow perceived in the prototypical gangster's drive to succeed. There is little if anything in Slim's behavior that conforms to Warshow's expectation that "the gangster's activity is actually a form of rational enterprise, involving fairly definite goals and various techniques for achieving them." In the end, the gangster, according to Aldrich, is just a hick trying to get by and make points with a girl, a young man bred to be a thug, inured to violence, and as lovesick as a puppy. In that context, existential cries like "I ain't so tough" or "Is this the end of Rico?" are unnecessary and inappropriate. Slim goes out a simple victim of love.

Note

1. Andrew Sarris, *The American Cinema: Directors and Directions, 1929 to 1968* (New York: E. P. Dutton, 1968), 84.

Young Vito (Robert De Niro) "dispenses justice" in *Godfather II*.

A Study in Ambiguity: *The Godfather* and the American Gangster Movie Tradition

Geoff Fordham

Introduction

It is perhaps stating the obvious to say that issues surrounding law and order have traditionally been a central theme of crime movies in general and gangster movies in particular. That is what the films are about, since the central characters operate outside the law, the narratives encompass their relationships with the agencies of law enforcement, while the plots are (generally) structured around the processes by which they are brought to justice or otherwise get their comeuppance. But running through what has been characterized as the gangster sub-genre is a series of ambiguities about the definition and enforcement of laws and social norms more generally, reflecting a fundamental ambivalence in audiences' (and indeed society's) stance towards the gangster-hero.[1]

These ambiguities are displayed in a variety of ways. Firstly, as Thomas Leitch points out, the dynamic of every crime film focuses on the relationship between three sets of characters: the perpetrator, the victim and the avenger, (official or otherwise)—but typically gangster narratives seek to "undermine and blur the boundaries (between) the typological figures."[2] So, the captain of police is routinely corrupt (as with Captain McCluskey [Sterling Hayden] in *The Godfather* [Coppola, 1972]); the gangster dispenses justice (passim throughout the sub-genre, but for example the young Vito [Robert De Niro] in *The Godfather Part II* [Coppola, 1974]); while the gangster becomes victim (again passim, but as an example, Tony Montana [Al Pacino] in *Scarface* [De Palma, 1983].[3])

These ambiguities also infect audiences' response to the gangster. A central and broadly universal foundation on which Hollywood's portrayal of the underworld is constructed is the moral imperative to demonstrate that crime does not pay. This imperative provides the moral underpinning to the "rise and fall" narrative that characterizes many gangster movies (for example *The Public Enemy* [Wellman, 1931], *White Heat* [Walsh, 1949] and *Al Capone* [Wilson, 1959]). But it is an imperative that has often been respected grudgingly, and at critical points in the development of the gangster film, only after external intervention. Munby explains how Hawks' *Scarface* was released after two years' negotiation with the censors, leading to the insertion of moralizing homilies and a name change (through the addition of a sub-title: *The Shame of the Nation*).[4] But despite these genuflections, Paul Muni's Tony (and George Raft's Guino) are more attractive than any of the representatives of the forces of law and order—a characteristic of the gangster film perhaps reaching its apotheosis with *Bonnie and Clyde* (Penn, 1967). Particularly in that subset of the gangster film that focuses on the Prohibition era, audiences' ambivalence reflects that of society more generally: "law-abiding" members of the community started to associate with the gangster who has become a preferred supplier.[5]

The ambiguities extend further to the gangsters' own stance toward the law and its enforcement. Although in many gangster movies the gang leader is himself a source of law enforcement within a closed gangster society, a powerful theme running through much of the sub-genre explores the gangsters' desire for acceptance in the straight and official world, particularly in those

An apotheosis of attractiveness: Faye Dunaway in Arthur Penn's *Bonnie and Clyde*.

films which locate gangster activity within immigrant communities. Since the "classic" gangster cycle of the early thirties, the ambitions of those from immigrant families to use lawlessness to secure the wealth, power, and prestige of "official" society commingle with a profound longing for assimilation and acceptance.

Finally this use of the gangster film as a device to explore the tensions between economic disadvantage and the illusory promises of acquisitive capitalism (brutally symbolized by the neon sign promising "the world is yours" in the Hawks *Scarface*) points to the most significant of the ambiguities that pervade the subgenre, displayed in the ambivalence of its stance towards the social, political, and economic context in which its narratives are worked out. Browne argues that Jack Shadoian is correct to say that the crime movie is "the central paradigm for investigating the inherent contradictions of the American dream of success."[6] For others however, the emphasis on the family as metaphor for social order, the extensive religious iconography that pervades the sub-genre, and the perverse imitations of capitalist organization which characterize movie gangsters' approach to business development, all serve to show how the subgenre is typically, if not inevitably, fundamentally supportive of the status quo.[7]

This paper focuses on how these themes are explored in an epic gangster movie of the early seventies: *The Godfather* (drawing where appropriate on the development of its core themes in the rest of the trilogy). The paper seeks to locate these films in the traditions of the gangster movie, exploring in particular how the themes, emblems, and motifs which support its claim to authentic subgenre status have responded to the changing socio-economic context in which it developed.

A Subgenre of Dissent?

The genre theorists' approach to the analysis of film stresses those elements of continuity which provide the unifying features that establish the films as legitimate candidates for genre status, irrespective of the social, political, and economic circumstances under which they were made. Andrew Tudor has pointed out the contradiction at the heart of this process: we can only identify the common features by examining the films; but until we have decided on those features we do not know which films belong to the genre and which therefore deserve examination.[8] According to Mason, implicit in genre theory is the notion that a genre is a "common set of practices that can be identified by its iconography, narrative formulae and semiotic codes."[9]

This approach to gangster movies is adopted by Edward Mitchell, when he argues that "Most of the study of film genres is taken up with an examination of formulas, icons, motifs—in short, the elements of repetitive patterning common to all films that we call detective films, or Westerns, or gangster films. This is as it should be. Indeed, no serious discussion of genre is possible without recourse to those elements that a particular genre film shares with others of its kind."[10]

But a number of critics have challenged this view, arguing that to focus on generic continuities distracts us from an analysis of those shifts and variations, albeit within a common framework, that show how films of particular eras respond to the economic, political, and importantly industrial circumstances prevailing at the time they were made. Leitch argues that "genres are best thought of as contexts that evolve in both personal and social history . . . rather than eternally fixed and mutually exclusive categories."[11] For Munby, gangster movies are "analogous to a Venn diagram with both areas of overlap and areas of distinctiveness."[12]

Munby, among other writers, sees the development of the American gangster movie as a series of cycles, each drawing on and evolving from its predecessors, but at the same time reflecting the distinctive concerns and characteristics of its time.[13] The "classic" cycle of the early thirties was—and more importantly was seen by audiences as—an explicit response to the Depression, and more explicitly, the "widespread despair over the value of public policy and the institutions of government, finance and the law."[14] This helps explain the appeal of the central figures (like Muni's Tony in *Scarface* or Robinson's Rico in *Little Caesar* [Le Roy, 1931]), strong figures who succeed (at least until the final reel) in the face of official opposition, by their own efforts.

Following the controversy over *Scarface* there was a brief moratorium in the production of gangster movies, though some of the impetus behind the classic cycle had evaporated with the abolition of the Volstead Act (which had introduced Prohibition) in 1933. But by the mid-thirties a new cycle of post-Prohibition, post–Production Code gangster movies was under way, exploring similar themes and using many of the same actors—but shifting the focus away from the gangsters, concentrating instead on the enforcers. The pessimism of the Depression gave way to the optimism of the New Deal (introduced after Roosevelt's election in 1933), and the gangster movie sought to reassert the legitimacy of official authority through films like *G-Men* (Keighley, 1935). But this cycle was still able to provide audiences with the same vicarious experience of heroic violence and corruption as their predecessors, even though the violence now was carried on (more or less) lawfully. Warner's publicity for *G-Men* stressed the continuity: "Hollywood's most famous bad man (Cagney) joins the *G-Men* and halts the march of crime."[15] The message was clear: adopt their tactics or fail, explicitly echoed 50 years later in *The Untouchables* (De Palma, 1987), through Malone's (Sean Connery) streetwise cop's advice to the purist Elliot Ness (Kevin Costner); and Ness' response later in the film when he pushes Malone's murderer off a courtroom roof ("I am in contempt of all that I swore to uphold")—another example of crime films blurring the boundaries between gangster and law enforcer.

Gangster movies within the post-war film noir cycle may have displayed a shared iconography with their predecessors from the thirties, but they brought a distinctive mood, and a tone darker than anything that had gone before. As many commentators have observed,[16] film noir offered a clear reflection of a darkening and pessimistic mood in the aftermath of World War II, amid the challenges to "traditional" values that returning servicemen experienced.

Although the film noir cycle has been "posited as aesthetically experimental and deviant," displaying little connections to what went before, for Munby noir gangster films picked up where pre-war crime films had left off, and were "received as an awkward reminder of problems whose resolution had been postponed by the need to prosecute the war,"[17] a sentiment echoed by Muller, who sees noir as incorporating "a bundle of unfinished business (that) lingered from the Depression."[18]

Although it co-existed with the noir cycle, Leitch argues that increasingly through the fifties and early sixties the gangster movie supported the Establishment[19]—with Hollywood galvanized by the perceptions of the threat of the Cold War: no more bent cops, no more romanticized villains. But by the late sixties, Hollywood's gangster movies put "the Establishment on trial," most completely through *Bonnie and Clyde*, which "managed to demonize the same American institutions as the gangster cycle of the thirties—the police, the banks, the law—but this time in metaphoric terms, using a pair of criminals of the thirties to attack the moral injustice of the draft and the violent injustice of the American experience in Vietnam."[20]

So within certain generic conventions, the gangster movie provided a format in which contemporary social and political concerns could be explored. For Munby however, paradoxically given his insistence on the mutability of the format over time, within these variations there is a crucial constant theme: for all the "conservative" elements which have been in evidence in gangster

Sean Connery's street-wise cop Malone teaches the purist Elliot Ness (Kevin Costner) how to blur the boundaries between gangster and law enforcer.

movies throughout their history, and the ambiguities these generate, the format is inherently subversive. He insists that the gangster film "has mediated perhaps the most profound periods of crisis and transformation in twentieth century US history, from the Depression to the cold war"[21]—to which one could add Vietnam, since the period of his review predates American involvement. Other writers have expressed similar views: Leitch for example, though he perhaps overstates his case when he says that "every crime in every crime film represents a larger critique of the social and constitutional order."[22] However, these subversive strands express themselves in a variety of ways:

> Through a critique of the acquisitive society which is implicit in gangsters' heady ambitions and, once successful, their grotesque and excessive lifestyles: Hardy describes De Palma's *Scarface* as "an infantile celebration of the gaudiness of wealth."[23]
>
> The romanticization of the anti-hero despite the requirements of the Production Code: however immoral their means, gangsters nevertheless offer practical (often "real life") examples of the dispossessed triumphing over the Establishment.
>
> Frequent demonstrations that society's official institutions are as corrupt as the criminal institutions they oppose (politicians in *The Untouchables*, multi-national corporations in *Scarface*, the church in *The Godfather III*, the police just about everywhere.)

Amsterdam Vallon (Leonardo DiCaprio) and Bill "the Butcher" Cutting (Daniel Day-Lewis) in Scorsese's turn-of-the-century Irish *Gangs of New York*.

Exposing the gap between "ideology" (America as the land of equal opportunity for all), and the actuality: success is not for the dispossessed or immigrant, unless pursued violently and illegitimately.

These strands are to be observed throughout the subgenre, in most if not all its cyclical variations, and are to be observed today. Munby notes that black gangster movies continue to provide "an uncomfortable reminder of the racist nature of economic and spatial destitution"[24]—like many other movies that have chronicled the same phenomena from the perspective not just of Italians, but Hispanics (*Scarface*), Irish (*Gangs of New York* [Scorsese, 2002]), and Jews (*Once Upon a Time in America* [Leone, 1984]).

But offering yet a further example of the ambiguities that run through the genre, the gang structures that provide the route out for all these groups, embody and are emblematic of the discriminatory economic structures against which gang members are rebelling. Gangsters may rebel against conventional moral codes and create alternative systems of governance and morality; but this does not necessarily mean they are subversive. As Leitch says, "gangsters cannot help imitate the society whose norms they seek to violate."[25]

In the next section we consider how these strands are developed in *The Godfather*: does the film justify Coppola's claims that it "was always a loose metaphor: Michael for America"?[26]

The Godfather: A Metaphor for America?

In his study of *The Godfather* trilogy, Nick Browne sees the three films as "deeply rooted in the conventions of the American crime film and the social experience of the ambitious outsider that shapes that genre's attitudes."[27] Presented on an epic scale the cycle portrays the rise of a "family" of Sicilian immigrants from the point where Vito Corleone (De Niro, then Marlon Brando) arrives as a young boy, to Michael (Al Pacino), his son's emergence as one of the richest and most powerful men in America. Although Coppola uses a variety of cinematic techniques (many consciously harking back to earlier examples of American gangster films) in his exposition of narrative, including montage, and in *The Godfather II*, flashback, the film's power derives from a deceptively simple narrative structure, assisted by powerful ensemble acting, with superb performances from Brando, De Niro (both of whom won Best Actor Oscars), and Pacino. Within its narrative structure the films explore the tensions between first and second generation immigrants (even successful ones), and the dominant WASP culture to which they aspire; and contrasts the highly regulated and ruthlessly enforced codes of honor and obedience imported from Sicily, with the ineffectual and corrupt structures of authority that immigrants encounter in America.

We saw earlier in this paper that throughout its history the American gangster movie has been characterized by ambiguities, in the way criminals have been presented, in the blurring of boundaries between outlaw and law enforcer, and in the perspective the films take on the social and economic

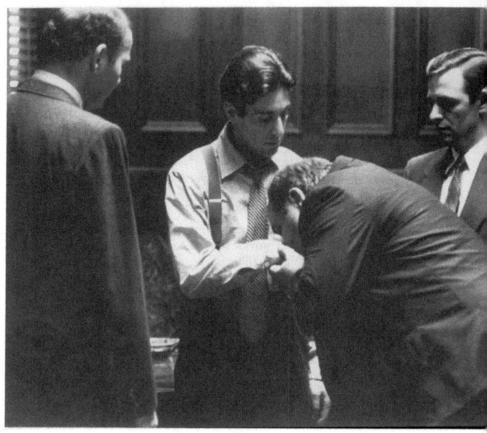

After Michael Corleone's "emergence as one of the richest and most powerful men in America."

circumstances from which gangsters emerge and in which the films were made. *The Godfather* trilogy is no exception.

The films have been seen by many commentators as a critique of American capitalism. Man for example, argues that while the gangster genre has generally displayed a "prosocial ideology supportive of the status quo" (if grudgingly), the *Godfather* films challenge this dominant ideology (if grudgingly as well). "On the whole, the trilogy indicts American capitalism for the rampant materialism within society and subverts the dominant prosocial myth."[28] But the films' pre-eminent and enduring themes and images offer powerful emblems of stability, order, tradition, and hierarchy.

The films' central theme focuses on the family (in two senses, including the role and significance of the blood family, and in the context of the gangster format, the structure and significance of the business Family) while their narrative explores both Vito's and more significantly Michael's (ultimately unsuccessful) attempts to protect and maintain the integrity of their families. This focus reflects one of Coppola's personal obsessions,[29] which he integrated directly into the film, not just through its narrative and thematic explorations, but through his casting, choice of associates, and source material: his father provided the music, his grandfather wrote the turn-of-the-century melodrama

("Senza Mama"—"Without Mama") which the young Vito watches in *Godfather II*, and his daughter Sofia plays Michael's daughter Mary.

One of the distinctive features of Coppola's direction of the trilogy and especially the first two films is his use of set-piece mise-en-scènes, which invariably help establish the family structure, as well as the relationship between the Corleone family and its wider Family business. *The Godfather* opens with an extended set-piece which introduces us to the Corleone family through the wedding feast of Vito's daughter Connie (Talia Shire). The sequence deftly establishes the key elements of characterization, context, and plot—all within a family occasion. Traditional Italian music sets the ethnic context (what Vera Dika has called the films' "Italianicity");[30] we see Don Corleone dispensing "justice" to a supplicant (in an exchange which contrasts the value of official legal structures with the Godfather's traditional methods); the police taking down the registration numbers of guests' cars establishes the nature of the family's relationship with the forces of law and order; Sonny Corleone (James Caan), Vito's hot-headed eldest son, reveals the rash and compulsive nature (through his seduction of a bridesmaid and his impulsive attacks on the agents) which will lead to his death later in the film; Michael and his fiancée Kaye (Diane Keaton) are introduced as outsiders; but critically, Vito is established as above all a family man whose abiding concern is to keep the whole family together: he refuses to have the group picture taken until Michael has arrived. He is also established as the patriarch—his authority over both his family and his Family is absolute.

(A similar family gathering set-piece opens *Godfather II*, after the family has relocated to Lake Tahoe as part of Michael's doomed attempt to distance himself from the Family's criminal past. Its contrast with the wedding scene— the traditional Italian musicians replaced by an anonymous "show-biz" band that turns an Italian folk-song into a nursery rhyme for example—offers ironic comment on what has happened to the family in the intervening period.)

The films' apparent endorsement of a traditional and conservative view of the family is also established by their exploration of the roles of women and their place within family (and Family) decision-making structures. Until Connie intervenes to sanction an assassination after Michael is taken ill in *Godfather III*, women's presence in any decision-making exercise is restricted to serving refreshments. In one sequence in *Godfather II*, Michael visits Hyman Roth (Lee Strasberg); as the two men sit discussing business Roth's wife serves sandwiches—but since the camera remains fixed on the men, we never see above her shoulders: she remains invisible. With the exception of Kay (whose WASP origins leave her permanently excluded from the family even before her divorce), the women in the films are either subservient domestics (beaten by their husbands if they fail in these duties) or whores. The brutal murder of a prostitute in *Godfather II* (contrived as part of the Family's plot to blackmail Senator Geary [G. D. Spradlin]) provides a graphic account of the violent commodification of women the films display: she is found tied, naked, to a bed, with a large gash running from her groin to her breasts. Of course this dual view of women formed a traditional element within the American gangster movie: for example in both versions of *Scarface*, Camonte/Montana demands chastity from his sister—exerting quasi-paternal authority in doing so—while following a quite different set of values himself.

A second traditional authority pillar which features significantly in the film's imagery is the church—once again, a traditional source of iconography in the gangster genre. (In the near contemporary *Mean Streets* [Scorsese, 1973], Charlie (Harvey Keitel) at one point faced a choice between becoming a priest or a gangster.) Throughout, the church appears to offer a route to redemption, contrasted with the venality of the gangsters' business operations. We see Michael in the baptism sequence that closes the first film (which we deal with in more detail later in the paper); a parallel sequence in *Godfather III* where Michael is invested with a Papal medal; and in the final movie we are introduced to Fr. Andrew Hagen (John Savage), whose father Tom (Robert Duvall) had been Vito's *consigliere*, entrusted for example with making an offer he couldn't refuse to the film producer threatening the career of Vito's godson Johnny Fontane (Al Mancino)—an episode culminating of course in the famous horse's head scene. The Hagen family, unlike the Corleones, appears to have completed the transition to legitimacy.

But within the films' embrace of these essentially conservative themes there is an ambiguity that reflects the ambivalence of the immigrant, torn

"A similar family gathering set-piece opens *Godfather II*, after the family has relocated to Lake Tahoe."

between the pursuit of assimilation within and recognition by his adopted culture, and the maintenance and defense of traditional customs and values. This extends to the notion of patriotism itself: the opening sequence of *The Godfather*, in which the camera pans back from a shot of the supplicant slowly to reveal Brando exuding authority, has the undertaker saying "I believe in America," even as he reveals how American justice has failed his family. Michael returns as a war hero who served what he clearly regards as "his" country; but in the flashback scene where we learn of his decision to enlist, Sonny expresses his anger and astonishment that anyone would risk their life for anything other than their family.

This reflects one of the key underlying tensions within the films, which, Dika argues, "take as a central theme the order and power of traditional Italian ways in confrontation with the corroding effects of America."[31] But this perception that America's effects can be corrosive—Don Vito refuses to become involved in the drugs trade for broadly this reason—does not inhibit the family's desire for acceptance within their adopted community, corrosive or otherwise. Vito tells Michael that he dreams one day his son could become "Senator Corleone, Governor Corleone," while much of Michael's efforts are directed explicitly towards accommodation, receiving "respect" from the rest of America as well as his own people (the drive to legitimatize the business, the charitable work through the Vito Corleone Foundation, the Papal medal).

But a similar ambiguity suffuses the Family's attitude to the law more generally: codes of fierce (if often unfulfilled) loyalty and obedience within the Family co-exist with a complete disdain and disregard for "official" structures, which are there to be ignored, corrupted or purchased. The ambiguity surrounding order and lawlessness that characterizes organized crime on the screen is, according to Alessandro Camon, intrinsic to the Mafia itself: "At the same time that it rapes and pillages a land and a population, the Mafia has always claimed to protect them and evince a sense of belonging."[32] This dual morality—absolute ruthlessness to enemies, absolute devotion to friends—is brilliantly expressed in the baptism sequence at the end of *The Godfather* (which also encapsulates the tensions between assimilation and tradition). In a montage reminiscent of Eisenstein, Michael, in the process of becoming Godfather (in the original sense) to Connie's child, renounces, in separate vows, the Devil, his works, his pomp, each vow intercut with one of the executions he has ordered to consolidate his control in his new role as Godfather in the Mafia sense.

So, the *Godfather* films focus on a series of the traditional icons associated with conservatism: the family, church, country, hierarchy. But, given the traditions of the gangster movie it is perhaps almost inevitable that their treatment should reflect ambiguity. For as the films' narrative unfolds each of these symbols of authority systematically disintegrates. As we saw earlier, the principal leitmotif of the films is the sanctity of the family, continually alluded to by Vito and Michael (and indeed Sonny during his brief period as Don after his father has been shot). But the pursuit of family stability is illusory, rendered impossible because of the treachery and cruelty with which it is surrounded. "If you're strong for your family you can lose it," says Michael, which is precisely what happens. The conflicts within the Family and between business and blood families directly or indirectly lead to the execution of Michael's brother and brother-in-law, Kay's decision to abort his child, and his daughter's killing on the steps of the theater in Palermo.

Similarly, the moral authority of the church is eroded as the narrative unfurls. The institutions of the church are revealed as corrupt: Michael's investiture with the Papal medal at the start of *Godfather III* suggests that even Michael, with all his sins can purchase redemption, as though from a mediaeval pardoner. Ultimately Michael's plans to legitimize his business through investments with the Vatican are defeated by criminality and corruption within the church (though the suggested murder of a Pope is perhaps a little melodramatic). Dika even suggests that Michael's commitment to his roots is undermined as a result of his corruption. With his commercial involvement with the Vatican, "Michael comes full circle. As a landowner in association with northern (Italian) businessmen and the church, he becomes the symbolic exploiter of his own people."[33]

There is a strongly nostalgic feel to Coppola's cinematography, set decoration, and direction, in both the urban sequences and the rural idylls of Sicily. For Browne, these nostalgic historical settings, and the perverse American dream they portray, gave audiences in the early seventies "a reality substitute—an imaginative vehicle for occluding and reworking contemporary anxiety and discontent with the changes in America wrought by the Vietnam war."[34] Dika echoes this when she argues that the films' focus on family chimed with a collective wish for something lost in "an era that saw not only the disintegration of the family, but also the deterioration of America's faith in government."

It is the films' underlying ambiguities that create the opportunities for audiences to work through contemporary issues—in the process of course also creating the scope for conflicting readings. For example, although as we have already seen, the films portray women mainly as either servants or mistresses, they do not do so uncritically. The men's relationships with their women are displayed through a variety of pathologies (possessiveness, jealousy, protectiveness), many of which are used to reinforce ethnic stereotypes of the traditional Italian male. But as Camon argues, Kaye's relationship to Michael shows the limits to the preservation of tradition alongside assimilation: his expectations and values are challenged by Kaye's

Michael Corleone, recipient of the Papal medal, looking forward to gangster retirement in *Godfather III*.

contemporary, non-Sicilian, "proto-feminist" view of conjugal roles and relationships.[35] Moreover as the family disintegrates, and with it Michael's authority, the behavior of the women changes: Kay resumes a position of equality with Michael in their relationship with their children, while Connie, in an assumption of responsibility that would have been unthinkable to her mother, effectively assumes the role of Don during Michael's illness.

Similar ambiguities are to be observed in the films' stance toward the economic and power structures of contemporary America. The gangsters in the *Godfather* movies may be rebels but they are hardly freedom-fighters or radicals (despite De Niro's performance as an urban Robin Hood in *Godfather II*): as Hyman Roth says, "We're not Communists." As we discuss in our conclusions, the ambiguities reflect a dilemma that has beset Hollywood beyond *The Godfather* and indeed the gangster movie. So far as this trilogy is concerned, we see a massive and powerful business empire created through corruption, intimidation, and murder; and we also see the consequences, in the disintegration of the main architect and all he holds dear. But whether this signifies (even in extremis) the corruption inherent in American corporate capitalism, or a sign of what can happen if unscrupulous individuals step beyond the boundaries of competition, is less clear.

But what is clear is that as the narrative progresses, and as Michael's empire grows, he becomes less and less distinguishable from the "straight" businessmen with whom he associates. When challenged by the corrupt politician Geary about both his ethnic background and his real business, Michael replies: "We're all part of the same hypocrisy, Senator." When he joins the consortium seeking to do business with Batista's Cuba, Michael sits, with equal and indistinguishable status alongside representatives of "legitimate" corporate capitalism like AT&T.

Conservative symbols may dominate the films' imagery, but are ultimately shown to be illusory because of the corruption of the Corleone family. We are left under no illusion that for Coppola, the Family's business, if not identical to, is at least sufficiently close to mainstream U.S. corporate capitalism to provide a vehicle within which to explore its excesses. Finally Man sees the trilogy as subversive since it "undermines wholesome family relationships, attacks the capitalistic base within American society as malevolent aggression"[36] and we may add, also exposes the corruption of authority, the hypocrisy of the church, and the misogyny at the heart of gender relations.

Conclusion

The Godfather trilogy shares many of the themes that have characterized gangster films throughout their history: the lack of clarity in the distinction between outlaw, victim, and enforcer; the attractiveness of the gangsters, linked with their inevitable demise to ensure crime is seen not to pay; the difficulties faced by immigrants seeking a foothold in the New World. Although Coppola pushed it further than other directors, his focus on family also reflects themes from earlier films including *Scarface* and *The Brotherhood* (Ritt, 1969). Also like its predecessors, the trilogy's presentation of these critical themes is shrouded in ambiguities which may reflect directors' intentions, but which, as Leitch points out, have often been interpreted as "anti-intentionalist," since the various critical approaches to gangster films have sought "the meaning of popular genres not in the avowed purposes of their creators, but in something broader and deeper—universalistic myths, patriarchal hegemony, industry-wide production styles, material and cultural forces beyond the creators' control and sometimes their understanding."[37]

Nowhere is this more apparent than in interpretations of gangster movies' stance towards the structures of 20th-century U.S. capitalism—these variations supported by the films' inherent ambiguities. The uncertainties surrounding the underlying critique within *The Godfather* trilogy reflect the same dilemma running through many of its predecessors in the genre—and indeed much else that Hollywood has produced. It may be legitimate to criticize specific aspects of a specific example of the system at work: but explanations typically shy away from a systemic critique, focusing instead on individual hubris (as an explanation of criminal behavior instead of one based on inequality and deprivation), or individual greed and corruption. Coppola's insistence on showing the growing similarities between Michael and his legitimate associates hints at broader systemic criticism; but ultimately, in *The Godfather* movies, just as with all their predecessors, neither the gangsters nor the films pose any serious threat to the American way of life whose shortcomings they reveal.

The *Godfather* lineage: Vito, Michael, and Vincent (Andy Garcia).

Notes

1. Fran Mason, *American Gangster Cinema: From Little Caesar to Pulp Fiction* (New York: Palgrave Macmillan, 2002), xiv.

2. Thomas Leitch, *Crime Films* (Cambridge: Cambridge University Press, 2002), 13.

3. Pacino's Scarface character belongs more clearly in this category than does Paul Muni's earlier version (*Scarface*, Hawks, 1932), since in the later film Montana is killed by other gangsters; Camonte is killed by the police. It is perhaps worth mentioning that there is a subset of the crime genre in which the victim becomes the avenger—particularly to be observed in the work of Hitchcock (*North by Northwest* [1959], *The Man Who Knew Too Much* [1934 and 1955]).

4. Jonathan Munby, *Public Enemies, Public Heroes* (Chicago: University of Chicago Press, 1999), 19.

5. Kenneth Allsop, *The Bootleggers* (London: Hutchinson, 1961).

6. Jack Shadoian, *Dreams and Dead Ends: The American Gangster/Crime Film* (Cambridge, MA: MIT Press, 1977); cited in *Francis Ford Coppola's* The Godfather *Trilogy*, ed. Nick Browne (Cambridge: Cambridge University Press, 2000), 14.

7. Glenn Man, "Ideology and Genre in the *Godfather* Films," in Browne, 109–10.

8. Andrew Tudor, "Genre," in *Film Genre Reader III*, ed. Barry Keith Grant (Austin: University of Texas Press, 2003).

9. Mason, xiii.

10. Edward Mitchell, "Apes and Essences: Some Sources of Significance in the American Gangster Film," in Grant, 219.

11. Leitch, 5.

12. Munby, xv.

13. This categorization characterizes the approaches of Leitch and Mason as well as Munby.

14. Leitch, 24.

15. Mason, 35.

16. E.g., James Chapman, "Film Noir and Society," in *Popular American Film, 1945–1995*, ed. James Chapman (Open University, 2000), 26–29.

17. Munby, 10.

18. Eddie Muller, *Dark City: The Lost World of Film Noir* (New York: St. Martins Griffin, 1998).

19. Leitch, 35.

20. Ibid., 41.

21. Munby, 1.

22. Leitch, 14.

23. Phil Hardy, "Crime Movies," in *The Oxford History of World Cinema*, ed. Geoffrey Nowell-Smith (Oxford: Oxford University Press, 1997), 306.

24. Munby, 225.

25. Leitch, 103.

26. Ibid., 122.

27. Nick Browne, "Fearful A-Symmetries: Violence as History in the *Godfather* films," in Browne.

28. Man, 111–13.

29. Peter Cowie, *Coppola* (London: Faber & Faber, 1995), 63.

30. Vera Dika, "The Representation of Ethnicity in *The Godfather*," in Browne, 76.

31. Dika, 77.

32. Alessandro Camon, "*The Godfather* and the Myth of the Mafia," in Browne, 59.

33. Dika, 100.

34. Browne, 19.

35. Camon, 70.

36. Man, 129.

37. Leitch, 53.

"Say hello to my little friend."

De Palma's Postmodern *Scarface* and the Simulacrum of Class

Ronald Bogue

From its initial articulation as an architectural style, postmodernism has been extended to describe a number of aesthetic, social, and intellectual movements and tendencies of the last three decades.[1] Among the most notable theorists of the concept are Jean-François Lyotard, Jean Baudrillard, and Fredric Jameson, who have formulated general accounts of postmodernity that encompass several dimensions of contemporary social life.[2] Each provides a perspective on postmodernism that is representative of one of three basic approaches dominant in the field of discussion—Lyotard, a philosophical approach, in which postmodernism is opposed to the modernist project of the Enlightenment; Baudrillard, a cultural approach, in which postmodernism is said to characterize certain features of *la société de consommation* or late capitalist society; and Jameson, an aesthetic approach, in which postmodernism is opposed to the high modernism of the decades between the two world wars. It is within the context of these three approaches to postmodernism that Brian De Palma's 1983 film *Scarface* may be viewed as a postmodern film about postmodern culture, and in particular as a commentary on class that can be understood from a postmodern theoretical perspective.

Postmodern philosophy has been described in various ways, but perhaps its most widely discussed characterization has been that of Lyotard, who argues in *La condition postmoderne* that the decisive aspect of postmodern thought is its "incredulity toward metanarratives."[3] As Lyotard specifies elsewhere,

> The "metanarratives" I was concerned with in *The Postmodern Condition* are those that have marked modernity: the progressive emancipation of reason and freedom, the progressive or catastrophic emancipation of labor (source of alienated value in capitalism), the enrichment of all humanity through the progress of capitalist technoscience.[4]

In the absence of such metanarratives, postmodern thought abandons the search for a universal ground of knowledge and accepts the existence of plural, incommensurable local language games whose legitimization can never be securely anchored in truths that lie outside a given discursive field. Decisive especially for Lyotard is his incredulity toward the metanarrative of

Marxism, to which he had subscribed in his early work, but which he eventually had come to see as merely one discursive mode among others. What is of particular note for us is that Lyotard's disenchantment with the Marxian metanarrative brought with it a loss of belief in the centrality of class and class struggle as formative forces of thought.

Although Lyotard has written extensively about various aspects of postmodernism, his approach to postmodernity remains primarily philosophical and centered on questions of epistemology. Jean Baudrillard, by contrast, is a theorist of postmodernity whose views on aesthetics, philosophy, and politics are basically functions of his social theory and his interpretation of history. According to Baudrillard, we live in an age of universal simulation and simulacra, of hypersigns and the hyperreal. The traditional logic of model and copy has been thoroughly undermined in our age of global mediation, primarily (but not exclusively) through advertising, the mass media, and the ubiquity of aestheticized commodities. Signs now refer only to other signs, images to other images, and the real as ultimate referent has disappeared. Like Lyotard, Baudrillard sees postmodernism as a challenge to Marxian analysis, not because it questions the epistemological status of metanarratives, but because it provides a context in which the privilege of such concepts as production, use value, class struggle, etc., can no longer be maintained. Class differences do not explain social relations in such a world, but emerge from the circulation of signs as mere secondary products of semiotic exchange.

Fredric Jameson, like Baudrillard, sees simulation and the play of simulacra as central features of postmodernism, but he adds to the postmodern profile a number of features that Baudrillard does not touch on, features that Jameson delineates in the aesthetic productions of diverse practitioners of the arts. Jameson's aim is to delineate a "cultural dominant" that emerges in late multinational capitalism, and hence to offer a comprehensive explanation of the logic governing all dimensions of contemporary life, but his conception of postmodernism is essentially grounded in an aesthetic conception of the term. In postmodern art Jameson finds a fascination with simulacra and mass-produced images; a depthlessness that eschews interpretation and emotional expression; a predilection for pastiche; and a "derealization" of history that privileges space over time and treats historical references as mere citations of present clichés about the past. Postmodern art, in Jameson's final analysis, is an expression of a schizophrenic consciousness, i.e., the consciousness of a decentered self disoriented in time, traversed by disorganized corporeal affects, seized by the intensity of immediate sensations and surface appearances, and filled with an overwhelming sense of the unreality and disconnectedness of the world. In his analysis of postmodernism, Jameson does not dwell on its relationship to class formation or class analysis, but his Marxian stance commits him to a view of class struggle and exploitation as the ultimate determinants of social relations in postmodernism. In his essay "Periodizing the 60s," Jameson recognizes the emergence in the postmodern era of several "new 'subjects of history' of a nonclass type,"[5] such as women, blacks, gays, students, and Third World peoples, yet these decentered, non-class forms of resistance he views as simply temporarily disguised instances of ongoing class struggle that will eventually reveal their true nature as relations of exploitation inevitably intensify.

At this juncture, we may draw the following basic conclusions. Lyotard's philosophical postmodernism is essentially epistemological in orientation, committed to no particular stance on the question of class in postmodernity, but incredulous of the Marxist metanarrative of exploitation and class struggle. Baudrillard's sociocultural postmodernism focuses on simulation and treats class distinctions as simulacral images with no more claim to our attention than other surface ephemera of the hyperreal. Jameson's aesthetic postmodernism includes Baudrillard's simulacra within it, but only as one aspect of the schizophrenic world that emerges in late multinational capitalism. Jameson seems tacitly to second Baudrillard's observations on the disappearance of clearly delineated class allegiances in postmodernism, but Jameson's un-postmodern Marxism allows him to subsume this tendency within a broader metanarrative of the inevitable struggle of the exploited to overcome relations of domination.

Although these three approaches to postmodernism are interrelated, they cannot be assimilated within a single model, a point that needs to be emphasized particularly when considering Jameson's account of the relationship between postmodern culture and postmodern art. Jameson's point of departure is a broad-ranging catalogue of postmodern aesthetic features, which he then reads as mediated symptoms of the postmodern social world, which in turn he relates to a particular stage in the development of capitalism. Yet as

"A predilection for pastiche."

Jameson realizes, there are two broad tendencies within postmodern art, one that celebrates the play of simulacra and the loss of the real (a Baudrillardian strain), and another that uses simulation and fragmentation as means of questioning social codes and cultural norms. This second type of postmodern art, which Hal Foster has labeled an "oppositional postmodernism,"[6] strives for a certain critical distance from the postmodern social world, even though it is committed to the subversion of distinctions between high and low culture and the abandonment of any appeal to a metanarrative as the ground of its critique. Jameson, I believe, pays insufficient attention to this distinction, and as a result, in his composite portrait of postmodernism he combines traits from divergent tendencies in postmodern art that are not compatible. Specifically, what Jameson labels the schizophrenic fragmentation of postmodern art and culture should be seen as typical primarily of "oppositional postmodernism," and it should be differentiated from Baudrillardian simulacral postmodernism on the basis of its ironic, critical stance toward the simulacra with which it plays.

To demonstrate in a cursory fashion the critical potential of oppositional postmodern works of art, I would like to look briefly at Brian De Palma's *Scarface* as a postmodern artistic critique of postmodern culture. I must preface this discussion, however, with a brief excursion into the theoretical domain outlined by Gilles Deleuze and Félix Guattari in their *Anti-Oedipus*, in part because their characterization of capitalism will help us to understand what De Palma is doing in *Scarface*, but also because their remarks about class in capitalism provide a means of bringing to bear on De Palma's film the Baudrillardian notion of class as simulacrum.

In *Anti-Oedipus*, Deleuze and Guattari posit the existence of a ubiquitous "desiring-production," a fusion of action and libidinal affect that permeates the social world. Traditional societies of various sorts try to regulate and control circuits and networks of desiring-production by imposing restrictive codes on them—kinship systems, religious rituals, castes, classes, clans, guilds, legal systems, tacit behavioral codes, etc. With the advent of capitalism, however, an anarchic process of decoding is set loose that threatens all restrictive codings of desiring-production. In the universal equivalence of capitalist exchange, everything is a commodity that may be exchanged for anything else. Yet capitalism depends for its functioning on a minimal stability that can only be maintained through a frantic recoding of the world, one that proceeds via ad hoc institutions and the *bricolage* of scraps and pieces of the decimated codes of previous traditional societies. Hence, two tendencies are always present in capitalism, a schizophrenic tendency toward dissolution, universal circulation, and the decoding of codes, and a paranoiac tendency toward the imposition of ever new recodings of previous codes. In its function as a force of decoding, capitalism is "the *negative* of all social formations," just as the bourgeoisie, in a parallel fashion, is the negative of all traditional castes and social groups: "Classes are *the* negative of castes and statuses; classes are orders, castes, and statuses that have been decoded. To reread history through the class struggle is to read it in terms of the bourgeoisie as the decoding and decoded class. It is the *only* class as such, inasmuch as it leads the struggle against codes, and merges with the generalized decoding of flows."[7]

In De Palma's *Scarface*, we have a postmodern film about postmodern culture, a study of desiring-production in the realm of simulacra, which consists of a constant and insatiable circulation of money, drugs, images, desire, and power. Several aspects of the film attest to its postmodern sensibility, chief of which is its frequent use of pastiche. Throughout his career, De Palma has incorporated cinematic citations in his work, so much so that he has often been accused of being a derivative director, who, for example, rips off Hitchcock in *Sisters*, *The Fury*, *Obsession*, and *Dressed to Kill* and Antonioni in *Blow Out*. Yet De Palma always quotes his sources with an ironic self-awareness and a humorous, unapologetic élan that makes audiences constantly ask whether the images they see are to be taken seriously, discounted as mere citations, or read as commentaries on the clichéd images of what we take to be the real. In *Scarface*, cinematic allusions abound—one can find clear references to Hitchcock, Antonioni, Minnelli, and Visconti, among others—but what sets this film apart from De Palma's earlier work is that it is his first remake of another film (Hawks' 1932 *Scarface: The Shame of a Nation*). Remakes, of course, are common in Hollywood, and not necessarily citational, but De Palma knowingly nods toward the original *Scarface* throughout the film, always forcing the audience to question at what level the action is taking place and whose images are being presented, De Palma's or Hawks' or

Tony sits morosely on the throne of his criminal empire.

Coppola's or those of any other gangster film director, for *Scarface* is as much a commentary on the cliché-ridden genre it participates in as a response to the Hawks original.

The look of the film is aggressively pop, a dizzying whirl of pastels and schlock that is at once compelling in its energy and inventiveness and repelling in its insistent bad taste. De Palma's visual consultant Ferdinando Scarfiotti turns Miami into a tropical Las Vegas which, as one reviewer puts it, is bathed in a "kitsch-glitz riot of evocative colors" and finds its fullest architectural embodiment in the Babylon Club, "a gaudy Erechtheum stocked with black Naugahyde banquettes, pink and blue ribbons of neon, black-marble toilet stalls, and mirrors, mirrors everywhere."[8]

This playfully critical fascination with pop culture contributes to a general "derealization" of the world, the invention of a universe whose surface sheen admits of no clear distinction between reality and artifice. Even the landscape is affected by this process of derealization. Early in the film, immediately after the hero, Tony Montana, has been released from the refugee detention camp, the camera focuses on a billboard of a Miami sunset, which seems real until the camera pulls back to reveal the frame of the billboard. As the camera descends, a Cuban restaurant sign decorated with palm trees comes into view, and finally the camera settles on the grimy eatery where Tony is washing dishes. It would seem that here we are being shown the difference between the dream and the reality of Miami, the promise of freedom and its grim fulfillment, but only a few minutes later, following Tony's successful but bloody confrontation with Colombian drug dealers, we see him silhouetted against a real sunset that De Palma's camera renders every bit as unreal as the early billboard sky. The sunset mural of Frank Lopez's office and the various skyline scenes painted on Tony's Hawaiian shirts are finally indistinguishable from the real Miami and the billboard Miami, all part of a single simulacral city.

History, too, is derealized in the film, particularly in the initial video sequences interspersed between the opening credits. The footage of the Marielitos arriving in Miami apparently establishes the historical context for the action, but the exaggerated contrast, distorted colors, and unconventional cutting turn this video reportage into a sign of video technology. The clips of Castro saying "They cannot adapt to the spirit of our revolution, . . . We don't want them," merely provide us with a pop icon whose remarks give added punch to Tony's initial statements of his anti-Communist sentiments and his desire to preserve his "human rights." The documentary footage does not ground the film in an historical situation, but simply resonates with the other video images that mediate reality at various points in the film: the police footage of Tony's bust, the multiple, paranoiac surveillance monitors in Tony's mansion, the five-screen television in Tony's bathroom, the large-screen monitor in Sosa's living room.

Scarface, however, is more than a mere play of appearances, for it is also a commentary on contemporary American capitalism. Most of the classic gangster films, including Hawks' *Scarface*, in one way or another draw parallels between organized crime and legitimate business (perhaps none more so than Coppola's *Godfather* films), but what sets De Palma's film apart from earlier gangster movies is the addition of cocaine to the equation of power, greed, violence, and capital. In the original *Scarface*, alcohol is simply the means whereby Tony Camonte gains his fortune, but in De Palma's remake cocaine is as much the subject of the film as is crime. It is no accident that Tony Montana breaks Frank Lopez's rule of "never getting high on your own supply," for in *Scarface* cocaine is capital and capital is cocaine.

Critics have complained that we never see Tony working for his fortune, maneuvering and scheming to gain his wealth, but the whole point is that there is no anchor to this inflationary economy, no equivalence between labor and profit. The transformation of cocaine into money is miraculous and instantaneous. In a montage sequence of less than three minutes, De Palma traces Tony's rise to the top: as a voice sings "Take it to the limit" (and of course, the point is that there *is* no limit), we see a bill-counting machine whirring through a stack of twenties, duffel bags of cash arriving at the bank, Tony and Sosa laughing as they talk on the phone, Tony in front of his new Montana Properties building, his sister Gina at the opening of the new beauty salon Tony has bought her, another shot of the money machine, more duffel bags of money at the bank, and the marriage of Tony and Elvira at their new mansion. As this and other sequences reveal, cocaine is the ultimate capitalist fantasy, a pure money machine that spews out cash faster than human hands and eyes can count.

But capital is also like cocaine, an amalgam of power, consumption, pleasure, and insatiable desire. Unlike other major substances of abuse, cocaine in its early stages of use is not experienced as a distraction from work, but as an enhancer of cognitive functioning. One therapist has observed that with most drug addictions, work is the first thing addicts give up, but with cocaine, work is the last thing they surrender before giving up their drug.[9] Users report that "vision seems sharper; sounds are clearer; odors are more distinctive and colors seem warmer, richer, and more intense"; they feel "more competent, optimistic, and self-assured"; they believe the drug "enhances social relationships" and "increases sexual desire, prolongs intercourse, and produces more intense and satisfying orgasms."[10] Yet, according to Spotts and Shontz, "despite its reputation as the caviar of drugs, our findings indicate that cocaine is the *most unsatisfying drug* of all the major substances of abuse. It induces ecstatic experiences, but it does not and can never produce satisfaction, completion, or fulfillment. . . . [I]ts only residual is the desire for more."[11] In prolonged use, cocaine ceases to enhance sexual pleasure, becoming itself a substitute for sexual activity, and the initial narcissistic expansion of the ego is often succeeded by intense states of paranoia.

Cocaine, then, is a distillation of eros, power, and insatiable desire, an addictive and all-consuming substance that induces narcissistic ego expansion and ultimately delusional paranoia. Cocaine, in short, is like capital, a point that is reinforced throughout *Scarface* as Tony's cocaine addiction becomes inseparable from his limitless desire for "the world and everything in it" (as he puts it). Money itself is explicitly linked to desire and power when Tony explains to his friend Manolo that "first you got to get the money; when you get money, you get the power; then when you get the power, you get the women." But at every point in the film the fusion of eros, violence, power, and money is reinforced through the ubiquitous expletive "fuck." (One reviewer reports that the word is used at least 181 times in the film.) "Fuck" is frequently used in a sexual sense in the film (Tony thinks that Elvira needs to be fucked, she responds that he'd be the last guy she'd fuck, etc.), but it is also used to refer to economic relations (Tony remarks that the banks have been fucking Miami for seventy-two years) and to power relations ("Don't fuck with me," Tony says at several points; "Never fuck me, Tony," Sosa warns his associate). All senses of the word come together when Tony remarks that "this town is like a great big pussy just waiting to be fucked," and it is clear that his desire to fuck Miami eventually becomes one with his cocaine business and habit.

In this world of limitless desire, in which, as Elvira says, "nothing exceeds like excess," concerns about class and status are frequently expressed, but it is evident that social class has no real functional importance. One can find a representative of the South American aristocracy in the European-educated cocaine baron Sosa, a typical bourgeois in the car dealer and mid-level pusher Frank Lopez, and in Tony a "peasant" (as Omar calls him) who "comes from the gutter" (as Tony himself says). Yet ultimately there is little that distinguishes the three from each other, all wearing similar clothes, displaying various forms of bad taste, and sharing the same naked desire for power and wealth. In many gangster films, the working-class origins and economic motivations of the criminal are explicitly thematized, and in some cases celebrated. In the *Godfather* films, for example, Don Corleone's Sicilian peasant roots, his struggle as a lower-class immigrant to support his family with dignity, and his solidarity with his extended crime family are central to the story that Coppola tells. In *Scarface*, by contrast, one never gets the impression that the Cuban drug dealers belong to a community, or that they have roots in a social class. Even in Hawks' *Scarface*, which tends to emphasize the autonomy and isolation of the criminal, one senses, in the scenes with Tony Camonte's mother, in the Ward One Social Club and in the Italian restaurants, that Camonte belongs to an ethnic working-class world that has shaped him and that guides his actions. The only sign of such a traditional social world in De Palma's film is Tony Montana's mother, but she seems a mere *citation*, an allusion to the original *Scarface* and a clichéd Latin mother whose isolated bungalow stands against the unreal Miami skyline like a displaced fragment of some lost and archaic world. Talk of class distinctions abounds in De Palma's *Scarface*, but essentially such talk focuses on commodity distinctions—$800 suits, $43,000 cars, $400 bottles of champagne. Class differences are constantly produced and distributed in this world, but only as signs of an inflationary exchange and as simulations of a traditional class society that has long disappeared.

In essence, what De Palma presents in *Scarface* is a world of universal Baudrillardian simulation and Deleuzoguattarian capitalist desiring-

"The marriage of Tony and Elvira at their new mansion."

production. Everywhere capital, desire, and power form free-floating circuits that dissolve social codes and retranscribe them in simulations of traditional codes, observing no law but that of limitless excess. The world of *Scarface* is a postmodern world, whose features mirror those of cocaine consciousness, a hyperreal of sensual and libidinal intensities imbued with the surface gloss of ecstatic perception and the simulacral unreality of drug-induced experience. The "look" of the film is finally the look of cocaine experience, which, however, is also the look of late capitalist, simulacral postmodernity. Yet De Palma's film is not simply a symptomatic reflection of postmodernity. It adopts a critical stance toward postmodern culture, but without stepping outside it or presuming the existence of a metanarrative, Marxian or otherwise, that explains it in any definitive way. De Palma's strategy is to play with the simulacra of postmodernity, to question them but without proposing a programmatic alternative.

De Palma, in sum, is an oppositional postmodern artist commenting on Baudrillardian postmodern culture from a theoretical position that is, like Lyotard's and Deleuze-Guattari's, decidedly postmodern. It would be inaccurate to assert that De Palma's film points toward a possible synthesis of the views of Lyotard, Baudrillard, Jameson, and Deleuze-Guattari on postmodernism and capitalism, but it does indicate that areas of common concern and intersecting interests inform all these discussions of contemporary culture. The philosophical, sociocultural, and aesthetic approaches to postmodernism must be carefully distinguished from one another, as must their privileged

Tony Montana (Al Pacino) and Elvira (Michelle Pfeiffer).

objects of analysis, yet they must not be isolated from one another, but set in differential resonance. Perhaps that is the great service of art works such as *Scarface*, which finally may tell us as much about postmodernity as any theoretical commentary.

Notes

1. For an intelligent discussion of postmodernism and the history of the term, see Matei Calinescu, *Five Faces of Modernity: Modernism, Avant-Garde, Decadence, Kitsch, Postmodernism* (Durham, NC: Duke University Press, 1987), 265–312.

2. For Lyotard's conception of postmodernism, see *The Postmodern Condition*, trans. Geoff Bennington and Brian Massumi (Minneapolis: University of Minnesota Press, 1984), and *The Postmodern Explained*, trans. Don Barry et al. (Minneapolis: University of Minnesota Press, 1992); for Jameson's seminal articulation of postmodernism, see "Postmodernism, or the Cultural Logic of Late Capitalism," *New Left Review* 146 (1984): 53–92; for Baudrillard's positions on postmodernism, see esp. *Simulacra and Simulation*, trans. Sheila Faria Glaser (Ann Arbor: University of Michigan Press, 1995).

3. Lyotard, *Postmodern Condition*, xxiv.

4. Lyotard, *Postmodern Explained*, 17.

5. Fredric Jameson, "Periodizing the 60s," in *The Ideologies of Theory: Essays, 1971–1986*, vol. 2, *The Syntax of History* (Minneapolis: University of Minnesota Press, 1988), 181.

6. Hal Foster, ed., *The Anti-Aesthetic* (Port Townsend, WA: Bay Press, 1983), xi.

7. *Anti-Oedipus*, trans. Robert Hurley, Mark Seem, and Helen R. Lane (Minneapolis: University of Minnesota Press, 1983), 153, 254.

8. Richard Corliss, "Say Good Night to the Bad Guy," *Time*, December 5, 1983, 96.

9. Calvin Chatlos, *Crack: What You Should Know about the Cocaine Epidemic* (New York: Putnam, 1987), 71.

10. James V. Spotts and Franklin C. Shontz, "Drug-Induced Ego States. I. Cocaine: Phenomenology and Implications," *International Journal of the Addictions* 19, no. 2 (1984): 129–30.

11. Ibid., 143.

Playing the hit man's "profession for laughs": Irene Walker (Kathleen Turner) and Charley Partanna (Jack Nicholson) drag a body in *Prizzi's Honor*.

Yoked Together by Violence:
Prizzi's Honor as a Generic Hybrid

Tricia Welsch

John Huston's 1985 gangster film *Prizzi's Honor* annexes two competing generic traditions to consider what acceptable role a woman might play in the world of crime. The film presents itself as a screwball comedy detailing the antic courtship and exuberant marriage of a (male) New York mobster and a (female) professional assassin, playing their compatibility for laughs before discrediting the wife's talents, questioning her wifely—and especially maternal—qualifications, and finally bumping her off. The anxiety about female authority in the work place is managed here by the film's recourse to strategies familiar from film noir: a second powerful woman manipulates and (fatally) controls events from behind the scenes, setting up the career woman in much the same way as the male noir protagonist is generically positioned. This second woman, however, reasserts traditional values which the first has challenged; her machinations are ultimately more successful and less threatening than those used by the professional hit woman who becomes—briefly—the Mafia wife. The regenerative possibilities of marriage, which screwball comedy affirms, film noir rejects, and the gangster film conventionally ignores, frame this story. The husband's initial quandary about his intended—"Do I ice her? Do I marry her? Which one of these?"—is resolved by his crime family's inability to absorb the new, threatening talent: first he marries her, *then* he "ices" her. The triumph of the second, sexually duplicitous woman, who accomplishes her ends quietly, denies the possibility of equality extended in the screwball romance by eliminating its representative, the feminist heroine. The film flirts with the screwball genre but stops short of commitment, carried away by the fatal charms of the gangster genre and film noir. This essay considers *Prizzi's Honor* as a generic hybrid, and argues that its mixed genres—the gangster film, the screwball comedy, and film noir—reflected cultural anxiety about female power in the 1980s. Further, articulating the ways in which one hybrid film manages multiple genres bears out what Stephen Neale has argued about generic specificity, that it is less a question of "particular and exclusive elements" than it is a matter of "combinations and articulations of elements, of the exclusive and particular weight given in any one genre to elements which in fact it shares with other genres"

(*Genre* 22–23). As Neale states elsewhere, "The elements and conventions of a genre are always *in* play rather than being simply *re*played"; this flexible understanding of generic change both allows for hybrids and indicates the extent to which the hybrid can reshape a genre's dominant tendencies ("Questions" 170).

Irene (played by Kathleen Turner) and Charley (Jack Nicholson's character) work in the same profession: he is a gangster, in line for leadership of the Prizzi crime family, and she is a freelance hit man. They meet at a Prizzi family wedding after Irene has been hired by the family, though Charley does not know that she is on the payroll, let alone for what kind of work. The couple's compatibility is first an advantage, then an obstacle, to their union, but the early part of the film treats it strictly as comedy. Specifically, the film plays Irene's choice of profession for laughs; her clear abilities are, variously, a source of pride and anxiety for her gangster husband. His continually befuddled expression and macho expostulations ("I didn't get married so's my wife could keep working!") are intended as humor: his traditional values are at odds with his pride in Irene's intelligence and his surprised enjoyment at having found a truly compatible mate. In keeping with the trajectory of thirties screwball comedies, when Charley proposes to Irene, he explicitly notes their equality: "Everything being equal, will you marry me?" Irene responds in kind, "Everything being equal, I'll marry you, Charley." However, Charley does not anticipate actually working alongside his wife. The task of the classic screwball comedy would be to make Charley realize what it might mean to

A *Godfather* parody: Irene and Charley meet at a mob wedding.

share life and work equally with a mate, a prospect that is a source of continued tension in this film.

Two images from the opening credits of *Prizzi's Honor* succinctly demonstrate the ways in which the values of the gangster film will pull against the film's comic impulses. The first image shows Charley as a motherless infant who is adopted by his Mafia godfather; Don Prizzi says soothingly, "He lost his mother but he's got another father. I'm his father now, with you" (and he gestures toward Charley's biological father). The absence or passivity of the criminal's mother is iconographic in the gangster genre, and this film calls attention to her loss, before immediately declaring her irrelevance. Two fathers are deemed better than a mother; this child is delivered directly from the hospital nursery into the Prizzi crime family, bypassing any maternal care. A second image in this sequence finds young Charley opening a Christmas gift of brass knuckles: even the toys in this family are deadly serious.[1]

A childhood overshadowed by Mafia business—all work and no play make Jack a dull boy—will be rewritten, albeit briefly, by Irene's playfulness. Screwball romances and marriages consistently include transgressive images of courtship as play and renewer of innocence, concepts that are anathema to a gangster family consumed by the serious business of crime. Repeatedly in thirties comedies we see work (temporarily) displaced by play, the result an enriched sense of what each has to offer. (*Bringing Up Baby* is the most perfect example of this paradigm.) Stanley Cavell has observed, "Almost without exception [screwball comedies] allow the principal pair to express the wish to be children again, or perhaps to be children together" (60). *Prizzi's Honor* offers an exemplary case of a marriage which serves this function: in addition to the general kookiness of the couple's courtship, in one telephone conversation Irene transforms Charley's baffled theorizing about how love fills unsatisfied needs from childhood by enticing him instead to play doctor with her. She offhandedly tells Charley that she doesn't even remember her mother as he puzzles out a magazine story he has read about love: "That's the amazing part," he responds. "There's something in you that knows anyways—the magazine said so. That's what love is: when you find someone who will give you what you think you wanted when you were a baby—but you didn't get it." As a direct response to his wistful reflections about childhood loss, she suggests a game (doctor), one that may be played by either children or adults, and one that deemphasizes sexual demands as it celebrates mutual discovery. The colorful, exuberant spirit of play which Irene introduces into Charley's life threatens to disrupt the family business, however, even as it offers to restore her partner's youth. The healing reconciliation of work and play, romance and partnership characteristic of the screwball comedy and available in such tender scenes cannot be sustained. *Prizzi's Honor* holds that the gangster's world cannot, finally, be a comic realm where trust is possible and in which successful enterprise is regenerative. Further, the film's pervasive distrust of partnership is, in the end, antithetical to the project of the screwball comedy. By setting these two generic traditions side by side, and noting how and when one dominates or displaces the other—and in what larger historical context

Irene and Charley's relationship anticipates 2005's *Mr. and Mrs. Smith* by two decades.

this occurs—we recognize genres as dynamic processes rather than stable taxonomies to be catalogued.

In addition to its fears about women in the work place, the film also registers anxiety about the prospects for marriage and maternity, even as it affirms a commitment to a strongly patriarchal Mafia family. Mothers are absent, forgotten by their offspring; fathers and godfathers abound. Just as the wedding which begins *Prizzi's Honor* sets the stage for brutality and murder, a crucial scheme in the film in which the Mafia wife pretends to be a mother goes desperately awry. Two scenes, one the planning of a kidnapping over dinner and the other its execution, feature the use of a baby as an aid to crime and propose mothering as itself problematic, deceptive. Charley and his father are laboriously blocking out a ruse to get an intended victim away from his bodyguard when Irene emerges from the kitchen, gorgeously attired and coiffed, and suggests that they need a woman on the job. She proposes to throw a baby at the bodyguard, who will catch it and be distracted from his duties long enough for Charley to nab his prey. Charley is skeptical; eyeing her askance, he asks, "For Christ's sake, where we gonna get a baby? Where we gonna find a broad would do something like this?" She answers delightedly, "Here! Me! We get a fake baby. You guys work it out—I got a terrific dinner almost ready." She heads back to the kitchen, the model of the 1980s superwoman who can finesse a tricky work assignment—one that puzzles her husband—with a flash of (female) intuition while juggling pots and pans, and without mussing her hair. His father regards Irene with pleased admiration, calling her scheme "a masterpiece," while Charley gripes that he will be the laughingstock of every Mafia family in New York if anyone learns he's used his wife on the job.

Charley alone expresses outrage at the (mis)use of a baby, as if to call attention to—or even compensate for—Irene's lack of "womanly" feeling; he specifically shows bewilderment at the "kind of broad" who would take part in a plan like the one Irene proposes. Further, the introduction of a baby into the "family" throws everything off-kilter. When the couple attempts the ruse, it fails miserably: the bodyguard does not catch the doll, and two people end up dead, one of them the police commissioner's wife, which will cause untold trouble for the Prizzi family. Irene's error stuns her: her female intuition, which seemed to afford new opportunities for creativity in crime, is rebuked by the disaster. The plastic baby in *Prizzi's Honor*, for whom no one accepts responsibility and who helps precipitate a catastrophe, has first a comic and then an ironic function in the narrative: we are meant to laugh at the introduction of the completely anomalous (an infant) into a traditional crime plot (a kidnapping), itself a stratagem conceived by a humorously deviant entity (a woman gangster). That the baby is artificial, a mechanism replacing a living body, is appropriate: the film sees its "mother" as unnatural, too. As Andrew Sarris has noted, children, and particularly babies, are not at issue in the screwball comedy, and for all the recurrent preoccupation with familial structures in the recent gangster film, the same is true of this genre, too.[2] But while for Stanley Cavell, the absence of children from the screwball comedy "purifies the discussion of marriage," the baby in *Prizzi's Honor* is introduced in order to rebuke a woman's failure to be maternal (58).

At the same time, the elaboration of a gag built around a false body chastises Irene: if such gags both "interrupt" and "reconstitute" subject identity, as Neale asserts, representing the body as first "fragmented/distorted/unco-ordinated/unbalanced" before restoring equilibrium as "bodily integrity/unity/co-ordination and balance" (*Genre* 61), then the tone of outrage or disbelief that Charley strikes when protesting the inclusion of the false baby posits him as balanced from the outset and identifies Irene with disequilibrium. Further, the inscription of suspense, established through the planning and execution of the kidnapping scheme, is a conventional way the gangster film manages time, while the disruption of equilibrium which characterizes screwball comedy is not contingent on a plan being fulfilled or aborted, and time tends to be elastic rather than strictly linear.[3] Increasingly in this film, as the consequences of the abortive kidnapping become manifest, the crime drama will dominate, challenging or displacing the expectations created by the presence of the contending generic system (comedy).

The "fake baby" which Irene conceives also stands as a metaphor for the final sterility of her marriage to Charley. Where the screwball comedy often located the couple's rejuvenation in shared work, with the woman having a clear stake in this labor, in the gangster/comedy hybrid Irene's skill makes her untrustworthy in direct proportion to the independence it promotes. The regenerative possibilities suggested by a woman's inclusion in this work place are stillborn because of Charley's fear that Irene is not on the level.[4] Here, her

Don Prizzi (William Hickey) does not immediately realize that
Irene is "a woman intent on equal opportunity employment."

status as a motherless child again provides a crux: she is not reined in by the authority of the family as Charley is. Irene appears out of the blue, has no living relations, possesses no obviously ethnic identity. She is radically unaffiliated, no one's child. Cavell argues that one consequence of the missing mothers in thirties comedies is the relative freedom of daughters; he further conflates the fate of the motherless female child with the potential for independence and equality associated with the New World, where what he calls a "new woman" is possible (57). But where the screwball comedy celebrates ad hoc communities and cross-class associations (think of the bus full of singing travelers in *It Happened One Night*, for instance), the gangster film consistently explores the tenacious hold of extended ethnic communities in the U.S. As a comedy, *Prizzi's Honor* presents Irene's lack of a mother and a motherland as an opportunity rather than an obstacle. As a gangster film, it construes her freedom as a troubling rootlessness that will be answered by the ever-more stifling control of the patriarchal family. An outsider to the Prizzis because she is not Sicilian, Irene is even more alienated because she is a woman intent on equal opportunity employment. Although early in the film Irene is called "outside talent," part of the project of *Prizzi's Honor* is ultimately to denigrate her talent in order to keep her outside.

To resolve the generic impasse—that is, the tension between its gangster and comic strategies—the film has recourse to another set of conventions, those of film noir. The film's sunny, playful first half gives way to a much darker resolution, in which a woman more dangerous than Irene works behind the scenes, adroitly manipulating both men and women for her own murderous ends, and doing so the more successfully for her willingness to appear powerless. *Prizzi's Honor* reflects an eighties audience's anxiety about either accepting or killing off its visibly powerful female figure (Irene) by reassigning her power to a more traditional female character. Irene is effectively replaced by Maerose Prizzi (played by Anjelica Huston), another woman who knows the crime business intimately but who does not sue overtly for power within the clan. An antidote to Irene, she represents not freedom but rooted-ness and traditional behaviors.

Maerose has some of the same functions as a noir femme fatale: for instance, she uses sexual manipulation as part of a long-term, murderous strategy that will leave her both blameless and more powerful. The odd twist here, though, is that she is driven by competition with another woman, Irene, although she carefully keeps her jealousy hidden. Unlike the traditional femme fatale, an outsider whose seductive charm renders her dangerous, Maerose gains power because she knows—better than anyone else—how to operate within the confines of the family. In fact, Maerose is the consummate insider, the Mafia princess, and she cleverly manipulates her family members until Irene is forced out. By fashioning Maerose as the smartest, most devious of all the Prizzis, the one most clearly capable of running the family business, the film registers another level to its ambivalence about female power. While the juxtaposition of gangster and screwball comedy formulas sees the female mobster by turns as a humorous anomaly and as a dangerous challenge to accepted social standards, film noir conventions consistently indicate that powerful women are not to be trusted, are always deadly. At the same time, however, since these female characters are seldom involved in explicit bids for control but tend to make their moves behind the scenes, they do not insist on visible change in the status quo and are thus, in some palpable way, less threatening even when they are more deadly. Maerose's actions help reinstate the male gangsters' authority; she herself can never claim leadership in the Prizzi family. The adoption of the noir strategy repudiates the promise of equality held out in the screwball romance by destroying the feminist hero-ine. It demonstrates an awed fascination with female power even as it works to contain the manifestations of such power.

Maerose (Anjelica Huston) is Charley's mob fiancée.

Prizzi's Honor in fact positions its ostensible heroine, Irene, in much the same way as film noir sets up its beleaguered male protagonist—as the unwitting (if not exactly innocent) victim of a woman who has figured out all the angles. The noir audience is led to identify with the male protagonist and to despise the femme fatale who has victimized him; similarly, Irene is an inventive, ambitious, likable character who never knows what hit her. The film presents the brooding, malevolent Maerose as shrewder and more deadly than even a professional assassin, thus placing the responsibility for reinstating patriarchal authority and traditional roles within marriage squarely on her (female) intervention.[5] In the beginning, the film presents the struggle to create a marriage between equals as a comic enterprise, with the husband's recalcitrance a source of humor; in its second half, it struggles to reassert the status quo—the authority of the Prizzi family—and achieves this end through the agency of a woman who has herself been contained by its authority.[6]

Prizzi's Honor fears that women are dangerous, that they render men powerless and that men don't even know it. The gangster's world is murderous to begin with but—as this film shows—the inclusion of women, whether as competitors or as partners, makes it twice as hazardous. *Prizzi's Honor* has it both ways: although the feminist woman is killed, ostensibly ending the threat she has posed to the traditional family, we identify with her as a victim and dislike the anti-feminist woman who has destroyed her—even as we also admire that woman's cunning.[7] Women are thus held responsible for both the disruption of the status quo (as caused by Irene's ambition) and its reinstatement (Maerose's Machiavellian tactics in service of the family). Throughout *Prizzi's Honor*, women cause all the upheaval, whether with comic or deadly results.

Where the gangster film persistently relegates romantic unions to the sidelines in favor of business concerns and the needs of an extended patriarchal family, and the screwball comedy tries to work out a balance between love and work, partnership and ownership in marriage, *Prizzi's Honor* has a more equivocal job: to show the value of a marriage between equals and then to disavow it.[8] In so doing the film reflects the eighties audience's discomfort with self-declared feminists and the strain of accommodating a newly powerful female work force. In order to displace the likable Irene, however, and make the final pairing of Charley with Maerose satisfying, the film must negotiate a tricky compromise between competing generic strategies. *Prizzi's Honor* finally acknowledges the claim of the family which the gangster film alleges over the freedom of association characteristic of the screwball comedy. This comes about oddly, through another twist of the generic screw. Even as the tale turns darkest, as Charley prepares to kill his killer wife, the film reinvokes the screwball comedy in its guise as the comedy of remarriage. A persistent motif in thirties comedy is the repairing of a marriage when one or both partners have already found replacements for their spouses. In *The Philadelphia Story* a young socialite must remarry her former husband, which entails leaving a new fiancé at the altar; in *My Favorite Wife* a woman is rescued after long years shipwrecked at sea and promptly sets about getting rid of her husband's brand-new wife. The pattern recurs in *The Awful Truth*, *His Girl Friday*, *The Palm Beach Story*, and many others. *Prizzi's Honor* also adopts the screwball comedy's practice of re-partnering an estranged couple, only here it is the comically compatible partner (Irene) who must make way for the reinstatement of the anti-feminist woman (Maerose), which in turn illustrates the more compelling family claim on Charley. The attachment between Charley and Maerose is practically incestuous: romantic partners years earlier, they were raised together, as closely as brother and sister. Maerose even claims at one point that she and Charley are "the same person," which goes beyond the screwball couple's desire to play at being children together. His return to her

A protoype of "the screwball couple's desire to play at being children together": Gerry (Claudette Colbert) and Tom Jeffers (Joel McCrea) in *The Palm Beach Story*.

represents his willingness to stay within the confines of his ethnic heritage and his extended family; it is a move toward the safety of enclosure.

Stanley Cavell touches on the Prizzi family's dilemma when he observes of thirties comedies that "marriage is always divorce, always entails rupture . . . is always a transgression" (103). When pushed to decide between his outsider wife, Irene, and his loyalty to the Prizzis, Charley confesses, "I know that I can never live outside the family."[9] The vow of loyalty he takes to the family on coming of age is more binding than his marriage vow to Irene, the male ritual coming before and superseding the heterosexual one. The either/or of Charley's early dilemma—"Do I ice her? Do I marry her?"—is resolved by the crime plot's inability to absorb the new talent: when Irene comes between Charley and his family, she has to go.[10] Having established Irene's competence, however, the film must go to some lengths to discredit her: her enterprising theft from the Prizzis gets construed as greed, her creative intuition in planning a crime backfires, and her husband is finally faster at the draw than she is. But the film, in comic fashion, gives us another marriage to take the place of the first one: Irene's "retirement" leaves Charley free for remarriage to Maerose, in a union that cements their childhood ties even as it guarantees a Prizzi dynasty.

A wedding opens this film, and in its closing moments we learn that the newly married couple has just returned from their honeymoon. "Where'd they go—Mars?" Charley asks incredulously, himself having met, courted,

Charley in work mode.

married, and murdered his wife during the other couple's vacation. *Prizzi's Honor* betrays a mystified fascination with the source and limits of female power and a striking ambivalence about the function of contemporary marriage and motherhood, especially when confronted by female ambition in the work place. First offering an exuberant marriage between equals that rejuvenates its members, the film then elaborately dismantles that union by subduing the woman. She is made to compare unfavorably with a more traditional woman, who exercises her power by scheming behind the scenes rather than posing a direct threat to the structure of the Mafia family. The film's penultimate sequence shows Irene and Charley preparing to kill each other, acting for the last time in tandem, a final reminder of the couple's uncanny compatibility that turns into a demonstration of the husband's superior skill (he ices her).[11] A canny hybrid, *Prizzi's Honor* scrutinizes the female by yoking together—violently—a range of generic stratagems. The film can best be understood by considering it within this range of systems, and by acknowledging its appearance at a moment in American history when anxiety about gender roles was pervasive.[12] It liberally mixes gangster and screwball comedy conventions with those of film noir. While it owes its laughter to the romantic antics of the screwball genre, the film's flirtation with thirties-style comedy closes on a distinctly sour note with the reestablishment of the gangster generic dominant. The aggression and violent ambition of that world finally compel the narrative in a lethal direction, which mirrors film noir's paranoid fear that women are unknowable, uncontrollable—and in charge.

Notes

1. Charley's absorption into the male society of the family is reinforced by the next sequence, when he and Don Prizzi cut their fingers and swear a blood oath by candlelight. Don Prizzi's speech declares this ritual a metaphoric genesis: "This drop of blood symbolizes your birth into our family." Slyly mixing solemnity and wit, Huston frames their two fingers touching to look like Michelangelo's *Creation of Adam*, with Don Prizzi standing in for God in another motherless creation scenario. And at the moment Prizzi's life-giving digit begins to bleed, we hear a bass voice swell out operatically, reinforcing the religious nature of this compact.

2. Sarris in fact calls the 1930s films "comedies of courtship" which only "anticipat[e] the quarrels that characterize most real marriages" (14).

3. Neale comments, "It is the play with this anticipation, the tension in the potential or actual difference between what is planned and what occurs, which provides a major means by which suspense is engendered and articulated in the gangster film, both at the micro-narrative level (the level of scene or segment) and at the level of the structure of the narrative as a whole" (*Genre*, 28).

4. Of course, her putative dishonesty is normal behavior for a criminal, an irony lost on her suspicious spouse. She pops up unexpectedly and disappears mysteriously throughout, and the film's repeated recourse to a shot of a jetliner traveling either east or west as Charley tries to keep up with Irene's movements

reminds us of her freedom, which to the Prizzis connotes instead her furtive restlessness and unreliability.

5. Maerose is associated visually with the dramatic chiaroscuro of film noir, while sunny Californian Irene is brightly lit and dressed in flowery pastels.

6. Maerose initially appears less threatening to family stability than Irene, both because her base of operations—an interior design business—is traditional and because her own position within the Prizzi family is shaky. Maerose has been in disgrace since a sexual escapade years earlier. Her father will not speak to her at the wedding: he insults Mae for not being "dressed right" and calls her a whore in Italian. Mae calls herself "the family scandal," and at first her status as its scarlet woman is literally rendered in her clothing: making no concession to Prizzi sobriety, she wears a dramatic strapless black gown with a brilliant crimson sash. Later, when she is determined to be accepted back into the fold, she wears circumspect black garb.

7. This type of resolution recalls the early feminist embrace of film noir as open to subversive readings and celebratory (to whatever limited extent) of female power. As Janey Place writes, film noir presents "one of the few periods of film in which women are active, not static symbols, are intelligent and powerful, if destructively so, and derive power, not weakness, from their sexuality" (35).

8. Frank Tomasulo has described this "calculated ambivalence" in his work on both *Apocalypse Now* and *Tootsie.*

9. Normal courtship rituals involve going "outside," making a commitment to someone new and thus enlarging the family circle. Charley, however, accepts the despotism of the family, unable to envision a future free of its strangling but familiar demands. He acquiesces after Don Prizzi declares vehemently, "She is your wife. We are your life." The Don's logic implicitly rejects both the "new woman" and the New World.

10. Shumway argues that "the major cultural work [of the screwball comedy] is not the stimulation of thought about marriage, but the affirmation of marriage in the face of the threat of a growing divorce rate and liberalized divorce laws" (381). These films "construct a romantic mystification of marriage" (393). *Prizzi's Honor* registers its discomfort with divorce by Charley's refusal to consider it as an option: he can only marry Irene or kill her.

11. Charley throws a knife at Irene, hitting her in the throat and pinning her to a wall. Huston holds this grotesque image for a long beat, and the next shots of Charley dumping Irene's body into the trunk of her fabulous car, sign of her success, are gratuitous but for their subtext: look what happens to an ambitious woman.

12. As Ralph Cohen says, "[Genres] do not exist by themselves . . . each is defined by reference to the system [of genres] and its members" (207).

Works Cited

Cavell, Stanley. Pursuits of Happiness: The Hollywood Comedy of Remarriage. Cambridge: Harvard University Press, 1981.

Cohen, Ralph. "History and Genre." *New Literary History* 17, no. 2 (Winter 1986): 203–32.

Neale, Stephen. *Genre.* London: BFI, 1980.

———. "Questions of Genre." In *Film Genre Reader II*, ed. Barry Keith Grant. Austin: University of Texas Press, 1995. 159–83.

Place, J. A. "Women in Film Noir." in *Women in Film Noir*, ed. E. Ann Kaplan. London: BFI, 1980. 35–54.

Sarris, Andrew. "The Sex Comedy without Sex." *American Film* 3 (March 1978): 8–15.

Shumway, David R. "Screwball Comedies: Constructing Romance, Mystifying Marriage." In *Film Genre Reader II*, ed. Barry Keith Grant. Austin: University of Texas Press, 1995. 381–401.

Tomasulo, Frank. "Masculine/Feminine: The 'New Masculinity' in *Tootsie*." *Velvet Light Trap* 38 (Fall 1996): 4–13.

———. "The Politics of Ambivalence: *Apocalypse Now* as Prowar and Antiwar Film." In *From Hanoi to Hollywood*, ed. Linda Dittmar and Gene Michaud. New Brunswick, NJ: Rutgers University Press, 1991. 145–58.

Robert De Niro as Sam "Ace" Rothstein in *Casino*.

Way of Life: *GoodFellas* and *Casino*

Constantine Verevis

In the early 1970s Martin Scorsese exploded on the filmmaking scene with his second feature, *Mean Streets* (1973), a film based on his experience of growing up in the Italian neighborhood of New York's Lower East Side. Scorsese described *Mean Streets* as "an anthropological study," a fiction film depicting Italian-Americans on "the everyday scale, the everyday level."[1] Some twenty years later Scorsese returned to the familiar terrain and criminal milieu of *Mean Streets* with the companion pieces *GoodFellas* (1990) and *Casino* (1995), films adapted from Nicholas Pileggi's journalistic books *Wiseguy: Life in a Mafia Family* (1985) and *Casino: Love and Honor in Las Vegas* (1995), respectively.[2] Following a comment that says what the film titles in Scorsese's "gangster trilogy" literally signify—"*Mean Streets* is about territory, *GoodFellas* about tribe, and *Casino* about a sacred place, or religion"[3]—this chapter interrogates the two later films in terms of their accumulation of ethnographic detail and expression of a way of life. In particular, this chapter takes an interest in the way Scorsese recreates the inner workings of the gangster lifestyle through a careful mixture of documentary reality (life) and expressive fiction (style).

Tribe

Scorsese says that he read Pileggi's *Wiseguy* while directing *The Color of Money* (1986) and was struck not only by its "narrative ability" but also the documentary element of its factual reportage, the way it expressed a particular lifestyle.[4] "I [was] interested in the book's structure," says Scorsese. "The subtitle is *Life in a Mafia Family*, and the documentary approach interested me. . . . *Wise Guy* [*sic*] gives you a sense of the day-to-day life [of gangsters] . . . how they work . . . and for what reasons."[5] *Wiseguy* recounts the factual experiences of Henry Hill, a middle-level Irish-Sicilian gangster who worked, alongside his friends and partners James "Jimmy the Gent" Burke and Tommy DeSimone, under the authority of local Mafia boss Paul Vario (renamed Jimmy Conway, Tommy De Vito, and Paulie Cicero, respectively, in the film). Through transcribed, first-person interviews with Hill, his wife Karen, and others, *Wiseguy* describes a way of life, from the moment in 1955 when the 11-year-old Hill wanders into the mob's cabstand looking for work, through to the time of his decision (May 22, 1980) to testify against Burke and Vario, and leave the gangster life to join the Justice Department's Federal Witness Protection Program. Essential to Pileggi's reportage was that it offered a true picture of criminal life, one focused not on the codes and behavior of the "godfathers" that ran the operation, but rather on the ethos of the tribe, the lower-echelon gangsters who actually worked the streets.[6] Describing this aspect of his book, Pileggi said:

> No books [about the Mafia had] told [it] from the point of view of a really little guy. . . . I thought of Henry [Hill] as a G.I. in a little crew in Queens. They never even got to Manhattan. . . . Once in a while they'd come to the Copacabana, and that's a big day in the city. Everything they robbed was at Kennedy [formerly Idlewild] Airport. . . . And when they finally made a huge, $5 million score, they all just came apart. They came apart on coke, they came apart on greed. They all started killing each other because they didn't trust each other. And that's the end of *GoodFellas* because it starts happy, and it ends bad.[7]

GoodFellas comes across as a remarkably faithful adaptation of Pileggi's book, a film that takes an interest not only in the quality of the lifestyle, but in the document's "feeling of truth":[8] "I knew it [*Wiseguy*] would make a fascinating film if we just could keep the same sense of a way of life that Nick [Pileggi] had in the book—what Henry Hill had given him—and . . . be as close to the truth as possible in a fiction film. . . . Throughout the [making of *GoodFellas*] I was always telling people, 'There's no sense in making another gangster picture, unless it is as close as possible to a certain kind of reality, to the spirit of a documentary.'"[9] As in Pileggi's *Wiseguy*, *GoodFellas* sets out to present a *realistic* portrayal of organized crime and how it operates by approaching the social milieu and attitudes of the Mafia not from the top, but rather by taking up its position at the bottom, alongside the rank and file—"the Mafia foot soldiers"—who have to work within the conventions and power relations of the system. More particularly, while *GoodFellas* does not shy away from the violence and mayhem of street life, it wants to interrogate the nature of criminal enterprise, its "profit motive": "People think gangsters kill people. Yes, of course they do. But the main purpose of the gangster, especially in *GoodFellas*, is to make money. That's why . . . Tommy [De Vito] is killed. After a while, he was making more noise than money. He was killing people for no reason . . . He was messing up the whole plan."[10]

Additionally, Scorsese determined to inject a feeling of realism into *GoodFellas* by adopting a number of formal techniques commonly associated with the documentary style, including high levels of voice-over narration, captions, and intertitles to indicate place and date, and specific references to historical events and locations. Scorsese admitted that the use of some of these techniques—voice-over and freeze frames—was influenced by the innovations of the French New Wave (especially *Jules et Jim*, 1963), but he employed these in order to shape the film "like a *staged* documentary":[11] "I wanted a very fluid style . . . but I also wanted it [*GoodFellas*] to be as if I had been doing a . . . Maysles cinéma-vérité documentary on these [wise] guys for twenty-five years with the ability to walk in and out of rooms with cameras."[12] At the same time, Scorsese claims he "found the style" for *GoodFellas* in two 1980s Armani commercials he made with cinematographers Nestor Almendros and Michael Ballhaus,[13] discovering in those concentrated pieces of filmmaking "how short [a time] a shot can be on the screen for an audience to register the image and understand its meaning. . . . The commercials crystallized my concept of moving the action much quicker."[14] Accordingly, Scorsese describes the process whereby, during the development of the script with Pileggi, he encouraged his co-writer to continually compact selected episodes from the book so that there was "a constant accumulation of [ethnographic] details, [and a realization] that if the scenes were kept short, the impact after about an hour and a half would be terrific."[15] The process of layering scene upon scene not only enabled Scorsese to recreate the documentary reality (the detail) of *Wiseguy*, but to transform the material through his own expressive and kinetic signature style.

In order to chronicle the twenty-five year tenure of career-criminal Henry Hill, Scorsese not only developed a brand of *expressive realism*, but also adopted the classical (if ironically inflected), biographical, rise-and-fall structure of the traditional gangster film.[16] Echoing Robert Warshow's classic formulation of the gangster movie—"a story of enterprise and success ending in precipitate failure"[17]—Scorsese described the life cycle of his Mafia foot soldiers: "wise guys have . . . an enjoyment cycle of maybe eight or nine years . . . before they either get killed or go to jail and start that long process of going in and out

Ace and his lieutenant Billy Sherbert (Don Rickles).

[of prison] like a revolving door. . . . The first few years are the exuberance of youth. They have a great time—until they start to pay for it."[18] This classical structure enables Scorsese to present his gangster story as a "mature version of the modern American success story,"[19] a cautionary tale which mixes loyalty and greed (power and profit) to focus on a handful of central characters—Henry Hill (Ray Liotta), Jimmy Conway (Robert De Niro) and Tommy De Vito (Joe Pesci)—and their ultimate (and tragic) downfall. The gangster life cycle—from success through to breakdown—in turn provides an opportunity to reflect upon the broader values and attitudes expressed in and through the film's period setting, with the friendship and prosperity of the 1960s gradually giving way to corruption and disintegration in the 1970s.[20]

Although Scorsese closely followed the spirit of *Wiseguy*, he calculated that the story of Henry Hill's rise and fall did not need to follow the straight chronology of Pileggi's book. Specifically, Scorsese decided to relocate Hill's account of Tommy De Vito's murder of a Gambino gang member and "made man," Billy Batts, from the middle pages of *Wiseguy* to the very beginning of his film.[21] Following some opening credits and (then) two intertitles that read "This film is based on a true story" and "New York, 1970," the opening (largely pre-credit) sequence of *GoodFellas* introduces Henry, who, after helping Jimmy and Tommy dispose of the body of Batts by stowing it in the boot of their car, watches with mild aversion as his companions finish the job, assailing the still breathing Batts with butcher knife and handgun. The unnecessary murder of Billy Batts stands as a symbol of the reckless acts that attract unwanted attention and come to threaten the stability of the life and also functions as a temporal marker and hinge between the rise and fall (1960s and 1970s) panels of the film. Its significance may not be apparent until it is replayed in its wider context (and more precisely dated to June 11, 1970) later in the film, but by placing the Batts killing at the beginning Scorsese builds a sense of inevitability into the decline of his three central characters.[22]

The pre-credit sequence of *GoodFellas* ends with a freeze frame on Henry's face as his voice-over announces: "As far back as I can remember I always wanted to be a gangster."[23] Following the credits, *GoodFellas* steps back to 1955 to show a young Henry Hill at his tenement window surveying the world of gangsterdom that is laid out before him in his East New York, Brooklyn neighborhood. Identifying the gangster life as an extreme version of the American dream,[24] Henry's voice-over (in a line lifted directly from Pileggi's book)[25] declares: "To me, being a gangster was even better than being president of the United States." On the street, outside the cabstand run by Paulie Cicero's brother, Tuddy, Henry sees an intoxicating display of "wealth, power and girth,"[26] of gleaming Cadillacs and Lincolns, and of burly visitors in silk suits and expensive jewelry. From the outset, the use of voice-over is determined by the interview transcripts of *Wiseguy*, but Scorsese focuses the device, reducing the narrating voices to those of Henry and (to a lesser extent) Karen and restricting events to cover only those of Henry operating within the mob. Henry's voice-over effectively guides the viewer through the narrative, providing an insider's knowledge and perspective on the world of the gangster, at once shaping the film as "a piece of documentary journalism" and providing "contextual and narrative connections . . . so that most scenes require no beginning and no ending but merely a few illustrative, emblematic shots."[27] But at the same time, Henry's mixed Irish-Sicilian background marks him as an outsider, a lower ranked gangster who can never be a "made-man," or full member of the Italian inner circle.[28] In *GoodFellas*, it is exactly Henry's status as a detached observer—a narrator at once inside *and* outside the systems of conduct that he documents—which positions him as a "quasi-anthropological commentator on the mob's codes and mores."[29] This in turn enables Scorsese to effect an important shift from an interest in the identity of an individual to a concern with the expression of a general way of life: "Henry's [function] in *GoodFellas* [is] to anatomize a collective lifestyle [by] chronicling an individual life. Scorsese depersonalizes Henry, denying him an independent existence apart from the Mob. By pluralizing Pileggi's book title, Scorsese locks his focus on the ethos of the group rather than the identity of the individual."[30]

In *GoodFellas*, Henry's voice is not just a demonstration of character, but an expression of behavior and of the *"rush of the lifestyle."*[31] From the opening moments, in which the youngster's attraction to the life is underscored by the

Jimmy Conway (Robert De Niro) with his young protégés in *GoodFellas*.

song, "Rags to Riches" (by Tony Bennett), Henry is irresistibly drawn *into* the life: "I was the luckiest kid in the world," he says, "I was part of something. I Belonged. I was treated like I was a grown-up. I was living a fantasy." Henry describes the 1950s as "a glorious time [when] wiseguys were all over the place." As the film moves forward several years to pick up Henry as a young adult (a caption reads "Idlewild Airport, 1963"), his fascination and sense of belonging is captured in a lengthy tracking shot through the mob hangout, Sonny's Bamboo Lounge. Henry's voice-over identifies the crew—Frankie the Wop, Freddie No Nose, Nicky Eyes, Jimmy Two Times, and others—as they acknowledge (in a reprise of *Mean Streets*)[32] the camera's point of view and mutter Sicilian greetings: "Eh, che se dice?" "Come si va?" "Ci vendiamo." At this point, Scorsese's interest in creating a realistic appraisal of organized crime and its daily workings becomes a determination "to show [gangster life] not just through facts . . . [but] through the everyday, seemingly unimportant details . . . how they dressed, [and] what [food] they ate."[33] As the camera tracks along an elaborately laid table, wiseguys and their partners seated each side, Henry's voice resumes: "For us to live any other way was nuts. To us those goody-good people who worked shitty jobs for bum paychecks and took the subway to work every day, and worried about their bills, were dead.

"A glorious time [when] wiseguys were all over the place": Henry Hill (Ray Liotta) with Tommy De Vito (Joe Pesci) in *GoodFellas*.

I mean they were suckers. . . . If we wanted something we just took it. . . . It was just all routine, and you didn't even think about it."

The Bamboo Lounge segment communicates the glamour and privilege of mob life, but its seductive nature is nowhere better rendered than in the Copacabana segment, an intricately choreographed, Steadicam sequence-shot (scored with the Crystals' "Then He Kissed Me") that follows Henry and his girlfriend, Karen, on their labyrinthine route through the service entrance of the nightclub to a special front-row table. The sequence begins as Henry guides Karen from his car, parked across the street, straight through the lengthy queue of patrons waiting to get into the club, and then down a flight of stairs. The camera continues to follow the couple as they make their way along a maze of narrow corridors, past service elevators into a bustling kitchen, then through a curtain and into the club where a maître d' welcomes the couple. He immediately signals a waiter, and Henry and Karen are guided to a specially set, front row table where a nearby group of wiseguys raise their glasses in salute as Henry and Karen settle into the evening's entertainment. Scorsese comments on the "marvellous cinematic acting-out of power and seduction" inscribed in the Copacabana sequence-shot:[34]

> There was a reason to do it all in one shot. Henry's whole life is ahead of
> him. He's the young American ready to take over the world and he's met
> a girl he likes. Because he works with these guys and he's smart . . . his
> reward . . . is getting into the Copa that way, having the table fly over the
> heads of the other patrons and being seated right in front of the singer. . . .
> So it had to be done in one sweeping shot, because it's his seduction of her
> and it's also the lifestyle seducing him.[35]

Henry and Karen marry and enjoy the rewards and privilege of the life, but (as the film moves into the 1970s) ostentatious living, drug abuse, and random acts of greed and violence (not only the Batts murder that leads to Tommy's death, but also Jimmy's determination to eliminate everyone involved in the Lufthansa airlines heist) increasingly threaten the stability of the life. Scorsese reported that he wanted the 1970s sequences to express a sense of disillusion and disintegration: "I wanted the style to kind of break down by the end . . . so that by [Henry's] last days as a wiseguy, it's as if the whole picture would be out of control."[36] This culminates in the extended "Sunday, May 11, 1980" sequence, a passage (extensively narrated by a sweaty and coked-up Henry) that chronicles his frantic "last day" and ends with his being arrested by federal agents on drug trafficking charges. The frenetic pace of the sequence—which is organized around Henry's various domestic and business commitments: preparing the evening meal, getting his disabled brother to a hospital appointment, delivering a shipment of guns, arranging for the dispatch of a quantity of drugs—takes place under the surveillance of the ominous hovering of a police helicopter and is designed to reflect Henry's cocaine-induced condition. Rapid camera movements and reframings add to the acceleration of the segment, as does the nerve-jangling selection of songs—"Jump into the Fire" (Harry Nilsson), "Memo for Turner" (Rolling Stones), "What Is Life" (George Harrison), "Mannish Boy" (Muddy Waters), and others—that seem to attend every moment of Henry's strung-out day. Scorsese maintained that he "wanted to create . . . the state of anxiety and the way the mind races when on drugs . . . [so that] you become functionally insane and that's your downfall":[37]

> I wanted to get the impression of that craziness. Especially that last day, [Henry] starts at six in the morning. The first thing he does is gets the guns, takes a hit of coke, gets in the car. I mean, you're already wired, you're wired for the day. And his day is like crazy. Everything is at the same importance. The sauce is just as important as the guns, is as important as Jimmy, the drugs, the helicopter.[38]

With Henry's arrest *GoodFellas* comes to an abrupt and crushing halt, the expressive use of camera and music giving way to the bland mise-en-scène—the terrifying "normality"[39]—of Henry and Karen's meeting with (actual) FBI agent Ed McDonald. Henry decides to testify against Jimmy and Paulie in exchange for protection, and over the ensuing scenes (which show Henry in the witness box) his monologue resumes as a lament for a lost way of life: "It was easy for all of us to disappear. . . . [But] the hardest thing for me was leaving the life. I still love the life. . . . We were treated like movie stars with muscle. We had it all, just for the asking. . . . Anything I wanted was a phone call away. Free cars. The keys to a dozen hideout flats all over the city. I bet twenty, thirty grand over a weekend and then I'd either blow the winnings in a week or go to the sharks to pay the bookies." Henry then leaves the stand to address the camera directly, saying "Didn't matter. It didn't mean anything. When I was broke I would go out and rob some more. We ran everything. . . . Everything was for the taking. And now it's all over." With that, the scene cuts to a tracking shot of outer-suburban, newly constructed, identikit homes which comes to settle upon Henry in a toweling robe, emerging from his front door to pick up his morning newspaper. His voice continues: "That's the hardest part. Today everything is different. There's no action. I have to wait around like everyone else. Can't even get decent food. . . . I'm an average nobody. I get to live the rest of my life like a schnook." As Scorsese puts it: "Henry . . . [is] just left out in God knows where, annoyed because he's not a wiseguy anymore. I was more interested in the irony of that. There wasn't a last paragraph in [Pileggi's] book saying, 'Now I know what I did. I was a bad guy, and I'm really sorry for it'—none of that. Just, 'Gee, I can't get the right food here.'"[40] If there is any doubt that Henry's lament is about the loss of "the life," *GoodFellas* ends with an exhilarating shot (a reprise of both *The Great Train Robbery*, 1903 and *The Great Rock 'n' Roll Swindle*, 1980) of a resurrected Tommy contemptuously firing his gun directly toward the camera, to the sound of the Sid Vicious cover of "My Way," and implicitly at every "average nobody"—at every worthless "schnook"—in the audience.

Temple

Scorsese followed *GoodFellas* with remakings of *Cape Fear* (1991) and *The Age of Innocence* (1993) before being drawn (irresistibly)[41] back to the gangster genre with *Casino*, a second Scorsese project based on a factual book by Nicholas Pileggi, and one that can be understood as a kind of sequel to *GoodFellas*. Pileggi's follow-up to *Wiseguy*, *Casino* tells the story of Frank "Lefty" Rosenthal, one of the most powerful and influential men in Las Vegas in the 1970s, his wife, Geri McGee; and his strong-arm man, Anthony "Tony the Ant" Spilotro (for legal reasons, renamed Sam "Ace" Rothstein, Ginger McKenna, and Nicky Santoro, respectively, in Scorsese's film). As in the earlier *Wiseguy*, *Casino* is based on firsthand accounts, but the later book opens up Rosenthal's story to describe the larger political, economic, and social implications of the mob's attempt to control the Las Vegas gambling scene during the 1970s. Pileggi describes the project:

> *Wiseguy* is a book about organized crime and how it works. . . . *Casino* [is] . . . the story of an industry, how that industry works and the history of that industry. . . . I worked on *Casino* for years until I found the people through whom I could tell the story of the casino industry. I had the man [Rosenthal] who was the master gambler who they needed to run the casinos, the mobsters who put together the connections, the Teamsters to make the loan, the front man who got the money from the mobsters, and the

Remo (Pasquale Cajano) watches as Nicky gambles.

Mafia muscleman [Spilotro] who was there to keep everybody in place. And he [Spilotro] falls in love with the gambler's wife [McGee] and it brings everything down. *It was the perfect dramatic story through which we could tell the story of the casino industry,* and that's what we made a movie about.[42]

As in the earlier *GoodFellas,* Scorsese was drawn to the drama of *Casino,* grounding it in the traditional structure of the gangster film to document the rise and fall of its principal characters and the "last days" of the mob in Las Vegas. The first part of the film tells the story of Sam "Ace" Rothstein (Robert De Niro), an expert handicapper from Chicago who rises to the upper ranks of the Las Vegas gambling scene and crime world when he is selected by Kansas City Mafia bosses to head the Tangiers Corporation (the fictional equivalent of the four casinos—Stardust, Fremont, Frontier, and Marina—headed by Rosenthal in the 1970s). Accompanying Rothstein during his rise in making the Tangiers into one of the most successful operations in Las Vegas are his longtime friend and mob enforcer, Nicky Santoro (Joe Pesci), and the beautiful Ginger McKenna (Sharon Stone), a veteran hustler who is enticed to marry Ace for financial security and (the appearance of) respectability. In the second part, the trio's accession to a life of privilege and excess gradually leads to their (inescapable) downfall. Increasingly unhappy in her marriage to Rothstein, Ginger turns to alcohol and drug abuse, and looks for comfort in adulterous relationships, first with her former pimp, Lester Diamond (James Woods), and then with Rothstein's protector, Santoro. The latter puts in place a bizarre love triangle, one that queers Rothstein's relationship with Santoro, and triggers events that bring down all three main characters and (eventually) the empire built around them. Scorsese emphasizes the tragic and *religious* dimension of his (mob) morality play, describing it as an "Old Testament story: [one of] gaining paradise and losing it, through pride and through greed."[43]

Jonathan Romney describes *Casino* as Scorsese's "flashiest, most superficial film," but adds that this is a way of saying that its style is perfectly matched to its theme: "Las Vegas is a construction of flashing, seductive surfaces that conceal a tawdry machinery. . . . [The main characters] move in a world that obliges them to be simply embodiments of desire, appetite-driven cogs in the Vegas machine."[44] This approach is immediately signaled in the film's audacious opening sequence. Following two intertitles that announce "Adapted from a true story" and "1983," the opening shows Rothstein, impeccably dressed in pastel shades of pink, leaving the Tangiers and headed for his parked car. As he walks from the building his voice-over explains: "When you love someone, you've gotta trust them. There is no other way. You've gotta give them the key to everything that's yours. Otherwise what's the point? And for a while I believed that's the kind of love I had."[45] Ace gets into his Cadillac and turns the ignition, and the vehicle explodes. As flames fill the screen the final chorus of J. S. Bach's *St. Matthew Passion* is heard and (as the credits begin) Ace's silhouetted figure periodically hurls in slow motion through the flames, "like a soul about to take a dive into hell."[46] At the end of the credits, a resurrected Ace is seen standing in his casino. His voice-over resumes:

"Before I ever ran a casino or got myself blown up Ace Rothstein was a hell of a handicapper. . . . I had it down so cold that I was given paradise on earth. I was given one of the biggest casinos in Las Vegas to run, the Tangiers, by the only kind of guys [the mob] that can actually get you that kind of money." There follows a shot of Nicky Santoro and he takes up the narration: "It should have been perfect. I mean he had me, Nicky Santoro, his best friend watching his ass. And he had Ginger, the woman he loved on his arm." In a paraphrase of the Frank Cullotta words that end Pileggi's book,[47] Santoro continues: "But in the end we fucked it all up. It should have been so sweet too but it turned out to be the last time street guys like us were ever given anything that fuckin' valuable again." The sequence is followed by an establishing shot of a glitzy nightscape, and a series of superimposed captions: "The Strip," "Las Vegas," "Ten Years Earlier."

As in *GoodFellas*, the opening of *Casino* at once signals the inevitable downfall of the (three) main characters and announces itself—in the narrating voices of Ace Rothstein and Nicky Santoro—as another "insider's tour of the world of gangsters, [one] spotlighting the fascinating era when organized crime families of the Midwest came to Las Vegas in the seventies and early 1980s."[48] Additionally, with its extended voice-over narration and interest in small details, *Casino* takes up the non-fiction impulse of the earlier Scorsese-Pileggi collaboration to document "the (d)evolution of Las Vegas

"'He had me, Nicky Santoro, his best friend watching his ass'": Joe Pesci as Nicky.

and the arcane workings of [the] casinos."[49] Scorsese shot *Casino* during working hours in an actual casino (the 1970s-built Riviera), and the first section
of the film plays like "a non-fiction [semidocumentary] prologue" devoted to
demonstrating and analyzing the methods of casino operation under the control of the mob.[50] The Tangiers is run as a perfect system, an early sequence
demonstrating how coins and bills are channeled and counted, packed and
weighed, stored and skimmed in the windowless, bare bones, and double
locked work rooms of the casino. In an extended sequence-shot (jointly narrated by Rothstein and Santoro) the camera follows an unassuming mob
courier as he enters the sacred count room, walks past the deadened gaze of
count room workers, to fill his suitcase with hundreds of thousands of dollars
in skim, and casually exits the casino. He then takes a chartered flight to go
on to deliver the tribute to a (seemingly) humble group of mid-West crime
bosses assembled in a produce store backroom in Kansas City.

Alongside its documentary impulse, *Casino* sets out to render a way of life,
or (better) a *new* life of respectability at the seat of the Temple. As Rothstein
says at the beginning of the film, "Anywhere else in the country I was a
bookie, a gambler, always looking over my shoulder.... But here I'm Mr.
Rothstein. I'm not only legitimate, but running a casino and that's like selling
people dreams for cash.... For guys like me Las Vegas washes away your
sins. It's like a morality car wash." Rothstein takes up a position of power
and influence alongside other Las Vegas "royalty"—investment bankers and
Nevada politicians—and his glittering prize is the showgirl, Ginger, introduced in dazzling style in a freeze frame and then to the sounds of "Love Is
Strange" (Mickey and Sylvia), "Heart of Stone" (Rolling Stones), and "Love
Is the Drug" (Roxy Music). Rothstein secures his investment, offering Ginger
a multi-million-dollar house with a housekeeper and a swimming pool, furs,
jewelry, and a key to his safety deposit box. But Ginger's drunkenness and
infidelity test the patience of the otherwise unflappable Rothstein, and when
she eventually comes between him and his boyhood friend, Santoro, everything turns bad. The glamour of "the life" rapidly degenerates, culminating
in Ginger's lethal drug-overdose in the corridors of a sleazy motel, Santoro's
brutal murder at the hands of the mob, and the car-bomb attempt on
Rothstein's life. The explosion of Rothstein's automobile (repeated at the end
of the film, again to chorus of "St Matthew Passion") is followed by a series of
(near-apocalyptic) images of the old casinos collapsing like decks of cards, as
developers blast their way through to make for the new corporate-owned and
"family-oriented" Las Vegas of the later 1980s (and beyond). Gerald Forshey
underlines the biblical dimension of the tragedy: "In *GoodFellas*, Pileggi and
Scorsese examined New York as a modern Babylon, a place with power as
the fundamental force, existing with a fragile veneer of codes of silence and a
communal morality. In *Casino*, Las Vegas becomes Gomorrah. Here, everything is out of control."[51]

Casino ends with a brief epilogue that shows an aged Rothstein, living in
San Diego (the real-life Rosenthal retreated to Boca Raton) and once again
working as a handicapper for the mob. The film's credits roll, first to the

"Love Is the Drug": Ginger (Sharon Stone) and Ace.

sound of Georges Delerue's "Theme de Camille" (from Jean-Luc Godard's *Contempt* [1963]) and then Hoagy Carmichael's spoken rendition of "Stardust" ("Sometimes I wonder why / I spend the lonely nights / Dreaming of a song / The melody haunts my reverie / And I am once again with you / When our love was new / And each kiss an inspiration / But that was long ago / And now my consolation / Is in the stardust of a song"), described as "the only piece [of music] that could sum up the emotions and thoughts about what [the viewer has] seen."[52] Scorsese adds that at the end (as in the beginning), it was essential to communicate the sense that something grand had been lost: "I'm not asking you to agree with the morality—but there was the sense of an empire being lost, and it needed music [Bach, Delerue, Carmichael] worthy of that. . . . Even though you may not like the people and what they did, they're still human beings and it's a tragedy."[53] Here, as in *GoodFellas*, the lament is for the loss of a lifestyle, the passing of a (gangster) way of life. At the same time, the end of *Casino* is a culmination and summation of Scorsese's own life- or auteur-style: "a blistering and haunting last word on the culture of American violence, criminal enterprise, and civic life [Scorsese had] mined since *Mean Streets*."[54]

Notes

1. Anthony DeCurtis, "What the Streets Mean: An Interview with Martin Scorsese," *South Atlantic Quarterly* 91, no. 2 (Spring 1992): 434.

2. Nicholas Pileggi, *Wiseguy: Life in a Mafia Family* (New York: Simon & Schuster, 1985), and *Casino: Love and Honor in Las Vegas* (New York: Simon & Schuster, 1995).

3. Gavin Smith, "Two Thousand Light Years from Home: Scorsese's Big *Casino,*" *Film Comment* 32, no. 1 (January–February 1996): 59.

4. See DeCurtis, 432; Gavin Smith, "Interview with Martin Scorsese," *Film Comment* 26, no. 5 (September–October 1990):, 27–28.

5. Mary Pat Kelly, *Martin Scorsese: A Journey*, with forewords by Steven Spielberg and Michael Powell (New York: Thunder's Mouth Press, 1996), 259.

6. Mario Puzo, author of *The Godfather*, described *Wiseguy* as "one of the few true pictures of the criminal life." Quoted in David Konow, "A Real Good Fella: Interview with Nicholas Pileggi," *Creative Screenwriting* 8, no. 2 (March–April 2001): 38.

7. Konow, 39.

8. Maurizio Viano, "Review of *GoodFellas,*" *Film Quarterly* 44, no. 3 (Spring 1991): 44–45.

9. Scorsese, quoted in David Thompson and Ian Christie, eds., *Scorsese on Scorsese* (London: Faber & Faber, 1996), 151.

10. Scorsese, quoted in Kelly, *Martin Scorsese*, 262–63.

11. Quoted in Smith, "Interview," 28.

12. Thompson and Christie, *Scorsese on Scorsese*, 154.

13. *GoodFellas* was photographed by Ballhaus.

14. Quoted in Les Keyser, *Martin Scorsese* (New York: Twayne, 1992), 196.

15. Quoted in Thompson and Christie, *Scorsese on Scorsese*, 151.

16. Steve Neale, "Westerns and Gangster Films Since the 1970s," in *Genre and Contemporary Hollywood*, ed. Steve Neale (London: BFI, 2002), 35.

17. Robert Warshow, "Movie Chronicle: The Westerner," in *The Immediate Experience: Movies, Comics, Theatre and Other Aspects of Popular Culture* (New York: Atheneum, 1972), 135.

18. DeCurtis, 438.

19. *GoodFellas* producer IrwinWinkler, quoted in Kelly, *Martin Scorsese*, 260.

20. See Smith, "Interview," 29; Leonard Quart, review of *GoodFellas*, *Cinéaste* 18, no. 2 (1991): 44–45.

21. Pileggi, *Wiseguy*, 117–20.

22. Lawrence S. Friedman, *The Cinema of Martin Scorsese* (New York: Continuum, 1998), 174.

23. Dialogue from *GoodFellas* is taken from Martin Scorsese and Nicholas Pileggi, *GoodFellas* (London: Faber & Faber), 1993.

24. See DeCurtis, 437, and Thompson and Christie, *Scorsese on Scorsese*, 155, where Scorsese describes the gangster life as "the American dream gone completely mad and twisted."

25. Pileggi, *Wiseguy*, 19.

26. Tom Milne, review of *GoodFellas, Monthly Film Bulletin* 57, no. 683 (December 1990): 356.

27. Viano, "Review of *GoodFellas*," 45.

28. Marie Katheryn Connelly, *Martin Scorsese: An Analysis of His Feature Films* (Jefferson, NC: McFarland, 1993), 139.

29. Quart, "Review of *GoodFellas*," 43.

30. Friedman, 172.

31. Scorsese, quoted in DeCurtis, 432, emphasis added.

32. Kathleen Murphy notes the similarity to the scene from *Mean Streets* in which Charlie (Harvey Keitel) "floats[s] euphorically through a barful of acquaintances." See "Made Men," *Film Comment* 26, no. 5 (September–October 1990): 26.

33. Quoted in Keyser, *Martin Scorsese*, 200–201.

34. Lesley Stern, *The Scorsese Connection* (London: BFI, 1995), 9.

35. Thompson and Christie, 155.

36. Friedman, 170.

37. Thompson and Christie, 158–60.

38. Smith, "Interview," 30.

39. Stern, 9.

40. DeCurtis, 439–40.

41. See Scorsese's comments on his interest in, and attraction to, the gangster film in Martin Scorsese and Michael Henry Wilson, *A Personal Journey with Martin Scorsese through American Movies* (New York: Miramax/Hyperion with BFI, 1997), 47–58.

42. Konow, 42; emphasis added.

43. Thompson and Christie, 200.

44. Jonathan Romney, "Review of *Casino*," *Sight and Sound* 6, no. 3 (March 1996): 40.

45. Dialogue from *Casino* is transcribed from Universal Pictures Region 1 DVD, 1998.

46. Scorsese, quoted in Thompson and Christie, 200.

47. See *Casino*, 348. Cullotta, chief lieutenant to Spilotro, entered the Witness Protection Program and has a cameo in Scorsese's film.

48. Victoria Alexander, review of *Casino, Films in Review* 47, nos. 3–4 (March–April 1996): 57.

49. Friedman, 176.

50. Todd McCarthy, "*Casino* a Stone Cold Winner," *Variety*, November 20–26, 1995, 47.

51. Gerald E. Forshey, "*Casino*: The Uses of Narrative Voice-Over," *Creative Screenwriting* 2, no. 4 (Winter 1995): 61.

52. Scorsese, quoted in Thompson and Christie, 208.

53. Thompson and Christie, 206–7.

54. Smith, "Two Thousand Light Years," 59.

Kitano as Yamamoto in *Brother*.

Takeshi Kitano:
Melancholy Poet of the Yakuza Film

James Ursini

The yakuza film is, like the British and French gangster films, a relative of the American gangster movie, but not a close one. In his seminal article in 1974 (reprinted in the first part of this volume) "*Yakuza-eiga*: A Primer," Paul Schrader describes the main difference: "The yakuza film does not reflect the dilemma of social mobility seen in the thirties gangster films. . . . The Japanese gangster film aims for a higher purpose." He then goes on to discuss how the genre evolved in the 1960s as an offshoot of the time-honored samurai film (*jidai-geki*), of which audiences were, by that time, beginning to become weary of. Like the samurai film, the yakuza movie also focused on the concepts of duty and humanity (*giri* and *ninjō*), an integral part of the ideal code of the samurai, and, at least initially, equated the protagonist of the film, the lead yakuza gangster, with the historical and mythical figure of the samurai.

Many of the earliest yakuza films, particularly those developed and produced at Toei Studios, followed a ritualistic formula, which Schrader also delineates: including, the release from prison of the protagonist yakuza, his moral dilemma regarding actions he is ordered to perform by his yakuza boss (again, the theme of duty vs. humanity), and the climactic bloody battle in which he comes down on the side of humanity. By the middle 1970s, however, after Schrader's article was written, the ritualistic, moralistic yakuza film had given way to the more documentary-style yakuza, in the vein of Kinji Fukasaku's multipart *Battles without Honor and Humanity* (1973–74). These films were violent and naturalistic, more interested in exposing the brutality and corruption of the yakuza lifestyle than in spreading a romantic patina over the image of the modern-day Japanese gangster.

With the collapse of the Japanese studio system in the 1980s, the production of yakuza films, as well as most types of Japanese movies, was drastically reduced, with some filmmakers migrating to television to continue their explorations of the genre. This situation continued until the early 1990s, when the genre was given new credibility, in the eyes of Japanese audiences as well as the world critical community, through the timely intervention of two transgressive postmodern filmmakers from a new generation: Takashi

225

Miike (*Shinjuku Triad Society* [1995], *Full Metal Yakuza* [1997], *Ichi, the Killer* [2000], etc.) and the subject of this study, Takeshi Kitano.

Kitano, born in 1947, is thirteen years older than Miike and had a long career as an actor, comedian, writer, artist, and TV star (most often billed as "Beat" Takeshi) before he began directing movies in 1989 with *Violent Cop*. His style is less showy and surrealistic than Miike's, drawing heavily on his background in television comedy for his slapstick scenes and on earlier classic directors such as Yasujiro Ozu (*Early Spring, Tokyo Twilight*) for his more Zen-like contemplative moments and Akira Kurosawa (*Seven Samurai, Throne of Blood*) for his naturalistic bursts of violence. But what is most remarkable about Kitano's films is not what he has borrowed from others but his unique sense of poetic melancholy which suffuses almost every scene in his films, even the funniest ones.

Originally, Kitano was slated to star in *Violent Cop*, which was to be a *Dirty Harry*–ish film directed by yakuza film veteran Fukasaku. However, when Fukasaku discovered that the workaholic Kitano demanded time to continue shooting his televisions shows while doing the movie, he bowed out of the film, fearing that the actor would not be able to commit himself totally to the part. In an act of bravura typical of the man, Kitano volunteered to take over the helm and direct the film himself, even though he had never directed a feature film before.

Completely rewriting the original script, Kitano created a film which contains all the elements, in embryonic form, which would characterize Kitano's later movies. The original script had attempted to capitalize on Kitano's fame as a comedian and so had designed the rogue cop Azuma as a comic character. However, Kitano saw the film differently. He saw it as an opportunity to break out of the pigeonhole in which Japanese audiences and producers had enclosed him. In 1983 a friend, director Nagisa Oshima, had cast him as the conflicted prison guard in *Merry Christmas, Mr. Lawrence* and had continued to encourage the actor to take on more dramatic parts. In *Violent Cop*, Kitano took his advice to heart.

The protagonist, Azuma, is a vigilante cop whose deadpan expression hides a psyche riddled with grief and anger. We first see Azuma entering the house of a middle-class teenager who participated in the beating of a homeless person. Kitano does not arrest the boy; instead, he treats the teen to a little of his own medicine. Calmly returning to headquarters, he is reprimanded by the new "gung-ho" chief, who has just told his men that "police are sacred," even though we soon learn that several of his officers are on the payroll of the local yakuza boss. Azuma of course ignores the warnings of his chief as he does most of his colleagues and continues to mete out justice his own way, beating suspects to a bloody pulp in the locker room, assassinating a yakuza boss, and kicking down the street a man who makes the mistake of having sex with his mentally disturbed sister Akari (Maiko Kawakami).

Azuma's quasi-incestuous obsession with his sister is the key to Azuma's actions. The only tenderness we see in the movie comes in the few scenes with

Azuma, the title character in *Violent Cop*, ritually crosses a bridge
after administering the third degree.

his sister: picking her up from the mental hospital, gazing at the sea with her
("a scene at the sea" is not only a constant motif in Kitano's films but the name
of a 1991 movie by the director), walking through a local fair. With Akari he
seems at peace, complete. So when she is kidnapped by the psychotic yakuza
thug Kiyohiro (Hakuryu), shot up with heroin, and raped repeatedly, Azuma
reaches critical mass and instigates the climactic bloodbath of the finale.

It is appropriate that the only person who truly understands Azuma is not
his beloved sister but the psychotic Kiyohiro, his nemesis. Kitano purposely
dresses them in similar clothes for their final drawn-out bloodbath which
begins in the streets and ends in the warehouse where his sister is being held.
Kiyohiro tells him, "You're crazy like your sister." This little bit of truth is
too much for Azuma and only aggravates his rage. When he does finally
see his sister, she has been turned into a crazed addict, clawing at the dying
Kioyhiro for more drugs. The director then cuts to a close-up of Azuma's
melancholy expression and then to a long shot when, unable to bear the sight
of her crawling on the ground like an animal, Azuma shoots his sister. Once
again and for the last time he has taken the law into his own hands. The new
yakuza boss enters and executes Azuma. Turning on the glaring lights in the
warehouse, the boss pronounces them all "crazy." And to him they are. For
to the ideal yakuza all that matters is "business" and this is not business but
emotions gone awry (or as Michael tells his brother in *The Godfather*, "It's not
personal, Sonny. This is strictly business.")

Boiling Point (1990) is a much looser film than its predecessor, *Violent Cop*.
In it Kitano decided to play with the form, inserting scenes which are open
for interpretation and abandoning at times the linear format of his first film,
e.g., flashforwards and a shot (Masaki exiting an out house on a baseball field)
repeated at the beginning and end which calls into doubt for the viewer the

reality of what has gone on before in the movie. It is in many ways his most experimental film and for that reason his least aesthetically satisfying movie.

Kitano has claimed, in an interview on the American DVD release of his version of *Zatoichi*, that real-life yakuzas have approached him several times, wondering how he knew so much about their lifestyle. He of course answers cryptically, as is his wont. But wherever his knowledge comes from, Kitano is unrelentingly naturalistic and brutal in his depiction of yakuza life. In *Boiling Point* Kitano exchanges the role of the cop for that of the yakuza. The character he incarnates for this role, Uehara, is arguably the most repellent portrait of a yakuza found in any of his films to date.

Uehara is a rogue yakuza (a vicious variation on the rogue cop Kitano played in his previous movie) who cannot control his temper, his drinking, or his innate sadism. One might conjecture that at least some of the inspiration for the character comes from Kitano's father who was an abusive alcoholic who deserted his family. Uehara cuts off his best friend's finger instead of his own, in order to present it to the yakuza boss he has offended (a time-honored form of reparation among the yakuza). He forces his "moll" to have sex with his friend and then rapes the man himself. That same girlfriend he humiliates constantly, kicking her, slapping her, and eventually abandoning her by the side of the road. As disturbing as the scenes are to watch, Kitano still manages to inject his own dark, sadistic humor (a mainstay of his wildly popular comedy shows on television), as when, in an improvised game of baseball, he repeatedly pitches the ball at his girlfriend rather than across the invisible plate.

Uehara's only act of humanity is when he befriends the slow-witted Masaki (Yurei Yanagi) and his pal Iguchi (Gadarukanaru Taka) when they arrive in Okinawa to buy guns to fight the yakuzas threatening them back home. He finds them their guns and takes a few for himself. In a scene reminiscent of 1930s gangster movies, he wraps the automatic weapon in flowers (birds of paradise) and presents them to the yakuza boss. He then opens fire killing all the yakuza in the room. The situation as well as the sound of the weapon reminds one of the "ra-ta-tat-tat" of the "tommy gun" used in so many gangster films of the classic period and evokes particularly James Cagney's single-handed attack on a nightclub where his rivals are ensconced in *The Public Enemy* (a scene to which he will pay homage again in *Sonatine*).

Sonatine (1993) is the yakuza film that put Kitano on the international cinema map. It garnered rave reviews on the festival circuit, won several national and international awards, and secured Kitano's position as a world-class auteur. Originally sold to producers as a *Die Hard*–style movie, Kitano, in a typical act of rebellion, transported his crew to a remote island and proceeded to make a small film in the style of the French New Wave, taking as his inspiration Jean-Luc Godard's *Pierrot le fou*. At the same time, Kitano used the film to shift gears and paint the portrait of a sympathetic yakuza, light years away from the brutal Uehara of *Boiling Point*.

The protagonist of the movie, Murakawa (Kitano), is an aging and weary yakuza who wants out. Kitano establishes his world-weariness throughout the film by means of his facial expressions and his walk. Whether threatening a recalcitrant small businessman by dunking him repeatedly in the ocean, listening to his boss finesse him into taking on the unpleasant job of mediating a clan war between two gangs on Okinawa, or walking the beaches of the island, Murakawa maintains a melancholy cast to his face (reminiscent of the masks used in Japanese traditional theater) and a walk in which he drags his body as if it were an unbearable weight.

Murakawa, of course, does not hide his feelings from those closest to him. He tells his chief lieutenant directly, "I'm worn out." And later he tells Miiyuki (Aya Kokumai), a woman who has fallen for his yakuza image, "When you're scared all the time, it gets to the point where you wish you were dead." The thread of suicide runs throughout the movie. Murakawa plays a game of Russian roulette with his gang members, he dreams his own suicide during the night, and ultimately kills himself in the final minutes of the movie. In fact, his earlier attack on the yakuza bosses who set him up in Okinawa is really an act of suicide gone awry, for although he survives, he is outnumbered and outgunned. It is also a scene of subtle power and true mastery. Murakawa enters the darkened restaurant where the gang is enjoying a traditional banquet, a convention American and Japanese gangster films share. What the audience then sees is the flash of weapons inside the darkened restaurant intercut with brief shots from the point of view of the victims of Murakawa's automatic weapon, which we see blazing into the camera, and even briefer shots of the victims falling to the ground. When this act still does not alleviate his feelings of angst, he returns to the only place he has been happy, the beach at Okinawa, and shoots himself in a borrowed car.

The ocean and beach play a major role in Kitano's films, as mentioned earlier. Kitano described his fascination with the ocean in an article by Tim Smedley, "A Divine Comedy: The Films of Takeshi Kitano": "I do love the

Dream sequence from *Sonatine.*

sea, but at the same time, something inside tells me to keep a distance from it. We all know our origin is in the sea and it feels to me as though Mother Nature is calling us home. . . ." In *Sonatine* scenes of the yakuzas cavorting at the beach take up the whole middle of the film as he and his cohorts hide out in an abandoned shack near the ocean. There he rescues Miyuki from a rapist and forms an attachment to her as well as for the motley group of yakuzas he has found himself allied with. It is during these scenes that we see Murakawa change in demeanor and in personality. His mask slowly cracks as he smiles honestly and openly. He even moves at a more rapid or frenetic pace at times. He laughs. Through a series of silly games ("Boss, isn't this too childish?" "What else can I do?"), Murakawa finds his "inner child." The importance of games as a theme (obviously based on his own background as a comedian) runs through many of his films, including non-yakuza works like *Kikujiro* and *A Scene at the Sea*. For example, when Miyuki flashes her breasts in a playful moment, Murakawa smiles like an innocent child in medium close-up (a type of shot Kitano uses in all his films sparingly and for emphasis, favoring instead longer shots) and says, "Isn't indecent exposure fun?"

Many friends believe *Sonatine* was Kitano's dry run for his own attempted suicide in 1994 when he ran his motorcycle into a railroad divider (source: http://www.kitanotakeshi.com). He suffered brain contusions and multiple skull fractures and went through a series of surgeries that left him with altered features and nervous tics, which are in evidence in his performances. Kitano, however, used this traumatic incident to reevaluate his life and develop his more personal aesthetic talents, including painting and writing.

The result of this period of self-examination and aesthetic development was *Hana-bi* (*Fireworks* [1997]). As in *Violent Cop*, Kitano is this time on the side of the law in its battle against the yakuza gangs. However, unlike its predecessor, the film centers on the psychological and physical toll these violent and brutal confrontations take on the police themselves. Kitano plays Nishi, an ex-cop who is haunted not only by the deaths and near-deaths of

A recurrent flashback to the shooting of his partners in *Hana-bi*.

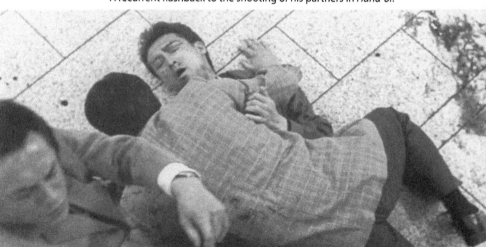

his cohorts, but also by the demise of his child and the imminent death of his wife from cancer. Unlike his former films, in which the actor was, for the most part, able to hide his suffering behind a mask, here the scars and facial twitches from his surgeries work for the character in externalizing the depths of sorrow this character feels but is unable to verbalize.

Throughout the film Nishi tries to make reparations for the damage done to others around him. He borrows money from the local yakuza boss and eventually even robs a bank in order to support the widow of a cop killed by a yakuza thug (seen several times in flashback and in slow motion) and to aid his close friend Horibe (Ren Osugi), who was crippled by a yakuza bullet and is now suicidal. (Parenthetically, Kitano has projected his own struggle with recovery on to the character of Horibe. Like Kitano, Horibe takes up painting to re-ignite his interest in life. Kitano's own paintings act as decor not only for the titles but much of the film.)

In the second half of the movie Kitano shifts gears and grafts on a noir fugitive couple theme to the gangster film structure. After the bank robbery, Nishi and his wife Miyuki (Kayoko Kishimoto) buy a van and take off into the country while being pursued by yakuzas as well as police. During the flight they find the love which they had buried under all their sorrow. They share moments of whimsy and happiness while playing Kitano's beloved games and immersing themselves in nature. But as in most fugitive couple films from *You Only Live Once* to *Gun Crazy*, fate is never far behind. In a clear homage to Francois Truffaut's own fugitive couple film *Mississippi Mermaid*, the pair ends up hiding out in the snow-packed mountains where Nishi dispatches the yakuzas sent to retrieve him.

Predictably for a Kitano film, the pursuit ends at the ocean where Nishi's cop pals finally find them. In a poignant final scene, Nishi loads two bullets into his gun and asks his comrades for "a little time." They, of course, agree. Nishi returns to his wife and as they embrace, she thanks him for the first time. As the camera pans discreetly away to the blue expanse of the "mother ocean" two shots are heard. The camera then cuts to a little girl who has been flying a kite on the beach as she stares in shock at what she can see but what Kitano refuses to show the audience. It is a moment of horror, like the other violent acts in the movie, but, unlike those other acts, so tender and emotional that Kitano cannot bear to show it to his audience.

After the worldwide success of *Hana-bi* (it won the Golden Lion Award at the Venice Film Festival), the director made *Kikujiro* (1999), named after his father. With this film Kitano purposely disappointed expectations once again by turning to a gentle comedy about the relationship between a lonely boy and idiosyncratic man. His only reference to the yakuza lifestyle is the upper-body tattoo we see briefly when Kikujiro undresses, indicating that he may have been a yakuza in the past.

Offered a chance by producer Jeremy Thomas to shoot in the prototypi-cal homeland of film noir and the cinema gangster, Los Angeles, Kitano reworked the elements of *Sonatine* for the English language movie *Brother*

Denny (Omar Epps) and Yamamoto posed in a traditional Japanese manner in *Brother*.

(2000). Kitano makes full use of the "city of the angels" in this film. *Brother* opens in the modernistic Los Angeles International Airport as a contemplative Yamamoto (Kitano), a yakuza in exile from his home for being a loose cannon, waits for a taxi to take him to his brother. He finds clues to his brother's whereabouts in a Japanese restaurant on the Miracle Mile of Wilshire Boulevard. This lead takes him to the center of downtown where he is accosted by an African-American named Denny (Omar Epps) who tries to extort money from a man who seems like a rich helpless Japanese tourist in a designer suit. Yamamoto responds with an outburst of extreme violence. In a reworking of the gouging out of the yakuza's eye with chopsticks in *Hana-bi*, Yamamoto takes a broken bottle and leaves the man one-eyed.

Yamamoto eventually does find his brother (Claude Maki), holed up in a derelict landmark, the Pacific Electric Building in downtown. He is now a member of a multiethnic gang of drug dealers, which ironically includes Denny—Yamamoto's first American casualty. Gradually Yamamoto grows fond of this group of misfits and their depressed industrial neighborhood because, as he says, it reminds him of where he grew up (again like so much in Kitano's films, autobiographically accurate). In the long Zen-like scenes the yakuza flies paper airplanes from the roof of his headquarters, cheats at games with Denny (who does not seem to recognize Yamamoto as his assailant), and stares at the Amtrak railroad yard in the distance while around him are the corporate high rises of the unseen executives, both Western and Asian, who have no contact with his world of the streets.

Intercut with these alienated and contemplative sequences are scenes of stylized violence as Yamamoto and his gang systematically defeat their rivals, first the Cholos and the African Americans and then the Japanese mobsters of Little Tokyo, until the most powerful yakuza joins Yamamoto's family. But when Yamamoto and his "brothers" (*aniki*) finally go up against the Italian mafia, they are out of their depth. In an elegiac series of shoot-outs, Yamamoto's gang is eliminated. The exile must even watch helplessly as his girlfriend and his brother are both cut down. In one strikingly poetic and horrific scene, shot under a bridge in downtown, all the audience sees are the flashes of gunfire which illuminate the dead bodies (similar to the restaurant shoot-out in *Sonatine*).

Convinced fatalistically that the end is near, Yamamoto tells Denny, with whom he has formed a bond, to "run away," then immediately makes a joke of it when Denny reacts with shock. The final scene of the movie takes place in

Palmdale in a deserted motel and nearby diner. There Yamamoto awaits his fate at the hands of the Mafia. He has sent Denny on his way, out of the "gang hell" with a gym bag full of money, and so rescued at least one "brother." As a line of limousines pulls up outside, he gives the owner of the diner some money to cover the impending damage and walks out into the desert sun in slow motion. The audience sees only a barrage of bullets as they shatter the red doors of the diner, in a scene which echoes the end of Howard Hawks' classic noir gangster film *The Big Sleep.*

The last film to date in which Kitano deals with the yakuza ethos is his boldly artistic *Dolls* (2002) which is based on bunraku theater in style and story. In one of its episodes an aging yakuza Hiro (Tatsuya Mihashi) tries to recapture the love of his youth, a woman he had deserted for the exciting gangster life. He finds her again but it is too late. His violent lifestyle claims him as he is shot down in the road.

Kitano has now moved on to new areas. He has done two samurai films based on the Shintaro Katsu's famous *Zatoichi* films of the 1960s and 1970s and has finished a film with his daughter, as well as another, called *Takeshis*, in which Kitano confronts his own doppelgänger. But as restless as this direct or is, one might safely predict that he will return to the world of the yakuza in the not-too-distant future.

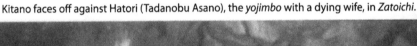

Kitano faces off against Hatori (Tadanobu Asano), the *yojimbo* with a dying wife, in *Zatoichi*.

PART
THREE

Contemporary
Views

Richard Attenborough as the 1940s "spiv" in *Brighton Rock*.

The British Gangster Film

Tony Williams

During an early scene in Edmond T. Greville's *The Noose* (1948), English newspaper editor (Reginald Tate) denies the claims of spunky American fashion journalist Linda Medbury (Carole Landis) that an underworld exists in post-war black market British society. "There are no gangsters in England." However, aided by her boyfriend, ex-commando Jumbo Hoyle (Derek Farr), she proves him wrong. Neglecting her assigned task to report on Dior's "New Look," Linda unveils the heinous activities of Sugiani (Joseph Calleia), "the nastiest thug in Europe." After a thirty-year career in the British underworld, this Italian-British "capo" now wishes to become a Renaissance prince like Cesare Borgia. Both Linda and Jumbo's team of World War I and World War II veterans foil Sugiani. Despite *The Noose*'s marginal status as a gangster film, it does reveal an interesting mixture of American and British themes still influencing British gangster films today. The presence of American actors Brad Pitt and Dennis Farina alongside "laddish" British actors such as Jason Statham, Jason Flemyng, and Vinnie Jones in Guy Ritchie's "mockney" (or "mock cockney") Tarantino-inspired revision of the genre in *Snatch* (2000) as well as the appearance of Ray Liotta alongside Jason Statham in *Revolver* (2005) is really nothing new. Nor does it result from purely box-office considerations such as *Brannigan* (1975), where John Wayne, tourist views of London, and the dominance of American gangsters played by Mel Ferrer and John Vernon overshadow their British counterparts. Certain British gangster films contain Hollywood influences but others do manage to develop their own form of national identity.

Crime and the criminal underworld were not unknown to British society, as the 19th-century fiction of Charles Dickens and his contemporaries reveal. But the gangster film is a fairly recent phenomenon within British cinema. Although the existence of individual criminals and specialized activities such as stealing jewels were around in the past, a fully defined British gangster film genre did not really develop until after 1945 in a cinema attempting to assert its own sense of national identity apart from Hollywood. Many well-known Hollywood stars such as Douglas Fairbanks Jr., Alan Hale, and Jack LaRue made crime movies in England during the 1930s such as *Jump for Glory* (1935) and *Murder in Soho* (1938). But pre-war censorship attempted to suppress any English imitations of Hollywood gangster films such as *Little Caesar* (1930),

Public Enemy (1931) and *Scarface* (1932). However, despite the successful attempt of banning the making of a film version of Edgar Wallace's pulp novel *When the Gangs Came to London* and the creation of home-grown alternatives such as Sexton Blake to counter the influence of American fictional private eyes such as Sam Spade and Philip Marlowe, some examples escaped censorship. In 1930, American actor Bernard Nedell played the title role in *The Man from Chicago*. The film depicted an ex-racketeer arriving in London to buy a nightclub (like LaRue in *Murder in Soho*) who successfully robs a bank and attracts the attention of the Flying Squad, a body whose activities would be featured in the later successful television series *The Sweeney* and its movie spin-offs in the 1970s.

Except for Ken Hughes' *Joe Macbeth* (1955) and St. John Clowes' *No Orchids for Miss Blandish* (1948), direct copies of American gangster movies were rare. Unlike America in the Prohibition era, an organized crime network along the lines of the Mafia in America and the Triads in China did not exist in pre-war British society.[1] But British readers and movie audiences had a fascination for the real thing. British National's weak attempt at parody with Maclean Rogers' *Don Chicago* (1945) is one example. Featuring American song and dance man Jackie Hunter in the title role, it chronicled the misadventures of a timid youth who cannot live up to his father's image. Fleeing to London, he masquerades as a tough guy, sets up a nightclub, and attempts to steal the Crown Jewels until his mother arrives to stop his activities. Lupino Lane's *The Innocents of Chicago* (1932) anticipated *Mickey Blue Eyes* (1999) with its comic narrative of the misadventures of Henry Kendall's English gentleman who inherits a Chicago bootlegging plant from his uncle and finds himself the target of two rival gangs. In Donovan Pedalty's comedy *Irish and Proud of It* (1936), a Chicago gang of whiskey distillers operates in the heart of London. In the crime musical *Rhythm Racketeer* (1937), Chicago gangster Nap Connors finds he has a double in bandleader Harry Grand (both played by Harry Roy in a dual role) and uses the resemblance to commit further crimes. Although these films never treat the gangster world seriously, their very British sense of humor reveals disavowal mechanisms designed to combat deep fears concerning the contaminating influences of American culture.

Criminal activities appeared in earlier British films usually involving the activities of jewel thieves such as *Checkmate* (1935) and *Crime Unlimited* (1935) as well as those depicting the exploits of E. W. Hornung's gentleman crook A. J. Raffles in Mansfield Markham's *The Return of Raffles* (1932). Debonair British star Ronald Colman had already portrayed the aristocratic thief in the Hollywood production *Raffles* (1930) and David Niven would follow in his footsteps a decade later. Raffles was after all an amateur and a gentleman. Jewel thieves were usually from more refined classes. So their criminal activities presented no threat to the dominant order especially when Raffles eventually dies a patriotic death in the Boer War. But the existence of a criminal proletariat on screen could evoke nightmare visions of Karl Marx's workers of the world uniting and throwing off their chains by equipping themselves with machine guns like those used by Paul Muni in *Scarface*.

Several ingredients which formed key elements of the later British gangster films did appear. But they lacked a threatening working-class context.
Scripted by Edgar Wallace from his own novel, *The Crimson Circle* (1929)
depicted the activities of a blackmail gang run by a criminal mastermind
resembling those in Fritz Lang's 1922 *Dr. Mabuse* films and *Spies* (1928). Like
Haghi in *Spies*, Edgar Wallace's title character in Walter Forde's *The Ringer*
(1931) is also a master of disguise. Wallace's Fellowship of the Frog in *The Frog*
(1937) is really an upper-class terrorist organization. In both film versions of
Wallace's *The Squeaker* (1930, 1937), the title character is an upper-class jewel
fence. Debonair Ivor Novello played a French Apache gangster in *The Rat*
(1925) and *The Return of the Rat* (1929) while Anton Walbrook portrayed a
much more refined European version in *The Rat* (1937). Lower-class excep-
tions certainly existed as in the racetrack gang depicted in *The Green Cockatoo*
(1937). Produced and directed by two Americans, William K. Howard and
William Cameron Menzies, from a story and screenplay by Graham Greene,
the film combined European and American elements. Photographed by the
great cinematographer Mutz Greenbaum (later Max Greene), it is one of the
early examples of British film noir.[2] John Mills first appears in a London
nightclub singing a British type song. He then performs a James Cagney
dance routine before meeting his brother (Robert Newton) and engaging in
American slang. This film features different cultural associations which later
gangster films develop.

Like its American counterpart, the British gangster movie involves an
organized crime network. It differs from narratives dealing with individual
criminals such as *The Life of Charles Peace* (1905) and those concerning the
participation of formerly separate characters engaged in isolated criminal
activities. *The Good Die Young* (1954), *A Prize of Gold* (1954) and *The League of
Gentlemen* (1960) involve a group of individuals forming a criminal alliance
before they intend going their separate ways. Lewis Gilbert's *The Good Die
Young* involves a group of British (Stanley Baker) and Americans (Richard
Basehart, John Ireland) down on their luck recruited for a robbery planned
by ruthless playboy Rave (Laurence Harvey). In Mark Robson's *A Prize of
Gold* Richard Widmark's United States Air Force sergeant plans a robbery so
that he can help a German girl take a group of orphans to Brazil. With the
exception of Basil Dearden's *The League of Gentlemen*, thieves eventually fall
out. Although the participants in *Robbery* (1967) and *The Italian Job* (1969) may
have had criminal records and prior involvement in organized crime, it is
the distinctive nature of the heist itself rather than the presence of a criminal
underworld that characterizes these films.

Censorship certainly affected the lack of British gangster films in the
1930s. *The Noose* was based on a popular play by Richard Llewellyn (best
known for the novel *How Green Was My Valley*) which he also co-scripted. As
Robert Murphy notes, Llewellyn had submitted a similar script titled *Murder
in Soho* (having no relation to the 1938 Jack LaRue film) to the British Board of
Film Censors in 1937 which they promptly rejected.[3] Since the crime involved
vice organized by gang boss Luciani, a subject paralleling the Warner Bros.

David Niven as the title character in *Raffles*.

production *Marked Woman* (1937) involving the activities of Mafia boss Lucky Luciano, the content was regarded as too offensive for British sensibilities. Although gangs existed in England such as the race-track gangs that influenced Graham Greene's *Brighton Rock* (1938), officialdom usually engaged in denial.[4] This would soon change in the bleak conditions of post-war Britain. An "age of austerity" involving rationing and the black market influenced not only the development of British film noir but also the recognition of many problems in a society recovering from an economically devastating war.

As Brian McFarlane comments, once "Trevor Howard, icon of British decency in so many British war films as well as the gentlemanly lover in *Brief Encounter*, turns up as an unshaven non-hero fleeing from the law in Cavalcanti's *They Made Me a Fugitive* (1947), one knows that something has gone terribly wrong with life in postwar Britain."[5] Directed by a Brazilian acquainted with surrealism and documentary, *They Made Me a Fugitive* reveals a different type of society from that promoted in contemporary official discourses. Far from being a home fit for heroes and the socialist paradise envisaged in the film version of J. B. Priestley's *They Came to a City* (1944), post-war Britain was a grim world of rationing, food shortages, power failures, coupons, the bleak winter of 1947, the black market, and "spivs" eager to supply popular demands. Associated with the vaudeville performances of Arthur English, who appeared on stage wearing American zoot suits, fedora hat, Hollywood matinee-idol pencil-thin moustache, and huge, garishly colored tie, the "spiv" was generally recognizable by his flashy style of dress which advertised access to well-fitting clothes and consumer goods usually unavailable in an era of strict rationing. This system was designed to institute equality among the classes but it was more often than not broken by all social groups thanks to a flourishing post-war black market. Generally, the "spiv" operated as an individual engaging in both legal and illegal enterprises like George Cole's Arthur Daley in the later popular television series *Minder*.[6] As Robert Murphy notes, Stewart Granger's Ted Purvis in *Waterloo Road* (1945) is probably "British cinema's first spiv."[7] Attempts were made to model the "spiv" on Hollywood models, but they were generally not successful because the British actors were not as charismatic as their American counterparts. In John Harlow's *Appointment with Crime* (1946), William Hartnell's Leo Martin describes himself as a "spiv" in contrast to Robert Beatty's Canadian "copper." But he resembles more of a working-class, sociopathic petty criminal eager to avenge himself on treacherous upper-class crime bosses such as Raymond Lovell's Loman and Herbert Lom's art dealer more than he does those charismatic upwardly mobile figures represented by James Cagney and Edward G. Robinson.

Despite failing to make Hartnell a British James Cagney, *Appointment in Crime* contains significant transitional elements.[8] Lovell and Lom represent those upper-class crime bosses from 1930s crime films. Lom is involved in a gay relationship with his artist accomplice Noel (Alan Wheatley) who comforts him by suggesting "a little drinkie." Noel employs the Dickensian figure of Victor Woolf's Josiah Crackle to do his dirty work. Crackle also anticipates another Dickensian criminal: Hay Petrie's "The Barber" in *The Noose*. Petrie had earlier portrayed the evil Mr. Quilp in *The Old Curiosity Shop* (1934). However, the film's chief distinction lies in depicting the gangster as a proletarian threat. Although Martin has not been conscripted, he has served time and feels himself betrayed for keeping quiet. Loman angers him when he mentions that the injury to Martin's wrists have now made him useless. The comment contains obvious parallels to the situation of disabled ex-servicemen. Before justice prevails at the climax, Martin manages to avenge himself on establishment figures responsible for his condition.

They Made Me a Fugitive is one of the bleakest post-war crime films contradicting the new post-war utopian society promised by the recently elected Labour Government in 1945. Unlike American film noirs such as William Keighley's *The Street with No Name* (1948) which comments upon the emergence of a new type of gangster in the post-war era but never examines *why* this has happened, *They Made Me a Fugitive* reveals the causes. Margaret Butler notes problems veterans had with re-adjusting to a new world in which their old life of comradeship was now over and that films were more aware of this than the actual establishment. "As time passed, the ex-serviceman was portrayed as cynical, world-weary and alienated. He descended from an existence where responsibility towards others was critical to a life in which self-seeking individualism predominated."[9]

Clem Morgan (Trevor Howard) is an ex-R.A.F. serviceman and former P.O.W. He drifts into post-war alcoholic oblivion until black marketer "spiv" Narcy (Griffith Jones) recruits him into his organization. On their first meeting, Clem describes himself as bored and having suicidal tendencies. His girlfriend Ellen tells Narcy that Clem needs "another war." But he soon becomes involved in what Narcy terms "free enterprise," an activity Charles Barr sees as inimical to the wartime spirit recreated in *Passport to Pimlico* (1949).[10] Narcy sees Clem as an ideal recruit who will infuse a "bit of class" into his gang. He also wishes to contribute to the patriotic spirit of post-war society by offering "a job to an ex-serviceman" and parodies Labour policies. "Don't be so reactionary. This is the century of the common man." Like later ex-servicemen in *The Ship That Died of Shame* (1955), Clem participates in the black economy until commodities become more deadly. After Clem objects to drug smuggling, Narcy frames him for the murder of a policeman. Clem escapes from Dartmoor but he encounters an England little different from Narcy's world. A frustrated housewife attempts to make him murder her husband. A lorry driver complains about the state of the country and then offers Clem black market items. Inspector Rockliffe (Ballard Berkely) accepts a cigar from Fidgety Phil (Peter Bull) clearly obtained from the black market and reveals his own violent wartime background to Clem. "Don't try to get rough. I learned as many parlor tricks as you did during the war." Unlike most American film noirs, *They Made Me a Fugitive* ends on a pessimistic note. The dying Narcy refuses to clear him. Inspector Rockliffe refuses to deceive Clem by telling him that there is hope for his exoneration since it involves millions of forms to go to the Home Office "depending on fresh evidence." The arrested members of Narcy's gang are clearly not going to provide this.

Dancing with Crime (1947) is another British film noir featuring Bill Owen in a Cagney influenced "spiv" role of Dave Robinson, a former veteran now involved in organized crime. When we first see him, he is flashily dressed like an affluent American in contrast to his former Tobruk Army buddy Ted (Richard Attenborough) who refuses temptations to make easy money in a black market world involving "No checks, no coupons, no questions" in order to "retire for life." Like John Mills in *The Green Cockatoo*, Dave represents flashy American values. We first see him playing jazz on a piano in a nightclub. But his cocky working-class attitude is clearly resented by upper-class bosses Gregory (Barry Jones) and Paul Baker (Barry K. Barnes), who first attempt to cheat him out of his fair share from a robbery and then murder him. Although Dave occupies only the first fifteen minutes of the film, he is a memorable dynamic presence who can find an outlet for his energies only in the criminal underworld. As Detective-Sergeant Murray (Garry Marsh) later tells Ted, "Civvy street seems pretty strange for some of you boys." Ted's girlfriend, Joy (Sheila Sim), also remarks that things have got so expensive since 1939. Honest Ted saves up to get married and wears his military blouse (rather than a suit) for most of the film since he refuses to participate in the black market. In Harold Huth's *Night Beat* (1947) two ex-commandos, Don (Hector Ross) and Andy (Ronald Howard), also encounter difficulties readjusting to civilian life. Don's girlfriend Julie (Ann Crawford) works for black

Christine Norden as Jackie and Ronald Howard as Andy Kendall in *Night Beat.*

market racketeer and nightclub owner Felix (Maxwell Reed) in a job different
from her pre-war employment. "This one is twice the pay and half the work."
Both veterans join the police force but Andy drops out after his involvement
with femme fatale Jackie (Christine Norden). Like the upper-class P.C. 49
(Hugh Latimer) in *The Adventures of P.C. 49* (1949), Don may see the police
as "the only legitimate way to get action in peace time." Felix obtained his
nightclub after its legitimate owner was deported as an enemy alien during
World War II. He and Jackie often speak in American slang which marks
them as dangerous outsiders for traditional British culture. Had not Norden's
screen career dissipated in the early 1950s, she had the potential to become
Britain's own femme fatale. But at this period, society began to react against
women doing male occupations as in wartime and the very concept of the
independent "good time girl." *The Adventures of P.C. 49* (1949) also contains
British cinema's only image of a female gang leader in Pat Nye's Ma Brady
who runs a black market hi-jacking gang. She is, of course, working class.

Officer and gentleman types such as Clem Morgan and Bill Glennon
(David Farrar) in Basil Dearden's *Cage of Gold* (1950) present another threat
to the establishment since they come from its own ranks. Like Clem, Bill is
an ex-R.A.F. officer but he is more unredeemable. He deserts his wife Judy
(Jean Simmons) on their wedding night after impregnating her and becomes
a major threat to the community not only by his criminal activities but also
by his involvement with a French mistress.[11] In Lance Comfort's *Silent Dust*
(1948), Nigel Patrick's Simon Rawley is a dead hero who has a memorial
pavilion erected in his honor until he returns to life as a coward, deserter,
sadist, and murderer. Glennon and Rawley are represented as "bad eggs"
within an upper-class nest. Their deaths will restore the status quo. But other
films are more complicated.

Following the end of World War II, some 20,000 deserters were on the
loose in Britain. As Murphy comments, they were unable "to go into legitimate employment and without ration books, they were easily recruited to
serve the black market."[12] Richard Grey's *A Gunman Has Escaped* (1948) reflects
this situation. John Harvey's gangster kills a Soho jeweler during a robbery.
Although he has underworld connections, the other members of his team
do not. They are former servicemen who have drifted into a life of crime.
But not all deserters joined the underworld. Lawrence Huntington's *Man on
the Run* (1948) presents a more sympathetic picture. Peter Burdon (Derek
Farr) deserted the army after he was refused compassionate leave to go to his
dying wife's bedside. He then went on the run, paying high prices for fake
identity cards and rationing books as well as facing blackmail from former
comrades (Kenneth More), who find that the only trade they learned in the
Army—killing—is no longer suitable in the post-war world. Forced to flee to
London, Burdon finds himself accidentally involved in a robbery, which leads
to the exposure of his real identity. Despite having helped the police track the
criminals, he finds himself court-martialed and facing hard labor despite the
pleas of a police inspector (Edward Chapman) on his behalf. *Man on the Run* is
a rare plea for sympathetic treatment of deserters, who may be forced to drift

into crime. But this is probably due to the date of its appearance. As Murphy notes, later British films blame the downfall of veterans on "personal weakness rather than on an unjust or ungrateful society."[13]

Juvenile delinquency also characterized post-war society. Although the Boulting Brothers' *Brighton Rock* (1947) is a relatively faithful adaptation of Graham Greene's novel, the 1940s "spiv" suit worn by Richard Attenborough's Pinkie and his relative youth as a Brighton gang leader would evoke fears in the minds of the audience concerning negative foreign influences in British society such as the activities of American deserter Karl Hulton and his British girlfriend Elizabeth Jones who terrorized England in 1944 in the "Cleft Chin Murder" incident.[14] Delinquent young women were often described by the term "good time girl." They were usually regarded as being led astray and not really gangsters. In David MacDonald's *Good Time Girl* (1948), Jean Kent's Gwen Rawlings becomes the mistress of gangster Griffith Jones. She finally

Richard Attenborough as Pinkie in *Brighton Rock*.

encounters two American deserters modeled on Karl Hulton (Bonar Colleano and Hugh McDermott). Although her involvement in murder is accidental, she is sentenced to fifteen years in prison—a salutary warning to any young woman attracted to a life of crime and the "poisonous" influence of American culture. Basil Dearden's *The Blue Lamp* (1949) is even more censorious. Like Gwen Rawlings, Peggy Evans' young delinquent has fled from a dysfunctional home. But she runs into the arms of a new breed of post-war criminal, personified by Dirk Bogarde and Patric Doonan. The opening commentary in the film regards the three as dangerous "extreme cases" lacking "the code, experience and self-discipline of the professional thief—this sets them as a class apart, all the more dangerous because of their immaturity." Dirk Bogarde's Riley commits the unforgivable sin by shooting P.C. George Dixon (Jack Warner). Dixon was played by an actor who also portrayed black marketers and hardened criminals in *Hue and Cry* (1947) and *My Brother's Keeper* (1948). He later became permanently identified with the role in the long-running BBC TV series *Dixon of Dock Green* (1955–76). *The Blue Lamp* moves towards what Charles Barr describes as an "extraordinary climax" where police, stadium authorities, the anonymous crowd, *and* the underworld unite in bringing a young gangster to justice.[15] As in Lewis Gilbert's *Cosh Boy* (1952), patriarchal authority successfully routs the threat of a juvenile delinquent who has obviously seen too many Hollywood gangster films. Before going to jail, James Kenney's cosh boy receives a thrashing from his future stepfather while Riley is destined for hanging.

During a brief scene in Fritz Lang's *The Big Heat* (1953), John Crawford appears as a veteran helping Dave Bannion (Glenn Ford) against the underworld. He later became one of many American actors who played gangsters in British cinema most notably in Val Guest's *Hell Is a City* (1960). Set in Manchester, the film casts Crawford as local gangster Don Starling who has supposedly gone to school and fought in World War II alongside Stanley Baker's Inspector Martineau. But the film provides no explanation for his American accent. Before committing murder, Starling is a jewel thief and rapist but not really an underworld mobster. However, Crawford's persona and accent immediately evoke associations of the American threat to British institutions feared by George Orwell and other establishment critics. The casting of Crawford may have been unconscious on the part of Val Guest.[16] However, Crawford's associations as a criminal version of Mike Hammer, a character created by another "bad taste" novelist, Mickey Spillane, are clearly evident.

During the 1960s two films managed to transcend established clichés thanks to the innovative involvement of directors and screenwriters. Joseph Losey's *The Criminal* (1960) began life as a pastiche of a Warner Bros. prison movie until the director hired the playwright Alun Owen to rewrite the screenplay to reflect his observations on the British class system, the criminal underworld, and prisons.[17] Stanley Baker's Johnny Bannion was based on the Italian Soho gangster Albert Dimes, who had gained notoriety some years before by defeating his rival Jack Spot in a brutal knife fight. Owen retained the individualist character of Dimes but made Bannion an Irish Catholic gangster who finds himself at odds with the corporate systems of class, prison, and the underworld that echo each other. Sam Wanamaker's crime boss, Michael Carter, may represent another American influence in this film. But the whole emphasis falls upon the oppressive nature of a British social structure where incarcerated bosses such as Greek criminal Frank Saffron (Gregoire Aslan), Chief Warder Barrows (Patrick Magee), the prison governor (Noel Willman), and Carter are all part of the same corporate system. Originally, Donald Cammell intended *Performance* (1970) to feature Marlon Brando as an American gangster on the run and Mick Jagger as the reclusive pop star in whose house he stays.[18] A series of happy accidents led to the current version. Shot in 1968 but released two years later, it mixed a dying swinging London, popular mythology surrounding the Rolling Stones, and the contemporary star status of the Kray brothers into Cammell's Jorge Luis Borges–influenced vision of a gangster film. With James Fox playing an East End gangster on the run from his boss, Harry Flowers (Johnny Shannon), clearly modeled on Ronnie Kray, *Performance* represented a transgressive blurring of class, gender, and generic boundaries.[19] It displayed a unique personal vision that still demands "a very wide range of cultural references for its interpretation," tied "to the whole legacy of a generation."[20]

If *Performance* represented a dark swan song for a passing era, Mike Hodges *Get Carter* (1971) depicted a brutal world foreshadowing the ruthless advent of Thatcherism and its adverse effects on British culture. Like *They Made Me a Fugitive*, *The Criminal*, and *Performance*, the British gangster film is often at its best when it manages to escape its American influences by holding a mirror up to the actual nature of a corrupt British society in all its contemporary manifestations. Such films seldom date, as the justly celebrated status of *Get Carter* today demonstrates. Criticized on initial release for its "bad taste," the film has become a cult classic not only as a gangster film but also in its ruthless methods of demolishing those deceptive illusions affecting British society in the later 1960s. It revealed that that the rampant materialism, corruption, and violence characterizing the later Thatcher and Blair eras had already begun. As Steve Chibnall points out, after the arrest and conviction of the Kray and Richardson brothers, the spotlight fell upon the darker recesses of the criminal underworld. It also became evident that "swinging England" was really rotten to the core. *Get Carter* also reveals the business relationship between the London underworld, represented in the film by the Fletcher brothers (modeled on the Krays), and the northeast of England, already affected by local government corruption. Michael Caine's Jack Carter may embody the traditional gangster code by avenging family violations, but he is also a sick individual who finally perishes at the hands of the corporation.[21] Michael Tuchner's *Villain* (1971) is another neglected film representing the decline of the individual gangster. Richard Burton's Vic Dakin combines Reggie and Ronnie Kray in one psychopathic, homosexual persona. But although he has previously flourished in a culture in which blackmail and money can buy anything, his days will soon be numbered. His own hubris and paranoia, as well as witnesses who will not be intimidated, bring his reign to an end.

Bob Hoskins' Harold Shand in *The Long Good Friday* (1980) is an East End gangster availing himself of the materialist upward mobility the Thatcher era promised. He regards his firm as a "corporation" and wishes to court American interests in the same manner as the Krays and Margaret Thatcher.[22] However,

Harold finds his dream of moving from gangster to businessmen thwarted by the I.R.A. Appalled by uncontrollable violence described by Mafioso "Charlie" (Eddie Constantine) and his corporate lawyer as "a bad night in Vietnam" and "worse than Cuba," the Americans finally decide that they do not want "to deal with gangsters." Before eventually meeting his fate, Harold delivers a patriotic British attack on his former allies, whom he terms "wankers," and extols the vitality of the new European Economic Community as opposed to a failed American empire now encountering an "energy crisis." *The Long Good Friday* is another key British gangster film where the American influence now becomes redundant in a national community experiencing a new era of history and violence.[23]

Bob Hoskins as moddish gangster Harold Shand in *The Long Good Friday*.

The early 1990s engaged in a retrospective examination of British gangster culture as well as continuing the ongoing dialectical relationship between the two cultural influences affecting the genre. Set in *Get Carter*'s now-changing Newcastle, *Stormy Monday* (1987) dealt with tensions between American cultural imperialism personified by Tommy Lee Jones' Cosmo and feelings concerning national sovereignty in the figures of local nightclub owner Finney (Sting) and Cosmo's employee Brendan (Sean Bean). Although the casting of Americans Jones and Melanie Griffith evoked the era of the 1950s, the tensions in the film developed those within *The Long Good Friday*. Hollywood influence also returned to the British gangster film. Danny Cannon's aptly titled *The Young Americans* (1993) featured Harvey Keitel as drug enforcement agent John Harris on the trail of Carl Frazier (Viggo Mortensen) engaged in his own dark version of cultural imperialism by Americanizing young Brits into the violent ways of urban criminality. These British "young Americans" become a threat to traditional villains as well as to an establishment world represented by *The Blue Lamp* (which Harris sees as an in-flight movie). These worlds are now gone for ever.

Peter Medak's *The Krays* (1990) and *Let Him Have It* (1991) examined two well-known historical examples from British gangster history. But the director also blamed the British establishment in the same manner he did in *The Ruling Class* (1972) which ironically equated the British class structure with the murderous activities of Jack the Ripper! *The Krays* documents its own version of "The Terrible Twins" but one scene evocatively suggests that the traumatic World War II era, evoked by Churchill as "Their Finest Hour," had disastrous effects on both men and women in the post-war era. It also indirectly echoes George Orwell's comments about the popularity of the violent *No Orchids for Miss Blandish* during the Blitz. As Mary Desjardins shows, the film also operates as a "doppelganger" of a vicious Thatcherite society.[24] By contrast, *Let Him Have It* deals with one of the most scandalous cases involving the British establishment which only recently gave a young victim of British justice a posthumous pardon. The film details the petty criminal activities of two youths influenced by Hollywood movies in a repressive era of 1950s Britain most recently documented by Mike Leigh in *Vera Drake* (2004). Although Christopher Craig kills a policeman when he misinterprets the cry of Derek Bentley (Christopher Eccleston) to hand over his gun, it is Bentley who faces trial and execution because he is old enough to hang, despite the fact that he did not fire the fatal shot. This ruthless depiction of the British judicial system echoes an era when the establishment became tired of treating deserters and criminals as victims of society. The film also reflects the later Thatcher ideology of regarding any threat to the official order as evil and incapable of reform. Thatcher's political victory in 1979 led to the "Victorian

Gary and Martin Kemp as the sword-wielding gangster twins Reggie and Ronald Kray in *The Krays*.

values" return of a different form of social Darwinism, which in turn led to more violent gangster movies. Paul McGuigan's *Gangster No. 1* (2000) and the films of Guy Ritchie represent two such examples. Ritchie's brand of violent gangster films is merely just "a bit of a laugh with the lads," according to his comments on the *Snatch* DVD featurette. *Gangster No. 1* features a historical montage beginning with the image of Margaret Thatcher and showing Paul Bettany's change from "young gangster" to Malcolm McDowell's "old gangster." However, Antonia Bird's *Face* (1997) more significantly reflected "the 1990s loss of political faith and belief in the possibility of change, the defeat of collective values by individualism and greed and the widespread nihilism and cynicism that it sees as resulting from these losses."[25] Featuring Robert Carlyle as a disillusioned ex-Communist turned gangster, the film depicted tensions between contaminating influences of post-Thatcherism and "New Labour" and the faint hope of continuing struggle represented by his mother and girlfriend.

Hollywood influences still challenge British gangster films. Despite national "laddish" tones in Guy Ritchie gangster films such as *Lock, Stock and Two Smoking Barrels* (1998), his work is nothing less than a derivative mixture

Michael Caine as the title character in *Get Carter*.

of Tarantino-meets-new-British-eccentricity. But unlike in the Ealing Studios comedies, eccentricity is a new, violent threat represented by the new breed of young gangster "animals" Michael Caine refers to in his DVD audio commentary on *Get Carter*. Some recent films do attempt to pioneer different patterns of meaning. They aim at a more original aesthetic generic style and also critique the corrupt nature of British society far more thoroughly than anything depicted in Ritchie's shallow, postmodernist manner. This is particularly true of the later work of director Mike Hodges, who follows the modernist trend represented by Joseph Losey's *The Criminal* to depict the dark world of contemporary British society via alternative cinematic styles. Both *Croupier* (1998) and *I'll Sleep When I Die* (2004) employ a deliberate minimalist style and emphasize character rather than violent action to draw the viewer into considering the damaging effects of materialism and violence within a changed British society.

Although not actually a gangster film, *Croupier* links the gradual dehumanization of aspiring writer Jack Manfred (Clive Owen) to the devious machinations of a manipulative father and unseen criminal underworld. Jack's moral collapse also results from his own willing complicity in the corruption surrounding him. Like *Get Carter*, *I'll Sleep When I Die* is another contemporary revenge tragedy. But Hodges succinctly depicts the damaging psychological effects of the power mechanisms contained in the underworld community. Clive Owen's Will Graham suffers a nervous breakdown and retreats into the rural wilderness of Wales until the suicide of his brother Davey (Jonathan Rhys Meyers) calls him back to London. When he returns, Will not only confronts his past associates, who wish him to return to his former life as a violent gang leader, but also again those damaging features of power and violence that caused his original breakdown. The film suggests that dark psychological mechanisms involving power, dominance, perverse sexuality, and self-loathing drove him away in the first place. When Will learns the reasons behind the death of his brother and confronts the person responsible, he returns to his former self. But he also will experience his own type of personal damnation.

Jonathan Glazer's *Sexy Beast* (2000) imaginatively merges gangster and horror genres in a insightful manner. The demonic figure of Don Logan (Ben Kingsley) forces retired gangster Gal (Ray Winstone) to participate in a robbery organized by Teddy Bass (Ian McShane), referred to as "Mr. Black Magic." Although it follows the structure of a heist movie, *Sexy Beast*

Ben Kingsley as Don Logan in *Sexy Beast.*

also contains dark supernatural overtones involving the themes of power and sexuality found in several other gangster films. Teddy is a satanic figure who resents the affluent and crooked figure of the aristocratic banker Harry (James Fox), echoing Leo Martin's class hatred in *Appointment with Crime* (1949). Logan is Harry's demonic servant, who will haunt Gal from beyond the grave. *Sexy Beast* also conflates images of a demonic Logan and Teddy in one scene and intimates that Teddy can read Gal's mind concerning Logan's absence in London.

Sexy Beast and Hodges' two films represent new possibilities for original developments in British gangster films that transcend previous influences. Only time will tell. The social dimensions will always be crucial for any major achievements within this genre. Although Malcolm Needs' *Charlie* (2004) falls far short of the innovative approaches brought to the genre by Joseph Losey, Peter Medak, and Mike Hodges, it does relate gangster culture to its wider social context. Depicting the rise and fall of notorious 1960s criminal Charlie Richardson (Luke Goss), who combined middle-class business dealings with brutal torture of any villain who offended him, the film depicts a dark relationship between the South African ruling elite and the British criminal underworld. Unfortunately, the film is unable to develop the rich potentials of its historical background preferring instead to borrow anachronistic techniques associated with the films of Guy Ritchie as well as referring to earlier films when the Kray Brothers, George Cornell, and Jack McVitie all make enigmatic cameo appearances. Unfortunately, Charlie never deals with the clash between the Richardson brothers and the Krays during this period nor does it develop suggestions concerning the British government's fear of organized crime at this time that led to savage life sentences imposed on the Krays.[26] By contrast, Charlie Richardson receives a prison term of eighteen years after which he is free to enjoy his current life as a respectable businessman commuting between London and South Africa. *Charlie* thus combines the stylistic traits of Guy Ritchie films with nostalgic references to British gangster life in the 1960s but ultimately becomes flawed in its conception. Unlike *Villain*, which suggestively hinted at the dark relationship between the Krays and the British ruling elite, *Charlie* can never develop the rich implications of its material, especially occurring in one scene involving Winnie Mandela's collaboration with the South African security establishment, to reveal why the British establishment savagely turned upon the Richardsons and the Krays in the 1960s. Hopefully, other British gangster films will later develop revealing implications concerning the British establishment and organized crime in future years.

Notes

1. James C. Robertson notes that during the 1930s the British Board of Film Censorship's "chief fear was that the American gangster dramas would spawn equivalents set in Britain, even though no large-scale British organized crime on the American model seems to have existed." See Robertson, "The Censors

and British Gangland, 1913–1990," in *British Crime Cinema*, ed. Steve Chibnall and Robert Murphy (London: Routledge, 1999), 16. Robert Murphy also notes that a powerful police force was able to overcome the old "rough house" gangs which had terrorized the poorer districts of Victorian cities, but the pre-war era saw the emergence of "more sophisticated criminal gangs such as the Darby Sabini mob and the Messina Brothers, who paid protection money to the police out of the fat profits they made from illegal gambling and organized prostitution. Little of this found its way into British films." See Murphy, "Riff-Raff: British Cinema and the Underworld," in *All Our Yesterdays: 90 Years of British Cinema*, ed. Charles Barr (London: British Film Institute, 1986), 286.

2. See Tony Williams, "British Film Noir," in *Film Noir Reader 2*, ed. Alain Silver and James Ursini (New York: Limelight Editions, 1999), 243–70.

3. Robert Murphy, *Realism and Tinsel: Cinema and Society in Britain, 1939–49* (London: Routledge, 1989), 161. Murphy earlier noted that the British writer Edgar Wallace became fascinated with the American crime scene. His 1930 gangster play *On the Spot* ran for a year in London's West End and his novel *When the Gangs Came to London* aroused the hostility of the British Board of Film Censors. Unlike Agatha Christie, Dorothy L. Sayers, and P. D. James, Wallace's crime novels were condemned for "bad taste." But they were popular at the time and led to later American-influenced crime fiction by Peter Cheyney and James Hadley Chase. Also, the American school of naturalist, realist, and hardboiled crime fiction influenced working-class novelists such as James Hanley, George Garrett, and Jim Phelan. See "Riff-Raff," 286–78. The British proletarian gangster film and the recent work of Guy Ritchie may also represent derivations of this tradition. For the British underworld film's constant struggle with the conventions of the Hollywood gangster film, see Charlotte Brunsdon, "Space in the British Crime Film," in *British Crime Cinema*, 148–59; Steve Chibnall, *Get Carter* (London: I. B. Tauris, 2003), 8.

4. For an informative study of the British underworld see Robert Murphy, *Smash and Grab: Gangsters in the London Underworld, 1920–1960* (London: Faber & Faber, 1993). British gangsters were also active in race-track and protection rackets during the 1930s. See also R. Samuel, *East End Underworld* (London: Routledge, 1981); James Morrison, *Gangland: London's Underworld* (London: Warner Books, 1993); *Frankie* Fraser, *Mad Frank* (London: Warner Books, 1995); Wensley Clarkson, *Hit 'em Hard: Jack Spot, King of the Underworld* (London: Harper/Collins, 2002); and Steve Chibnall, *Brighton Rock* (London: I. B. Tauris, 2005), 15–18.

5. See Brian McFarlane, "Losing the Peace: Some British Films of Postwar Adjustment," in *Screening the Past*, ed. Tony Barta (New York: Praeger, 1998), 93. The term "Age of Austerity" derives from a key description of the post-war era which forms the title of a highly informative edited collection of essays. See *The Age of Austerity*, ed. Philip French and Michael Sissons (Oxford: Oxford University Press, 1986). For further information on circumstances in the post-war era influencing crime films, see Murphy, *British Cinema and the Second World War* (London: Continuum, 2000), 179–80; Margaret Butler, *Film and Community in Britain and France: From* La règle du jeu *to* Room at the Top (London: I. B. Tauris, 2004), 98–99.

6. For the role of the "spiv" in post-war British society see David Hughes, "The Spivs," in *Age of Austerity*, 87–105. As a veteran actor who began his career in 1940s British cinema, George Cole's performance as the well-dressed con man Arthur Daley is an obvious incarnation of the "spiv" in later years. Shown on Thames television during 1979-1985, followed by feature length specials such as *Minder on the Orient Express* (1985) and *Minder: An Officer and a Car Salesman* (1988), the series was produced by Euston Films which was also responsible for many innovative crime series during the 1970s such as *Special Branch* (1973–74), *The Sweeney* (1975–78), *Out* (1978), and the female gangster series *Widows* (1983). See Manuel Alvarado, *Made for Television: Euston Films Limited* (London: British Film Institute, 1985). The intriguing relationship between film and television versions of the underworld is outside the scope of this study but mention may be made of the Granada television series *Big Breadwinner Hog* (1969) and BBC 1's *Gangsters* (1976, 1978), the latter dealing with British Asian Gangsters in Birmingham. Derived from Philip Martin's 1975 contribution to Play for Today, the second series suffered due to its creator's self-indulgence. After dying as gangster boss Rawlinson in the pilot episode, Martin returned to life in the second series playing a different character and engaging in derivative Godardian avant-garde techniques. Despite this, the series was the first to feature a Pakistani narcotics agent played by Ahmed Khalil as hero.

7. See Murphy, 148.

8. See Chibnall and Murphy, *British Crime Cinema*, 8, 81. During this period, attempts were made to launch Hartnell into major stardom following his role as the tough sergeant in Carol Reed's *The Way Ahead* (1944). Although the actor distinguished himself as the leading actor in *The Agitator, Strawberry Roan, and Murder in Reverse* (all 1945), *Appointment with Crime* did not receive adequate promotion, despite one reviewer's championship of an actor he believed "had all the toughness worthy of his being developed into a British Cagney or Bogart." See Jessica Carney, *Who's There? The Life and Career of William Hartnell* (London: Virgin Books, 1996), 101. From then on, Hartnell played supporting roles in *Temptation Harbour, Odd Man Out, Brighton Rock* (all 1947) and *Escape* (1948) before turning to character roles and eventually becoming BBC's first Dr. Who in the early 1960s.

9. Butler, 99. See also Murphy, *Realism and Tinsel*, 153–57, 168, and *British Cinema*, 186–88, for the reactions of establishment critics such as Arthur Vesselo and C. A. Lejeune toward films such as *They Made Me a Fugitive*. For the comments made in 1948 by the president of the Board of Trade, Harold Wilson, condemning gangster movies and calling for "more films which genuinely show our way of life," see Chibnall and Murphy, 1.

10. See Charles Barr, *Ealing Studios* (London: Cameron & Tayleur, 1977), 97–107. Narcy is the criminal counterpart to Garland in this Ealing comedy.

11. See Murphy, *British Cinema*, 186–90; Butler, 148–49; and Murphy, "Cage of Gold," in *Liberal Directions: Basil Dearden and British Postwar Film Culture* (Wiltshire: Flicks Books, 1997), 154–61.

12. Murphy, *British Cinema*, 180.

13. Ibid., 189.

14. See Murphy, *Realism and Tinsel*, 178. The story was later depicted in *Chicago Joe and the Showgirl* (1985), starring Kiefer Sutherland and Emily Watson. George

Orwell referred to the case in his celebrated essay "Decline of the English Murder," comparing it to the more genteel versions of British crimes. By contrast, he described the incident as the result of "the anonymous life of the dance halls and the false values of the American film" (127). Referring to Elizabeth Jones as "an English girl who had become partly Americanized," Orwell believed "the whole meaningless story, with its atmosphere of dance-halls, movie palaces, cheap perfume, false names and stolen cards belongs essentially to a war period" (128). However, films such as *Appointment with Crime*, *Dancing with Crime*, and *Night Beat* reveal that this was also a post-war phenomenon. Despite Orwell's puritanical tone, he does intuitively reveal many intuitive components of the 1940s British gangster film. See "Decline of the English Murder," in *The Collected Essays, Journalism and Letters of George Orwell*, ed. Sonia Orwell and Ian Angus, vol. 4, *In Front of Your Nose* (London: Penguin Books, 1978), 124–28. He also notes that *No Orchids for Miss Blandish* enjoyed its greatest success during the Battle of Britain and the Blitz. Orwell also recognizes that Edgar Wallace represented the transition between genteel detective fiction and the worship of brute force he sees in the Americanized crime fiction of writers such as Peter Cheyney and James Hadley Chase. See Orwell, "Raffles and Miss Blandish," in *The Collected Essays, Journalism and Letters of George Orwell*, ed. Sonia Orwell and Ian Angus, vol. 3, *As I Please* (London: Penguin Books, 1971), 246–60. Mrs. Kray's monologue in the final part of *The Krays* (1990) intuitively links the Blitz shown on her television and the violent activities of her terrible twins in the brutal murder of Jack McVitie (Tom Bell).

15. Barr, 85.

16. On the audio commentary of the 2002 DVD version of *Hell Is a City*, Guest mentions that Crawford was "a good character actor" resident in England at the time "so I used him." Guest mentions his indebtedness to Jules Dassin's *Naked City* (1948). Dassin also shot *Night and the City* (1950) in England with a predominantly American cast but featuring Herbert Lom in one of his many contemporary villainous roles as Greek gangster Kristo. The Czech-born actor later remarked, "I was a foreigner and in all English eyes, all foreigners are villains." He also played a White Russian businessman who becomes involved in the underworld in *The Frightened City* (1961). See "Herbert Lom," in *An Autobiography of British Cinema*, ed. Brian McFarlane (London: Methuen, 1997), 377. Crawford also appeared in Wolf Rilla's *Piccadilly Third Stop* (1960) as a non-gangster, but thuggish, American who becomes involved with Terence Morgan's playboy in an embassy heist. A year before, in *The Shakedown*, Morgan played an Italian pimp, Augie, involved in a pornography racket (aided by Bill Owen!) and competing with a Maltese vice boss (played by Harry H. Corbett) obviously modeled on the Messina brothers, like Sugiani in *The Noose* (1948). In Vernon Sewell's *Soho Incident* (1956), Martin Benson co-stars as betting-shop gangster Rico with Canadian Lee Patterson and American Faith Domergue. Sydney Tafler's various roles as a Jewish gangster in *The Scarlet Thread* (1951) and *Wide Boy* (1952) also deserve further attention.

17. See Michel Ciment, *Conversations with Losey* (London: Methuen, 1985), 184; Andrew Spicer, "The Emergence of the British Tough Guy: Stanly Baker, Masculinity, and the Crime Thriller," in *British Crime Cinema*, 88–89. Losey had already explored the British class system in *Blind Date* (1959), his first collaboration with Stanley Baker. The reappearance of *Blind Date*'s snobbish cop

John Van Eyssen as an upper-class prisoner in *The Criminal* may represent Losey's Marxist sense of humor.

18. See Colin McCabe, *Performance* (London: BFI, 1998), 20.

19. For the role of Johnny Shannon and the mythological significance of East End gangsters Ronnie and Reggie Kray, see McCabe, 40–41; Reg and Ron Kray with Fred Dineage, *Our Story* (London: Pam Books, 1988); John Pearson, *The Profession of Violence: The Rise and Fall of the Kray Twins*, new ed. (London: HarperCollins, 1995). Photographed by David Bailey, the Kray brothers were as much a part of the so-called swinging sixties as their pop-star counterparts. Johnny Shannon went on to play many gangsters in British film and television. He appears briefly as one of the heavy mob from Newcastle in *Villain* (1971)

20. McCabe, 73.

21. Michael Caine and Mike Hodges discuss these issues in the audio commentary of the 2000 DVD release of *Get Carter*. See also "Mike Hodges Discusses *Get Carter* with the NFT Audience, 23 September 1997"; Robert Murphy, "A Revenger's Tragedy: *Get Carter*," *British Crime Cinema*, 117–22, 123–33; Chibnall, *Get Carter*.

22. See Chibnall, *Get Carter*, 43–44.

23. See also John Hill, "Allegorising the Nation: British Gangster Films of the 1980s," in *British Crime Cinema*, 160–71.

24. See Mary Desjardins, "Free from the Apron Strings: Representations of Mothers in the Maternal British State," in *Fires Were Started: British Cinema and Thatcherism* (Minneapolis: University of Minnesota Press, 1993), 130–44.

25. Claire Monk, "From Underworld to Underclass," in *British Crime Cinema*, 182.

26. See Pearson, 215–18.

"This Gun for Hire depicts psychologically volatile criminal anti-hero, Raven (Alan Ladd)."

Reforming Hollywood Gangsters: Crime and Morality from Populism to Patriotism

Sheri Chinen Biesen

When a Hollywood mogul makes a horrific discovery—the severed bloodied head of his favorite horse in bed with him in Francis Ford Coppola's sweeping epic underworld saga *The Godfather*—it was a day of reckoning with 1940s celluloid gangsters. In March 1943 when real life gangsters known as Al Capone's "gangland successors" were indicted and notorious syndicate leader Frank Nitti was found shot dead along a railroad track—a "suicide"—it seemed to be the stuff of gangster film lore.[1] Hollywood gangster pictures were changing by the 1940s. By the time Robert Warshow wrote his influential crime film essay, "The Gangster as Tragic Hero," in 1948, Hollywood gangsters had taken on a variety of cinematic permutations. Unlike Warshow's existential anti-hero, some of the earliest silent-era American gangster protagonists were not nearly so tragic. D. W. Griffith's *The Musketeers of Pig Alley* (1912), for example, was recognized for its documentary-style realism based on newspaper accounts of actual street crime and portrayed a scrappy, charming, playfully cynical gangster hero with a wicked sense of humor and keen survival skills who cunningly outwits the law. Greater pathos, a more brooding tone, sensational violence, and trademark atmospheric urban milieu evolved in gangster films of the Prohibition era and Depression years. By the late 1930s and early 1940s crime pictures had responded to changes in Production Code censorship and federal regulation. Screen gangsters were adapted and "reformed" in new and innovative ways. Hollywood reformulated gangster anti-heroes in a fascinating array of experimental crime films as World War II broke out and filmmakers responded to social, cultural, and industrial changes in the film industry in a new era.

Inspired by classic Hollywood gangster films of the early 1930s such as *Little Caesar*, *Public Enemy*, and *Scarface* these crime pictures featured volatile, unstable crime heroes who inhabited Hollywood's cinematic incarnation of a menacing American city. The gangster genre powerfully critiqued the American dream, raised issues of social class, and showcased the ultimately tragic fate of its self-destructive crime anti-hero. Warshow described the screen gangster's futile quest for upward mobility in these Hollywood crime films: "for the gangster there is only the city, not the real city, but that

dangerous and sad city of the imagination . . . which is the modern world."
Trapped in the alluring, deceptive, and harsh climate of the urban jungle,
the gangster's struggle for success by means of crime and violence ends in his
demise, terminating his pursuit of the American dream: "In the deeper layers
of the modern consciousness . . . every attempt to succeed is an act of aggression, leaving one alone and guilty and defenseless among enemies: one is
punished for success. This is our intolerable dilemma: that failure is a kind of
death and success is evil and dangerous, is—ultimately—impossible."[2] This
moral retribution was, of course, encouraged and reinforced by Hollywood's
Production Code censorship and would ultimately lead to a remarkable transformation of the gangster genre itself.

Drawn from sensational tales of real street crime in 1920s and 1930s
America, early crime films—often depicting the gangster as an urban Robin
Hood—coincided with Prohibition (1919–33), when the public regarded
gangsters with some ambivalence. Even in the permissive censorship climate of Pre-Code Hollywood, these gangster pictures were often considered
exceedingly censorable as they conveyed tough hard-hitting verisimilitude.
Throughout American popular culture—radio dramas, hardboiled crime
novels, magazine serials, short stories, comics, dime novels, and gangster
films—artists and hacks alike portrayed "real life" Jazz Age crime with gritty
realism that relied on tabloid and pulp fiction sensation. Like pulp stories
and contemporary newsreels on actual gangsters, crime films showed sadistic
violence (toward women, even animals) with a distinctive fast-paced style and
shadowy "look" to convey its seedy atmosphere of speakeasies, cabarets, jazz,
and booze.

Gangster pictures enjoyed popularity during the Great Depression—in a
bleak era when many felt helpless, impotent, and incapable of effecting any
economic or social change, and the system seemed on the verge of collapse.
Hollywood anti-heroes took action, tried to beat the system, did something
with their lot in life and seemed to articulate cultural issues intrinsically
embedded in American society. Tracing the criminal's poor beginnings, ill-
gotten gains, rising prominence, and inevitable demise, these tough male-
oriented films dealt with working-class struggles, portraying the common
man or ethnic immigrant experience seeking success or acculturation in
mainstream America. Set on the streets of a magnetic, corrupt American city,
crime pictures featured visual iconography—guns, car chases, cops, crooks,
nightclubs, swanky apartments, urbane clothes—documenting the gangster's
wealth and power, and peripheral women's roles (mothers, sisters or loose
"moll" girlfriends). As Warshow observes, the gangster genre critiques the
American dream to suggest it is no dream, but rather an unpredictable urban
nightmare of futility that dooms the gangster criminal.

Known for its corrupt setting and distinct visual style, these films tack-
led real life crime issues and critiqued social problems in a brooding, seedy
urban environment. In particular, the Hollywood gangster genre developed
an innovative visual style at Paramount and Warner Bros. At Paramount,
director Josef von Sternberg, a sensuous pictorialist, collaborated with UFA

alumnus Hans Dreier on silent-era films like the influential gangster classic *Underworld* (1927, written by former reporter Ben Hecht), *The Drag Net* (1928, now "lost"), and *The Docks of New York* (1928). Sternberg's atmospheric crime pictures included what Rudolph Arnheim called "uncannily lewd detail" as a prostitute "lustfully strokes" a sailor's "naked arm with indecent tattoo marks all over it, as he ripples the muscles on it for her amusement. . . . This woman sees nothing of the man but power, nudity, muscle."[3] In the lax censorship climate of pre-Code Hollywood, suggestive visual innuendo heightened rough, raw, working-class sex and crime "in the shadows"—achieved without dialogue. Stylized mise-en-scène metaphorically captured a forbidden, sordid milieu.

In the sound era, crime films gained immense sensory appeal and enormous popularity—reproducing sirens, screams, and gunfire, while relying on tough, urban dialogue. Warner Bros. became known for its gangster pictures such as Mervin Leroy's *Little Caesar* (1930) starring Edward G. Robinson and William Wellman's *Public Enemy* (1931) starring James Cagney, and for realistic "social problem" films like LeRoy's powerful *I Am a Fugitive from a Chain Gang* (1932). Warner Bros. production chief Darryl Zanuck championed hard-edged social realism and in January 1931 explained, "Prohibition did not cause crime, gang violence, or a corrupt environment, but rather Prohibition merely served to bring crime before the public eye."[4] Referring to *Public Enemy* and linking Warners' successful gangster cycle to Dashiell Hammett's hardboiled detective narrative, *The Maltese Falcon*, Zanuck considered crime films and pulp fiction exemplary social critique of a growing urban American crime problem that did not therefore violate the Production Code. *Scarface* (1932), directed by Howard Hawks, adapted by Hecht, produced by Howard Hughes and released through United Artists, starred Paul Muni as the quintessential gangster anti-hero. Its lethal finale (one of several endings shot to appease censors) shows Muni gunned down by authorities—riddled with about 20 machine gun bullets—falling dead on a shadowy rain-soaked city street. *Scarface* was controversial to the Hays Office because it sympathetically portrayed crime and criminals, and suggested an incestuous relationship between the gangster (Muni) and his sister (Ann Dvorak). Negotiations with censors delayed the 1931 production an entire year before a revised ending was finally released in 1932.

Many crime films like *Public Enemy*, *I Am a Fugitive from a Chain Gang* and *Heroes for Sale* (1933) depicted World War I veterans scarred by the brutality of war returning to a Prohibition (and, later, Depression) era America where violence, social injustice, and corruption is rampant and basic day-to-day survival is a challenge. Gangster films tapped into social and cultural changes taking place in the United States between World War I and World War II influenced by 1920s and 1930s American popular culture, newsreels, social-realist theater, and working-class fiction and dealt with the dashed hopes and meager existence that so many endured during the Great Depression. The crime film genre embraced these working-class themes, which flourished during a time when many were down on their luck and survived because they were willing to do the humblest work. Championing individuals, the working-class hero—or anti-hero like the gangster, ex-con, tough everyman turning to crime just to survive, or the street-wise hardboiled detective—was a man who lived by his wits and challenged corrupt institutions in a hard-scrabble world. Emerging from the Depression, many ordinary people surviving the 1930s could identify with such working-class populist themes.

Despite the popularity of crime in American popular culture, mid-1930s film censorship banned Hollywood from adapting hardboiled crime stories and diluted the sexual content and excessive violence in crime pictures. While tough guy heroes and corrupt urban settings dominated screens in early gangster films, once the Hollywood motion picture industry established the Production Code Administration (PCA) and began enforcing censorship by late 1934, censors were more inclined to discourage promiscuity, brutality, and romantic portrayals of gangsters involved in "unsavory" illegal activity (such as labor racketeering and prostitution).

After *Public Enemy* made Cagney a star as a gangster in the pre-Code era, Warner Bros. recast him as crime-fighting FBI enforcer in *G-Men* (1935); gangster-turned-cop Robinson went undercover to break up the mob opposite tough-guy Humphrey Bogart in *Bullets or Ballots* (1936). Responding to a changing censorial, cultural, and production climate, the gangster/crime genre was often transformed into social problem "message" pictures. Crime

Cagney "recast . . . as crime-fighting FBI enforcer in *G-Men*," with Margaret Lindsay as Kay.

themes were featured in social realist films like Fritz Lang's *Fury* (1936), *You Only Live Once* (1937, starring Henry Fonda as an ex-con futilely trying and failing to "go straight"), William Wyler's *Dead End* (1937, where Bogart plays an unsympathetic gangster who corrupts street kids), Michael Curtiz's *Angels with Dirty Faces* (1938, starring repeat offender ex-con and former gangster Cagney redeeming himself by dying like a coward while going to the electric chair to show the "Dead End" kids that his tough gangster was not admirable, revealing he had a conscience to his best friend-turned-priest Pat O'Brien) and Anatole Litvak's *Confessions of a Nazi Spy* (1939, gangsters-turned-espionage hunt, based on an actual spy case).

In *You Only Live Once* the gangster criminal is a kind of Depression-era tragic hero trying to survive who becomes an ex-con struggling to make it on the up and up; he doesn't get a break and instead goes bad, flees, is on the run, then is framed, gets caught, goes back to jail, busts out, and in paranoid desperation kills his friend the prison priest who tries to help him—even after he's been exonerated and can go free. When he runs off with his pregnant

Angels with Dirty Faces: Laurie (Anne Sheridan) watches a discussion between mobster Rocky Sullivan (Cagney) and his childhood friend Father Connelly (Pat O'Brien).

sweetheart and the couple robs just to stay alive, the crime narrative evolves into a bizarre Bonnie and Clyde tale. In other films, World War I veterans adapted their combat skills and turned to a violent life of crime as in *They Gave Him a Gun* (1937) and Raoul Walsh's *The Roaring Twenties* (1939), starring Cagney and real-life World War I veteran Bogart. In *The Roaring Twenties*, Cagney's combat veteran and former gangster meets his demise and is sadly described: "he used to be a big shot." The famous line seems to suggest Warner Bros.' swan song bidding farewell to the studio's renowned gangster genre and notorious crime star. It is also no coincidence that Edward G. Robinson was no longer playing a gangster but a federal agent hunting subversive totalitarian enemies in another Warners' film, *Confessions of a Nazi Spy*, that same year. Warners "declared war" on Germany recasting gangster Robinson as FBI G-Man ferreting out Nazi spies in America in Litvak's topical *Confessions of a Nazi Spy* as World War II broke out in Europe.

Confessions of a Nazi Spy was influential in challenging Production Code censorship of political propaganda in favor of publicizing the growing Nazi menace. Indeed, America's renowned Depression-era "menace to society" was no longer the gangster. "The gangster pictures performed a great service. . . . They aroused the public's consciousness of a rank and reckless state of affairs as nothing else could have done. They were, I believe, largely responsible for the repeal of prohibition and consequent abolition of the big mobs," famed *Little Caesar* star Robinson explained in 1939, adding: "Today we are in a war much more serious than we were in then. We've got to fight to preserve our rights. The world is faced with the menace of gangsters who are much more dangerous than any we have ever known. And there's no reason why the motion pictures shouldn't be used to combat them, the same as they formerly were. I tell you, the motion pictures could dwarf any League of Nations ever devised by man if they were allowed to use their full power. Films and the radio are the most immediate and powerful forces in the world for informing men and shaping public opinion." Bosley Crowther of the *New York Times* opined, "Robinson has no desire to reinvest old ghosts. He is through with gangster pictures, as most every one except the C-producers are. He would like to go on now and tackle the more fearsome ogres which confront the world. And although there is no immediate prospect of the Warners permitting him to appear in an outright anti-fascist picture, he would if he had his way. And—who knows?—'Little Caesar' was always a tough guy with the opposition." In a revealing piece, "Little Caesar Waits His Chance," Crowthers observed: "It has been just exactly eight years since 'Little Caesar' blazed his chilling way across half the motion picture screens in this country and thereby earned for Edward G. Robinson not only a lasting sobriquet but also a reputation as one of the toughest guys in the world. His subsequent screen impersonations were not fashioned to detract from this fame, and it soon became also embarrassing for Mr. Robinson to appear abroad. People instinctively suspected him and cautiously steered clear lest that inevitable hail of bullets should suddenly rattle from a swiftly passing car . . . what was then a terrifying and sinister social problem—the menace of gang rule—

The Roaring Twenties: Cagney and Bogart in "Warner Bros.' swan song to the studio's renowned gangster genre."

has since been effectively submerged while greater problems have risen to challenge man. Al Capone has been stored away in prison and the old mobs have either been liquidated or retired. Only 'Little Caesar' is as great as he ever was, and—ably represented by his mouthpiece, Mr. R.—pleads guilty to a desire to change his territory and go on fighting."[5]

The atmospheric milieu of the gangster genre was conveyed in moody visuals in experimental crime films like Robert Florey's *Daughter of Shanghai* (1938), designed by Hans Dreier and Robert Odell, starring sleuth Anna May Wong, *The Face Behind the Mask* (1941), co-scripted by Paul Jarrico, starring Peter Lorre as an immigrant-turned-disfigured crime boss, and Sternberg's *The Shanghai Gesture* (1941), starring Gene Tierney. Low-budget "B" crime films included German emigré John Brahm's *Rio* (1939), *Let Us Live* (1939), recasting Fonda as an innocent wrong man framed by circumstances on death row, and Charles Vidor's *Blind Alley* (1939), starring hoodlum Chester Morris, moll Dvorak, and psychology professor Ralph Bellamy. In *Blind Alley*, gangster Chester Morris' psychotic criminal mind, corrupted by the city, is revealed in vivid style through reverse-exposure images of his recurring nightmares. MGM originally tried to adapt the play on which it was based, *Smoke Screen*, in 1935, but censors nixed the project and told the studio to "dismiss it entirely from further consideration" because its gangster hero was "thoroughly unacceptable," insisting the story violated the Code "so bad . . . that it was irrevocably beyond its pale" especially "the *suicide* of the gangster, as a means of escape from the consequences of his crimes."[6] Because it depicted crime, suicide, and psychotic insanity, *Blind Alley* was shelved for several years until Columbia filmed it in 1939, when the PCA advised against displaying weapons or showing crime details and warned that British censors would reject "any material dealing with insane characters and the use of an asylum as a background."[7]

By 1939 Crowther announced in the *New York Times* "sensational news— Mr. Robinson revealed that Hitler himself will appear in his . . . next picture, 'Confessions of a Nazi Spy.' This will be a story about Nazi spy activities in America with Mr. Robinson as a G-Man who nabs them; and actual newsreel shots of Hitler will be thrown on a process screen, with the characters of the picture in the foreground, to give the illusion of actual proximity. Der Fuehrer might even be invited to pay dues to the Screen Actors Guild. After that, Mr. Robinson will make a picture which is now called 'Brother Orchid.' It is the story of an ex-gangster who becomes a resident in a monastery where all the brothers engage in floriculture. When an outside gangster begins to cut in on the humble brothers' modest trade in flowers, Mr. Robinson—or 'Brother Orchid'—goes forth to handle the situation. A lively farce."[8]

Beyond the social realist variations on the gangster genre seen in such films as *You Only Live Once, Dead End, Angels with Dirty Faces, Let Us Live, Blind Alley,* and *Out of the Fog,* several films like Warners' *Brother Orchid, Blues in the Night,* and Columbia's *The Face Behind the Mask* are fascinating examples of genre experimentation and reveal Hollywood's effort by studios to reformulate gangster films. A notable Warner crime picture, Lloyd Bacon's *Brother*

Orchid (1940), parodied Warners' gangster cycle when hoodlum crime boss and rival Humphrey Bogart nearly kills off mobster and former crime boss Edward G. Robinson who barely escapes death, then is revived and reformed into a monk at the serene Monastery of the Little Brothers of the Flowers. (Little Caesar's conversion from a kingpin to a divine pacifist—resembling Friar Tuck—combines gangster-comedy and social drama, seemingly accommodating PCA piety.) While *Brother Orchid* begins by paying homage to the gangster genre and casting some of Warner Bros.' famed crime stars (Robinson, Bogart), it soon descends into parody and lighthearted comedy tempered by social realism that seems to also draw on the studio's successful period adventure pictures with Donald Crisp as the monk heading the monastery and literally reforming the gangster.

Another Warner crime film, Raoul Walsh's *High Sierra* (1941) transposed the gangster genre from the urban jungle to the parched California high desert of the Sierra Nevada mountains, stunningly shot on location amid the rugged terrain, steep cliffs, and bright sands in broad daylight, showcasing Bogart in his first lead. It fittingly seemed to write the epitaph for the gangster genre heralding in a new kind of crime film and presenting a new image of screen masculinity, Bogart's sentimental hero, rugged as his rough surroundings but with a heart, an iconic image of the 1940s. Not only was tough

Parodying the Warner Bros. gangster cycle: Edward G. Robinson as Johnny Sarto and Allen Jenkins as Willie "the Knife" Corson in *Brother Orchid*.

guy gangster Bogart reformed into a hardboiled dick in *The Maltese Falcon*, associate producer Henry Blanke (a UFA alumnus who worked as production manager on Lang's *Metropolis*) dealt more directly with the social ill of the gangster as cultural menace in experimental crime pictures like Anatole Litvak's *Out of the Fog* (1941), a moody racketeer yarn with glistening water, black nights, and abundant fog shot by James Wong Howe, starring hoodlum John Garfield—after Bogart was rejected—with Ida Lupino. Another experimental film that reformulated gangsters was Litvak's *Blues in the Night* (1941, also produced by Blanke), a shadowy rain-drenched "gangster musical" jazz *noir* filmed by Ernest Haller, starring heavies Lloyd Nolan and Howard Da Silva, Richard Whorf, Priscilla Lane, Betty Field, Jack Carson, "Dead End" kid Billy Hallop, and a young Elia Kazan.

Blues in the Night fuses the gangster crime genre with populist melodrama and a brooding noir jazz musical that seems to include more elements of crime, psychological instability, and even stylized conventions of the horror genre than any typical upbeat musical. In many ways *Blues in the Night*'s reformulated gangster film is a forerunner of early noir crime films. Gangsters turned ex-cons are ambiguous criminal antagonists who befriend and betray friends. Everyone is double-dealing everyone else: a gangster's moll turns murderous femme fatale, and a self-destructive jazz musician starts brawls, goes to jail, and ends up going insane in an asylum after tangling with the femme fatale, who guns down her ex-con criminal-gangster former lover and is killed by a dubious disabled suitor who drives her off a cliff in a thundering rain-soaked night. *Blues in the Night* seemed steeped in the milieu and streetwise social realist critique of the gangster genre, and Warners even tried to tap into the success of the big band era by originally considering starring Duke Ellington and his jazz orchestra in the film, and ultimately casting Jimmy Lunceford and his big band. While the dark brooding film had its foot firmly planted in the social plight of the Depression era, however, its gritty stylized class critique fell flat when it opened on December 12, 1941, just five days after the Pearl Harbor attack. The film's reception context had been completely transformed as a nation grappled with the collective shock of wartime. Nonetheless, the film ends as it begins, as the cast of *Blues in the Night* continued to ride the rails like a band of drifters, a gang of scrappy Depression-era hobos traveling in circles playing music in a boxcar.

Another fascinating example of genre experimentation is Robert Florey's *The Face Behind the Mask*. Although it does not start out at all resembling a gangster picture, it soon takes on a far more brooding tone and bleak narrative path. Lorre's newly arrived immigrant to America exudes innocence and touching naiveté early on in the film; he merely wants to begin a new life in a new land of opportunity. The New York setting becomes an urban jungle, and the film itself seems to invoke conventions of the horror genre. A raging fire breaks out that destroys the young man's apartment building, nearly killing and permanently disfiguring the protagonist. His future is also scarred by his horrifying appearance, which denies him employment and ultimately contributes to his literally becoming a monster and turning to a violent life of crime to survive. The picture evolves into a very unconventional gangster film: Lorre rises and metamorphoses into a ruthless, vicious crime boss until his inevitable demise, where he redeems himself in an existential finale. Removed from the East Coast urban jungle and aware that he cannot control his own self-destructive actions or those of his men, he chooses to strand himself and the other criminals to die in the parched sands of the southwest desert. The final setting seems to anticipate the stark barren terrain of later male-oriented war pictures like another Columbia film, *Sahara* (1943), starring Bogart on loan from Warner Bros. following his fame in *The Maltese Falcon* and *Casablanca*, and his transition from hardboiled crime hero to private dick and reluctant patriot.

The tough, scrappy independence, isolation, and irreverence of hardboiled gangster anti-heroes were ideal pre-war Depression-era figures readily adaptable to more politically-charged protagonists in topical espionage pictures with the escalation of World War II. Political propaganda potboilers and espionage thrillers by emigrés like Alfred Hitchcock, Anatole Litvak, and Fritz Lang were influential prototypes for a violent, paranoid crime trend in wartime—particularly vis-à-vis psychological crime films, federal censorship, and reformed gangsters. Bogart's image of tormented tough guy, former crime hero, and model of 1940s masculinity, related not only to hardboiled crime material like *The Maltese Falcon*, but also to reworking the gangster cycle as warfare neared.

Screen gangsters and their unethical, often illegal, activity were considered "un-American," banned as unpatriotic, and censored by the government's Office of Censorship in the World War II years.[9] Previously the industry's self-regulation by PCA censors discouraged crime, violence, sex, adultery, and political content in Hollywood films. Yet, the federal Office of Censorship encouraged political content, showing war-related crimes and violence to stiffen patriotic resolve. This shift in regulatory principles produced an odd pairing of espionage themes and "disguised" gangster heroes; crime films supporting World War II (and evading PCA censorship with "realistic" war-related crime material) appeared even before America entered the conflict. Espionage narratives established graphic patriotic crime, gratuitous violence, often sexual violence, gaining censorship approval while ushering in paranoid criminal psychology and unstable anti-heroes (as in gangster cycles) in a corrupt setting.

In retooling to support America's war effort, as censors tolerated growing screen violence but viewed gangsters as "anti-American" and potential fodder for Nazi propaganda, Hollywood transformed criminals into more patriotic, guilt-ridden, unstable, and self-destructive crime protagonists—a variation on mobsters, combating espionage, sabotage, "fifth columnists" and evading censorship.[10] Filmmakers repackaged gangster-crime conventions to conform with regulatory restrictions. Personal sacrifice, sense of duty, and love of America redeemed criminals, adapted as "disguised" gangsters, reformed for the national good to support the cause. Many gangster crime films seemed to morph into espionage narratives with "patriotic" crime, paranoid psychology, subjective point-of-view, and a tough masculine psyche simulating combat. Instead of loose gangster's molls, spy crime thrillers included mysterious undercover operatives—multifaceted counterespionage career women—in a world of intrigue with brooding visual style. As World War II neared, Hollywood's gangsters and psychological crime anti-heroes conveyed a "crisis of masculinity" with strong, independent—often working—femme "threats" to patriotic male crime figures. Crime anti-heroes were reformed into patriotic gangsters in cynical espionage crime films.

This Gun for Hire depicts psychologically volatile criminal anti-hero, Raven (Alan Ladd), who spurns women, relishes cold-blooded murder and illegal activities, in a film that straddled Hollywood's wartime transition. Paramount purchased Graham Greene's 1936 crime novel *A Gun for Sale* (retitled *This Gun for Hire* in the U.S.) for $12,000 in 1941.[11] While Greene's book was set during the interwar 1930s in Britain, the studio changed its setting to wartime 1940s California, then redirected its unsavory plot to instead support America's Allied war effort by adding topical themes about Japanese chemical bombs against the U.S. Raven is reformed from a hit man being hunted by police to an unlikely patriotic martyr battling the enemy. W. R. Burnett (who wrote *Little Caesar, High Sierra*, and *Asphalt Jungle* and co-scripted *Scarface*) and Albert Maltz adapted the investigative thriller that centered on an assassin's violent quest for revenge, murdering criminals—even shooting and slapping women—after being double-crossed.

Raven meets a beautiful woman, Ellen (Veronica Lake), recruited by a senator to serve as an undercover agent and kidnapped by a lewd crime operative, Bates (Laird Cregar), a subversive "fifth columnist" conspiring to sell poison gas and chemical weapons formulas to the Axis enemy in Japan to bomb American cities. Tough guy Raven foils the plot, saves the alluring agent, but is still gunned down by authorities (and her police detective fiancé, Robert Preston). Greene was not thrilled by the film's topical subplot involving a "female conjurer working for the FBI" which had nothing to do with his novel; yet, on the brink of World War II Paramount was sold with the premise of Greene's book—where protagonist Raven murders a government minister and instigates a war.[12] In the novel, Raven was scarred by a harelip, which fueled his sociopathy. The topicality of *This Gun for Hire* successfully won over Production Code censors as the U.S. entered the global conflict and enabled Paramount to justify a violent story and patriotic criminal with a war-related sabotage plot to attack America.

Adapting the gangster genre for wartime, *This Gun for Hire* reformed gangsters and criminal assassins. Crime now related directly to World War II and accentuated tracking domestic sabotage and chemical warfare by a foreign enemy. The film's criminal milieu gets darker and darker as events progress to unravel more insidious details about the conflict and espionage, visually conveying anxiety over fifth columnists via its shrouded mise-en-scène as it goes on. Rather than the social critique of "The World Is Yours" as the gangster lies shot dead by police on a dark, wet city street at the finale of *Scarface*, gangster crime, imagery, and thematics in *This Gun for Hire* are adapted to serve wartime, becoming blacker as the narrative unfolds to reveal domestic corruption aiding the evil Axis powers and subverting the American way, coinciding with the film's narrative shift from isolationism to greater involvement in the war effort, and the risky domestic consequences of ignoring such a call to military action. In a nearly pitch-black scene Raven and his kidnapped hostage hide out in an abandoned shack from the authorities. Raven's tormented killer remained a study in contradictions. Paranoid and on the run, despite his disturbed psychology, criminal acts, and brutality, he is ultimately not the perceived threat or agent of danger. Guilt and remorse haunt him, authorities punish him, and he patriotically aids the country. World War II redeems Raven's reformed assassin.

Like earlier gangster pictures, in the tradition of "padding" scripts with salacious material—or simply to make the movie more interesting and sell tickets—Paramount added sexualized violence to the film. Before Raven executes a traitorous old man's lover—firing through a door—for witnessing his murder, censors wanted the woman's attire changed from a negligee to a dress to reduce the suggestion of illicit sex. (Paramount instead dressed her in a satiny black dress to suggest a gangster's "moll.") They also wanted to minimize the suggestive delivery of the old man's line "my—er, wife" when introducing his mistress. The attractive young woman in a slinky black dress whom Raven murders was originally an old lady in Greene's novel.

The studio also added a new character not in the book. The saboteur's tough-guy assistant, Tommy (played by Marc Lawrence, frequently called upon to play hoodlums, as in *Blind Alley* and *Dillinger*), is a fairly obvious gangster figure—"disguised" to avoid censorship and comply with pro-American political propaganda. Though dressed as a chauffeur, bellboy, or manservant wearing a prim uniform, Tommy talks like a gangster, using recognizable slang dialogue and exhibiting violent behavior—especially toward women. In a job suggestive of a mob hit, Tommy is to kill the kidnapped Ellen and dump her body into the reservoir. Relishing his task, Tommy praises his own scheme as "a work of art—up she'll bob without a mark on her . . . a suicide. Beautiful!"[13]

The film's March–June 1942 publicity drew on gangster crime conventions and capitalized on the war in a big way. In reforming gangsters, Paramount promoted patriotic crime with a distinctively masculine psychological ethos and "combat mentality" that vicariously tapped into the war effort. Publicity referred to Alan Ladd as "Trigger Man," "Wary with a woman . . . Tender with a kitten . . . But a terror with a trigger! He's the 'KISS and KILL' Ladd they're all talking about!" Ads read: "A Lone Wolf . . . dynamite with a girl or a gun!," "Killer without a Conscience! Lover without a Heart?," and "Kiss Her . . . or Kill Her! Which will he do?" The pressbook exclaimed Lake "Finds a Guy too Tough to Take!" and "Don's Boy's Garb for Role . . . quite fashionable in Hollywood these days."[14] *Motion Picture Herald* called *This Gun for Hire* a "gangster film with patriotic twist," noting the story's topical "interest" added a sense of wartime immediacy.

Three months into World War II, America's mobilization effort was in full throttle. *Motion Picture Daily* outlined Paramount's formula for success: "Director Frank Tuttle skillfully blended a blood-and-thunder spy melodrama with psychopathic overtones" and Lake and Ladd to produce "taut action and suspense." Ladd's unstable mercenary anti-hero is described as a "psychopathic killer" hiring out his "services to the highest bidder," yet "tormented by nightmares of a killing which he committed as a youth, he derives satisfaction during the day from the sheer lust of murder."[15] *Look*'s April 1942 *This Gun for Hire* review plays up the military angle, calling Ladd a "professional killer" hired by "enemy agents" to retrieve the secret formula for producing "poison gas" in a California factory and murder treasonous informants. It exploited the film's "Japanese plot to shower deadly chemical bombs on American cities" with a "cold-blooded lone gunman" who aids a night club singer working for the government to combat a saboteur.

On May 29, Philip Hartung of *Commonwealth* noted the story's "cold violence" was "natural cinema material." Espionage was at the heart of *Life*'s June 22, 1942 *This Gun for Hire* feature. Primed for action, Ladd's Raven is repeatedly called "the killer" who (alluding to the draft for military combat) "receives orders by mail to do a little job of murder and tests out his only friend: his automatic." Tapping into home-front anxieties and paranoia about espionage, sabotage, and chemical warfare, the piece even shows killer Ladd disguised in a gas mask to pull off his ultimate coup against subversives in the chemical plant. Like Rosie the Riveter and female factory workers, Lake's photo is surprisingly androgynous, cloaked in male garb and fedora in which she "hides her hair under a man's hat."[16] Reflecting shifting gender roles during World War II, both male and female characters in *This Gun for Hire* are complex, unpredictable, defying stereotypes, even duplicitous.

As Warner Bros. reformed gangsters and adapted crime heavies, Bogart became a rising star, and after *High Sierra* he gained fame in the wake of *The Maltese Falcon* as private detective Sam Spade. After Pearl Harbor, Warners wanted another *Maltese Falcon*, but like Paramount preferred patriotic themes, as in espionage crime films like *This Gun for Hire* with more topical narrative propaganda. Bogart's hardboiled screen persona was adapted, becoming an anti-Nazi gambler opposite Peter Lorre and Conrad Veidt in *All Through the Night* (1942), followed by *Across the Pacific* and *Casablanca*. Warners publicity called Bogart, "the male star that says excitement," and capitalized on the film's hardboiled patriotism: "the brand newest twist in big-time action—gangsters vs. Gestapo—*and it is welcome now!*"[17] Ultimately, the sociopathic patriot assassin seen in Greene's topical hit man in *This Gun for Hire* showed how Hollywood's wartime climate reformed, and in many ways reinvented, the gangster genre in a fascinating convergence of PCA censorship, propaganda, and the emergence of reformulated gangsters as genres changed in response to the industry's process of mobilization. While real-life gangsters and Capone aides were indicted for racketeering in wartime, tough guy screen criminals and reformed gangsters evolved and became a staple of noir crime anti-heroes in the war years and in the aftermath of World War II.[18]

"Both male and female characters in *This Gun for Hire* are complex, unpredictable, defying stereotypes, even duplicitous": Alan Ladd with Veronica Lake as Ellen.

VERONICA LAKE · ROBERT PRESTON

THIS GUN FOR HIRE

LAIRD CREGAR · ALAN LADD

Screen Play by Albert Maltz and W. R. Burnett · · · Based on the Novel by Graham Greene
DIRECTED BY FRANK TUTTLE · · · A PARAMOUNT PICTURE

Notes

1. "8 Capone's Aides Indicted in Fraud; One Kills Himself," *New York Times*, March 20, 1943.

2. Robert Warshow, "The Gangster as Tragic Hero," *Partisan Review*, February 1948; reprinted in *The Immediate Experience* (1970).

3. Rudolph Arnheim, quoted in Marilyn Yaquinto, *Pump 'Em Full of Lead: A Look at Gangsters on Film* (New York: Twayne, 1998), 20. Many crime films and other genres like the horror picture benefited from creative emigrés from overseas and the aesthetic cross-fertilization between Germany and the United States as a result of ParUfaMet, and later the war in Germany, as expatriate talent flocked to Hollywood.

4. Darryl Zanuck, letter to Jason Joy, MPAA/MPPDA, MHL, January 6, 1931.

5. Bosley Crowther, "Little Caesar Waits His Chance," *New York Times*, January 22, 1939.

6. *Blind Alley* memos, MPAA/MPPDA, MHL, 1935–39.

7. Ibid.

8. Crowther, "Little Caesar," *New York Times*, January 22, 1939.

9. Fred Stanley, "Hollywood Peeks Into the Future," *New York Times*, February 21, 1943.

10. Ibid.

11. Budget and story files for *This Gun for Hire*, PCPF, MHL, 1941.

12. PCPF, MHL, 1941; Gene D. Phillips, "Graham Greene: The Films of His Fiction," excerpt, Los Angeles County Museum of Art Program Notes, MHL, September 18, 1980.

13. Breen, letters to Luigi Luraschi, MPAA/MPPDA, MHL, October 23–30 – November 7, 1941.

14. Paramount Press Book for *This Gun For Hire*, USC PBC, 1942. MPAA/MPPDA, MHL, January 29, 1942.

15. Edward Greif, "*This Gun for Hire*," *Motion Picture Daily*, March 17, 1942; "*This Gun for Hire*," *Motion Picture Herald*, March 21, 1942.

16. Review of *This Gun for Hire*, *Look*, April 12, 1942; Philip Hartung, "*This Gun for Hire*," *Commonwealth*, May 29, 1942; "Movie of the Week: *This Gun for Hire*, Ladd and Lake Make an Unusual Melodrama," *Life*, June 22, 1942, 48, 50, 53. *This Gun for Hire* solidified Ladd and Lake's stardom and spun off sequel pairings of the couple in adaptations of Dashiell Hammett's *The Glass Key* (1942) and Raymond Chandler's *The Blue Dahlia* (1946) at Paramount.

17. WB Press Book for *All Through the Night*, WBA, USC, 1942.

18. Sheri Chinen Biesen, *Blackout: World War II and the Origins of Film Noir* (Baltimore, Md.: Johns Hopkins University Press, 2005).

The cigar-chomping Faye Dunaway as Bonnie in *Bonnie and Clyde*.

A New Kind of Girl for a New Kind of World

Dominique Mainon

The shift from silent to talking films in the late 1920s and early 1930s brought far greater means of artistic expression to articulate society's discontent. Rakish urban rebel characters personified many of the traits of ambitious immigrants and began to stamp a new mark of glamour upon the ethnic anti-hero that even the suffocating Production Code would be unable to truly stifle.

Within the blurred lines of an increasingly chaotic caste system and the repressive order of Prohibition, a new type of morally adventurous and morally confused heroine entered the fray, casting her female gaze upon the anti-hero. She is the wanton nightclub performer, the bored heiress, a greedy hustler, or a rebellious Daddy's girl gone bad. She is an integral part of the image of a gangster even up to present day, an objectified measurement of power, a bridge to incorporation with higher society, but also a ticking time bomb that could bring down an entire operation.

Gangster movies are rarely complete without the requisite "moll" making her appearance. The term "moll" is derived from the name Molly, which is a nickname for Mary. Having long been used as reference to prostitutes, ("johns" being their customers), some even say the expression draws back to famous alleged prostitute of the bible, Mary Magdalene, although in the U.S. the name was used more often as reference to women who are simply attracted to criminals and gangsters. Fur-clad high society molls drawn to the subversive elements of gang life, as well as hardened gun molls with their classic sweaters and berets, who were ruthless as the gangsters themselves, made numerous appearances in early cinema.

The cliché montage scenes of a gangster's rise to success almost inevitably include a scene of the gangster hero being fitted with a brand new suit, as he attempts to rewrite his rough past as a thug and gain entrance to a new economic and social class. A new woman will make an appearance after the new suit, serving as evidence of his newfound power. She may even be the trigger for his seduction into gangland, having admired mob bosses for their access to these exceptional women. The society moll could be his bridge to further success and higher reputation, his tool, his decoy—and at the very end—usually his downfall.

"It ain't polite, but it's what you want," Clark Gable's character "Ace" Wilfong tells Jan Ashe (Norma Shearer), the headstrong daughter of a high society attorney in *A Free Soul* (1931). Ace embodies the erotic fantasy object of a rebellious female's desire, which unfolds as the underworld character Ace resorts to force to regain control of Jan. She inadvertently pits her bad-boy lover Ace against Leslie Howard's more gentle and impotent character, her fiancé Dwight Winthrop. These two men will be famously juxtaposed with a free-spirited woman again eight years later as Rhett Butler and Ashley Wilkes in the epic *Gone with the Wind*.

Many titles during the early 1930s really didn't strictly stick to the traditional gangster territory of rise-and-fall themes of urban crime, intergang warfare, social/economic unrest, and corruption. The gangster figure breached the realms of society melodrama and in many cases even embodied the definition of the standard "chick film" for a time, in female-centered narratives. In addition, films being assessed by the Studio Relations Committee in 1931 (a group that advised and assisted studios in producing films that would meet code requirements) were often modified in ways that would allow them to bend the rules and avoid distribution problems. Films that came under the classification of "Gangster Theme" were likely to cause many problems with censors. However, there were distinctions between a "gangster film" and films that simply dealt with crime as a source of drama that were not so specifically defined and articulated, other than to make clear that it was unacceptable to depict crime without clearly showing adverse consequences and the reign of law and order in the end. Reign over the libido was a different matter to be dealt with more forcefully later.

As it is, a number of early films exist which have not been thoroughly studied as "gangster films"; however they clearly crossed the lines into gang territory and the development of the gangster persona. They also clearly crossed

Clark Gable as mobster Ace Wilfong, defended by lawyer Stephen Ashe (Lionel Barrymore, left), and in a three-way liaison with Ashe's daughter Jan (Norma Shearer, right) and her fiancé Winthrop (Leslie Howard).

the traditional gangster film will bring crime, the fallen woman, and society melodrama into the genre of film noir.

The high society heiress character offers a potent and eroticized power exchange that is not based solely on sex, but more on the intoxicating rise in status and reputation that the woman represents, which in turn brings a sexual charge to the relationship. To the gangster she could be his ticket into a world that was still above him, despite whatever wealth he might achieve. To the socialite, the rough gangster could be an outlet for unfulfilled erotic desires and an opportunity to enjoy the degradation of the act and/or the sexual power it granted. The risk to her that comes with indulging in deviant desires is the threat of social ostracism, becoming a "marked woman," which intensifies the danger and excitement of the union. To the lower-class or middle-class domesticated woman, entrance into the gangster world might increase her socioeconomic status, an option not available to her through more conventional means. In either case, after the stock market crash of 1929 confronted the privileged classes with a new, far less stable reality, it was clear how quickly changes in status do occur.

Going back to *A Free Soul*, Jan Ashe's compulsive sexual desires for Ace Wilfong are alluded to by her father as a "sickness" or infirmity, similar to his own alcoholism. We witness her gender confusion and unconcealed desire triggered into action during a telling scene when she first meets Ace in her father's office. Though the love triangle at the outset appears to be between the seductive gangster Ace Wilfong and her ineffective fiancé, Dwight Winthrop, the true clash for Jan is between Ace and her father, the famous attorney Stephen Ashe (Lionel Barrymore). The film boldly presents their close father-daughter relationship in an almost incestuous light during the opening scene, which shows an older man eating breakfast in a hotel room while a woman gets dressed in the bathroom. The two chat and joke casually, the woman calling him by his first name and requesting that he bring her an article of clothing to put on as she stands waiting in her undergarments. The audience is led to believe the two are casual lovers, when in fact it is soon revealed that they are instead father and daughter, both outgoing, adventurous types who like to live life to the fullest.

When the tall, dark, and handsome Ace later makes his first appearance, Jan casually exposes her naïve sense of gender equality, brought about by the unique relationship with her father. She does not exhibit any customary female coyness, but rather gazes directly at Ace with the intensity of a traditional male gaze. She sizes him up in a brazenly objectifying manner, and then immediately acts to stake a claim on him by suggesting they trade ties for luck before he goes into court. Esther Sonnet explains the significance of the scene in *Mob Culture: Hidden Histories of the American Gangster Film.*

> That Jan and Ace exchange ties when they first meet confirms that she is unaware at this stage, as Freud would insist of all female pregenital sexuality, that she does not own the phallus, but *acts as if she does.* In other words, Jan believes she is her father's equal in possessing the symbol of male

authority, the phallus/tie, which keeps the father/daughter relation in a state that is undifferentiated by gender inequality. Offering her tie to Ace is a gesture grounded in understanding that she is his equal, too, and in the belief that it is hers to offer.

The tie-exchange may not only place her as his equal, but in combination with her strong female gaze, it is as if she is symbolically placing her collar about his neck and claiming him. The pathway to her later domination is in place. "You're the first really exciting man I have ever met," she tells him later, after being shot at while driving in his car.

These sort of courtship and exchange rituals are repeated in many gangster/crime/melodrama films to follow, often showing an alternative exchange of vows that strays from the traditional marital relationship. In the 1949 film *Gun Crazy* (a.k.a. *Deadly is the Female*) a similar scene takes place when the two main characters, Annie (Peggy Cummins) and Bart (John Dall), first meet and participate in a shooting contest together. Once again there is a distinct phallic symbol utilized in the shared fascination with guns, and strong female gaze of desire from Annie to Bart, which is even set at a distinct angle to show her above him, gazing down. The intensity of the exchange in the gun contest is much more of a binding ritual than their actual marriage vows are later, which is never even shown on screen. Because Annie doesn't have the

Bart (John Dall) and Annie Laurie Starr (Peggy Cummins), gun fetishists and criminals.

cash to pay up on her bet when she loses, she gives her ring to him as a prize for winning the contest, although Bart gives it back to her again, thereby symbolically completing the ceremony.

In *A Free Soul*, the dashing and virile gangster Ace, despite having his choice of women, becomes fixated upon Jan Ashe and determines to marry her. But Jan won't marry either him or her upright fiancé Dwight. "I don't want to get married yet," she proclaims sadly. "I don't want life to settle down around me like a pan of sourdough."

For Ace though, her refusals and humiliation only seem to arouse him more, eroding his thinly veiled disguise of manners and exposing the coarseness and violence of his true nature. "I never was as nuts about you as I am right now," he tells her when she refuses him. Lying back on the couch, she gazes up at him, clearly enjoying his torment and her own power over him. The forbidden element of their affair eroticizes the union even more, and her willingness to continue to see him on a regular basis acts as a cycle of tease and denial that breaks him down further in frustration.

Like most female characters, Jan will definitely be punished in the end for her indulgences, and order restored. Ace gets out of control, threatening Jan with social and economic ruin, and Dwight must nobly and quietly kill him in order to save Jan's reputation from being sullied. The father dies of alcoholism (punishment for his own sins after his impassioned court appearance where he takes blame for the union between Ace and Jan, for not "protecting" her, as a father should). But the film still stands as unique for reasons that Esther Sonnet also clearly outlines:

> *A Free Soul* is a highly distinctive narrative because it so explicitly represents the psychical foundations of hegemonic heterosexual female identity. Although the conventionality of its conclusion cannot be contested, the film does challenge the prevalent view within film studies that Hollywood cinema offers only Oedipal dramas from the point of view of the male spectator. The metonymic use of the gangster figure is a potent indication of unconscious pleasures addressed to the *female* spectator.

The roughhouse charms of Ace as an objectified male become more of a tool for the female character to develop further. Rather than finding depth in Ace's character as the film progresses, we find him increasingly shallow as he is reduced more into simply a means of coercion for Jan to split from her father and enter adult sexuality. Clark Gable will serve well in these type of shady character roles again and again, especially later on when his "coercion" puts a rare smile on Scarlett O'Hara's face the next morning, solidifying his already swooning female fan base.

The bored, uninspired, and adventure-seeking socialite makes many appearances in early gangster-related films such as *Dance, Fools, Dance* (1931). This one starts with another risqué father-daughter sequence. Joan Crawford plays the part of Bonnie Jordan, a rebellious socialite who, in order to combat boredom at a party on a ship, resorts to stripping to her underclothes and encouraging the guests to jump off the boat with her and go swimming. Disobeying her father's orders to return on board immediately, instead she swims to shore. However, the harsh reality of the stock market crash jolts her out of her easy lifestyle, and with her father out of the picture due to a fatal heart attack, her "protection" is removed and she is forced into work as a news reporter. Based on the gangland killings at the time, the story shifts to Bonnie's experience working undercover as a cheap moll in the underworld where she performs expert tap dancing and gains the lewd attentions of yet another Clark Gable gangster character, a mob boss named Jake Luva.

Once again we see the father-daughter relationship split, and the positioning of two completely opposite male characters—Jake Luva, the mob boss, and her brother Rodney, a weak-willed man who allows himself to be lured into working for Jake selling bootleg alcohol. Joan Crawford, who so often played women facing severe economic and moral challenges, again embodies a role that presents a sexually liberated modern woman resisting the chains of marriage. She refuses the rather loveless, forced proposal of her boyfriend Bob, advising "I like my freedom as much as you do, Bob, and I intend to keep it."

The "commercialization of stimulation" (E. W. Burgess) of the era provided a rampant breeding ground for the development of transgressive and deviant sexuality. Even prior to the 1930s a number of films were produced that perpetuated this feminized cycle of melodramas, including those with semi-gangster themes. Titles such as *Ladies of the Mob* and *Romance of the Underworld* depicted women "forced" into a life of sin by circumstance, which is really an ideal role for many female-centered fantasies. It allows female audiences to furtively enjoy relating to the subversive pleasures in which the heroines of these films partake without being bound by any moral guilt for doing so. The heroines pushed moral boundaries by voluntarily giving themselves over to sinful activities—but all in the name of a noble cause, of course,

Bonnie Jordan (Joan Crawford), "working undercover as a cheap moll"
and muzzled by Jake Luva (Clark Gable).

such as the undercover reporter trying to solve a crime or attempting to help a loved one who got in too deep with the wrong people.

On the surface these roles could appear belittling to women, but the advent of box-office smash hits such as *The Public Enemy* (1931) that exemplified the true misogynist tradition of gangster films brought these romantic gangster-involved melodramas pretty much to a halt. The masochistic male roles that might appeal to female audiences are overpowered by scenes such the one in *The Public Enemy* depicting James Cagney's male character, Tom Powers, commanding his girlfriend Kitty (Mae Clark) to bring him a beer.

Tom: Ain't you got a drink in the house?

Kitty: Well, not before breakfast, dear.

Tom: I didn't ask you for any lip. I asked you if you had a drink.

In a shockingly crude and telling act, Tom grabs a grapefruit and mashes it into her face. And that signals the end of their union. However, Tom immediately picks up a new girlfriend while cruising in his roadster, the flashy and emotionally elusive blonde Gwen Allen, played by Jean Harlow. Even though she retains some level of power over Tom initially by denying him, the moment she indulges her own somewhat strange needs and attraction, she is cut off and abandoned. Gwen shows maternal tendencies toward him in her desire, commanding him as a mother might, yet serving him. Tom reacts to most situations in rather infantile ways in general. His emotional responses are instantaneous. He becomes impatient with Gwen's elusive nature and chooses to leave.

Gwen: Where are you going?

Tom: I wanna blow.

Gwen: You're a spoiled boy, Tommy. You want things and you're not content until you get them. Well, maybe I'm spoiled too. Maybe I feel that way, too. But you're not running away from me. Come here. *(She points and orders him to sit on her chaise. She removes his hat, tosses it away, and then sits on his lap)* Now, you stay put, if you know what that means. Oh, my bashful boy. *(Mothering him, she holds him to her breast)* You are different, Tommy, very different. And I've discovered it isn't only a difference in manner and outward appearances, it's a difference in basic character. The men I know, and I've known dozens of them, oh, they're so nice, so polished, so considerate. Most women like that type. I guess they're afraid of the other kind. I thought I was, too. But you're so strong. You don't give. You take. Oh, Tommy, I could love you to death. *(She kisses him and they fall into each other's arms.)*

This passionate moment is interrupted by an intrusion, and Tom is informed that "Nails" Nathan has been accidentally thrown by his horse in the park and killed. Tom walks out, never to come back, leaving Gwen standing sadly in the doorway, shocked by the abrupt termination of the union.

"You're a spoiled boy, Tommy":
Gwen (Jean Harlow) in *The Public Enemy*.

Tom's mama's-boy complex continues with yet another girl, Jane (it will be an even stronger tendency in another later James Cagney film, *White Heat* [1949]). Tom's courtship attempts are either undeveloped on any adult level or simply nonexistent. In each case the women seek to seduce him. Gwen asks for his phone number, and Jane makes use of his drunkenness to have her way with him to some degree. "Be a good boy and sit down," she tells him. "I'll take your shoes off, too. I want to do things for you, Tommy. You don't think I'm old, do you, Tommy?" She cradles his chin in her hand.

Aside from this mollycoddling, Tommy-boy really does have a unique and very significant mother figure in the film, Ma Powers (Beryl Mercer) who is a more benign version of the infamous real life "Mother Barker," heav-

Tom Powers has money for his doting mother
(Beryl Mercer) in *The Public Enemy*.

ily demonized by FBI director J. Edgar Hoover as "the most vicious, dangerous, and resourceful brain this country [had] produced in many years." (*American Magazine*, 1936) Whereas many society melodramas films portrayed the importance of a strong father-daughter relationship, relying upon paternal leadership for protection and guidance (even if the father's morals are questionable), in this film the perils of a boy relying upon a maternal figure is shown as a lesson.

Queen of the Mob (1940) presented yet another incarnation of Ma Barker, but test audiences found it too reprehensible to kill off the Ma character (played by Blanche Yurk in this case), either because she was a maternal figure or because she was so charismatic. Resurrected multiple times on screen, a Ma character made appearances in other films such as *Guns Don't Argue* (1957), *Ma Barker's Killer Brood* (1960), and *Bloody Mama* (1970). It interesting to note the choice of wording on these films, which bring to mind the horror genre's consistent projection of women as monstrous often in relation

Shelley Winters as Ma Barker, "'the most vicious, dangerous, and resourceful brain [in] this country,'" in *Bloody Mama*.

to their reproductive capabilities and organs. David Cronenberg's *The Brood* (1979) involves a psychotic wife and mutant children along with various disturbing bloody, birth-related imagery. The psychological lesson that is upheld throughout the years is almost always the same: the boy must break away from the mother and join the dominant patriarchal order. The consequences of challenging this order can be deadly not only to the individual, but a threat to society as a whole.

The Production Code was not the only force to mold Hollywood into producing films that conformed to national ideals; dominant society dictated it purely by economics as well. By portraying deviant behavior in films, the shining example of "normal" non-aberrant behavior is reinforced constantly by contrasting characters who exemplify the rewards of obedience to patri-archal authority. There is always a hyperbolic moment injected into scripts when the consequences of bad and good are placed side by side for analysis. In *Gun Crazy*, the heroine, a gun fetishist and criminal on the run peeps into the snow-covered window of a warm, cozy middle-class residence, while standing shivering and hungry in the darkness outside. She is clearly outcast, whereas the happy family inside enjoys the modest rewards of obedience to society rules. The woman is punished for wishing to reach far beyond the means of her class, and the man who is lured to follow and feeds her seem-ingly uncontrollable desire for more is punished for indulging her needs.

The envelope is pushed though, by the "fallen women" of gangster films, who defy gender expectations. When contrasted against hardworking lower-class "good girls," the appeal of the fallen women is clearly more seductive. Joan Crawford, who would come to define the classic femme fatale, plays the character Ethel Whitehead in the noir-melodrama *The Damned Don't Cry* (1950). She is a working-class woman stuck in a miserable marriage. She appears old, tired, and burned out in the beginning. But after she takes charge of her destiny and gains entrance into the dangerous world of gangsters, she transforms herself into a new figure, changing her name and taking on the persona of a rich heiress. Becoming an icon of glamour, she lives the good life as she climbs her way up the crime syndicate. Until of course her indulgences inevitable blow up in her face.

The fallen woman's power is usually false, controlled by the man. In the case of *The Damned Don't Cry*, Ethel is even humiliated over her choice in perfume and accessories, and must be guided by a powerful older male figure in how to dress, act, and speak like a cultured woman. After an initial flash of anger, she accepts the trade off of her own physical commodities for entrance into a socio-economic realm previously denied to her.

Again and again we see the importance of a woman's physical assets, quick wit, and proper adornment and display of herself as an integral part of gangster films and the formulation of the gangster himself. Furs, jewels, and evening gowns all serve as key signs of power, but masculine and phallic imagery is also incorporated in many cases. Beyond the obvious female use of guns in films, other practices like smoking take on erotic appeal. The heroines tease with long cigarettes, blowing smoke in men's faces or even chewing on a cigar in more aggressive masculine affectations, such as Faye Dunaway's style in the landmark film, *Bonnie and Clyde* (1967). Her boyish hats and pseudo masculine ways triggered a fashion craze after the film was released. Her aggressive sexuality is made all the more clear in a conversation with the more sexually ambiguous Clyde.

All right. All right. If all you want's a stud service, you get on back to West Dallas and you stay there the rest of your life. You're worth more than that. A lot more than that. You know it and that's why you come along with me. You could find a lover boy on every damn corner in town. It don't make a damn to them whether you're waitin' on tables or pickin' cotton, but it does make a damn to me.

The cuckolded male is a mainstay of the gangster film, whether he is willingly cuckolded or not. In Martin Scorsese's *Casino* (1995), Robert De Niro's character, Sam "Ace" Rothstein, falls for the beautiful hustler Ginger (Sharon Stone) as he watches her expert interaction in cheating another man out of some money and then punishing him for not paying her off further in an ingenious spontaneous reaction. She tosses trays of poker chips up in the air, causing havoc as everyone greedily scrambles to pick them up.

Later on Sam quietly accepts her hustling lifestyle with a sort of admiration. She can do things like keep a businessman up on drugs for three days straight while draining his bank account and sending him back to his wife empty-handed. The camera shows the small details of how she operates, zooming up multiple times on her hands, showing the way she folds a hundred dollar bill into her palm, flexing it to make sure it's just right, the endless smooth handoffs of tips, pills and payments to everyone around. Though she is essentially a hooker and drug dealer, as a hustler himself Sam admires her game.

The one man Sam cannot abide, though, is her greasy pimp-boyfriend, who seems to drain her of all her funds and has the ability to reach into her usually inaccessible heart with his sweet talk—something Sam is incapable of doing. This same type of character is also the Achilles' heel of many a heroine as far back as the masterful mobster Mahlon Keane (Robert Armstrong) in *The Racketeer* (1929). Mahlon becomes stuck in a love triangle with Rhoda (Carole Lombard), a strong-willed ex–society girl. Rhoda is in turn in love with a sickly, alcoholic concert violinist. In this particular case of cuckoldry, the powerful gangster is reduced to the point of actually helping get the hapless musician back on his feet and into society in return for Rhoda's allegiance. It seems a further insult that she clearly sacrifices herself by agreeing to marry Mahlon only because of his having helped the musician. Even as Mahlon discusses their union, the sound of violin plays in the background.

In *Casino*, despite the fact that Sam knows that Ginger doesn't love him, Sam is so obsessed with her that he essentially buys his way into marriage with her, hoping that one day she will grow to love him. He spoils her with everything he can. The movie even begins with his words about her in narration as he opens up his car door and gets in: "When you love someone, you gotta trust them. There's no other way. You gotta give them the key to everything that is yours. Otherwise, what's the point?" The car abruptly blows up in a ball of fire after he turns the ignition key.

Sam Rothstein made the mistake of having Ginger's beloved low-life boyfriend beat up, causing Ginger to hate him and spiral down into severe alcoholism and drug addiction which will eventually kill her. But she also commits a grandiose act of revenge by having an affair with Sam's long time friend/partner Nicky Santoro (Joe Pesci), driving a wedge in the fraternal order that had long been established between them. Even the intensely vicious and ruthless Nicky appears visibly shaken after an explosive encounter with the drug-addled Ginger as she leaves his restaurant. "I fucked up, Frankie," he confesses to his friend. "I fucked up good this time. I should have never started with this fucking broad."

And in this sort of negative relationship, the significance of the destructive power a woman also wields as symbol comes into play. Not only can she uplift the status of the gangster by her presence, even her lack of presence can make her into a tool of destruction, humiliation, and downfall when she allows herself to be taken under the wing of another man. The old mafia rule says: if someone "welshes" on a deal or betrays you, beat them up or kill them. Then as final ultimate insult, you take their woman. Even the now-deceased, real life gangsta rapper, Tupac Shakur tapped into this old-school code of misconduct in the vicious song "Hit 'Em Up," in which he sings about having sex with the R & B singer Faith, the wife of his enemy Biggie Smalls.

The female gangster-lover also serves as a decoy and/or henchman in many circumstances, to penetrate circles that might normally be inaccessible to the gangster. In some cases the women become so involved with the crime business that they actually run the show as the power behind the throne, like

Lester (James Woods), the "beloved low-life boyfriend" of Ginger (Sharon Stone) in *Casino*.

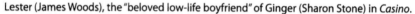

Lucy Liu plays the unlikely role of the yakuza boss, O-ren Ishii, in *Kill Bill*.

Catherine Zeta-Jones character Helena in *Traffic* (2000). Girls with guns make gangster-style appearances as early as in the 1921 silent movie *Outside the Law*, in which Priscilla Dean plays Molly Madden, a daughter of an underworld leader trying to save her father from a setup. She appears quite aggressive and vicious with her gun. Later we see a more direct version of active female participation in crime in *Lady Gangster* (1942), with the heroine, Dorothy Burton (Faye Emerson), using her stage-acting skills to become a smooth criminal and rob banks with a male gang that ends up trying to betray her. Though it wraps up to a neatly conventional ending, the movie includes some early women-in-prison scenes, and the head male gangster dressing in drag to come speak to her in prison.

Posing the female as hit man (or hit woman) is often tricky and rarely handled in any realistic way. *Prizzi's Honor* (1985) poses Kathleen Turner and Jack Nicholson as assassins for the Mafia who are hired to kill each other but fall for each other in the meantime, making the concept of professional female killers more into a cute comedic/action fantasy, much like the heavily hyped Brad Pitt and Angelina Jolie face-off in *Mr. and Mrs. Smith* (2005). The concept of female mob assassins is more surreal, although entertaining, in the recent *Kill Bill* movies by Quentin Tarantino. Lucy Liu plays the unlikely role of a yakuza boss who shows her unwillingness to accept insubordination by decapitating another yakuza leader.

Overall, the gangster's molls, flappers, twists, and broads of the early days have gone on to form new hybrids of characters that offer seditious fantasies to both male and female audiences. Although even in this day and age, most of these tales still show responsible and expected punishment for indulgence in crime, drugs, alternative sexual practices, and violence. Women are still cast women in dual roles that portray them as monstrously seductive, or as victim, or in some cases, both.

An apprehensive Tom Powers (James Cagney) brandishes a gun on a day-lit urban street.

The Gangster and Film Noir: Themes and Style

Alain Silver

> Say, listen, that's the attitude of too many morons in this country. They think these big hoodlums are some sort of demi-gods. What do they do about a guy like Camonte? They sentimentalize him, romance him, make jokes about him. They had some excuse for glorifying our old Western bad men. They met in the middle of the street at high noon and waited for each other to draw. But these things sneak up and shoot a guy in the back and then run away.
>
> Chief of Detectives, in Howard Hawks, *Scarface* (1932)

The style and substance of the gangster film in the late 1920s and 1930s are essential parts of the cinematic line that leads to the classic period of film noir. In transforming several genres of fiction into a movement, icons and characters mutate. Instead of tommy guns blazing out of car windows, gats are discreetly concealed under double-breasted suits. Molls wearing diamonds and furs to the speakeasy are succeeded by femmes fatales crooning love songs in smoky nightclubs. But the male protagonists of the pre-noir gangster film and many of those in the noir movement have the same character core: men driven to success and capable of extortion, larceny, or even murder to achieve it. The classic period of noir is rife with explicit gangster figures, mostly as antagonists to the alienated detectives or federal agents in pictures such as *T-Men* (1948), *The Big Heat* (1953), or *The Big Combo* (1955). Frequently, the gangster himself, from small-time gambler to hit man to syndicate mouthpiece, is the principal of the noir narrative: *This Gun for Hire* (1942), *Nobody Lives Forever* (1946), *The Gangster* (1947), *Force of Evil* (1948), *Kiss Tomorrow Goodbye* (1950), *Night and the City* (1950).

If one defines gangsters simply as criminals allied with others of like mind and intention—as opposed to the more complex structure of a Mafia-style group—then a movement as rife with criminal enterprise as film noir must also be full of gangsters. In noir, however, many if not most of the gangs are ad hoc: small, one-project entities put together with a mind to the requirements of the enterprise at hand. Films such as *The Asphalt Jungle* (1950) and *The Killing* (1956) are typical. Writers, producers, directors, cinematogra-

phers, and actors who began their association with criminal narratives in the
gangster genre continued to work in that vein when making film noir.

Purely in terms of visual style, the influence of the gangster film on noir is
even more striking. Conventional film history asserts that during the transition from the silent era visual options were severely restricted by the physical requirements of early sound recording, that the lighting and staging in
pictures by von Sternberg such as *Underworld, Thunderbolt*, and *Docks of New
York* became more difficult if not impossible to achieve. In fact, although
some early talkies did spend much of their screen time on soundstages, *Little
Caesar, The Public Enemy*, and *Scarface* went outside, as the location sequence
from *The Public Enemy* on page 90 or the scenes at the head of this essay and
on pages 60 and 324, which were shot on the streets and alleys of the Warner
Bros. back lot, confirm. Whether day or night, whether on actual locations
or the wet-down pavement of a studio New York Street, the perilous urban
landscape of film noir is fully anticipated. Although noir may be a movement
defined by style rather than a genre, icons and themes also contribute to its
identity. The movement's dark view of the world embraces a wide range of
plots and cuts across studios, budgets, and creative personnel; but certain
narrative consistencies are clear. The protagonists of noir are often caught in
a bind not of their making, falsely accused or otherwise entrapped, alienated

Von Sternberg's *Thunderbolt*.

from normal society, not anti-heroes, thugs, or megalomaniacs but ordinary Joes in extraordinary circumstances.

The most coincidental concept between the gangster film and the noir cycle is that of the underworld. In both genre and movement an essential presumption is that such an underworld exists, a parallel society outside the normal world (in which the people who go to the movies live). The reality with which this world is evoked—the use of characters inspired by real criminals who perpetrated the violence that scandalized newspaper readers but enthralled film audiences—lays the foundation for the world of film noir. For the viewers who watched town cars spraying bullets and careening across movie screens in the 1930s, the subtler but no less deadly dangers of film noir in the following decades were easy to accept.

As noted in the introduction, the other factor intervening in the through-line from *Little Caesar*, *The Public Enemy*, and *Scarface* to film noir was the empowering of the Hays Office in mid 1934. For a time, from the late 1930s through the beginning of World War II, the Code administration under Joe Breen prohibited many narratives, whether related to the gangster film or film noir, from going into production. Then, in the grisly context of a world

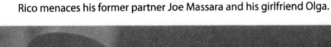

Rico menaces his former partner Joe Massara and his girlfriend Olga.

war, such "scandalous" narratives as James M. Cain's *Double Indemnity* (1944) and *The Postman Always Rings Twice* (1946), the rights to which their respective studios had held for over a decade, were finally permitted to go before the cameras.

Character Conventions

Joe Massara (Douglas Fairbanks) in *Little Caesar* is hardly an innocent man, but he seems unable to escape the grip of the underworld. Even after he parts with Rico (Edward G. Robinson) to focus on his parallel legitimate career as a dancer, events pull him back in. At one point, Rico decides to eliminate this liability and kill Joe. Rico's "soft spot"—read: his love for the handsome Joe— makes him change his mind at the last minute, with deadly consequences. As the now self-aware Rico says, "This is what I get for liking a guy too much." Such homoerotic relationships recur frequently in film noir, most notably in *Street with No Name* (1948) and its remake *House of Bamboo* (1955), where gang bosses portrayed by such hard-bitten noir actors as Richard Widmark and Robert Ryan respectively are taken by tough-talking, handsome undercover agents (Mark Stevens and Robert Stack).

The inability to escape the consequences of one's criminal past is also a common noir plot point in pictures from *You Only Live Once* (1937) to *The*

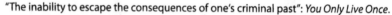

"The inability to escape the consequences of one's criminal past": *You Only Live Once.*

Reckless Moment (1949). Ironically, Joe Massara *does* escape. The fact that he lies prostrate next to a billboard with Massara's likeness adds another layer of comeuppance to Rico's death; and lost in the drama of the title character's violent rise and fall is the fact that contrary to the then unenforced tenets of the Production Code, Massara gets away with a lot of crimes and suffers no punishment.

Rico passes the billboard behind which he will shortly be shot.

"Mother of Mercy, is this the end of Rico?" dissolves to the billboard behind which the gangster lies.

Sergeant Flaherty in *Little Caesar* and Inspector Guarino in *Scarface* are both dogged cops, and their relentless pursuit of the gangster protagonists anticipates the obsessed noir detectives in *The Big Heat* and *The Big Combo*. Paul Muni's somewhat stereotyped portrayal of the Italian Camonte as a dandy and womanizer creates a through-line to Richard Conte as Mr. Brown in *The Big Combo*, or even, it could be argued, all the way to Conte's Barzini and James Caan's Sonny Corleone in *The Godfather*. In *The Big Heat*, a spurned and disfigured moll's empathy for the widowed detective suspected of being a rogue is the key to his triumph.

Cornel Wilde (left) as the obsessed noir detective in *The Big Combo*.

"A spurned and disfigured moll's empathy for the widowed detective suspected of being a rogue is the key to his triumph."

"The understated but equally obvious sexual avarice of noir gangsters":
a smooth Whit Sterling confronts Jeff Bailey and Kathie Moffat.

Veterans turned gangsters: Bogart and Cagney
in *The Roaring Twenties.*

The more understated but equally obvious sexual avarice of noir gangsters is a key plot point with figures such as Big Jim Colfax (Albert Dekker) in *The Killers* (1946), Whit Sterling (Kirk Douglas) in *Out of the Past* (1947), and Slim Dundee (Dan Duryea) in *Criss Cross* (1949). The parallels between Capone and Camonte in *Scarface*, from the trademark furrow in his cheek to his custom-tailored wardrobe or bulletproof limo, are pointedly drawn. But the tirade of the detective bureau chief (Edwin Maxwell)—cited in the epigraph at the head of this chapter—when a reporter asks him for comments on the "colorful" Camonte smacks of empty rhetoric. The sordid tale of Tom Powers in *The Public Enemy* anticipates the alienation of many protagonists in film noir. Although his father is a cop and his brother is a law-abiding veteran of World War I, the evolution of Powers from "dead end" kid to petty criminal to gangster is presented with a matter-of-fact style and a hint of empathy that is more troublesome in terms of the Production Code than more obviously ethnic quasi-caricatures such as Rico and Camonte. In contrast, the protagonists of *The Roaring Twenties* are themselves war veterans, men hardened to the use of weapons and to killing on the battlefields. As Eddie Bartlett (James Cagney) struggles to make a profit in the taxi business, his sense of entitlement for wartime sacrifice leads him to the more lucrative use of his cabs running bootleg liquor. The attitude of Powers and Bartlett carries forward into noir characters as diverse as "Lucky" Gagin in *Ride the Pink Horse* (1947), Joe Rolfe in *Kansas City Confidential* (1952), and Mike Hammer in *Kiss Me Deadly* (1955), all of whom are cynical, suspicious of any authority (which they believe is biased against them), and self-reliant in the extreme.

The portrayal of the adult Mike Powers (Donald Cook) is a dour one. Even before he joins the army, Mike is depicted in uniform (he works on a streetcar), so that his slender, dark-clad figure provides a graphic contract

A dour Donald Cook portrays Mike Powers in uniform as a streetcar conductor . . .   . . . and wounded army veteran.

with James Cagney's compact and energetic personification of Tom. As a returning veteran, Mike is grimmer than ever, so that he also anticipates aspects of the taciturn and alienated Gagin, as well as Johnny Morrison (Alan Ladd) in *The Blue Dahlia* (1946), and even the embittered bigot Montgomery (Robert Ryan) in *Crossfire* (1947). Cagney's later portrayals, from *Angels with Dirty Faces* (1938) through *Each Dawn I Die* and *The Roaring Twenties* (both 1939) to *White Heat* (1949), anticipate and echo many noir figures. Cagney's hoodlums become more psychopathic with age, so that the line from the baby-faced killer in *The Public Enemy* leads to the severely disturbed Cody

The taciturn and alienated Gagin (left), Johnny Morrison (right, top), and Montgomery (right, bottom).

Jarrett in *White Heat*. From those characters, from Enrico "Little Caesar" Bandello and Tony "Scarface" Camonte, it's a small step to portrayals of the purely sociopathic killers with colorful names in *The Killer Is Loose* (1956) and *The Lineup* (1958). And even though he portrays an innocent man, Cagney's iconic facial expression and posture are more sinister than those of George Raft's criminal character "Hood" Stacey in *Each Dawn I Die*.

Sociopathic killers with colorful names and guns in their hands:
Leon "Foggy" Poole (left) in *The Killer Is Loose* and Dancer, the hitman, in *The Lineup*.

Although he portrays an innocent man, Cagney's iconic facial expression and posture are more sinister than those of George Raft's criminal character, "Hood" Stacey, in *Each Dawn I Die.*

Visual Style

The early scenes of *Little Caesar* take place at night in proletarian milieus: a gas station and then a roadside diner. The celebrated opening of Robert Siodmak's adaptation of *The Killers* is also set in a diner. Although the interior shots of the later film are somewhat more stylized, both engage viewer identification and use everyday settings to underscore the narrative implication that "this could happen to anyone." As an early flashback reveals, the objects of the killers' search, the hapless Swede (Burt Lancaster), works in a gas station.

The opening gas-station hold-up in *Little Caesar.*   Rico and Massara inside a diner after the hold-up.

The arrival of Duke Mantee (Humphrey Bogart, center) at the diner in *The Petrified Forest*.

The nighttime neon sign of the diner and gas station (on a Warner Bros. sound stage) in *The Petrified Forest*.

The opening shot in *The Killers*.

As with the soundstage diner and gas station in *The Petrified Forest*, where the isolated structures in the middle of the desert add irony to the arrival of the gangster Duke Mantee and his minions, the gas stations in *The Killers*, *Out of the Past*, and *Kiss Me Deadly* (1955) are archetypes of plebeian life, the venues where a man hiding from a dark past chooses to work. In the grimmer irony of film noir, no job is mundane enough to provide a refuge.

Inside the diner.

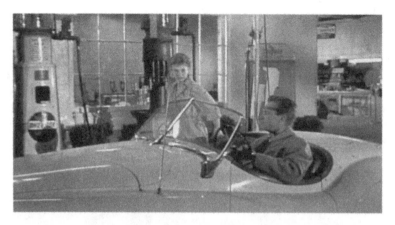

Night gas station in *Kiss Me Deadly*: Mike Hammer (Ralph Meeker) pulls his sports car into a Calabasas gas station after picking up the mysterious hitchhiker Christina (Cloris Leachman).

While the black sedans of the era slowly creeping down night-lit streets quickly became genre icons for an impending hail of bullets, filmmakers selected locations that reinforced the sense of the everyday and the implication that gangsters are among us. Day-lit shots—sometimes in documentary-style footage such as the "big funeral" from *Little Caesar* (page 87)—could be inserted at selected moments to reinforce the underlying impression of realistic mise-en-scène, which carried into certain noir films. Although there is considerable quasi-expressionistic staging inside it, a diner figures prominently as a flashback frame in *Detour*. When the gangster genre enjoyed a resurgence after the success of *Bonnie and Clyde* in 1967, the same icons—period cars (darker, retro variants of Bonnie and Clyde's Ford V-8), gas stations, diners, and nightclubs all reappeared, as in *The Grissom Gang* (1971).

Period gas station in *The Grissom Gang*.   Period diner in *The Grissom Gang*.

The fruit store sequence (first frame below) when the fugitive Rico seeks refuge in *Little Caesar* is an even more colorful evocation of proletarian context. The violence and viciousness of the underworld of Ma Madgalena (Lucille La Verne) is fully revealed in, for instance, the film noir *Thieves' Highway*, where ethnic characters such as Mike Figlia (Lee J. Cobb) and the matronly Midge (Hope Emerson) conspire to exploit growers and truckers like Nick Garcos, portrayed by Richard Conte (second frame below), whose iconic association with gangsters sets the audience up for Garcos' savage beating of Figlia at the movie's conclusion.

Much of *Thieves' Highway* is staged in long take by director Jules Dassin. An elaborate long take opens *Scarface*. In order to accomplish the shot on a soundstage, it opens with almost surreal staging using forced perspective and a wagon pulled by a pony for a midget milkman. The camera passes through several walls, first into the nightclub, then into the lounges and service rooms beyond that, where we see the shadow of the as-yet-unidentified Tony Camonte and hear him whistling.

From a forced-perspective prop lamppost and painted backdrop, the camera pans to a miniature milk wagon pulled by a pony.

The camera dollies "through" a wall as a tired janitor takes in the sign . . .

and picks up party detritus; Louie prattles on drunkenly with his last

guests, then heads for the telephone. The shadow appears at the end

of a corridor and comes forward, whistling, then says, "Hello, Louie,"

and shoots. The janitor finds the body and hurries away.

There are several equally elaborate openings in noir films, one of the most celebrated being in one of the last films of the classic period, *Touch of Evil*. Long takes were effective in many noir narratives, from the pictures of Max Ophuls to the lesser-known films of John Farrow, such as the tour-de-force sequence inside the title object during the opening sequence of *The Big Clock*.

From a nondescript city skyline at night, the camera pans to the Janoth Building. A traveling matte reveals a corridor behind the façade, when

the shadow of a guard, then the person himself, appears, and a man hides,

then hurries apprehensively across the corridor and into the clock mechanism. After checking the lobby (a process screen) through a viewing port, the

man moves to the other side. As the camera pulls back, his figure (at bottom

center) is obscured by the clock, and he begins his narration: "How did I get

into this anyway.... Thirty-six hours ago I was a decent, respectable, law-abiding citizen."

Long before it became a staple of the noir style, both *Little Caesar* and *Scarface* used neon and incandescent signage. In the latter, the promise of the Cook's Tour sign—"The World Is Yours" (see page 42)—is explicitly recapitulated with a pan up from Camonte's body lying crumpled on wet asphalt by some streetcar tracks. (Even wetter is the fall of Tom Powers, who, wounded while avenging his friend's murder, mutters "I ain't so tough" before collapsing. In the classic period of noir, a similar ending, such as the fugitive falling and dying in the gutter in *He Ran All the Way*, needs no embellishment.) There is a subtler usage in *Scarface* in the transition from the killing of the last rival, Gaffney, in a bowling alley. The image shifts from a ten-pin falling to a

Camonte crumpled on the wet asphalt.

Powers falls in the gutter.

Wounded fugitive Nick Robey (John Garfield) stumbles into the gutter in *He Ran All the Way*.

sign that reads "Paradise No. 2," the club where Camonte and his minions go to celebrate. The sign outside the Palermo Club in *Little Caesar* is initially just

a transition; but the scene lighting inside, punctuated by the pulsing of the sign outside (left three frames next page), is a usage that creates an undercurrent of instability that became a staple in film noir, most expressionistically in scenes where faces of killers were illuminated solely by muzzle blast. In *The Unsuspected* (1947) the lower-key lighting inside the killer's hotel room makes the graphic impact of the sign outside the window even more pronounced (right three frames next page).

In contrast, the day scenes in *Little Caesar, Scarface,* and *The Public Enemy* use narrative context, such as the everyday streets intercut with the morbid discussion inside the car during the funeral in *Little Caesar.* Although most of the shooting takes place at night, the ambushes in *The Public Enemy* and *Scarface*—the comic relief during the assault in the café where Camonte's

crony fumbles on the pay phone while terrified patrons scream and duck for cover—offer a disturbing juxtaposition. A subtler sequence is the first meeting of Camonte's sister, Cesca (Ann Dvorak), with his henchman Rinaldo (George Raft). She sees him with an organ grinder and several children through the decorative railing of a fire escape. When Cesca throws a quarter, Rinaldo catches it and substitutes one of his own, establishing Raft's signature gesture of tossing and catching a coin. The shot of Cesca behind the railing, demure and erotic at the same time with her face graphically entwined and partly cut off by the railing, is a metaphoric indicator that her fate is sealed. A similar mise-en-scène is used as a grinning Tom Powers lies in wait in the rain in *The Public Enemy*. Once the existence of the underworld is revealed, the audience realizes the city streets, even in broad daylight, can harbor unexpected

menace, a concept that informs numerous film noir such as *The Naked City* and *Side Street*.

Ultimately, in the gangster film and film noir, the night holds more peril. When Camonte first points out the Cook's Tour sign in daylight, his smug remark—"Some day I look at that sign, I say, 'Okay. She's a mine'"—creates irony dependent on dialogue and performance. When he lies dead beneath it, the irony is silent and purely graphic.

Motifs

Most if not all of the typical motifs of film noir first appear in the early gangster talkies.[1]

1. The simple use of shadows on walls, as in the opening of *Scarface*, in *The Public Enemy* or *Little Caesar*, or at the end of *Angels with Dirty Faces*, is a typical noir motif, as in *The Killers*. While the figures in

The Public Enemy and *Little Caesar* become anonymous during flight, the menace in *The Killers* is focused on the identifiable protagonist.

Rico's shadow leads him toward death in *Little Caesar*, and low light exaggerates the dark shapes on the wall in *Angels with Dirty Faces*. Fourteen

years after *Scarface*, director Howard Hawks creates a more complex motif in *The Big Sleep* by placing the shadow at the center of a noir triptych.

2. The model years may have changed, but the dark cars also prowled the streets of film noir. The night scenes, crowded with people and nightclubs, add a sense of constriction to the milieus of the gangster film. Those in *Scarface* and *Little Caesar* are crowded and more brightly lit than those of in film noir. As milieus they are pure background—as already noted, "Paradise No. 2" has metaphoric implications in *Scarface*—but they are never focal points, as in *Gilda* (1946) or *I Walk Alone* (1948). The high-key lighting

and Cesca's excited expression contrast markedly with the darker milieu and apprehensive gaze of Gloria Grahame in *Song of the Thin Man* (1947).

Except for the slightly off-center framing, the light and staging in *The Public Enemy* (below) do not suggest that Matt Doyle will soon be gunned down in the street. In *Criss Cross*, dynamic lighting and

framing immediately underscore the awkward relationship during a nightclub encounter (left). Massara's blonde girlfriend Olga Strassoff (Glenda Farrell, pictured on page 293) in *Little Caesar* may have a slightly exotic name and look, but she merely anticipates the blonde noir chanteuses such as Elizabeth Scott in *I Walk Alone* or Grahame in *Song of the Thin Man* or the gloved archetype in *Gilda* (1946).

In the later half of the classic period, even more exotic singers and locales appear, such as in Mady Comfort in *Kiss Me Deadly*.

Even in the fateful context of a roulette table, noir filmmakers used light and angle to accentuate the context of instability. And even with the wheel in the foreground, *Angels with Dirty Faces* has less of a sense of "mischance" than *Out of the Past*, where Jeff Bailey remarks that "there's a way to lose more slowly."

3. As Tom Powers brandishes a gun in broad daylight while he sits in the passenger seat in the scene at the head of this article, Cagney's expression creates apprehension. The context and low-key light create more menace in the vehicle interior at night (with Bogart holding the gun) in *The Roaring Twenties*. But even without a gun, the staging and shadows deepen the sense of peril in a shot from *I Walk Alone*.

4. The car is at once a refuge and an escape, but only when it starts, as Rico's hapless minion in *Little Caesar* discovers.

For Neff and Phyllis in *Double Indemnity*, the starter motor grinds and grinds until it finally catches.

On the nocturnal streets the camera tracks the doomed mobsters from side angles in *Little Caesar*. More diverse patterns are used in film noir

with figures sometimes disappearing into pools of light as in *The Killers*.

Some noir filmmakers, such as Robert Aldrich, spoke explicitly of reversing expectations, of standing the norm "on its head," so the sense of peril with similar shots of Hammer in *Kiss Me Deadly* is first made completely explicit with cutaways of the man following him, then revealed as misplaced when Hammer easily overcomes his pursuer. Even from the side angle, Hammer's size gives him visual dominance.

5. Hawks introduces the conceit of bullets fired through the door in *Scarface* (below left) and recapitulates it fourteen years later (below right) in the ending of his 1946 adaptation of Chandler's *The Big Sleep*.

6. When Camonte uses the phone in a store after he wrecks his car escaping an ambush (below left), the extreme backlight is typical of noir cinematography. The phone in film noir often suggests vulnerability, as in *Out of the Past* (below right).

7. The clock face has deterministic connotations both in *Little Caesar* (below left) and in *Raw Deal* (1948, below right). In the noir film, the face of Claire Trevor in the foreground makes the fatefulness more personal. The exterior

 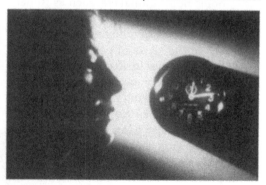

clock face in *The Set-Up* (1949) makes the same deterministic statement and
becomes a linking motif through several camera angles in *Kiss Me Deadly*.

In an alternate **angle** in *Raw Deal* the clock face mirrors a human face.

8. The mirror motif, which is part of a
    moment of comic relief in *Little Caesar*
    (above right), evolved into a more
    somber suggestion of doppelgängers
    and the perils of the parallel under-
    world in many noir films, including
    another starring Edward G. Robinson,
    John Farrow's adaptation of Cornell
    Woolrich's *Night has a Thousand Eyes*.

In noir, the mirror often permits interposing closer shots of antagonists in a single frame, as in the meeting of the conspirators in *The Killers* or the detective and a prime suspect in *Laura*. As in *Scarface*,

the mirror easily permits the ironic revelation of a character's expression and the figure that motivates it, as in *The Thief* (1952, below left) and *Kiss Me Deadly*.

9. Jail settings, with their bar motifs, and the even grimmer execution chambers frequently used in film noir recall earlier uses in the gangster film. The set in Von Sternberg's *Thunderbolt* on page 292 is mirrored in noir films such as *Try and Get Me* (1950) or *The Last Mile* (1959). Although

excised from the final cut, the gas chamber sequence in *Double Indemnity*

is an iconic reflection of Cagney's walk to the electric chair in *Angels with Dirty Faces*. The sequence in *Black Tuesday* (below right) is practically a restaging of this scene.

10. The symbolic "X" introduced in the main title of *Scarface* recurs frequently throughout the movie. In Gaffney's hideaway, the play of light across his body marks him as doomed.

A similar fatality is reinforced, using shadow or body placement, but without the overt symbolism, in *The Killers* and *Criss Cross*.

The cross motif in the rafters of the garage opens the St. Valentine's Day massacre in *Scarface*, where the figures are shadows. In Roger Corman's 1967 *St. Valentine's Day Massacre* the scene is more graphic.

In Stanley Kubrick's *The Killing* the bodies are piled more naturalistically. The death of gangster Whit Sterling in *Out of the Past* is revealed in

a stylized, open-eyed pose that is more subtly ironic than Camonte's in *Scarface*.

Twenty-five years after *Scarface* Aldrich used the X motif in *Kiss Me Deadly*, abstractly in the establishing shot of the beach house and more literally in the shape of Hammer's body tied to a bed, or Christina's pose on the highway as she flags down Hammer at the movie's beginning.

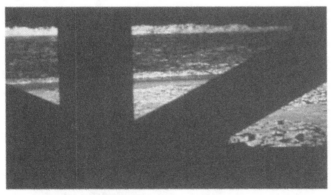

11. Of course, the deadliest women in film noir use guns, like Cesca at the end of *Scarface*. But while Cesca's semi-incestuous emotions prevent her from shooting her brother, no such sentiments inhibit a femme fatale like Lily Carver in *Kiss Me Deadly*.

Conclusion

Although this survey of the thematic and stylistic relationships between the gangster genre and film noir is of necessity brief, even a cursory selection of images reveals how large a pool of icons and motifs they share. Much as the gangster films of the 1930s influenced film noir, the classic period of that movement in turn influenced the filmmakers who helped revive the gangster genre in the late 1960s and early 1970s. Even in a post-Code era, in which there are no restrictions on the violence and no requirements for moral retribution, the gangsters depicted by Francis Ford Coppola and Martin Scorsese live in the world of Tony Camonte and Tom Powers but suffer the angst of noir. While the noir movement is over, neo-noir is itself a genre which easily uses elements of both noir movement and gangster genre. Many newer films, particularly remakes such as *Night and the City* (1992) or *Kiss of Death* (1995), often straddle, however uneasily, the hazy and inexact line between neo-noir and neo-gangster while incorporating elements with mixed success from the antecedent movement and genre.

Note

1. For more detailed descriptions and discussion of the key stylistic devices and motifs in film noir, see our book-length study of *The Noir Style* (New York: Overlook Press, 1999).

In All Its Fury
and Violence ...Like No
Other Picture
Since
"SCARFACE"
and
"LITTLE
CAESAR"!
"THE
KILLING"
Sterling
HAYDEN
COLEEN GRAY · VINCE EDWARDS
JAY C. FLIPPEN

"Explicit acts of terror": a shootout in broad daylight in *The Public Enemy*.

Hits, Whacks, and Smokes:
The Celluloid Gangster as Horror Icon

Catherine Don Diego

Horror films abound in contemporary cinema, enriching the genre with innumerable hybrids such as science-fiction horror (*Aliens, Virus, Pitch Black*), paranormal horror (*Stir of Echoes, The Sixth Sense*), teen horror (*The Faculty, I Know What You Did Last Summer*), and parody of teen horror (*Scary Movie*), not to mention new renditions of the good, old-fashioned monster movie (*Mary Shelley's Frankenstein, Interview with the Vampire, Bram Stoker's Dracula*). Despite their variations, all of these films rely at least in part on what is traditionally believed to be one of the essential ingredients of horror: the supernatural or mystical unknown. But horror cinema has always had its realist contributions, with Fritz Lang's *M* (1931), Alfred Hitchcock's *Psycho* (1960), Michael Powell's *Peeping Tom* (1960), and many others—films which lack a paranormal element, yet often get classified as horror due to their terrifying depiction of seriously disturbed human characters.

Many realist horror films (e.g., *The Silence of the Lambs* [1991], *Seven* [1995], and *Henry: Portrait of a Serial Killer* [1990]; even such "splatter" movies as *The Texas Chainsaw Massacre* [1974]) often transcend those that fall squarely in the genre due to their supernatural nature, which raises the question whether or not any generic boundaries can be employed to determine whether or not a particular film qualifies as horror. My own view is that some of the most terrifying realist horror offerings in the cinema are better known as gangster movies, and the primary suggestion of this essay is that we include the iconic celluloid gangster in the brotherhood of established American horror icons. A relatively recent and wildly popular example would be Brian De Palma's 1983 version of *Scarface*, a film which combines elements of suspense, horror, and mayhem far exceeding what many supernaturally based narratives could offer. This film's distinctive appeal to younger audiences can be traced to its grisly, stark depiction of gang violence, unlike the symbolically brutal 1932 original directed by Howard Hawks. However, the horrific elements of gangster films were in place decades before De Palma's remake.

Explicitly stylized scenes of carnage have been essential to this genre since the conclusion of *Bonnie and Clyde* (1967) and the toll booth scene in *The Godfather* (1972). Which is not to say that, prior to these films, the gangster

"Seriously disturbed human characters": Peter Lorre as Hans Becker in *M*.

genre was without its appalling, frightful sequences, whether overt or implied. An example of implied horror would be the scene from *The Public Enemy* (1931) in which a middle-aged man sits down at the piano and begins playing a song from his youth. The player laughs nervously as two younger men look on, one of them with a gun aimed at the player's head. In the frame, however, all we see is the second younger man with a countenance of fearful anticipation. The player continues with his song until he falls from a shot fired from the unseen gunman as the younger man looks on in horror. This scene would hardly evoke terror from today's audiences, and its deliberate pacing might even turn off less attentive viewers. But *The Public Enemy* also features more explicit acts of terror, including ruthless killers pumping metal from tommy guns into victims who refused to obey gang orders.

Ever since the early 1930s gangster cycle—a cycle which includes *Little Caesar* (1930), *The Public Enemy*, and *Scarface*—gangsters have been privileged members of Hollywood's human monster club, "real" killers who have frightened and bedazzled audiences with their seemingly omnipotent control over victims and limitless lust for blood. Although organized crime film icons such as Tony Camonte (Paul Muni), Rico Bandello (Edward G. Robinson), and Tom Powers (James Cagney) have captivated audiences for decades, as do their successors in numerous contemporary mob movies, they have not quite been regarded as "horror characters," those whom we generally regard as the genuine players of the genre, ranging from the Wolf Man to Freddy Krueger. But considering the filmic gangster's innate ability to terrorize his onscreen victims and shock his audiences, supernatural origin and powers would be superfluous here, since his breed already encompasses a side of humanity that few would label "normal." Even if a rival gangster whacks him, or if he winds up frying in the chair, there are dozens more ready to take his place. The very word "gangster," implying as it does one out of a possible many, can conjure up the image of an overwhelming number of monsters and an eternity of torture, whereas most ghostly or "undead" monsters (save for the zombie hordes in films such as *Night of the Living Dead* [1968]) strike alone and momentarily. Consequently, the supernatural element so crucial to horror films such as *Dracula* (1931), *Nightmare on Elm Street* (1984), or *Halloween* (1978) becomes somewhat redundant when a fully human antagonist leaves his audience with the threat of reincarnation through an upcoming protégé in the ranks.

So where does the gangster film stand with respect to the horror genre? Considering the violence inherent in fictional and non-fictional narratives of organized crime activities, the horrific nature of shakedowns, hits, and scare tactics that contribute to the morbid fascination audiences have with these films places many (though not all) of them at least within the periphery of the horror genre. Even at the moral level, gangsters are usually portrayed as subhuman abominations. Referring to the early thirties gangster cycle, Thomas Doherty points out that the three films listed above "evenhandedly parcel out social pathology and sexual aberration: homosexuality (*Little Caesar*), misogyny (*The Public Enemy*), and incest (*Scarface*)" (146). And there is little mystery why, by this time, gangster films were being systematically banned from theaters across the nation, thanks to "pressure from ministers, women's clubs and civic organizations" (Black, 1994: 121). Unlike horror films featuring vampires, zombies, gremlins, space aliens, ghosts, and a whole host of other stock monsters, the supernatural does not figure at all in the gangster film, nor is it an element necessary for terrifying viewers.

The quintessential icon in this case would be Tony Camonte, the avaricious nihilist of Howard Hawks' 1932 *Scarface*, who terrorizes Chicago not only with his quick-triggered ambition but his alien looks and manners. One cannot underestimate the significance of the immigrant's threat to white, Protestant American culture during the Depression era, when strict anti-immigration laws were checking the successive waves of impoverished southern Italians. Tony Camonte typifies the horror of facing a superflux of alterity in the darker races' immigration into major U.S. cities. In fact, both *Scarface* and *Little Caesar* magnify the perceived horror of unrestrained immorality descending upon this country by aliens, i.e., the southern Italians.

If the supernatural or fantasy worlds of traditional horror cinema rely on the unknown and on the personal fears of individual viewers, the swarthy immigrant gangster by contrast evokes public and societal anxieties. Jonathan Munby argues that with respect to the threats posed by early-20th-century immigrants, Prohibition "was an act born out of anxieties about consumerism's corrosion of the puritan work ethic. . . . [T]his fear cannot be separated from a concomitant fear of the 'new' and hyphenated American" (32). The "cultural Other," as Munby puts it, threatens the social and cultural status quo through his selling of drugs, alcohol, prostitutes, or gambling opportunities, vices that corrode the moral foundation of a community.

Doherty notes that "like most organs of American popular culture, Hollywood preferred to portray the gangster as a foreign infestation rather than a homegrown plague. In the city, from immigrant blood, he springs from alien sources and perverse impulses. Though a product of America, the gangster was demonized as a swarthy stranger whose name ended in a vowel" (140). Thus, even the origin of the cinematic gangster is associated with "perverse" and "alien" elements in the popular imagination, and is therefore unnatural and somehow not quite human. There is no mystery or element of the ethereal in this metaphoric plague, unlike the literal plague that strikes a community in *The Stand* (1994), nor is there an alien invasion as in *Independence Day* (1996). Gangsters are spawned from the community itself, and subsequently work from the inside. They peddle desired vice to their willing neighbors, which, considered holistically, is a more insidious danger than actual disease. Consequently, their horror is generated from moral and cultural fears, relying on the exaggerated imaginations of viewers. One need not "believe in" gangsters as one might consider the possible existence of monsters and space aliens. Gangster films captivate and frighten audiences without that "suspension of disbelief" required when watching a vampire movie. The gangster exists in reality as well as on the screen, whether as part of an organized crime family, neighborhood youth gangs, or the local high school's reprobate crowd. Their sheer numbers serve to magnify the fears of the mainstream.

Creating a moral monster out of a criminal celebrity increases his ability to terrorize not just his victims, but society as a whole. Al Capone is the prototype for Tony in 1932's *Scarface* and Rico in *Little Caesar*, but in order to underscore the cultural and moral terror he invoked in people, depicting his criminal behavior was insufficient. In both of these films, Capone's fictional counterparts became unnatural monsters at the level of sexuality. Though Rico's downfall is ultimately precipitated by greed and pride, he seems even more horrifying in scenes that strenuously suggest his homosexual desire for Joe (Douglas Fairbanks, Jr.) and his jealousy following Joe's rejection of him for Olga (Glenda Farrell). In one startling scene, Rico at the height of his power declares that he no longer needs Joe, while stretching out on the bed with his soldier crawling next to him.

Rico's homosexual proclivity is noted in Doherty's description of this iconic character: "A diminutive bandit whose single-minded ambition compensates less for his stature than his repressed homosexual desire, Caesar Enrico Bandello is compact, swarthy, and tightly wound; his golden boy pal Joe . . . is tall, patrician and easy going" (146). To read this film in terms of its subtextual medieval theology, it seems that the main culprit is Rico's monumental pride, since it affects every aspect of his being. Next to Joe, who has the desire to work legitimately (as a nightclub dancer) and love within the bounds of moral rectitude (his beautiful partner, Olga), Rico's desire is for absolute power, and this means that he stays only with men and insists that they stay with him. He even pursues Joe and urges him to return to the fold; and he perceives Olga as a threat not just to their friendship, but to his business as well. The upshot of *Little Caesar*'s homoerotic slant, then, is Rico's hold on the weak and ambivalent character who finds himself unable to escape the mob's web. The real horror of this film is not so much the disintegration of social welfare that Rico perpetrates on the city, but his own moral decay and the downfall of those he permeates with his moral poison.

To emphasize the depravity of Rico's wickedness, the supernatural symbolism of hellfire recurs between scenes of his personal and public crimes. In its focus on eschatological concerns, the film mediates elements of what is in effect a morality play. Sin itself is the true monster, and Rico is Everyman caught up in its grasp. The scriptural quote "Those who live by the sword die by the sword" precedes the narrative, suggesting that the following story should be taken allegorically as well as fictionally. Munby notes that *Little Caesar*'s author, W. R. Burnett, saw the narrative at an abstract or universal level as "allegoriz[ing] the corrosive features of modern capitalist society" (45–46). The sexually decentered representation of the mobster, then, validates the moral protocols of mainstream (i.e., WASP) America. As in medieval theology and fictional narratives starring that original band of moral gangsters, the Seven Deadly Sins, one sin always leads to another, greater sin, or else additional sins are already implicit in the initial act. The sexual depravity of the gangster here verifies his total degeneration and ultimate damnation. Compared to Marlowe's Faust, another willful sinner, Rico spurns last minute reprieves, and his physical death merely precipitates his spiritual damnation. He utters the famous line, "Mother of mercy! Is this the end of Rico?" after realizing what he has lost in his refusal to repent.

If *Little Caesar* depicts the alien gangster with what is coded as an inherently immoral preference for homosexuality, Hawks' *Scarface* expresses a similar moral depravity in Tony's obsession for his nubile sister, Cesca (Ann Dvorak). His unbridled lust for power leads him to treat his sister as a jealous husband would treat his flirtatious wife. The implied incestuous relationship is iterated in several scenes, and is almost mentioned explicitly when Cesca complains, "You don't treat me like a sister. You treat me like a, a . . . I don't know what . . . !" Her silence suggests that Tony's sin is too horrifying to utter and, perhaps, that she cannot bring herself to acknowledge that the desire is mutual. In the case of both Rico and Tony, the repulsive nature of their criminal souls intensifies exponentially with the decay of their sexuality, thereby making them monstrous and predatory in the moral sense as well as in the social sense.

Limitless terrorization and lethal consequences have always been essential facets of the gang film's appeal. Audiences are at once repulsed and fascinated by the cold-blooded mob bosses Rico and Tony, and partly in response to their robust attraction for many viewers, the film industry and its censors claimed in 1932 that *Scarface* would constitute the end rather than the beginning of the gangster film cycle. And just recently, David Remnick has predicted that with the real mob's gradual demise, the filmic mob's demise will soon follow (21). Nevertheless, the proliferation of "true crime" narratives featuring tell-all biographies of ex-mob members has spawned a legion of devoted viewers fascinated by their gruesome escapades, and may be eclipsed in popularity only by biographies of serial killers. But mobsters such as Sammy "the Bull" Gravano often boast of having more victims than many serial murderers, and the nature of their disposal methods can rival the worst in horror fiction. A recent episode of HBO's *America Undercover*, "The Iceman Confesses: Secrets of a Mafia Hit Man" (2001), not coincidentally following the hit series *The Sopranos*, features the infamous Richard Kulkinsky, who describes his gory occupation for the camera. The narrator meanwhile provides background on the Iceman's boss: "DeMeo's hideout was a shop of horrors where bodies were chopped up and prepared for disposal." Such horrific activities are just "part of the job" in gangland, as it were, and their fictionalization on the screen yields undeniably compelling entertainment.

But what keeps audiences attracted to these stories of criminals and their casual mayhem? It may have something to do with the presence of actual gangs in contemporary society. We read about them in gossip columns and watch their exploits almost daily on various news programs and documentaries, but they also offer a strange combination of glamour and horror that appeals to the imagination in a manner unlike the fantastic, preternatural monsters of traditional horror movies.

"Moral depravity in Tony's obsession for his nubile sister, Cesca (Ann Dvorak)," in *Scarface*.

Often the supernatural manifests itself in the realistic image of the arche-typal screen gangster. A recent episode of *The Sopranos* ("Pine Barrens") fea-tures a rival Russian gang member surviving both a strangling and a gunshot wound to the head, thereby haunting Paulie (Tony Sirico) and Chris (Michael Imperioli) as they leave the woods. The episode and the 2001 season conclude with no final word on their supposed victim, leaving both the audience and the characters wondering if the Russian is still alive. There is an indication that his Chechnyan commando training has instilled in him superhuman powers, or, as Paulie comments, "He's like fuckin' Rasputin!"

Perhaps just as essential as the mysterious and superhuman aspects of many horror icons is the aberrant mental state of others. Hannibal Lecter and Norman Bates naturally rule in the realm of realist horror, but gangster films have provided audiences with their own emblematic and terrifying lunatics. Capone-like figures such as Rico and Tony may represent the larger crime organization, but Tommy Udo (Richard Widmark) in *Kiss of Death* (1947) proves to be just as frightening at an individual level. Widmark's portrayal of this psychotic small-time hood raises a seemingly harmless figure to monster

"Widmark's portrayal of this psychotic small-time hood raises a seemingly harmless figure to monster status": Tommy Udo (Richard Widmark) confronts Nick Bianco (Victor Mature) at the conclusion of *Kiss of Death*.

status during the horrific scene in which he throws an invalid old woman down a flight of stairs. Next to Nick, played by the strapping Victor Mature, Udo seems weak and ineffectual, but he manages to terrorize his victims to desperation. He too continually manages to escape the law, though not in a superhuman manner. Although the district attorney assures Nick that Udo's murder trial will result in a sure conviction, Udo is found not guilty, thereby giving him another life.

The element of insanity in Udo's personality is captured and magnified by James Cagney as Cody Jarrett, the diminutive psychopathic gangster in *White Heat* (1949). Cody's horrific death comes in the violent conflagration of a gas fire, reflecting his destruction of his enemies and cohorts. Similarly, Johnny Rocco (Edward G. Robinson) in *Key Largo* (1948) taunts and terrorizes his captors more through his sadistic personality than through actual violence. Perhaps in keeping with the reigning MPAA Code, the anti-heroes of many later films emphasized the gangster's sadism and derangement rather than his penchant for actual violence (Dargis 16). Nevertheless, these characters' brutal natures loomed over the screen like toxic clouds or swarming insects in science fiction horror, or like hordes of the undead in supernatural horror.

Martin Scorsese's most celebrated mob characters also derive their penchant for terror from mental abnormalities. Johnny Boy (Robert De Niro) of *Mean Streets* (1973) and Tommy DeVito (Joe Pesci) of *GoodFellas* (1990) both border on insanity, which makes them even more threatening and unpredictable than their rational partners. Furthermore, the comedy that proceeds from these characters' mental instability magnifies the horror that they evoke by adding to it elements of suspense, surprise, and absurdity. In *GoodFellas*,

"Tommy's act is so horrific that he shocks even this group of inveterate gangsters": Tommy De Vito (Joe Pesci) murders a fellow card player in *GoodFellas*.

for example, Tommy is most lethal when he abruptly shifts from the role of amusing raconteur to unpredictable sadist, as when he suddenly smashes a glass into a restaurant proprietor's forehead, or when he launches into a vicious kicking attack on Billy Batts (Frank Vincent) after this made man teases Tommy about the latter's days as a shoeshine boy. Pesci's portrayal of this evil clown, whose crimes start out as jokes but end up as tragedies, is nothing short of macabre. In another scene, Tommy amuses his fellow card players by shooting Spider (Michael Imperioli), a young gofer, in the foot, but the joke becomes fatal when Spider later says, "Hey, Tommy. Go fuck yourself." Jimmy (Robert De Niro) and Henry (Ray Liotta) jocularly ask Tommy if he is going to take that from the kid, and Tommy responds by murdering Spider. Tommy's act is so horrific that he shocks even this group of inveterate gangsters.

Just as Scorsese co-opted paradigms of volatile characters from classic Hollywood gangster films, David Chase's *The Sopranos* is informed by the canonized horrors of Tommy Udo, Cody Jarrett, and Tommy DeVito, all of whom maim and kill at whim. In Episode 8, "The Legend of Tennessee Moltisanti," Chris shoots a bakery clerk in the foot for not having the right bread, commenting casually, "These things happen sometimes." Indeed they do, and a knowing audience catches both the allusion from *GoodFellas*

"*The Sopranos* is informed by the canonized horrors of Tommy Udo, Cody Jarrett, and Tommy DeVito, all of whom maim and kill at whim."

(the actor who originally played the victim now in the role of shooter) and the suggestion that Chris' violence has been learned from the screen.

Many of *The Sopranos*' episodes foreground grisly, terrifying violence in the comic mode. It is simply not enough to brutally murder a squealer, and Jimmy Altieri's (Joseph Badalucco Jr.) demise in "I Dream of Jeanie Cusamano" (1999) exemplifies the excessive outrages suffered by a mob's victim. Not only is Jimmy riddled with bullets, but the transgression is punctuated by the symbolic effect of a rat stuffed in his mouth. Satriale's meat market, a gang meeting place, also serves as a shredding and disposal preparation center for fatalities, bringing a whole new meaning to the term "waste management." In Episode 25, "The Knight in White Satin Armor," Tony's sister Janice (Aida Turturro) murders her fiancé, Richie Aprile (David Provale), and Tony takes the body to Satriale's for dismemberment prior to an assuredly anonymous burial. As the industrial saw severs the corpse's limbs, Chris comments to Furio (Federico Castelluccio), "I'm not eatin' anything from here for at least seven months." For almost every gruesome murder or shakedown on *The Sopranos*, there is a violent, absurdist comic element as well. After Richie runs over (and over and over) Beansie (Paul Herman) in a parking lot in Episode 16, he lands in the hospital with numerous metal braces; Tony asks, "Do you get the Jets on that thing?" But according to the gangster's code, reverence for the victim would transgress an honorable act, so a caustic, pitiless attitude preserves the survivors from the victims' fate.

This impassive approach to murder and mayhem implies that the criminal must be cavalier and relentless in degrading his victims. Tony Camonte says it best: "Do it first, do it yourself, and keep on doing it." But whereas *The Sopranos* features crude, dark humor to horrify audiences, Tony Camonte dehumanizes his victims by whistling the famous sextet from *Lucia di Lammermoor*, Donizetti's masterpiece concerning rival aristocratic Scottish "gangs" in the 17th century. To those familiar with Italian opera, the irony should not go unnoticed, especially considering the contrast between the horror of Lucia's insane assault on her bridegroom and Tony's lucid, calculating murders.

Many of Hollywood's post-Code gangsters, however, not only lost most of their horrific elements, they also became more levelheaded, perhaps signifying an effort to "clean up" the screen by making the leading mobster somewhat sympathetic, especially as juxtaposed with the hardened gangster who serves as his antagonist. Films such as *The Petrified Forest* (1936), *The Roaring Twenties* (1939), *High Sierra* (1941), *Angels with Dirty Faces* (1938), even the comically inept gangsters in *Each Dawn I Die* (1939) and the waggish thugs in *All Through the Night* (1942) lack the elements of horror and explicit carnage that branded the earlier mob films. Instead of a Rico or a Tony flashing his power through a rabid testosterone-induced spray of machine gun bullets, the post-Code gangster, such as Eddie Bartlett (James Cagney) in *The Roaring Twenties*, captivates the audience with his boyish charm and secret soft-hearted side. Eddie still has the macho tough guy persona that Cagney played in *The Public Enemy*, but he no longer terrifies the public space. In each of the above-mentioned films, the protagonist is a gangster (in *Each Dawn*

"The post-Code gangster, such as Eddie Bartlett (James Cagney) in *The Roaring Twenties*, captivates the audience with his boyish charm and secret soft-hearted side," here posed with Jean (Priscilla Lane).

I Die, the protagonist is aided by a gangster), but one who was coerced into crime by unfortunate circumstances and one who ultimately redeems himself by defeating a malevolent rival. Ironically, then, the post-Code gangster glorified the profession far more than his pre-Code counterpart.

But this moderating effect did not endure. In the seventies, gangsters assumed a patina of respectability with mild outward manners and pretensions of virtue, similar to the morphic powers of Dracula. In Francis Ford Coppola's *The Godfather*, Michael Corelone (Al Pacino) changes from a mild-mannered, college-educated war hero into a ruthless, "cold blooded monster," as his sister puts it after he murders her husband. Her choice of words signifies the random cruelty and mercilessness that afflicts anyone, regardless of blood or business, who transgresses the "Family" code of honor. *The Godfather: Part II* (1974) similarly concludes with Michael's fratricidal hit on Fredo (John Cazale)—an ultimate act of treachery.

In modifying the iconic cinematic gangster, Coppola portrayed a more elite class

"A ruthless, 'cold-blooded monster'": Michael Corleone in the *Godfather* series.

of thugs who adhered to a protocol of stylized violence. Although Vito Corleone (Marlon Brando in *Part I*; Robert De Niro in *Part II*) belongs to the same alien ethnic class as Tony Camonte, he and his second-generation heirs have managed to assimilate, perhaps not into the mainstream of American culture, but certainly into its legal and economic power structure. This sleek representation of Mafiosi does not glorify the mobster's image, but presents him as an even more terrifying, insidious monster who at times appears to be a noble, benevolent man of honor. In *The Godfather*, both Vito and Michael are alternately portrayed as gentle, wise family men and ruthless, degenerate killers. Our horrified reaction to the severed horse's head in the bed depends upon the element of sudden shock that dominates this scene, its owner screaming as if he himself had been mutilated. To conclude this ugly spectacle, Coppola cuts to a tight shot of the Don relaxing at home with a casual, even carefree, expression and an indifferent wave of his hand, as if to comment, "It's all in a day's work."

Just as *The Godfather* shows the mobster's mutating forays from monster to gentleman, *GoodFellas* emphasizes his innate seedy nihilism. A few choice scenes illustrate the dark comedic mode that is characteristic of Scorsese's art. The ad hoc burial and subsequent exhumation of Billy Batts exemplifies the normalcy with which the mob approaches acts usually reserved for ghoulish, undead monsters straight out of Stephen King novels, the only difference being that the mob operates in this manner in the "real" world. Every criminal act of Paulie Cicero's (Paul Sorvino) gang exemplifies routine procedure. Les Keyser explains that "Scorsese wanted to avoid the mythical dimensions of Coppola's *Godfather* saga and instead capture everyday actualities. He told Gavin Smith that for him *The Godfather* was 'epic poetry, like *Morte D'Arthur*'; his 'stuff,' Scorsese maintained, 'is like some guy on the streetcar talking'" (201). But for his audience, these ordinary guys operate in a paradigm of privilege and freedom that ordinary mortals can only imagine.

For this reason, Henry Hill's overt running commentary lends an almost humanizing note to his gory tale, although the ironic upshot of a career criminal justifying his actions to an uninitiated audience cannot go undetected. Seymour Chatman elucidates this narratological phenomenon in *Story and Discourse*: "The overt narrator's capacity to judge goes far beyond adjectives and descriptive phrases; it evokes a whole epistemology and argues the matter in a discursive, rhetorical way. In so doing it presupposes a set of norms quite contrary to the one that the implied audience presumably entertains" (243). Henry's wife, Karen (Lorraine Bracco), validates his rhetoric by commenting that it wasn't long before everything her husband did "seemed normal."

Prior to *GoodFellas*, though, one of the most enduring gangster icons of the last twenty years was *Scarface*'s Tony Montana, whom Brian De Palma and Oliver Stone (as screenwriter) depict as anything but normal. In her essay "Brian De Palma's Horror Films," Allison Graham only briefly refers to this filmmaker's most terrifying character; compared to the satanic, personal realm of the eponymous Carrie (Sissy Spacek), however, Tony threatens not only those who have injured him but society as a whole. He does this primarily with drugs, which effect a widespread, random mode of violence and destruction. Graham does point out, however, that De Palma's Tony reveals a monumental thirst for power when he says, "Me? I want what's coming to me . . . the world, Chico, and everything in it"; and she explains that the world does, indeed, come to him (142), establishing Tony's potential for terrorization of an entire society.

The traditional horror paradigm is fundamental to this film. De Palma sets up his notorious buzz-saw scene according to the traditional suspense structure of horror by panning off the victim a moment prior to the violent attack, thereby creating a false sense of security for the viewer. After several moments of frivolity between Manny (Steven Bauer) and a bikinied blonde on the street below, the camera returns to Angel (Pepe Serna)'s head half sawed off, accompanied by the obligatory splatter effects. As one victim goes down, the scene concludes with a spray of automatic gunfire, and Tony executes his rival at close range in the street. This scene helps to establish Tony's eventual stature as not only a seemingly indestructible despot, but an intrepid warrior. Such gradual character construction may not conform to traditional horror narratives whereby the monster arrives on the scene already endowed with superhuman powers, but it does demonstrate how a powerless, impoverished refugee can build a reputation for terror, and eventually menace a major American city.

Most importantly, the appeal of this film is grounded not only in its excessive violence and flashy contemporary setting, but in the perverse relationship that the audience develops with Tony. Although he is not a particularly sympathetic character, he is certainly a compelling and dazzling anti-hero, as much as Tom Powers in *The Public Enemy*. Of course, much of the allure in question derives from the intense, captivating acting styles of Pacino and Cagney, but the characters on the screen take on a life of their own and have become icons of popular culture.

It is particularly noteworthy that De Palma's Tony has evoked both admiration and horror in many viewers, and since this film adheres to the horror mode in so many respects, sympathy for the devil, as Noël Carroll puts it, is generated for the eponymous antagonist. Carroll explains that "sympathy for the devil is a recurring theme in horror fiction . . . generally due to the fact that the moral assessment of the monster in the story, or the grounds for the audience's moral evaluation of the monster, have been shifted in the monster's favor" (143). Tony does not elicit sympathy, nor does he merit morality points. Instead, he seduces the viewer with his overwhelming power as one man against a multitude of criminal forces, even though he is an inveterate criminal himself. Despite whatever identification the audience might form with Tony, his demise is essential to the narrative, since the conventional implication of his death would be that the social order is restored, at least temporarily, after a period of chaos. In this version of the film, however, Tony perishes at the hands of a rival gang rather than the police. Although such closure probably imitates life more accurately than the traditional denouement of death by police fire as in the 1932 *Scarface*, it leaves the careful viewer with a lingering impression of fear and uneasiness. Similar to the monsters of traditional horror narratives, the gangster always leaves a space for his return in various forms. They are the "undead" of social pariahs.

In *New Jack City* (1991), Nino Brown (Wesley Snipes) exemplifies yet another urban drug lord who terrorizes an entire community in the style of his cinematic mentor, Tony Montana, threatening his victims with random violence while ravishing them with crack. From a social standpoint, the Cash Money Brothers' grasp on the Carter building is no less frightening than King Kong on the Empire State Building or aliens attacking the White House. Even the renegade cops, Scotty (Ice-T) and Nick (Judd Nelson), fail to overpower the gang via unorthodox and perilous methods. Towards the end, the district attorney's case against Nino is dismissed on a technicality, and, like Tommy Udo, he seems as immortal as a vampire until a seemingly innocuous character guns him down.

The sympathy that such a character might elicit, however, does not imply that his downfall is tragic in the same manner as the Frankenstein monster's demise. Siegfried Kracauer argues that the gangster's "sufferings in the wake of adverse circumstances and unfortunate destiny are often called tragic," but "the gangster who prefers death at the hands of the police to capture and punishment [does not] bear any resemblance to the tragic hero" (265). Traditionally speaking, tragedy implies a sense of human nobility, as with the Frankenstein monster; whereas the iconic gangster, be it Tony Camonte or Tony Montana, proves to be inhumanly malicious and abjectly immoral.

"The renegade cops, Scotty (Ice-T) and Nick (Judd Nelson)," in *New Jack City*.

Rooting for a monster may not seem all that absurd when he disguises himself as an indulgent father or a caring son or brother. He can be a picaresque figure who holds the power to remedy social injustices and personal injuries. One can lose judicious perception quite easily when Tony Soprano (James Gandolfini) and his henchman rough up a remiss and indifferent doctor on a golf course. Likewise, viewers may hope that Tony will whack Ralphie (Joe Pantoliano) for beating to death his goomah, a young, rather pathetic "exotic dancer." Tony distinguishes himself from the gang by holding out some sympathy for her, if only as a result of his subconsciously comparing her with his temporarily estranged daughter, Meadow (Jamie-Lynn Sigler). The stripper approached him as a father figure, oddly enough, and Tony is not wholly offended. Such instances of compassion or empathy, no matter how brief, can lure viewers into a false sense of identification with the villain, and may cause them to forget that Tony is a ruthless crime boss who kills for business and pleasure ("I wish it was me in there," he confides to

"The iconic gangster, be it Tony Camonte or Tony Montana, proves to be inhumanly malicious and abjectly immoral."

his psychiatrist, referring to Furio's savage shakedown of a reluctant brothel proprietor). This is especially the case during sentimental, almost childlike moments when the villain is seen alone watching old movies, feeding ducks, or spoiling his children. But this dualistic representation makes him even more treacherous in that we may momentarily forget that he has killed his best friend, ruined his childhood companion's business, and burnt down another friend's restaurant.

As Bill Tonelli explains, "The men on *The Sopranos* do what most men, in their hearts, wish they could do: spend time with one another out and about, idle and unrestrained by the civilizing presence of women in their workplace, free to drink, smoke, curse, eat thick sandwiches of meat and cheese and carry guns and fat rolls of large-denomination bills. They freely commit violence and fornicate, the very things men still do best but are most vigorously denied by contemporary codes of acceptable conduct" (*New York Times*, March 2, 2001).

But if these men are mortal—and moral—monsters, is it only because they are not bound by conventional social etiquette? I think not. Most of their appeal, it seems, derives from the comedic paradigm in which they operate. Because of their highly caricatured personas, we find them perhaps more endearing than threatening, but this is, once again, the treachery of their appeal.

Recent episodes on *The Sopranos* have foregrounded the horrific side of the mob, departing little from the true-crime incidents this fiction represents. Another *Times* article claims that "with the mob's reality so emphasized and illustrated by convincing characterizations, viewers absorb both entertainment and horrific realism that rarely surfaces in traditional cinema." Regarding the level of violence on the series, Caryn James comments that "while the blood, beatings and deaths have kept everyone buzzing, from ordinary viewers to the president of NBC, the more important issue goes beyond how much splatter appears on screen. For the first time, this season's *Sopranos* relied heavily on violence directed against innocents, especially women, characters not involved in Tony's mob career. . . . [The] series creator, David Chase, has done more than escalate the brutality. He has kept the series honest, true to the lethal consequences of a mob boss's life" (May 19, 2001).

Not surprisingly, this emphasis on fierce reality has attracted more viewers than it has alienated. Bill Carter, also of the *Times*, has noted that "*The Sopranos* has been a bigger hit than ever this season, scoring ratings in its initial broadcasts on Sunday night that have frequently eclipsed those on the broadcast networks . . . [and] has achieved this despite being in only about a third as many homes as the networks" (May 21, 2001). Perhaps, then, the lure of the horrifying wields more fascination for a contemporary audience that has been desensitized to the big screen's violent spectacles. Similar to younger audiences' fascination with the De Palma *Scarface*, *Sopranos* viewers continue to be drawn in by the horrifying suspense generated by point-blank executions and whacks with nine irons, which are, in the long run, both shocking and absurdly comic.

The lure of gangland horrors will undoubtedly continue to captivate audiences for the foreseeable future. TBS is about to air yet another rendition of the John Gotti story, and with soldiers and consiglieri like Sammy the Bull (who boasts of having committed more than nineteen murders), the lone serial killer, or even the ever-recrudescent vampire, seems rather inefficient in the terror department.

Works Cited

Black, Gregory. *The Catholic Crusade against the Movies, 1940-1975*. New York: Cambridge University Press, 1997.

———. *Hollywood Censored: Morality Codes, Catholics, and the Movies*. Cambridge: Cambridge University Press, 1994.

Carroll, Noël. *The Philosophy of Horror; or, Paradoxes of the Heart*. London: Routledge, 1990.

Carter, Bill. "NBC Executive Raises Issues on *Sopranos*." *New York Times*, May 2, 2001: http://www.nytimes.com/2001/05/02/business/02NBC.html?ex=991530785& ei=1&en=91c7ceal14274047.

Chatman, Seymour. *Story and Discourse: Narrative Structure in Fiction and Film*. Ithaca, NY: Cornell University Press, 1978.

Dargis, Manohla. "Dark Side of the Dream." *Sight and Sound*, August 1996: 15+.

Doherty, Thomas. *Pre-Code Hollywood: Sex, Immorality, and Insurrection in American Cinema 1930-1934*. New York: Columbia University Press, 1999.

Graham, Allison. "'The Fallen Wonder of the World': Brian De Palma's Horror Films." *American Horrors: Essays on the Modern American Horror Film*, ed. Gregory Waller. Urbana: University of Illinois Press, 1987: 129-44.

James, Caryn. "The Sopranos: Violence Rises on TV, but on This HBO Show, It Makes a Point." *New York Times*, May 22, 2001. http://www. nytimes.com/2001/05/22/arts/22NOTE.html?ex=99 1530589&ie=&en= baffc 38a324e4056.

Keyser, Les. *Martin Scorsese*. Twayne's Filmmakers Series. New York: Twayne Publishers, 1995.

Kracauer, Siegfried. *The Theory of Film: The Redemption of Physical Reality*. Princeton, NJ: Oxford University Press, 1960.

Munby, Jonathan. *Public Enemies, Public Heroes: Screening the Gangster from* Little Caesar *to* Touch of Evil. Chicago: University of Chicago Press, 1999.

Remnick, David. "Is This the End of Rico?" *New Yorker*, April 1, 2001, 21+.

Teachout, Terry. "The Sopranos: Things We Can't Miss, and Things We Can't Forget." *New York Times*, May 20, 2001. http://www.nytimes.com/2001/05/20/ arts/20TEACH.html?ex=991541374&ei= &en=11cb59bc9b30806c.

Tonelli, Bill. "A 'Sopranos Secret': Given the Choice, We'd All Be Mobsters." *New York Times*, March 4, 2001. http://www.nytimes.Com/2001/03/04/arts/ 04TONE.html?ex=991541568&ei=1&en=3d.

Young men on the mean streets of Chicago.

Fukasaku and Scorsese: Yakuzas and Gangsters

Joaquín da Silva

As Mark Schilling points out, yakuza and Hollywood gangster films have long constituted distinct genres and have evolved differently over the years.[1] Paul Schrader argues that the yakuza film bears little resemblance to its American or European counterpart. More specifically, he asserts that the yakuza film does not reflect the dilemma of social mobility depicted in the 1930s American gangster film, nor does it reflect the despair of the post-war film noir. It aims for a higher moral purpose, one that springs from the *giri-ninjo* (*giri*, social obligation; *ninjo*, personal inclination) conflict, an essential theme in yakuza films.[2]

From a purely historical point of view, it is indisputable that the Japanese and Hollywood gangster films have had different periods of generic mutation and have focused on very different themes. Nonetheless there is a confluence between the individual national iterations of the genre. This is typified in two gangster films released in 1973, one Japanese, *Jingi Naki Tatakai* (*Battles without Honor and Humanity*), directed by Kinji Fukasaku, and the other American, *Mean Streets*, directed by Martin Scorsese. These two movies, which are part of very different national cinemas and backgrounds, use similar themes and techniques to arrive at similar conclusions. They also marked an important divergence in the evolutionary path of the gangster and yakuza genres to that point. This essay will examine these similarities and differences between the two genres and also consider how themes initially belonging to one or the other national genre have crossed over to its counterpart. Although both were released the same year, there is nothing to indicate that either filmmaker was aware of the other's project, so it is hardly possible that they directly influenced each other in any way. And although Scorsese's *Mean Streets* is at least partly an homage to gangster films of the 1930s such as *The Public Enemy*, a fable of young men on the make for power scrutinized with the added realism of hand-held camera and saturated colors and manipulated with techniques such as jump cuts and slow motion, Fukasaku's *Battles without Honor and Humanity* is a rejection of the idealized depiction of the yakuza in the *ninkyo-eiga* ("chivalry films") of the 1960s.

The American Great Depression and the coming of sound coincided with a new kind of realism in Hollywood films. New genres emerged that challenged the idea of the American Dream, with its possibilities of prosperity and social equality for all. The gangster film became, at the beginning of the 1930s, a reflection of society. As Robert Warshow asserted, the gangster became a sort of tragic hero, who rose to power through crime, the only alternative to succeed, but was ultimately immolated. At least, this could be so until the Production Code compelled the studios to shift the emphasis from the gangster as a tragic hero to the gangster as a social victim, emphasizing at the same time that crime does not pay.

The figure of the gangster changed radically in the 1940s and 1950s and was mostly subsumed in a new genre, film noir. The heroes in these movies were most often private or police detectives or some other enforcer of the law. Gangsters, even when in prominent roles, were always the antagonists. Not until 1967 with Arthur Penn's *Bonnie and Clyde*, a period film set again during the American Depression, were gangsters once more represented not just as tragic heroes but also as revolutionary ones. The release of Francis Ford Coppola's *The Godfather* in 1972 continued the trend toward mythologizing the figure of the gangster, in this case the Italian mafiosi who had been so crudely depicted four decades earlier in *Little Caesar* and *Scarface*.

In Japan, although critic Keiko McDonald cites earlier examples of yakuza films such as Daisuke Ito's *Chuji tabi nikki* (*Chuji's Travel Diary* [1927]) or Hiroshi Inagaki's *Mabuta no haha* (*The Mother He Never Knew* [1931]), the core period for yakuza films really began with *ninkyo-eiga*, a prototype of which is Tadashima Tadashi's *Jinsei Gekijo: Hishakaku* (*Theatre of Life: Hishakaku* [1963]). This film contained a new narrative formula for yakuza films that would be used in one variation or another in over three hundred subsequent motions pictures before the decade was out. It coincided with a revived star system in Japan.[3] The periods were usually late Taisho to early Showa (1923–40) and like the Hollywood gangster film the settings were usually urban, in modern Tokyo. Honorable yakuza are depicted as living—and dying—by the *jingi* code. *Jingi* is the moral and ethical equivalent of *bushido* ("the way of the warrior") by which the yakuza abide. As McDonald observes, "The yakuza experiences his own version of the characteristic Japanese tension between opposing values of *giri* and *ninjo*."[4] She further explains that "*Jin* expresses the Confucian virtue of benevolence; *gi*, the values of justice and rectitude . . . the element of rectitude yields the concept of absolute loyalty to the Organization, its boss (*oyabun*) especially."[5] The mythical stature of the *oyabun* is underlined by wearing traditional Japanese garments.

Gregory Barrett concludes that by combining elements of the samurai and the yakuza codes *jingi* can be seen as a modern equivalent to *bushido* and its proponents as modern samurai.[6] Like their samurai counterparts in the feudal era, the dishonorable yakuza are only interested in money and represent the worst aspects of modernization, Westernization, and corruption of traditional Japanese social values. Honorable and dishonorable individuals, good and bad men, must fight it out in a war of moral values.

According to Schrader the enormous success of *The Godfather* in Japan spurred Toei studios, the main producer of yakuza pictures, to shift emphasis to a more "documentary style" yakuza film or *jitsuroku eiga* (true story films).[7] This assertion is puzzling, if not contradictory, since the style of *The Godfather* is far from documentary. Its opening scenes cut back and forth between very dark tones in interior shots, a reflection on the machinations of the Mafia, and the bright exteriors of a wedding. *The Godfather* shares with the yakuza films of the 1960s a narrative stress on family loyalty, a criminal's sense of honor, and underworld justice. Schrader, quoting Tadao Sato, explains how duty can be more important than humanity in *ninkyo eiga*.[8] This could just as easily apply to *The Godfather* when, for example, Michael Corleone follows in his father's footsteps and becomes "godfather," then ignores his own sister's pleas and orders the death of her husband, Carlo, who helped in the murder of their elder brother, Sonny. While cross-cutting may occasionally be used in a documentary, the elaborate montage in the cycle of killings that concludes *The Godfather*, which is rife with extreme violence and ritualistic overtones, is far removed from any documentary style. The cycle of deceit into which Michael Corleone is drawn is thematically closer to the *giri-ninjo* conflicts than to a realistic portrait of a ruthless killer. If anything *jitsuroku eiga* finds its Western equivalent in a film such as *Mean Streets*.

In an interview Kinji Fukasaku explained that he believed his 1970s films were seen by society as too brutal and that he felt rejected by mass audiences.[9] In succeeding decades, his innovations in both technique and the depiction of violence became mainstream. Analogously, if Scorsese's *Mean Streets* brought freshness to the gangster film genre with his realistic and unglamorous view of the personas and lifestyles of small-time gangsters in Little Italy, by the time of *GoodFellas* (1990) Scorsese had appended mythical implications. *Mean Streets* in many ways shares the *giri-ninjo* conflict that prevails in the yakuza film. The *giri* is evoked as Charlie (Harvey Keitel) tries to remain loyal to his uncle Giovanni. The *ninjo* aspects are his deep-rooted Catholicism, which supports his inclination to help Johnny Boy (Robert de Niro), and his love for his cousin Teresa.

In his book *Hollywood Genres*, Thomas Schatz succinctly describes Charlie's internal conflict when he examines the downfall of the gangster hero:

> This internal conflict between individual accomplishment and the common good, between man's self-serving and communal instincts, between his savagery and his rational morality is mirrored in society, but the opposing impulses have reached a delicate and viable balance within the modern city. The gangster's efforts to realign that balance to suit his own particular needs are therefore destined to failure.[10]

In discussing the *giri-ninjo* conflict in the post-war samurai film, David Desser explains how "in Japanese life the *giri/ninjo* conflict is unresolvable," and consequently, "when confronted by the *giri/ninjo* conflict, the hero of the Nostalgic Samurai Drama makes his choice knowing full well the price to be paid in social alienation and/or self-abnegation."[11] In Charlie's case there are several conflicting things that threaten to destroy him. First of all, it is his loyalty to uncle Giovanni, seen as the authority figure of the neighborhood (the *oyabun* figure in the yakuza film), somebody who oversees order in the community. Secondly, it is Charlie's sense of penance, which is externalized in the form of Johnny Boy.

A more fundamental reason for Charlie to help Johnny Boy is family ties. Whether defined by blood or by gang affiliation, the family defines the core relationship for the protagonist in the gangster film, a core that, ironically, usually ensures the protagonist's destruction.[12] Charlie's religious convictions condemn his activities, such as collecting payments for his uncle Giovanni, and certain of his emotional attachments, such as his infatuation with the African American dancer at Tony's bar, which runs counter to the racism of his Italian American associates. These add to the existing burden of Catholic guilt, a longing to be punished. Thus conflicted and in the context of the genre, Charlie's struggle to achieve his goals is doomed. As Schatz points out, the main flaw in the gangster hero is "his inability to channel his considerable energies in a viable direction."[13] As the voice-over at the very beginning of the film elucidates: "You don't make up for your sins in the church, you do it in the streets, you do it at home." Charlie spends all his energy trying to do just that, to save Johnny Boy and to keep his uncle happy, but he cannot maintain the delicate balance between *giri* and *ninjo*.

In contrast, Fukasaku seems to take up the themes and purposes of the earlier Hollywood gangster films of the 1930s. As McDonald notes, he "puts its subject in a broad social context: modern Japan in the twenty-five year period ending in 1970."[14] Fukasaku's films question the values of post-war Japan

"Deep-rooted Catholicism": Charlie prays for guidance in *Mean Streets*.

by linking the ascension of
the Yamamori gang in *Battles
without Honor and Humanity*
with that of Japan itself. This
mirrors the rise to power of a
gangster such as Tom Powers,
the James Cagney character
in *The Public Enemy*. The conversion of the yakuza into
businessmen, and the fact that
it throws certain figures out
of step with the times, recalls
the position Burt Lancaster's
character Frankie Madison
in *I Walk Alone* (1948) or, in
the neo-noir adaptations of

Harvey Keitel (right) as Charlie, whose "sense of penance . . .
is externalized in the form of Johnny Boy"
(Robert De Niro).

Donald Westlake's *The Hunter*, Walker (Lee Marvin) in *Point Blank* (1967) or
Porter (Mel Gibson) in *Payback* (1999).

Shozo Hirono (Bunta Sugawara), the main character in *Battles without
Honor and Humanity*, is a brute who follows the *jingi* code. When Hirono gets
involved in a fight with a member of a rival gang he decides to follow the
ritual of cutting his little finger (*yubitsume*) and presents it wrapped in a white
cloth in appeasement to Yamamori, the rival gang's *oyabun*. Yamamori, in
fact, scorns Hirono and the value of the finger, while insisting that Hirono
pull some job to get money for the clan. Hirono, even though faithful to
the *jingi* code, has no idea of how to perform *yubitsume*. Fukasaku gives the
sequence a comical tone which parodies the yakuza ceremonies that permeate the *ninkyo-eiga*. The fact that this important ritual is not taken seriously
is highlighted when Hirono's offering is mocked as going to extremes over a

"Mirror[ing] the rise to power of a gangster such as Tom Powers":
the *Battles without Honor and Humanity* series.

frivolous dispute. Later Hirono will kill another rival *oyabun* to save his own boss and then agrees to go to jail when Yamamori offers him the control of the gang after he is released. Sticking to the code of *jingi*, Hirono is used and betrayed by his own boss. Like Madison, Walker, or Porter, Charlie and Hirono are anachronistic figures, "old school" mentalities trying to survive in a newer, more pragmatic gangsterism. Their codes are ignored or scorned by most of their contemporaries.

While *Mean Streets* shares common ground with the classical yakuza films and while Fukasaku takes on the social and historical issues that are normally seen in the classic American gangster film, *Mean Streets*, an independent production, is closer in style than in content to the conventions of Old Hollywood. *Battles without Honor and Humanity*, a studio production, challenges genre conventions. As Fukasaku himself has commented, his "contribution to the development of Japanese cinema was to abolish the star system."[15] Much like certain "B" film producers in the United States, by using expectations based on genre rather than performers Toei could compete for audiences by relying on more sensational content produced at lower budgets. Even though Fukasaku is a studio filmmaker, his yakuza films were made in the same context as *Mean Streets*: the Hollywood New Wave, in which the director was more prominent. Fukasaku was, despite this and for most of his career, a studio director working on studio assignments, many of them quite conventional.

In the wake of European art cinema and during the emergence of Hollywood *auteurism*, the end of the 1960s and beginning of the 1970s, directors acquired more control of their work. Certainly the work of the French *nouvelle vague* had an enormous influence on these American *auteurs*, especially the technical aspects of their filmmaking. Lightweight camera equipment and more sensitive film stock could be used in location shots with only available light, creating an aura that mimicked cinéma vérité. Editing that used jump cuts, direct and voice-over narration, parallel points-of-view, and the like had both theoretical and material underpinnings. Japan had its own New Wave with Nagisa Oshima in the forefront. Rather that acknowledging any influence from his French counterparts, Oshima cites the movies of Yasuzo Masumura and Ko Nakahira as having an enormous impact on his own work.[16]

Indisputably *Mean Streets* and *Battles without Honor and Humanity* were made under the influence of very different cultural contexts. However, the Classical Hollywood and European art cinema and the *ninkyo eiga* are film genotypes that can cut across cultural boundaries. Clearly also both filmmakers had been influenced by the style and substance of documentaries. Scorsese recalls that he "witnessed American daily life etched for the first time on American screens in unsanitized, ethnically diverse images by the New American Cinema documentarists."[17] Fukasaku's use of the hand-held camera started after he saw newsreels from the student movements, where grainy images showed college kids and farmers fighting the police.[18]

Fukasaku believes he first began to use a hand-held camera in *Hitokiri Yota* (1972). In fact, it was in a film made earlier that year, *Gunki Hatameku Mot Ni*, in which he intersperses photographic stills taken at the New Guinea front during World War II. The film follows the widow (Sachiko Hidari) of Sergeant Togashi (Tetsuro Tamba) in her search to discover what really happened to her husband, executed for desertion in New Guinea. Whereas the main story is shot in color, flashbacks of the interviews she made with her husband's comrades are shot in black-and-white to enhance the documentary feel.

So despite very different cinematic backgrounds, Scorsese's and Fukasaku's similar worldview emerged from their depiction of violence, their demystification of the gangster and his world, and their documentary-like visualizations, all of which infused their work with a greater sense of realism and immediacy to the people portrayed in their films. The concordance between both films is revealed in their first minutes. *Mean Streets* opens as Charlie is awakened by a voice-over that is quite disorientating, particularly since it is not Charlie's own voice (but, in fact, Martin Scorsese's voice). The voice-over confirms what the mise-en-scène suggests: an austere room and a spotlighted crucifix on the wall, Charlie's struggle between his religious convictions and his rough environment and unlawful activities and friends are all quickly established with the city as backdrop. The hand-held camerawork follows the tormented Charlie around the room. Jump cuts punctuated by the first notes of "Be My Baby" by the Ronettes are used after Charlie returns to bed and falls asleep again.

This sequence is followed by the main title credits: the song continues the soundtrack under mock home movie footage of the christening of a little boy from Charlie's family and the subsequent party where the main characters of the film are introduced. The home movie rendering of the rituals of life is in marked contrast, almost a parody of the elaborate sequences which open and close *The Godfather*. Once the title credits conclude, there is a long shot of a religious procession in Little Italy. The shaky and black-and-white faux 8mm is transformed into the normal world of the movie itself shot in color 35mm that perfectly situates the story in a specific spatial context. From this point, the elaborate introduction of the four main characters uses a dynamic

"Documentary-like visualizations" in the *Battles without Honor and Humanity* series.

introduced by Sergio Leone in *The Good, the Bad, and the Ugly* as the end of each sequence which establishes a character's personality—Charlie is the religiously repressed and guilty one; Tony runs a bar and also has a strong sense of morality; Michael is the racketeer, easily fooled; and Johnny Boy is the crazy one. Scorsese uses a freeze frame and superimposes the character's name on the screen.

The opening sequences of *Battles without Honor and Humanity* are remarkably similar. A still photograph of the mushroom cloud covering the sky of Hiroshima is the first image, accompanied by Toshiaki Tsushima's dramatic soundtrack. This photograph cedes to several others of the city right after the bombing. Then the narrative shifts to moving images, still in black and white, of a Hiroshima public market, which finally metamorphoses into the color and anamorphic images of the movie proper. The attempted rape of a Japanese girl by an American G.I. and the scuffles that follow are shot by Fukasaku with a shaky hand-held camera. The images come to an abrupt stop every time the main characters are introduced, one by one, in freeze frames with their names superimposed on the screen.

The beginnings of both films are far from identical but share a significant number of stylistic manipulations employed to similar purpose. The home-movie footage of *Mean Streets* and the black-and-white stills of Hiroshima in *Battles without Honor and Humanity* both invoke the sense of a found document, of authenticity, because they place the narrative in a very specific historical, cultural, and spatial context. The freeze frame and superimpositions underline the influence that documentary or cinéma vérité had on both directors. Generically both directors share these techniques as their respective plots demystify the gangster film genre. Mark Schilling notes that "in the late 1960s, directors such as Kinji Fukasaku, Kosaku Yamashita and Junya Sato began making yakuza movies that more nearly reflected contemporary

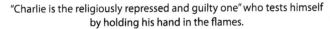

"Charlie is the religiously repressed and guilty one" who tests himself by holding his hand in the flames.

The craziness of Johnny Boy (Robert De Niro) upsets Tony (David Proval).

realities, with a gritty violence and brutality that had little to do with the ideals of *giri* and *ninjo*, everything to do with life and death on Japan's *mean streets* [emphasis mine]."[19]

Another aspect that bridges the cultural divide between Mean *Streets* and *Battles without Honor and Humanity* is their autobiographical context. This is more prominent in Scorsese's film, since some of its characters are based on friends of the director and some of events actually happened to him. As Scorsese himself has explained, "*Mean Streets* was an attempt to put myself and my old friends on the screen, to show how we lived, what life was in Little Italy. It was really an anthropological or a sociological tract."[20]

The autobiographical elements are less obvious in Fukasaku's film, but *Battles without Honor and Humanity* is also based on real events. The story is adapted from a novel by the journalist Koichi Iiboshi that was created using his interviews with the imprisoned and deposed *oyabun* of the Mino gang, Kozo Mino.[21] Just before his death Fukasaku remarked that in making a new sort of youthful and violent yakuza film, as with his last complete film, *Battle Royale*, he "wanted to replace the old techniques with a new kind of film, where I could overlay my own experiences of living in post-war Japan."[22] The end of that war had brought for the young Fukasaku a total collapse of all the values he had learnt at school: authority, nation, honor, etc.[23] Fukasaku saw the end of World War II as the beginning of a state of anarchy where friendship and camaraderie are put to the test, a view that becomes the main motif in *Battle Royale*. This theme also constitutes one of the main elements in *Mean Streets* as Charlie tries to help his closest friend Johnny Boy against a menacing environment that threatens to destroy their friendship.

The connections between *Mean Streets* and *Battles without Honor and Humanity* go beyond the immediate whether the subversion of genre conventions or atypical visual elements. These films have enormously influenced the yakuza and gangster films that followed. So it should not come as a surprise that *Battles without Honor and Humanity* was selected by the *Kinema Junpo*, the eminent Japanese cinema magazine, as one of the twenty best films in the history of Japanese cinema. *Mean Streets* is often taken with *The Godfather* as one of "the two most important gangster films of the seventies."[24]

The narrative and stylistic innovations of Fukasaku's film were soon co-opted by his own production company, Toei in making more *jitsuroku eiga*. To add more realism to these new yakuza films, former gangsters such as Noburo Ando were cast in significant roles. Ando had a small part in *Battles without Honor and Humanity* and starred in several films such as *Boriyoku Gai* (*The Violent Street* [1974]) and *Ando Noboru no Waga Tobo to Sex no Kiroku* (*Noboru Ando's Chronicle of Fugitive Days and Sex* [1976]). Later he directed his own films such as *Yakuza Zankoku Hiroku—Kataude Setsudan* (*Yakuza Cruel Secrets—Arm Dismemberment* [1976]). After a marked decline in popularity of yakuza stories made them bad box office in the mid-1970s, independent directors such as Ishii Takashi, Kitano Takeshi, and more recently Miike Takashi, have resurrected and redefined the genre in the 1990s. The graphic and surreal violence depicted in films such as Miike's *Koroshiya* (*Ichi the Killer* [2001]) and *Gokudô kyôfu dai-gekijô: Gozu* (*Yakuza Horror Theater: Gozu* [2003]), even the phantasmagorical and transgeneric explosion of *Izo* (2004), are all rooted in Fukasaku's original and anarchic view of the savage world of the yakuza. Aaron Gerow describes the groundwork laid by Kinji Fukasaku for Takashi as his "apocalyptic nihilism and sympathy for Japan's social marginals."[25] These characteristics are also shared by Ishii Takashi's film *Gonin* (1995), where the five main characters of the story represent five types of outcasts in the structure of Japanese society: a former pop singer, who is secretly gay; a disgraced policeman who has just been released from prison; a recently fired salaryman; a brain-damaged former boxer turned pimp; and his lover, a Filipino illegal immigrant.

Gonin has often been compared to Quentin Tarantino's *Pulp Fiction* (1994). Before his overt foray into the world of *giri* and *ninjo* with *Kill Bill*, Tarantino, just like his Japanese counterparts, had tried to redefine the gangster in his films from the 1990s. Narrative and visual anomalies and the extensive use of a soundtrack of popular songs are elements of Tarantino's work that clearly derive from the example of *Mean Streets*. Scorsese's soundtrack for *Mean Streets*, derived mainly from the songs of his youth, epitomized the drama; as Scorsese has said, "The whole movie was 'Jumping Jack Flash' and 'Be My Baby.'"[26] Another through-line from *Mean Streets* can be seen in the work of Guy Ritchie. One of the most obvious lifts from *Mean Streets* in Ritchie's first feature film, *Lock, Stock and Two Smoking Barrels*, is the use of the snorry-cam (a camera that is fixed to the actor's body) after one of the protagonists, Eddy (Nick Moran), loses 100,000 pounds on a bad poker hand. In *Mean Streets* the same technique was used to follow a drunken Charlie as he staggered around Tony's Bar. In his second film, *Snatch*, Ritchie's complicated narrative uses several interlocking stories, flashy camerawork, and an almost wall-to-wall soundtrack of popular tunes.

More than three decades after their almost simultaneous release, the technical and narrative innovations of *Battles without Honor and Humanity* and *Mean Streets* continue to inspire imitators and elaborators. Wherever new generations of filmmakers may take the American or Japanese gangster film, 1973 will certainly remain a milestone year in their histories.

In 2006 Scorsese directly bridged the gap between American and Asian depictions of contemporary gangsters when he used the Hong Kong production *Infernal Affairs* as the basis for his latest gangster film *The Departed*.

Matt Damon (left) and Leonardo DiCaprio as a crooked supervisor and an undercover Boston police officer in *The Departed*.

Notes

1. Mark Schilling, "Yakuza Films: Fading Celluloid Heroes," *Japan Quarterly* 43, no. 6 (July–September 1996): 30.

2. Paul Schrader, "*Yakuza-eiga*: A Primer," *Film Comment* 10, no. 1 (January–February 1974): 10.

3. Keiko Iwai McDonald, "The Yakuza Film: An Introduction," in *Reframing Japanese Cinema: Authorship, Genre, History*, ed. Arthur Nolleti and David Desser (Bloomington: Indiana University Press, 1992), 174.

4. Ibid., 167.

5. Ibid., 190.

6. Gregory Barrett, *Archetypes in Japanese Film* (London: Associated University Presses, 1989), 64.

7. Schrader, 10.

8. Ibid., 12.

9. Patrick Macias, *TokyoScope: The Japanese Cult Film Companion* (San Francisco: Cadence Books, 2001), 154.

10. Thomas Schatz, *Hollywood Genres* (Boston: MacGraw-Hill, 1981), 85.

11. Nolleti, 150.

12. Ibid., 94.

13. Ibid.

14. Nolleti, 184.

15. Macias, 185.

16. David Desser, *Eros Plus Massacre: An Introduction to the Japanese New Wave Cinema* (Bloomington: Indiana University Press, 1988), 41–43.

17. David Thompson and Ian Christie, *Scorsese on Scorsese* (London: Faber & Faber, 1989), 20.

18. Macias, 154. One can assume that Fukasaku meant the documentaries of Shinsuke Ogawa made between 1968 and 1973 and focusing on the protests of rural villagers and farmers around Sanrizuka against the construction of Narita International Airport (*Summer in Narita, The Three-Day War in Narita, Peasants of the Second Fortress, The Building of the Iwayama Tower*, and *Heta Village*).

19. Schilling, 40.

20. Thompson and Christie, 48.

21. Macias, 141.

22. Ibid., 153.

23. Aaron Gerow, *Fukasaku Kinji: Underworld Historiographer.*

24. Phil Hardy, *Gangsters* (London: Aurum Press, 1998).

25. Gerow.

26. Thompson and Christie, 45.

The Hong Kong Gangster Movie

Tony Williams

Most Western viewers associate the Hong Kong gangster film with the post-1986 films of John Woo, namely *A Better Tomorrow* (1986), *A Better Tomorrow 2* (1987), portions of *A Bullet in the Head* (1990), and *Hard Boiled* (1992). Although these films offered Woo his ticket to Hollywood and glamorized the ugly world of gangsters in a manner similar to their Hollywood competitors, the Hong Kong gangster film is more of a hybrid entity. It may encompass many different genres such as romance, comedy, prison movie, historical epic, the undercover agent narrative depicted in the *Infernal Affairs* trilogy and other types of films.[1] Stephen Chow's worldwide box-office success *Kung Fu Hustle* (2004) is a recent example of this tendency. Although it integrates the actor's well known Cantonese comedy persona into a semi-serious martial arts film indebted to recent developments in digital special effects, it also contains prolific references to different types of kung-fu fighting styles as well as that frequently filmed classic of Cantonese social melodrama *The House of 72 Tenants* last filmed by the Shaw Brothers in 1973. However, *Kung Fu Hustle* is also a gangster movie. Set in Shanghai during the 1930s, it features the notorious Axe Gang last seen in *Boxer from Shantung* (1972) directed by Zhang Che on which John Woo worked as assistant director. Chow plays a "wannabe" Triad (Chinese gangster) who joins the organization until he sees the light in the best manner of a hero from a 1950s Cantonese social melodrama. The Vice-President of the Axe Gang is played by Lam Suet, one of Hong Kong's most prolific character actors, who has portrayed Triads in serious films such as Johnny To's *A Hero Never Dies* (1998), *The Mission* (1999) and not-so-serious ones such as Herman Yau's *Shark Busters* (2001). He remains in office until defeated by the landlady played by former stuntwoman/actress Yuen Qiu, whose film credits include *Disciples of the 36th Chamber* (1984) and *The Man With the Golden Gun* (1974). Earlier in his career, Stephen Chow had played a serious role in the gangster drama *Just Heroes* (1989) which John Woo co-directed as a benefit film for veteran martial arts director Zhang Che.

Although the Hong Kong gangster film does have some similarities with its Western counterparts, it is a more diverse genre. Screen any Hong Kong

Opposite: A baby and a gun: Chow Yun-fat as Tequila in *Hard Boiled*.

The Heroic Trio: Chow Yun-fat, Ti Lung, and Dean Shek in *A Better Tomorrow 2*.

Stephen Chow defeats the Ax Gang in *Kung Fu Hustle*.

film and a Triad often appears whether in a major or minor capacity. Woo's *Bullet in the Head* deals with the adventures of three Hong Kong youngsters who have to flee their homeland to escape retribution for the death of a Triad loan shark. They relocate to Vietnam during 1967 and narrowly escape death at the hands of Saigon Triad leader Mr. Leong (Y. S. Lam Chung) and find themselves captives of demonic Viet Cong who re-enact those fictionalized Russian roulette deadly games earlier ascribed to them in Michael Cimino's *The Deer Hunter* (1978). When Ben (Tony Leung Chiu-wai) eventually discovers the friend who has betrayed him, the guilty party Frank (Waise Lee) is now in a corporate boardroom about to occupy the highest echelon in the Hong Kong Triad society in a scene evoking Ray Danton's discovery of a different organization in Budd Boetticher's *The Rise and Fall of Legs Diamond* (1960).

Although Woo's films are important, they represent the tip of an iceberg involving many directors, stars, genres, and locations intermingling in the most dazzling combinations. The Hong Kong gangster film often uses different locations such as America, China, Taiwan, Thailand, and Vietnam. Acclaimed director Wong Kar-wai began his career writing gangster movie screenplays before directing his first film *As Tears Go By* (1988), a gangster romance drama starring Andy Lau Tak-wah, Maggie Cheung Man-yuk, and Jackie Cheung Hok-yau. In David Lam's *Asian Connection* (1995) two Hong Kong cops, played by Danny Lee Sau-yin and Michael Chow Man-kin, form an alliance with their Taiwan and Mainland counterparts and travel to Taiwan to pursue the leaders of a drug syndicate. In Che-Kirk Wong's *Rock 'n Roll Cop* (1994), Hong Kong police join forces with their Mainland counterparts to pursue a brutal group of gangsters who operate on both sides of the border. By contrast, the action of Philip Chan's *Tongs: A Chinatown Story* (1986) takes place almost exclusively in New York. It charts the gradual corruption of a former Mainland Chinese refugee, Mickey (Simon Yam Tat-wah), after he arrives with his brother from Hong Kong. The film ends abruptly on an ambiguous note by suggesting that the supposedly incapacitated uncle who initially helped him escape from China may be a Tong leader himself. Directed by a former police officer who became an actor specializing in cops, *Tongs* is one of the few gangster films indirectly hinting at the threat the Triads present to today's global economy.

The Hong Kong gangster film is a genre having similarities with its Western counterparts. But, like its Japanese yakuza cousin, it has key associations with a Triad culture which has exercised a key role in Chinese history, both past and present. Unmentioned or not, a Chinese gangster film is also Triad in nature whether the underworld receives a realistically grim or romantic representation.

Like the Sicilian Mafia, the Triad underworld represents a formidable and efficient criminal organization with a particular history. But whereas the Mafia represents a small group of families often engaged in vendettas against each other, the Triads have a much more complex historical background. As Martin Booth notes, this organization "arose from and within the largest nation on earth, their genesis and, indeed, their fundamental psychology

A grimly determined Tequila (Chow Yun-fat) in *Hard Boiled*.

being located not in oscillating family or clan union and disunion but in reactions to the invasion and conquest of their land by outside forces."[2] But while the Mafia has experienced a serious loss of power in certain areas, the Triads are now becoming an international crime organization to the extent of even threatening Italian-American godfathers in certain areas of their turf. Although the Triads operate little differently from most criminal organizations today, they are "historically, if distantly descended from those secret associations and groups which fit into the long tradition of self-preservation through unity and patriotism dating back to the authoritarian Zhou dynasty (1027–221 BC)."[3] Probably few Triads know the purported history of their organization (or even the distinctive membership rituals of the past, let alone its patriotic origins), but the clannish and secret nature of the group still remains. As Booth recognizes, the organization's transition from a patriotic secret society to an international criminal organization began in Hong Kong, which still has the unjust reputation of being "Triad City." Even before Britain gained Hong Kong by the Treaty of Nanking in 1847, many Triads had emigrated there. Several immigrants set up trade associations and guilds to protect their interests, but mercenary Triads saw great potential in exploiting their own people. Although Triad membership was made illegal in 1845, the organization existed as an alternative power behind the throne. According to Booth, "By 1847 Hong Kong was seen as the nerve centre for Triad activity all over China and Triad membership in the colony was estimated to be as high as three-quarters of the local Chinese population."[4]

Although officially proscribed, the Triads had a long history of involvement in Chinese politics. Both Sun Yat-sen and Chiang Kai-shek used the organization during their various political careers and may even have joined it. Also, anticipating the role of Alden Pyle in Graham Greene's *The Quiet American* (1955), during 1946 America began to finance a so-called Third Force designed to remove both the Communists and Kuomintang as leading players in Chinese politics. This comprised the Man Chi Tong, or the Overseas Chinese Democratic Party, one of whose founding members was the Triad "Big Timer" Chiu Yuk. Booth maintains that "anyone wishing to join the Third Force was more or less obliged to become a Triad member—a fact the Americans were either ignorant of or deliberately chose to ignore."[5] When the Communists defeated the Kuomintang, many Mainland Triads were among those seeking refuge in Hong Kong. As Booth recognizes, politically the Triads have been right of center since the 1920s when they aided the Kuomintang against their Communist rivals: "Both socialism and communism are inimical to them. They thrive best in a free market democracy."[6] During the Hong Kong Chinese Cultural Revolution riots (briefly featured in *A Bullet in the Head*), they acted as anti-Communist informers, "letting the police know the whereabouts of Communist activists, their meeting places and the location of bomb makers who occasionally operated out of left-wing trade union offices. Of course, the Triads had a vested interest: the left-wing unions were their main competitors in control of the labor market."[7]

Triad infiltration of the police has been a major problem since the early days of the Royal Hong Kong Police force in the 1880s. Prior to Hong Kong's reunification with China, a small proportion of English officers commanded a high percentage of Chinese constables. It was not until the latter part of the 20th century that it became possible for Chinese to be promoted beyond the rank of sergeant-major. Bribery thus grew to be an inevitable way of life for many in an institution that soon became known as "the best police force money can buy."[8] The corruption extended not only to ordinary policemen, but even to high-ranking British officers, such as Superintendent Ernest "Taffy" Hunt and Chief Superintendent Peter Godber, who were both convicted of bribery in the early 1970s after having perverted the course of justice for several decades. The Godber incident later became the subject of one of Ng See-yeun's biggest commercial successes, *Anti-Corruption* (1975), as well as two films directed by David Lam, *The Powerful Four* (1991) and *First Shot* (1993). In the first film, an unnamed older superintendent (obviously modeled on Godber) turns a blind eye to the criminal activities of a younger inspector (modeled on Hunt), who takes bribes from a vicious new generation Triad intent on disseminating heroin into the colony, rather than opium, which only appeals to the older generation. *First Shot* continues Lam's indictment of the British police establishment by masquerading as a Hong Kong remake of Brian De Palma's *The Untouchables* (1987). The film fictionally recreates the foundation of the Independent Commission against Corruption (IACAC), set up after the Godber scandal in 1974 and the resignation in 1969 of Lee Rock, the most notorious and corrupt local figure in the Hong Kong police force,

A rare moment of peace for Tequila (Chow Yun-fat) in Mr. Woo's nightclub.

who rose from the rank of constable to chief Chinese officer in the force. This incident also spurred a fictional re-creation by the director Lawrence Ah Mon, whose two-part biopic *Lee Rock* (1991), starring Andy Lau in the title role, was filmed very much in the melodramatic, social-realist style of 1950s Cantonese cinema, as were his other crime films, *Gangs* (1986) and *Queen of Temple Street* (1990). Unlike the later *Young and Dangerous* series, the first film presented an unglamorous view of lower-level Triad society, while the second starred the Taiwanese actress and director Sylvia Chang as the madam of one of Hong Kong's most infamous red-light districts. By the time *First Shot* appeared, Lam could actually name Peter Godber. Lawrence Ah Mon suggested in an interview with the Hong Kong critic Stephen Teo that British authorities were fully aware of police corruption and had been forced to set up the IACAC.[9] The Organized Crime and Triad Bureau, which has featured in several Hong Kong gangster films, was set up soon afterward. However, Triad infiltration into the police force remained a major problem and is featured in several films, such as Che Kirk-wong's *Organized Crime and Triad Bureau* (1994) and the *Infernal Affairs* trilogy. This explains Kit's (Leslie Cheung) anger against his brother Ho (Ti Lung) in *A Better Tomorrow*: his blood ties to a known Triad immediately place him under suspicion in the police force.

Although Triads today operate in a less traditional hierarchy than before, both they and their movie counterparts are divided into three main groups. The lowest echelon is the "rank and file" *sze kau* or 49s. These represent the bulk of the membership equivalent to lowly foot soldiers who carry out most of the dirty work with meat cleavers and butcher knives often prominently displayed in gangster movies. They answer to the *hung kwan* or Red Pole official, a fighting-unit commander well versed in martial arts and in control of fifty men. But since today's Triads are as well versed in accountancy and computer technology, the *pak tsz sin* (White Paper Fan) is the business manager who keeps the books and banks the money. The second level of Triad bureaucracy is represented by the senior officials known as *sheung fa* (Double Flower) who control everyday business. These only exist in the most advanced Triad organizations. Ultimate authority lies with the *shan chu* (or Dragon Head) who exercises authority over every member and activity of his society. He may confer with a deputy, the *fu shan chu*, who acts as his proxy when he is absent. These levels differ in each Triad organization and may not appear in their cinematic counterparts.[10] Many Triad movies focus upon the lower ranks of 49s such as the *Young and Dangerous* series (1996–98), *Mongkok Story* (1996), and *Once Upon A Time in a Triad Society 2* (1996). Popularly known as the *goo wak jai* series (a term roughly translated as "young rascals" representing a younger version of the slang term "rascals" used by triad films), the *Young and Dangerous* films concentrated upon the younger members recruited between the ages of 15 and 18. During 1978–87, the biggest Hong Kong Triad organization, the Sun Yee On, tripled its membership by recruiting teenage students; it has also taken recruits as young as 12.[11] *Young and Dangerous 3* (1996) revealed the presence of young Triads in the classroom. As Martin Booth notes, it is quite possible for a *fei jai* (Cantonese slang for "spiv" or "wide boy") to climb the ladder of the Triad organization to become eventually a *taipan* (or tycoon), involved in both legitimate and illegitimate business enterprises.[12]

The film industry has long been influenced by Triad involvement that often extends to actually producing, casting, and investing in local films—a fact referred to during the opening sequence of Cha Chuen-yee's *Once Upon a Time in a Triad Society* (1996), where the evil but fascinating Kwan (Francis Ng) conducts a co-production deal with Japan and also produces X-rated movies in *Young and Dangerous* (1996).[13] Many actors such as Chow Yun-fat, Andy Lau, Stephen Chow, Danny Lee, Tony Leung Chiu-wai, Tony Leung Ka-fai, Eric Tsang, Anthony Wong, Ekin Cheng, Francis Ng, Jackie Cheung, Lam Suet, and Jordan Chan, have played gangsters at various stages of their careers. In many cases, actors often alternate between playing cops and gangsters as if indirectly acknowledging the historical problems of bribery in the Hong Kong police force. Others such as Simon Yam, Shing Fui-on, and, particularly Roy Cheung, have long been associated with their gangster roles in the Hong Kong film industry. Former gangsters have also become involved with the industry such as actor-producer Ng Chi-hung and veteran actor Michael Chan Wai-man. Like former Japanese yakuza Noboru Ando, he has the tattoos to prove it. He began his career in martial arts films such as *The Mysterious Footworks of Kung Fu* (1978), *Snake Deadly Act* (1980) and has portrayed gangsters for decades in films such as *Broken Oath* (1977), *The Club* (1981), *Royal Warriors* (1986), *Legacy of Rage* (1986), *Project A: 2* (1987), *Triads:*

Johnny Wong gets the drop on Alan (Tony Leung Chiu-wai).

The Inside Story (1989), *My Heart Is That Eternal Rose* (1989), *Lee Rock* (1991) *The Unmatchable Match* (1990) Once *Upon A Time in a Triad Society* (1996), *Mongkok Story* (1996), and *Young and Dangerous 3* (1996). *In My Darling, My Goddess* (1982), Michael Chan plays both cop and his Triad look-alike as if conscious of the thin line between gangsters and police worlds. He also played the starring role in *Carry on Yakuza* (1989) and satirized his gangster role in *Truant Heroes* (1992) by playing a former triad who has now become a teacher but finds it difficult to give up his old ways.[14]

The Hong Kong gangster film's parallels with Western counterparts are not surprising in an industry that has always been influenced by outside models. Yet, although Woo's gangster films reveal the influence of Jean-Pierre Melville, as Ken Hall and others have noted, they also contain traces of other diverse influences, such as the "heroic-bloodshed" model of the 1960s and 1970s films of Woo's mentor, Zhang Che.[15]

Woo worked as assistant director for Zhang Che on several Shaw Brothers films such as *Seven Blows of the Dragon* (1971), *Boxer from Shantung* (1972), *Four Riders* (1972), and *Blood Brothers* (1973). None of these films belonged to the gangster genre. With the exception of *Four Riders* which was set in the immediate post-war era, the rest were historical costume dramas. In his *Better Tomorrow* films, Woo reincorporated the "heroic bloodshed" motif long associated with Zhang Che into the Hong Kong gangster film thus giving the genre a much needed revitalization in terms of his concept of cinematic authorship. Also, as Stephen Teo has noted, *A Better Tomorrow* is also a new version of Lung Kong's *Story of a Discharged Prisoner* (1967).[16] Key cultural elements of loyalty, righteousness, and friendship constantly occur in his films, aspects

Shaw Brothers veteran Philip Kwok as Mad Dog in *Hard Boiled.*

for which the Triad underworld is not actually noted for as Francis Ng's Kwan discovers in *Once Upon A Time in a Triad Society*. Woo's films are highly romantic in nature concentrating on issues of male friendship and betrayal. The nearest Woo gets to the traditional Hong Kong gangster film occur in parts of *Hard Boiled*. Playing an early version of the undercover cop he will later depict in *Infernal Affairs*, Tony Leung Chiu-wai's Tony finds himself forced to betray and kill the older *shan chu* figure of Hui (Kwan Hoi-shan) now becoming anachronistic in the brutal, high-technology Triad world represented by Anthony Wong's Johnny Wong. When the showdown finally occurs in a Hong Kong hospital, Wong's brutal methods involving the shooting of hospital patients becomes too much for his henchman "Mad Dog" (played by Shaw Brothers veteran Phillip Kwok). When he protests at the breach of his former code of ethics Wong immediately shoots him. As Kenneth Hall has shown, *Hard Boiled* is a highly accomplished film.[17] However, it is also important to examine other examples of the genre if we are to do the Hong Kong gangster movie sufficient justice and not limit it to just one talent or a limited number of films.

Although the sheer diversity of Hong Kong generic cinema often makes classification exceedingly difficult, certain definable categories exist. These include the "Big Timer" films; the "Big Circle" Mainland Chinese gangster films represented by Johnny Mak's *Long Arm of the Law* series (1984–89); the teenage gangster film; prison movies; the undercover agent theme represented by *Infernal Affairs*; and several post-1997 gangster films.

"Big Timer" films resemble those American biopics dealing with well-known figures such as Al Capone, Legs Diamond, Dutch Schultz, and others

Alan (Tony Leung Chiu-wai) shoots his former boss to maintain his cover.

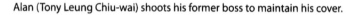

which, superficially, appear to resemble Robert Warshow's concept of "the gangster as tragic hero."[18] However, a closer examination reveals significant differences of a cultural nature. The gangster may not die in a hail of bullets like Edward G. Robinson in *Little Caesar* (1930), James Cagney in *Public Enemy* (1931) or Paul Muni in *Scarface* (1931), and may not even suffer a beating in the prison yard as does Rod Steiger in *Al Capone* (1959). Instead, the Eastern equivalent may die peacefully in his bed like the title figure in *Lord of the East China Sea* (1993) or heroically face incarceration as in *To Be Number One* (1991). A crooked cop has equal claims to be regarded as a "Big Timer" especially if he has the status of Lui Lok (or "Lee Rock" in the anglicized form of his name) still remaining in Taiwan enjoying his ill-gotten gains. These films often exhibit a deceptive romanticism resulting from historical and ideological issues absent from the more complex work of John Woo.

Although Johnny Mak produced the first "Big Timer" film, *To Be Number One*, his association with this project reveals a creative involvement very similar to the role of Tsui Hark as nominal producer in his Film Workshop products. Depicting the life of Triad godfather and drug baron Ng Sik-ho, or "Limpy" Ho as he was nicknamed following an attempt on his life resulting in a leg injury, the film romanticizes its title character in much the same way as *The Godfather* (1971) did with Marlon Brando's Vito Corleone. The real "Limpy" Ho was a brutal character who rose up the Triad hierarchy. He began as an impoverished *49* reaching the status of big boss by profiting from the international heroin trade prior to his arrest in 1974. Released from prison on compassionate grounds in 1991, he died a few months after his screen biography was released.[19] The film charts his life from his beginnings

Tony Leung Chiu-wai with his undercover opposite number Andy Lau in *Infernal Affairs*.

as a Chinese refugee in 1962 up to his eventual arrest in 1974. Ho was compellingly portrayed by Ray Lui (who, like Robert De Niro for *Raging Bull*, put on weight for the role to depict the result of Ho's later affluent lifestyle), but the film's romanticizing traits are not surprising in an industry affected by Triad involvement. Although the film opens with images of a contrite Ho in the prison chapel, these moralistic overtones are soon forgotten as the film glorifies his rise to power in a one-dimensional manner, a factor affecting most "Big Timer" films. The film also changes the actively complicit role of Ho's real-life spouse into that of Cecilia Yip's undiscerning figure and also redeems the role of the Lee Rock figure of Lui Ko-tin (who, in real life, was Ho's business partner) by allowing him to arrest Ho at the end of the film.

The commercial success of *To Be Number One* led to Johnny Mak reuniting its director and stars Ray Lui and Kent Cheng in another "Big Timer" biography, *Lord of the East China Sea*. Filmed in two parts, perhaps in homage to Coppola's *Godfather* films, the film charted the historical rise of one of the most notorious godfathers in Chinese history, Du Yueh-sheng (1887–1951). Born in a Chinese slum area adjoining Shanghai, the orphaned Du suffered child abuse from his uncle at the age of ten, became a hardened criminal by twelve, and quickly rose up the ladder of the Triad hierarchy to form connections with high society and the decadent Kuomintang leader Chiang Kai-shek (who was also a Triad member). Du's most infamous activity involved Triad's participation in Chiang's purge of Communists in the infamous Shanghai Massacre of 1927 when some 5,000 to 10,000 suspected Communists and innocent victims perished.[20] Both Du and Chiang were heavily involved in

Anthony Wong on the right side of the law in *Infernal Affairs II*.

the opium trade. By the late 1940s, he began to move his assets to Hong Kong when Communist victory looked inevitable in China. Despite his notoriety, the British authorities allowed him to settle there and even Mao Zedong attempted to tempt him to return to control the urban Triads. Fully aware of memories of the Shanghai Massacre, Du declined and died in his bed on August 16, 1951. Praised as a hero by the president of the free Republic of China in Taiwan, Du's remains were interred in the territory of his former partner in crime. As Martin Booth ironically comments, Du is now "regarded in Taiwan as a hero of the people, a patriot who fought the evil of Communism and upheld the basic tenet of the Triad societies of old: to restore China to her own, true citizens."[21]

Some knowledge of the real Du Yu-sheng can help viewers understand the one-dimensional, evasive structure governing *Lord of the East China Seas*. Since Hong Kong then depended on Taiwan as an overseas market, an accurate picture of the ugly incidents in Du's career were out of the question. Instead, Ray Lui's Luk Yu-san presents a mellow and naive image of this dangerous godfather figure, whom the film portrays more as a victim of circumstances and a pawn in the political machinations of the Nationalist Government than as the key player he actually was. The most infamous betrayal of historical fact presents Du and his criminal associates as totally innocent of any involvement in the Shanghai massacre and as mere victims of a political machine. Even after the end of World War II, the "upright" Du suffers further betrayals from the Kuomintang machine while, in reality, he was still exploiting his own people at this time. Chiang Kai-shek appears briefly at the end of Part One and the film suggests that he does not know what his own officials are doing to a gangster who only wishes to be a patriot to his country. The film also attempts to humanize an ugly character by the insertion of a romantic sub-plot even more unbelievable than that in *To Be Number One*. As Stephen Teo points out, the glaring historical inaccuracies and revisionist tendencies dominating these two films starring Ray Lui may be due to the Golden Harvest studio mythologizing the Triads as well as the vanity-press aspect of Triad involvement in the Hong Kong film industry itself.[22]

"Big Timers" may be crooked cops as well as gangsters, a fact illustrated by another two-part biopic, *Lee Rock* (1991), devoted to Hong Kong's extremely corrupt, native-born Lui Lok. Like Limpy Ho, Lee Rock was a refugee from the Chiuchow region of China. He arrived in Hong Kong in 1948. But, unlike his more notorious countryman, Lee joined the Hong Kong police force and reached the high position of chief of sergeant-majors before his resignation in 1969. Both John Charles and Stephen Teo have noted the melodramatic and glamorized depiction of this particular character, which owes much to Triad infiltration of the film industry and continuing problems of bribery and corruption in the police force.[23] Lee begins his career as an honest cop before realizing that the facts of life in the Hong Kong police involve bribery both to boost his low salary and the temporary loss of his first love (Chingmy Yau) once her father learns of his occupation. Lee's rise to the top of his profession as Hong Kong's most notorious crooked cop arises more from circumstances beyond his control than from conscious design. The second part of the film reunites him with his long-lost sweetheart, whose son becomes an investigating officer in the investigation of his father. From that point on, the film becomes more concerned with the rivalry between Lee and his nemesis, Ngan (Paul Chun-pui), both of whom are on the take. However, in true Hong Kong melodramatic fashion, father and son are reunited over the mother's deathbed, leading them both to engage in a typical action-movie shoot-out. The film ends with the now aged Lee living in Canada and about to leave for Taiwan to avoid extradition.

Although other "Big Timer" movies exist in Hong Kong cinema, mention should be made of Frankie Chan's *Burning Ambition* (1989) which resembles less of a traditional Hong Kong gangster movie but more of an updated version of a Jacobean revenge tragedy aiming to destroy all the usual romanticized premises of Triad movies. Like *Once Upon A Time in a Triad Society*, the film not only shows that there is no honor among thieves but also that even the most closely-bonded family unit can tear itself to pieces in the fight to be number one. An unscrupulous uncle Chau Hsiong (Ko Chuen-hsiang) murders his own "Big Timer" brother (Roy Chiao) to place his weak nephew Wai (Miu Kiu-wai) on the Triad throne rather than his more competent younger brother Tat-hwa (Simon Yam). If Francis Ng's Kwan discovers that righteousness does not exist among the Triads in *Once Upon A Time in a Triad Society*, *Burning Ambition* reveals an ugly picture of family betrayal probably closer to actual reality than the romantic imagery employed in big-budget "Big Timer" counterparts. The boss's widow betrays her own devoted goddaughter while Chau Hsiong uses his own children as disposable pawns in the deadly contest. After lying to his remaining son Chi-shau (Frankie Chan) about protecting his biker friends he has brought with him to Hong Kong, (who has lived in exile in Holland following an assassination ordered by his own father),[24] Chau Hsiong collapses into insanity when his betrayed son reveals the corpse of the heir-apparent during a Triad confirmation ceremony. The film ends on a note of poetic justice as the raving uncle embraces the bloodless corpse of his nephew. He had earlier forced his brother's widow to witness the murder of her younger son Tat-hwa. Although not as well known as major budgeted "Big Timer" productions, the film is unique in having no character to identify with, depicting the real world of Triad society where neither loyalty or family honor really matter in a manner similar to Takashi Miike's yakuza family melodrama *Fudoh: The New Generation* (1996).

Taylor Wong's *Triads: The Inside Story* (1989) is also a worthy addition to this group since it takes a different direction by focusing on a character who does not want "to be number one." After the murder of his gangster father Li Man-ho (Chow Yun-fat) reluctantly returns to Hong Kong to sort out the affairs of the Hung Hing Triads. Featuring well-known heavies such as Roy Cheung, Michael Chan, and Shing Fui-on, the film is unique in dealing not only with the reluctance of certain Triads to assume high office but also the reservations expressed by their wives. When Li Man-ho suggests that Kong (Roy Cheung) could move into legitimate business, the latter replies that he

A well-equipped Tequila (Chow Yun-fat) in *Hard Boiled*.

has been a Triad for most of his life. Due to his illiteracy, Kong's only options are working in 7-11 or McDonalds. "People like us can't do anything else." Earlier Kong was seen attempting to recruit a schoolboy into the organization. The wife of Shing (Michael Chan) urges him to retire since the younger Triads are "crazy" and "don't care for rightness." But this is also true for the older generation since Li Man-ho later discovers that his uncle was responsible for the death of his father. *Triads* is another rare film which takes a different look at the grim realities of this lifestyle.

The Mainland backgrounds of "Limpy" Ho and Lee Rock are key elements within Hong Kong gangster films revealing that the "two Chinas" are indissoluble even before 1997. Johnny Mak's *Long Arm of the Law* series again reveals the hybrid nature of the Hong Kong gangster film where no firm line can ever be drawn between Hong Kong, Mainland China, and Taiwan. Shot between 1984 and 1989, this four part series not only examines the fears facing reunification in the pre-1997 era but also interrogates the role of "Big Circle" Mainland gangsters who also terrorized Hong Kong. The founding members of this group were former Red Guards and demobilized soldiers from the People's Liberation Army who began their activities in the southern Chinese districts of Guangzhou province. Sometimes they were also professional criminals or labor-camp escapees who fled to Hong Kong. During the mid-1980s and early 1990s, "Big Circle" gangsters engaged in high-profile armed robbery against gold-dealers and up-market jewelers often paralleling the pyrotechnic activities of blockbuster action movies, by using weapons borrowed or stolen from the Chinese military.[25] Johnny Mak's *The Long Arm of the Law* (1984) deals with a group of "Big Circle" gangsters who botch a jewelry store robbery and appear to resemble Hong Kong's worst fears concerning Mainland Chinese infiltration thirteen years before 1997. However, despite their thuggish nature, the gangsters do express loyalty and concern for each other as opposed to the manipulative local Triads and crooked and greedy police force. The film ends inside the now-demolished Kowloon Walled City. Originally a "no-go" area for both British and Mainland authorities, it was a place one could purchase illicit drugs, hide from the police, and gain access to unofficial medical help. Mak also critiques the colonial-run police force which abandons the rule of law to eliminate its quarry. In one of the grimmest endings to a Hong Kong gangster film, the police massacre the Mainlanders with multiple automatic rounds leaving their bodies to rot alongside dead rats ironically reprising a Red Guard tune used earlier in the film.[26]

The following films in the series directed by Michael Mak continue this bleak imagery. In *Long Arm of the Law 2* (1987), the Hong Kong police force a group of Mainland prisoners to become informants and eventually betray them all in a bloody climax. *Long Arm of the Law 3* (1989) features Andy Lau portraying an innocent victim of Mainland justice who flees to Hong Kong. He not only has to deal with the Triads but an unforgiving cop ominously named Mao played by Elvis Tsui. *Long Arm of the Law IV* (1990) also features Elvis Tsui, this time playing a noble gangster involved in smuggling dissident students from China after the Tiananmen Square crack-down. He finds himself betrayed by the Hong Kong police (with the complicit support of the colony's Governor) while pursued by a vicious Mainland political commissar who threatens to stop Hong Kong food supplies unless authorities allow a convenient arrest of the fugitives outside territorial waters.

Based upon a comic book by Niu Lo, the unexpected success of the first *Young and Dangerous* film led to four sequels and a prequel. As critics have noted the film series appeals to a younger generation audience half of whom lived in the world of the "young rascals" and the other half attracted to triad gangs so much so that Tsui Hark described the series as "Triad recruitment films." Featuring young stars such as rock singer Ekin Cheng, Jordan Chan, and Jerry Lam, the films presented a semi-glamorized MTV version of younger generation Triads but, at the same time, did not entirely neglect the hazards of this lifestyle.[27] Beginning with the recruitment of young schoolboys by Triad leader Brother B (Ng Chi-hung) in 1985, the film immediately jumps a decade to show their twenty-something counterparts beginning their careers in the *49* category. However, while the series does glamorize its protagonists such as handsome, Versace-wearing Ho Nam (Ekin) Cheng and his loyal friend "Chicken" (Jordan Chan), the dark side of the Triad world is not entirely neglected. Brutal gangster Kwan (Francis Ng) takes over the Wanchai-based Hung Hing society (obviously based on the San Yee On group) after brutally murdering Brother B and his entire family. Loyalties frequently change in these films. Ho Nam is framed in the first and third episodes while "righteous" boss Chiang Tin-sung is respectively ousted and murdered in these episodes. *Young and Dangerous 2* (1996) covers Chicken's missing period in the first film

Anthony Wong as a younger-generation Triad boss.

when he fled to Taiwan, joined Taipei's San Luen Triads, rising to the status of branch leader, and explicitly depicts the well-known connections between Taiwanese politics and the gangster world, a subject in Michael Mak's *Island of Greed* (1997). *Young and Dangerous 3* also introduces violent Triad Crow (Roy Cheung) who smashes an image of the Triad deity Kwan-yu in the opening scene and murders his boss Camel Lok (Michael Chan) with the aid of Tiger (Ng Chi-hung). Even being a Triad girlfriend or mistress is dangerous. Ho Nam's "Smartie" (Gigi Lai) suffers brain damage, rape, and brutal murder in Parts Two and Three. Crow forces Chiang's mistress to participate in a pornographic film in Part Three.

The series often brings actors back in different roles and *Young and Dangerous* features two former Triads playing older versions of their former selves. *Young and Dangerous 5* (1998) sees Ho Nam moving up the corporate crime ladder. Now branch leader of Causeway Bay, he sees his territory threatened by his Mainland Triad counterpart Ho Nam Szeto and finds himself drawn into the more dangerous realms of transnational global capitalism when crooked Malaysian Chinese businessman Chan Datuk manipulates him into becoming involved in a housing development scam in Kuala Lumpur and cruise ship gambling. As Ho Nam's new boss Chiang Chung-sing tells him times are changing and high financial schemes will now replace the world of street fights, jeans, and T-shirts. However, Ho Nam eventually discovers that crooked billionaires "are more cunning than rascals" but he can no longer return to his former life since the "series and its progression, then reflect a shift from early capitalist accumulation to the global networking of late capital accumulation, moving like so many blips on a computer screen by a simple keystroke."[28]

The series proved so popular that it led to spin-offs. Francis Ng repeats his role as Kwan in *Once Upon A Time in a Triad Society* which exposes the thin line dividing reality from glamorized fantasy while in its sequel further deglamorizes the Triad lifestyle as does *Mongkok Story* where Edmond Leong's tentative recruit encounters an ugly world personified by Anthony Wong and Michael Chan. Female gangsters are by no means absent. In *Young and Dangerous 3*, a middle-aged branch manager supports Ho Nam during a meeting when he is accused of complicity in the death of his boss in Amsterdam. Parts four and five feature lesbian triad Sister 13 (Sandra Ng) who also appears in her own movie *Portland Street Blues* (1998) which, disappointedly, deals more with her sexual confusion rather than the qualities which make her a powerful boss in a man's world.[29]

Despite the incarceration of criminals, the Hong Kong prison movie often shows that the world inside differs little from the outside particularly in revealing a hierarchical society also dominated by the Triads. In Chen Yu-ping's Taiwanese prison drama *Island on Fire* (1990), Wang Yu's Triad leader Kui dominates the prison community until his eventual betrayal. Scripted by former prisoner Nam Yin, Ringo Lam's *Prison on Fire* films reveals a Darwinian society dominated by gang fights and national resentment. In *Prison on Fire* (1987), Hong Kong Triad leader Micky (William Ho)

Tequila (Chow Yun-fat) brandishes bigger hardware in *Hard Boiled*.

dominates the community, aided by the complicity of security chief "Scarface" Hung (Roy Cheung). *Prison on Fire 2* (1991) reveals the tensions between the Hong Kong and "Big Circle" Triad prisoners which the new security chief Zau (Elvis Tsui) manipulates to maintain his brutal control over the entire community. Chow Yun-fat's leading character Chung befriends Brother Dragon (Chen Sung-yung) who was formerly a captain in the People's Liberation Army which he joined to avoid starvation. Despite tensions, the film depicts a growing solidarity between the Hong Kong prisoners and their Chinese counterparts in a manner suggesting a more positive resolution of 1997 fears in Hong Kong cinemas. When a riot breaks out between both factions, a guard comments, "It's a civil war." But despite the treachery of Dragon's subordinate Skull, aided by Zau, the film ends by suggesting a "better tomorrow" for both factions while also ironically re-introducing the ominous presence of Roy Cheung from the previous film in an amusing cameo towards the end of the film.

Before *Infernal Affairs* focused upon the dilemmas of undercover agents both in the Triads and the police force, several films had already treated this theme. As mentioned, the Hong Kong police force had a record of corruption and many officers had Triad connections. In Che-Kirk Wong's *Organized Crime and Triad Bureau* (1994), dedicated Inspector Lee (Danny Lee) finds his status lowered in the eyes of his colleagues who prefer his subordinate officer Chiu (Roy Cheung) who has also acquired his former girlfriend. However, the film later reveals that Chiu is a Triad plant who has a more dedicated sense of brotherhood with gangster Tung (Anthony Wong) than Lee's colleagues have towards him. He dies heroically defending his boss from the police. But

Andy Lau's high-ranking police Triad informant in *Infernal Affairs* causes the death of both his former boss (Eric Tsang) and his alter-ego undercover cop (Tony Leung Chiu-wai). Rather than dying or facing arrest in the Mainland Chinese version, he undergoes a living hell of spiritual punishment for the rest of his existence. Andrew Lau's *To Live and Die in Tsimshatsui* (1994) had earlier depicted the mental anguish of undercover cops, one of whom (played by Tony Leung Ka-fai) had become totally identified with his alter ego. As Charles also notes, another merit of this film is depicting the younger Triads as little better than mindless animals doped up on cough syrup in contrast to the glamorized lifestyle of the *Young and Dangerous* series.[30] In *Cop on a Mission* (2001) Daniel Wu's character slowly turns from undercover cop to treacherous Triad until his betrayal of boss Ting (Eric Tsang) eventually rebounds against him.

Several post-1997 films continue Triad themes in distinctive ways. As well as containing his usual homoerotic themes Johnny To's *The Mission* (1999) provides a virtual galaxy of gangster stars such as Simon Yam, Francis Ng, Anthony Wong, Roy Cheung, and Lam Suet confronted with the problem of how to deal with a younger Triad (Jackie Lui) who has "screwed" the boss's wife. A year before To's *A Hero Never Dies* parodied John Woo's work as well as satirizing the genre's misogynistic and homophobic elements. In Dante Lam's *Jiang Hu—The Triad Zone* (2000), Tony Leung Ka-fai plays a middle-aged version of his earlier gangster heroes attempting to readjust to a changing world and humorously falling flat on his face in the process. It also features a cameo role by Anthony Wong as the god Kwan who returns to earth only to find that

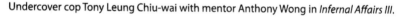

Undercover cop Tony Leung Chiu-wai with mentor Anthony Wong in *Infernal Affairs III*.

his Triad worshippers are far from being righteous. Perhaps the most recent bizarre version of a Triad movie is Edmund Pang's *Men Suddenly in Black* (2003) starring Eric Tsang and Jordan Chan. Ostensibly a comedy about four married men engaged in a "mission" of infidelity, it makes several references to Triad movies as well as featuring cameos by Lam Suet and Tony Leung Ka-fai as a former "Big Timer" now confined to house arrest by his wife. Featuring opening cameos by Lau Ching Wan and Francis Ng, Marco Mak and Wong Jing's *The Color of the Truth* (2003) involves Triad Jordan Chan manipulating young cop Raymond Wong to avenge the deaths of their fathers several years previously at the hands of Inspector Jiang (Anthony Wong), who may or may not have acted illegally. The film also involves the presence of Vietnamese Triads, who have featured in other films such as *Wild Search* (1989), *The Roar of the Vietnamese* (1991), *Phantom War* (1991), and *Run and Kill* (1993).

Notes

I wish to thank Art Black for his generous help in supplying me with videos to write this article.

1. See Charles Leary, *"Infernal Affairs: High Concept in Hong Kong,"* http://www.sensesofcinema.com 26 (2003); "What Goes Around, Comes Around: *Infernal Affairs II* and *III* and *Running on Karma,*" http://www.sensesofcinema.com/contents/03/26/internal_affairs.html, 30 (2004).

2. Martin Booth, *The Triads: The Chinese Criminal Fraternity* (London: Grafton Books, 1990), 2.

3. Martin Booth, *The Dragon Syndicates: The Global Phenomenon of the Triads* (New York: Carrol & Graf, 1999). This book updates the author's earlier work, but both are essential reading for any serious study of the Triads.

4. Booth, *Triads*, 40.

5. Ibid., 60–61.

6. Ibid., 90–91.

7. Booth, *Dragon Syndicates*, 169.

8. Booth, *Triads*, 89–92; *Dragon Syndicates*, 171–72.

9. See Tony Williams, "The Films and Social Significance of David Lam," *Asian Cult Cinema* 20 (1998): 15–19.

10. Booth, *Dragon Syndicates*, 129–32.

11. Ibid., 196, 262.

12. Ibid., 262–68.

13. The subject of Triad involvement in the Hong Kong film industry is well documented. See Booth, *Triads*, 103–4; *Dragon Syndicates*, 225–26, 248–52; Frederic Dannen and Barry Long, *Hong Kong Babylon: An Insider's Guide to the Hollywood of the East* (New York: Hyperion, 1997), 24–37; Lisa Odham Stokes and Michael Hoover, *City on Fire: Hong Kong Cinema* (London: Verso, 1999), 30–33; David Bordwell, *Planet Hong Kong: Popular Cinema and the Art of Entertainment* (Cambridge, Mass.: Harvard University Press, 2000), 41.

14. For the similar role of Noboru Ando in Japanese cinema, see T. D. C. Fujiki, "Noboru Ando: From Gangster to Gangster," *Tokyoscope*, ed. Patrick Macias (San Francisco: Cadence Books, 2001), 114–29; Mark Schilling, *The Yakuza Movie Book: A Guide to Japanese Gangster Films* (Berkeley, Calif.: Stone Bridge Press, 2003), 119–23. See also the interviews with former yakuzas now working in the Japanese film industry in the special features section of the Home Vision Entertainment DVD version of Kinji Fukasaku's *Street Mobster* (1972), also featuring Noboru Ando.

15. For an excellent study of John Woo and the key elements influencing his work see Kenneth E. Hall, *John Woo: The Films* (Jefferson, N.C.: McFarland, 1999).

16. Stephen Teo, *Hong Kong Cinema: The Extra Dimensions* (London: British Film Institute, 1997), 58, 175. For relevant information on this influential film now preserved in the Hong Kong Film Archive see *Cantonese Cinema Retrospective, 1960-1969*, revised ed., ed. Shu Kei (Hong Kong: Urban Council Publications, 1982), 81, 86–87, 181. Significantly, the director plays a police official in both versions. But while Kong's cop attempts to harass an ex-convict into becoming an informer, Woo's Taiwanese police chief is much more sympathetic. For other comparisons see also Karen Fang, *John Woo's* A Better Tomorrow (Hong Kong: Hong Kong University Press, 2004), 15, 19–220, 22.

17. Hall, 151–64.

18. Robert Warshow, *The Immediate Experience* (New York: Athenaeum, 171, 133.

19. For Ho's career see Booth, *Dragon Syndicates*, 182–92. As Teo points out, the film "makes the sociological point that the 60s and 70s were the era of big-time Chiuchow criminals who had come to Hong Kong as refugees in 1949, while the 80s, of course, were dominated by small-time Mainland Chinese criminals who had come to Hong Kong as illegal immigrants" (237).

20. See Booth, *Triads*, 129–30; *Dragon Syndicates*, 81–82.

21. Booth, *Dragon Syndicates*, 102. As Booth elsewhere notes, it is highly unlikely whether contemporary Triads know their own history, let alone their former traditional rituals.

22. Teo, 238.

23. John Charles, *Hong Kong Filmography, 1977-1997* (Jefferson, N.C.: McFarland, 2000), 563–64; Teo, 239–40.

24. According to Booth, Holland, especially Amsterdam, is one of the key international locations for Triads: "Dutch laws are still considered lenient compared to those of other European countries, the city is strategically placed, easily approached across national borders, and has a wide multi-racial, cosmopolitan community in which Chinese do not seem apparent." *Dragon Syndicates*, 281. After his temporary displacement as Triad boss by Kwan in *Young and Dangerous* (1996), Simon Yam's Chiang Tin-sung briefly moves there and eventually murdered there in *Young and Dangerous 3* (1996).

25. See Booth, *Triads*, 234, 280.

26. Mak's first film in this series has received close attention. See Esther Yau, "Border Crossing: Mainland China's Presence in Hong Kong Cinema," in *New Chinese Cinemas*, ed. Nick Browne et al. (Berkeley: University of California Press, 1992), 180–201; Stokes and Hoover, 260–61; Yingchi Chu, *Hong Kong Cinema: Colonizer, Motherland, and Self* (New York: Routledge, 2003), 98–105.

27. See, e.g., Stokes and Hoover, 79–85; Bordwell, 26–28; Miles Wood, *Cine East: Hong Kong Cinema Through the Looking Glass* (Surrey: Fab Press, 1998), 58–69; John Charles, 347–49.

28. Stokes and Hoover, 85.

29. See Booth, *Triads*, 119–21, for the role of May Wong in the 1970s heroin trade. Although not Triad related, many hookers formed their own "spinster societies" such as the Sworn Sisters Society. See Booth, *Dragon Syndicates*, 228. The wives of "Big Timers" such as "Limpy" Ho were, of course, fully aware of their husbands' activities.

30. Charles, 316.

"Ghost Dog, the gangsta figure, rejects his relation to this world and chooses heroic solitude": Forest Whitaker as the title figure in *Ghost Dog: The Way of the Samurai*.

Family Values and Feudal Codes: The Social Politics of America's Fin-de-Siècle Gangster

Ingrid Walker

I. The Spirit of an Age: 2000

> As far back as I can remember, I always wanted to be a gangster. To me, being a gangster was better than being President of the United States.
>
> Henry Hill, in Martin Scorsese, *GoodFellas* (1990)

> [Seeing that] America is a society of criminals might be more humanly interesting and morally satisfying than a society of empty routines, irresponsibly powerful organizations, widespread corruption, and meaningless violence.
>
> John G. Cawelti, *Adventure, Mystery, and Romance* (1976)

At the beginning of the 21st century, the social reality of one of popular culture's favorite figures—the gangster—is in decline. "The Mob is probably in the worst shape it's ever been since the 1930's," writes Stephen Fox, author of *Blood and Power: Organized Crime in Twentieth-Century America*, and the Italian American mob's once vital empires are crumbling.[1] Between the enforcement of RICO statutes, a concerted federal crackdown on organized crime, and increased outside competition, much of the Mafia's power base has been immobilized. The FBI has its eye on mob expansion into Internet commerce. In 1999, Operation Uptick shut down a securities firm scam that reached through New York's Five Families to "a virtual Who's Who of securities violators."[2] John Gotti and Carmine Persico, unable to manage their organizations from prison, appointed their sons as family bosses and watched helplessly as the inability of the next generation to lead created disastrous internal dissension in two of New York's top mob Families. In the ultimate act of Mafia heresy, the head of a Philadelphia family broke the law of omertà by turning federal witness—becoming the highest-ranking American Mafia member to defect. The writing is on the wall: dons who once seemed impervious to the law cannot withstand the vigilant pressure of state and federal officials. While a few mob microcosms persist, such as Youngstown, Ohio, in which the remains of established mob Families still maintain a stronghold, gangster life prevails not so much in the Italian American Mafia but in less pervasive manifestations of Russian and Asian organized crime.[3]

Similarly, the era of another late-20th-century gangster figure, the African American gangsta, also wanes. In the wake of a general truce between Crips and Bloods gangs in many major cities, the gangsta street warrior culture no longer threatens social order the way it did 10–15 years ago. After a period of intense warfare and media scrutiny, the inner-city killing fields have all but abated and law enforcement has become more adept at dealing with the tightly bounded world of street gangs. But, as Edward James Olmos depicts in *Lives in Hazard*, a documentary about gang life in East Los Angeles, gang-banging is a zero-sum game. Eventually the body count would all but decimate a generation. Yet, gang culture did not go away, it went underground. It survives in urban America as a sub-economy and flourishes in interstices across the nation as a social form. Proliferating outside the inner city in suburban (white middle-class) and rural areas, gangs have grown most steadily on Indian reservations. The Bureau of Indian Affairs estimates that in the last six years the number of known Indian gangs has tripled to 520, with over 6,000 members. With little economic activity or commercial crime, most gang activity on the reservation consists of gang members assaulting each other.[4] While this manifestation of youth gang culture—like the African American and Latino gang warfare of the 1980s—is just as likely to decimate that population, the localization of this activity to reservation life functions also as a kind of marginalization: Indian gangs threaten themselves far more than they threaten mainstream America.

Despite the steady deterioration of gangster and gangsta life on the street, gangsters' imaginary life thrives in film, television, fiction, music, and computer games. A unique mimesis between gangsters and their fictional representations enhances the popularity of gangster narratives. La Cosa Nostra has long been enamored of its public image portrayed in the media. Some, such as Al Capone, sought to influence or shape that characterization.[5] More recently, mafiosi taped by federal agents discussed how characters in *The Sopranos* directly reflect them and their work.[6] In their tell-all books, real wise-guys recall Francis Ford Coppola's adaptation of Mario Puzo's *The Godfather* as a seminal example of an idealized Mafia lifestyle. For Sammy "the Bull" Gravano, the fiction offers the only solace and meaning at the end of a mob career: "Now, years go by, and the only thing I can love about my life is the movie. There's no honor, there's no respect."[7] In a strange inversion of fiction and reality, many mafiosi have come to see gangster romances as the standard by which they live and measure their own lives.

Just as mob films have created Mafia icons, gangsta rap has solidified and popularized gangsta culture as a form nearly independent from but embraced by gangbangers. The gangsta's salience as a popular cultural figure was predicated on his forceful reality: the rise of gangsta rap paralleled the spread of gang warfare and the crack economy in L.A. and other cities in the 1980s. And, yet, our sense of the gangsta is more informed by the popular representation of gangsta rap than any social reality. Gangsta rappers themselves blur this line between street life and rap's discourse about it.[8] Gangsta rap has been both lauded and critiqued for its cyclical relationship in exhorting a political stance, characterizing it, and creating a culture in which it can exist.[9] Even as they cite real-life gangsta experience, rappers like Ice-T, Niggaz with Attitude, Snoop Doggy Dog, Tupac Shakur, and others personify the romanticization of street violence. They walk a fine line between laying claim to authenticity and glorifying that past life in a fictional present. This rhetorical characterization, it turns out, can have distinctly real consequences outside of that fiction. Both Shakur and [Christopher] Wallace died violently, caught up in the brutal culture promoted by their music. Thus, the gangsta rapper is a unique figure; he has a paradoxical stance as a musician in the recording industry and a speaker from the street. In performing, he inhabits an aestheticized, often materialist imitation of gangsta life. A distinctly promotional—if not causal—commercial relationship exists between gangsta rap and gangsta culture, one that has, according to Anthony Walton, both "galvanized and commercialized the already existing gang culture."[10] This cultural aesthetic has been absorbed by endless popular culture genres, from computer games like "Kingpin: Life of Crime" to haute couture where Parisian and New York design houses have appropriated 1980s gangsta street wear.[11]

Clearly, the larger-than-life personification of these lifestyles intrigues not only audiences, but gangsters of all sorts. In particular, the object of devotion is the narrative's depiction of a code or values by which mafiosi and gangstas live, an ethics that has been romantically expressed in gangster narratives. Gangster filmmaker Martin Scorsese has commented that "the reason for those codes—why people live that way—are very strong lessons. The most important reason is survival."[12] These codes have been so consistently mythologized in late-20th-century popular culture that they have become archetypal, something to which both real and fictional gangsters/gangstas subscribe. Although, as Albert Mobilio writes, the Mafia (and, by extension, gangsta) story provides "a rigged moral measuring stick" against which audience's own morality ranks high, its narrative's internal logic demands the respect of certain values seemingly absent in contemporary American life such as loyalty, honor, and respect.

As Mafia and gangsta representations evolve, they borrow from the codes of their antecedents and often revise and even subvert these codes. Two contemporary gangster/gangsta narratives, David Chase's television series *The Sopranos* and Jim Jarmusch's film *Ghost Dog: The Way of the Samurai* represent significant permutations of gangster mythology. A pragmatic portrayal of the Mafia in mainstream American culture, *The Sopranos* dramatizes the struggle of the middle-class American family *as* mob life. The Soprano clan's vitality lies not in the impermeability of its mob organization (plagued as it is by

RICO prosecution and infighting), so much as in its sense of entitlement to social status and financial success. David Chase's series sets out in broad strokes a complex portrait of a mob fully entrenched in American capitalism. Marginalized only by their transparent class-climbing ambition, the Sopranos have nearly achieved a suburban ability to "pass." Although Tony struggles to reconcile the imaginary world of his mob code—its expectations of agency and power—with his everyday suburban world, he and the other characters express a direct relevance to contemporary American life. As one reviewer has written, unlike Vito Corleone, the Sopranos don't worry about becoming legit—as far as they are concerned, they *are* legit.[13]

What *The Sopranos* is to family melodrama, *Ghost Dog* is to the romance and drama of the gangsta as street warrior. Jarmusch uses the Eastern mythos of the samurai to depict a black man's mode of survival in late-20th-century urban America. Ghost Dog, the gangsta figure, rejects his relation to this world and chooses heroic solitude. Not unlike the gangsta rapper, Ghost Dog's characterization removes the gangsta ethos from the gang concept entirely. Although he is clearly the most effective hip hop–styled assassin on the street, we do not see Ghost Dog as a gangsta in the context of the other gangstas depicted in the film. Instead, he finds brotherhood across the centuries in *Hagakure: The Way of the Samurai*, an ancient warrior code of values. Jarmusch creates a logical hybrid, fusing gangsta rap's aesthetic of individuality and violence with the samurai code found in *Hagakure*—a philosophy that prepares the samurai for battle and death. Juxtaposed against

"*The Sopranos* dramatizes the struggle of the middle-class American family *as* mob life."

an impotent Mafia (the cartoonish and cartoon-obsessed Vargo family) and a ghostly urban world, Ghost Dog radiates the power and serenity inherent to the strict observance of a code. The warrior's skill and art become the logical evolution and refinement of gangsta culture: more than a mode of survival of inner-city life, it is the path to self-fulfillment. Ghost Dog's "Way of the Samurai" becomes the function of a code that is at once alienating and a means of survival for the fin-de-siècle "gangsta." Gangsta culture has evolved to embrace the mysticism of the samurai's individualistic, selfless pursuit of his duty—his life in death.

Both gangsters embrace an idealized code, but while Ghost Dog seemingly inhabits some version of a bygone warrior era, Tony Soprano can only lament his inability to invoke a romanticized gangster past. Tony is paralyzed by his conflicting desires to inhabit an imaginary mob past and to be a successful 21st-century father and businessman. Caught in the web of responsibilities he has to his two families, he struggles with irreconcilable upper-middle-class family values and mob Family values, an ongoing friction expressed in his anxious dysfunctions as a Don. Tony's *Godfather*-esque code is outmoded, yet he insists to an underling that the new rules under his tenure as Don are the same old rules. While the tactics of running the organization's business pursuits have not changed much since the 1930s, the tension Tony experiences in applying those tactics to his suburban middle-class life belies the challenge of moving from the surety of that mob world to the complexity of social politics at the end of the 20th century. For Tony, contemporary suburban life breeds middle-class ennui. The boredom and anxiety of this life are mitigated by the patriarchal culture of violent rule and fear-induced respect he experiences in the mob. Tony's ongoing dilemma is that this sort of power has very limited currency in a culture of conspicuous consumption and progressive social changes.

Whereas *The Sopranos* is a hard look at the anxieties and hypocrisies of suburban American life, *Ghost Dog* functions as a commentary on the constricted cultural condition of the black American male. Jarmusch contrasts the samurai warrior's code with some of his film's alternatives for a young black man in urban America: from drug hustling or refuge in the gangsta fantasy to struggling as an entrepreneur. Of these possibilities, the Ghost Dog character most distinctly evokes and contrasts hip hop's hardcore gangsta figure. The individualism, brutally effective violence, and survival skills celebrated in gangsta rap form the basis for the samurai code Ghost Dog has come to embody.

Both *The Sopranos* and *Ghost Dog* portray the late-20th-century gangster as a figure significantly defined by a family or feudal code. The fantasy in each work is that of an idealized gangster world, one which reflects a social desire for the authoritative outlaw. This desire has been expressed in film and fiction throughout the century, but never so well as in Mario Puzo's *The Godfather*.

"Tony is paralyzed by his conflicting desires to inhabit an imaginary mob past and to be a successful 21st-century father and businessman."

"'In *The Godfather* . . . the Don is its theocratic center.
He is not only boss, but king, judge, and priest.'"

II. Famiglia Nostra

> Gangsters are [not] people who have imposed their will in our community.
> Their values are our values.
>
> Anthropologist Mark Shute, quoted in David Grann,
> "Crimetown U.S.A." (2000)

In his 1969 novel, *The Godfather*, Mario Puzo writes about the world of Vito Corleone and other mafiosi as though it were a parallel universe. The rationale by which Corleone claims the authority to design, build, and protect his own cosmos expresses a morality and values noticeably absent in mid-century American life: absolute allegiance to family and friendship, individual honor, vision, and social duty. Written in a tumultuous period of American social life when old-fashioned values were publicly rejected, the novel offers a compellingly secure moral foundation. At the same time, the Corleone organization presents a peculiar conflation of hardball mob tactics and strict social values in safeguarding a privileged way of life for a limited group of people. In the great tradition of American rebels, self-reliant men who refuse to be unjustly bullied for others' gain, Vito claims: "we are not responsible to . . . the *pezzonovantis* . . . who declare wars they wish us to fight in to protect what they own. Who is to say we should obey the laws they make for their own interest and to our hurt? And who are they then to meddle when we look after our own interests? *Sonna cosa nostra*, these are our own affairs."[14]

The gangster figure has come far since this seminal popular representation. Various permutations of the Italian American Mafia romance have made a powerful mark as a film genre: from the drama of Coppola's sumptuous adaptation of Puzo's trilogy, *GoodFellas*, and *Donnie Brasco* to overt parody such as *My Blue Heaven*, *Analyze This*, and *Bullets over Broadway*. Yet, despite their departures in plot or form, mob films in these subsequent generations lean heavily on Puzo's characterization of the Italian American Mafia in one way or another because his tale drew the mob's mythology so indelibly in our imagination. The myth's power draws not on its social reality (indeed, as late as 1980, the federal government struggled to prove La Cosa Nostra's existence in court), but on a fantasy about the underworld's figures and laws.

Cultural critics have noted the attributes Puzo brought to the gangster genre in this first novel. In his analysis of the significance of the introduction of family as a unifying structure in the wake of the rampant individualism of former gangster narratives, John Cawelti identifies the means by which Corleone's old-world values are expressed and upheld: "The Don and his authority represent an image of an organization that can be seen in opposition to those aspects of contemporary social institution commonly perceived as signs of social failure: the impersonality of the modern corporation on the one hand and the declining authority of the family on the other. . . . There is a tribal closeness about the criminal organization as it is portrayed in *The Godfather*, and the Don is its theocratic center. He is not only boss, but king, judge, and priest. . . . the tribe-family ruled by the Don is a patriarchy with absolutely clear roles and lines of authority."[15]

Cawelti argues that it is also Puzo's focus on the expression and wielding of power that marks this novel as a seminal gangster narrative. Vito Corleone's power is expressed both through his actual family (although Puzo notes the Don's displeasure with the limitations of his fatherly authority over his sons) and especially through his mob Family. It is in the latter that he can shape and maintain a world as his idyll, as his son Michael articulates:

> He doesn't accept the rules of the society we live in because those rules would have condemned him to a life not suitable to a man like himself, a man of extraordinary force and character. What you have to understand is that he considers himself the equal of all those great men like Presidents and Prime Ministers and Supreme Court Justices and Governors of the States. He refuses to live by the rules set up by others, rules which condemn him to a defeated life. But his ultimate aim is to enter that society with a certain power since society doesn't really protect its members who do not have their own individual power. In the meantime, he operates on a code of ethics he considers far superior to the legal structures of society.[16]

Indeed, the opening scene of the novel establishes this point with a petitioner who asks for "justice" when the courts have failed him. This sense of Corleone as a man with the vision and power to live by his code is perhaps the most compelling aspect of *The Godfather* and explains its lasting influence in popular culture's revision and development of gangster stories. The social history of the debate about morality and individual responsibility undergirds *The Godfather*'s timelessness as a popular narrative. Although the gangster film and pulp magazines and novels had designed amorality as free will, for the most part, Puzo's revision reinforces the sense that moral vision and the wherewithal to live according to one's code are acts of individual will. Vito Corleone's morality appeals because of its individual expression of authority and because of its universal application. The code *The Godfather* popularizes has to do with modeling the mob Family on the dynamics of the biological family. Seeming at times a benevolent patriarch, the Don exacts loyalty, friendship, and respect, but wields these as weapons, as well. His code calls for effective brutality even as it masquerades as generosity and good will.

In light of more recent Mafia narratives, Cawelti's analysis of *The Godfather*'s significance in presenting the family as the locus of this code seems particularly astute. If one is neither the author of a gangster code nor heir to its legacy, one is alienated from it entirely. The lesson of Martin Scorsese's film *GoodFellas* is in some ways the tragedy of Henry Hill's seduction by the gangster life from outside of its realm. Because Henry, Jimmy, and Tommy are not "family" in either sense of the word, they do not internalize the family's code. Alienated from the family, they are outsiders distinctly disadvantaged by their less-than-foot-soldier status. They mistakenly attempt to live the gangster life without the authority, demands, and privileges of its

"*GoodFellas* is in some ways the tragedy of Henry Hill's seduction by the gangster life from outside of its realm": Robert De Niro as Jimmy and Ray Liotta as Henry Hill.

value structure. The goodfellas' demise has to do with the absence of clear boundaries, discipline, and purpose codes like Don Corleone's provide.

One of the major functions of Don Corleone's code as Puzo articulates it, is to live life as a critique of mainstream America and its hypocrisies. It is interesting, then, that one of the most popular Mafia stories to come along since *The Godfather*—the television series *The Sopranos*—works directly against this impulse. In many ways, Tony Soprano and his family *are* middle America. They are not the logical extension of Vito Corleone's hoped-for professional-class future for his children. Instead, the Soprano family has made a more or less comfortable assimilation into suburban American life. Although Tony's waste management business and his strip club provide a typical front for his mob existence—one rooted in a working-class reality—the upscale suburban home, expensive vehicles, and his daughter's first-rate college suggest not professional-class concerns but an embracing of particular emblems of status and material success.

Unlike Henry Hill's family, the Sopranos are not merely class invaders; the schism in the moral compass of the show frequently reveals that their values are "our" values. Tony walks a fine line: he is a ruthless killer, but he is also a man concerned about his family and friends. He wants peace with his wife and a decent relationship with his children—even if he's not sure how to go about it. He sees a psychologist because he is anxious about these conflicting realms in his life. Tony's spiritual malaise aligns him with other baby boomers who feel cheated by the unfulfilled promises of their youth. He feels, as do many Americans of that generation, "that the best is gone, that I came in at the end." The irony is that he's talking about both American society in general and the decline of the Mafia. Tony struggles with his peers' lack of adherence to the code that he and other mobsters in his generation were supposed to internalize and carry on. In *The Sopranos*, the mob is besieged as much by inner infidelity as it is by the federal government. Early in the series, the greatest threat to Tony's Family is his own biological family. As the tag line to the show's second series proclaimed: "If one family doesn't get him, the other will." Tony attempts to preside over what seems to be the end of a legacy. One of his closest associates turns witness for the F.B.I., his mother colludes with his uncle to contract a hit on Tony, and his kids click through websites that track the events in Tony's gangland.

In *The Sopranos*, the family values central to Don Corleone's code are revealed to be fraught with tensions. What we see so little of in *The Godfather* is what has popularized the series—the dysfunctions of family and the raw brutality of mob life are the tension and focus of daily life in this world. In *The Godfather*, misogyny and ruthless violence control inner family life. By contrast, in *The Sopranos*, troublesome strong female characters (Tony's mother, wife, sister, and daughter) upset the balance of power and enhance the anxiety Tony experiences moving from the murderous world of his business Family to the unsympathetic family of his suburban home. Tony knows he wields no real authoritarian power. He wonders: "What kind of man am I that my own mother puts a hit on me?" In the many domestic scenes we see Tony's inability to lead as a Don, husband, or father, a characterization far from Puzo's image of a Don. In one scene in which Tony is frustrated by his sister's manipulation of their mother's estate, he reacts by beating the phone with the receiver, pulling it off the wall, and hurling it into the dishwasher his wife, Carmella, is emptying. As their teenage son, A. J., watches this outburst in silent horror, Carmella responds to Tony's lack of control much as she would to an unruly adolescent: "Why don't you grow the fuck up."

While Tony laments the end of a golden era in mob life, he also lacks Vito Corleone's imperialistic nature. His lack of control over both families is rooted in his inability to invoke the same order in each world. An episode called "The Executive Game" demonstrates this as a conflict between Tony's ascendance to the head of the Family and his attempt to keep a civilian friend away from the corruption of this life. When at a high school college recruiting event with Carmella and his daughter, Meadow, Tony's earnest attempt to leave business behind and be a family man for the evening is subverted by a gambling friend who asks who he "likes." Missing David's intent, Tony replies that the guy from Bowdoin makes a lot of sense. His friend says, "No I meant in the game tonight." David explains that now that Tony is mob boss, he would like some of the action. Tony demurs: "You're a nice guy—this game's not for you." It turns out that David is a compulsive gambler and he will soon owe Tony $45,000 for his failure in the executive poker game. Inevitably, Tony has to muscle David to collect the debt and impress upon him that this is business, not personal. The social niceties and similarities between Tony and David as business owners and fathers of high school seniors are stripped away when Tony extorts an SUV purchased for David's son in partial payment and beats David severely to make his point.

In this hands-on manner, Tony wields some of the power of the Family mob boss. But he frequently makes his point with force, not words or negotiation tactics. He may be running the executive game, but he's not able to live the life of an executive. Perhaps this explains his sense that "I got the world by the balls and I can't stop feeling like a fucking loser." Tony's efforts and actions are often undercut by slight failure: he's boss only because Uncle Junior is under house arrest. Meadow angrily rejects his graduation gift, the tainted SUV, because she recognizes it as belonging to her classmate. Because he either will not or cannot employ the Draconian measure he uses in running his organization to establish control of his family at home, Tony's domestic impotence undermines his ability to be a confident mob Family

"Troublesome strong female characters (Tony's mother, wife, and daughter) upset the balance of power."

boss. This is exacerbated by his sense of change in his social capital as a mobster. In an episode in which Tony takes Meadow to visit Northeast colleges, they have a moment of bonding in a conversation in which she confronts him about being in the Mafia. Tony tries to soft-pedal the issue but she is satisfied that her suspicions have been warranted. When she says the kids at school think it's cool, Tony interjects hopefully, "Like *The Godfather*?" Meadow dashes his romanticization of the mob by responding, "No, more like *Casino*, with the seventies clothes and the pills." Her generation's concept of the Mafia has its own updated aesthetic that rejects Puzo's code as conservative and unimportant.

As the series' second and third seasons demonstrate, the nature of Tony's personal conflicts is complex: he resents his anxiety and inability to be ruthlessly in control even as he wants to be a good, warm father to his children. He tells Dr. Melfi, his psychiatrist, that he resents the victimhood she imposes on him by naming it anxiety. Later on, as he seems to take control of the therapy sessions, Tony asserts, "I want . . . to direct my anger at the people who deserve it." Unable to do this, he unloads that anger on mistresses and underlings, instead. Without firm control, he cannot establish his authority. Unlike his idols, Michael and Vito Corleone, Tony lacks the founding sense of an unassailable value structure and clear rules, shared and internalized by both families. Tony's sister follows New Age trends and her own opportunism, Tony's kids adhere to mainstream American consumerism and social values as their moral compass, and his wife defers to the Catholic church. His nephew, Christopher—Tony's best bet for the next generation in the Family— is really a drug addict enacting a mobster role he's learned from the movies, not from his Family. Tony's capos understand and abide by the old ways, but they sit around the Bada Boom strip club and do *Godfather* imitations, impersonating an idyllic past they have never experienced.

Mobilio's comment that viewers and readers enjoy a false sense of moral superiority over the mob stories they enjoy reflects the duality in Tony Soprano's self-conception, as well. His conflicted social identity as a mob boss and an upper-middle-class businessman and father gives Tony a vantage point from which he judges others—both shortsighted, dated mobsters and suburban chumps like David, who will never be players. And, yet, Tony's sense of this schism is frequently painful. He knows his time as a godfather figure is not to be. Well aware of the ways in which that bygone patriarchal machismo has been neutered by social expectations, he laments: "Gary Cooper—now that was an American! He wasn't in touch with his feelings. He just did what he had to do. What they didn't know was that once they got Gary Cooper in touch with his feelings, they wouldn't be able to shut him up."

Early in the series, Tony's primary dilemma is the reconciliation of his psychological malaise with his macho Mafia role as a gang underboss. Dr. Melfi suggests that his depression is the manifestation of his distaste for the violence he must commit as well as the cutthroat politics of his business. Together, Tony and his psychiatrist trace his anxiety attacks to the childhood trauma of witnessing the violence in his father's world. Unlike Ghost Dog,

Tony cannot find solace in a stylized code of violence. As the series continues, Chase makes sure that Tony's violent acts, even his discourse with others, are raw, visceral, and immediate. It has little to do with a philosophy other than the basic tenants of Darwinian survival. Tony's unresolved desire for power, to fulfill his many lusts and to ameliorate his angst while being a good leader, all play against his overblown romantic notions of Mafia life, derived in large part from his obsession with Coppola's *Godfather* epic. Ultimately, Tony is left unfulfilled; he is caught between the discordant roles of his quotidian existence, unable to realize his dream of becoming the Godfather.

III. The Gangsta Way

> The samurai's life was like the cherry blossom's, beautiful and brief. For him, as for the flower, death followed naturally, gloriously.
>
> Hojo Shigetoki, *Ideals of the Samurai* (12th century)

> The gangsta myth, as it rises out of our legends of Western outlaws and immigrant crime syndicates, is a seductive fix for the cognitive dissonance that comes from growing up in an America that promises so much and delivers, to some, so little. It is a peculiarly American way of living with hopelessness.
>
> Anthony Walton, "The Gangsta Myth"

The gangsta's popular identity as a street warrior has, of course, been shaped by the gangster films and legends of the early 20th century. The mythologies of gangster and gangsta life are related: 1980s and 1990s gangsta rappers weaned on 1970s mob films derived much of their posturing and characterization from this vision of gangster life and its antecedents.[17] Not surprisingly, the gangsta's social role has been defined less by the actual gang-banger than by the hyperreal gangsta rapper. Although the life of street gangs made it to the big screen in films such as *Boyz in the Hood, American Me, Menace II Society*, and the propagandistic *New Jack City*, gangsta rap has done more to shape the gangsta's image as street and individual hero. This identity exists in the liminal space between authentic street knowledge and what can be borrowed from other gangster legacies.[18] Gangsta rappers like Ice-T, Snoopy Doggy Dogg, Ice Cube, and Tupac Shakur run a circuit that expresses the contradictions in that character. From the authenticity of lyrics like "Six in the Morning" (Ice-T) or "Fuck Tha Police" (N.W.A.)

Tyrin Turner as Kaydee Lawson in *Menace II Society.*

that presented life on the street as rough, unglamorous, and dangerous to the myriad of songs that send up the life of the gangsta as romantic and powerful, the gangsta rapper revels in the outlaw role. And, yet, even as they lionize the gangsta lifestyle, gangstas rap about the need to "Escape from the Killing Fields" (Ice-T). There is a double awareness

Wesley Snipes (center) as Nino Brown, "a gangsta who watches gangster films."

that the very social conditions that have helped distinguish hardcore hip hop and the gangsta personae have resulted in genocide for a whole generation of inner-city boys and men. The self-awareness of this feedback loop—playing the "playa" and romanticizing the "gangsta" with bravado—makes for a powerful and conflicted genre.

In his fictitious city, Jarmusch's Ghost Dog is a gangsta for the 21st century, a breed apart from both the red track-suited street runners doing business out of doorways and the Vargo family, mafiosi who sit idly in their social club watching cartoons, infantilized by their lack of social authority. Ghost Dog carries a subtle but unmistakable power as he follows the way of the samurai. He is exemplary in his adherence to an ancient code that calls for selflessness and daily meditation on death as the samurai's duty. As a development of the gangsta culture that permeates the entire aesthetic of the film, Ghost Dog's ascetic existence contrasts the materialist excess of gangsta fantasy even as it echoes Ghost Dog's relation to black street culture. Although his gangsta look fits the samurai stylization of his physical movements and he boosts the most luxurious cars to drive to his contracted jobs (listening to haunting hip hop and reggae music at full volume), Ghost Dog is distinct from that culture in important ways. Solitude marks Ghost Dog. He is a lone assassin without a gang or clan; instead, he has only a distant, attenuated relationship with his "master" and the centuries old code of a feudal Japanese samurai culture. Unlike the gangsta with his crew, Ghost Dog has and needs no one. His only friends are Raymond, a Haitian ice-cream vendor who "speaks" to Ghost Dog across a language gap, and Pearline, a young girl with whom he has brief but poignant literary discussions. He maintains a distant relationship with his master, Louie, via carrier pigeon. More like Mary Shelley's monster (whose fate he reads to Pearline), he is alienated, nearly friendless, and has made a unique but potentially problematic accommodation to the conditions postmodern American life offers the urban black man.

The gangsta persona in the film is understood most prevalently in its conflation with hip hop culture and gangsta rap. Hardcore/gangsta culture is portrayed as style, business, and as an empty promise. Although we briefly see the red-clad trio who hustle business on the street, the gangsta image has a more extended portrayal by a group of idle young black men, rapping for each other in the park while they drink from brown-bagged 40-ounce bottles. Would-be gangstas, their music and expressions convey a hopelessness that Ghost Dog observes at a distance. Later, in a comical scene among the mafiosi, an aging gangster enthusiastically conflates the hip hop music of Public Enemy with the reality of gangsta street life, thus confusing lyrics with a lifestyle. Upon hearing Ghost Dog's name, Mr. Vargo and the other wiseguys react in utter confusion, but Sonny explains: "He means like the rappers." He goes on to quote Flavor Flav—making the connection between rappers, gangsta rappers, and street warriors. Seconds later, Sonny calls to Johnny, without irony, to "Go outside and get Sonny the Snake, Joe Rags, and Big Angie," underscoring the similarity between these worlds where men are renamed as gangsters.

"A comical scene among the mafiosi": left to right, Cliff Gorman, Victor Argo, and John Tormey as Louie.

The implication of Sonny's confusion about music and the real world is that Ghost Dog, by virtue of his name and his ethnicity, must be one of hip hop's gangstas. Within the logic of the film and gangsta rap's self-characterization, his blunder makes sense; the simulacra of gangsta rap seems to have taken root for the young men in the park, as well, whose lyrics convey a lifestyle and agency they can only rap about. As far as white, mainstream America might be concerned, gangsta *life* has been subsumed into the rhetoric of gangsta rap, which has itself become hip hop stylization.

"The commonly silent Ghost Dog is a man of action: a powerful and fearsome assassin."

For Jarmusch's fantastical vision in *Ghost Dog*, the style expresses a passivity and distance from action by its very discursive nature. The park bench rappers underscore their social alienation moving as a limited and ghostly Greek chorus through the park, indirectly acknowledging Ghost Dog as an actor in the world to which they are condemned to be spectators.

Conversely, the commonly silent Ghost Dog is a man of action: a powerful and fearsome assassin.[19] Ghost Dog represents the bankruptcy of the gangsta figure socially even as he elevates gangsta rap's individualism to a means of spiritual actualization. Jarmusch creates a mythology for the gangsta by casting him as a samurai. It is a compelling representation, but potentially specious: while it addresses particular issues for urban black males, it offers a problematic resolution. Jarmusch's urban fantasy focuses specifically on the code of samurai life, aggrandizing the purpose of the killer's path as one that prepares him, spiritually, for death. Literally quoting passages from the 18th-century samurai text Tsunetomo Yamamoto's *Hagakure: The Way of the Samurai* in each major narrative development, Jarmusch emphasizes the significance of the samurai's philosophical preparation for death in Ghost Dog's actions. "The way of the samurai is found in death. Every day without fail, one should consider himself as dead. This is the substance of the way of the samurai." Ghost Dog's philosophical borrowing becomes a mysticism for gangstas—a way of romanticizing the inevitable violent end of this way of life. Anthony Walton writes that rappers like Shakur and Smalls "posited that to survive one had to be hard, cold, pragmatic, and willing to do violence at the slightest provocation." He argues that: "This style has become the preferred mode of self-expression among young blacks in the ghettos and elsewhere, as if it has been collectively decided that such a posture is the best way to oppose the frustration, lack of opportunity, and humiliation that plague so many young blacks—a nihilistic embrace of all the forces and circumstances against them."[20]

However, the way of the samurai adds a crucial element of Buddhism: the elimination of a sense of self. The absolute personal discipline, commitment to meditation and worship, and pursuit of truth intrinsic to this philosophy distinguishes it from other representations of gangsta life, particularly the narcissistic self-promotion of gangsta rap.

Perhaps the stronger implication of the samurai code has to do with the questions raised in the film's juxtaposition of scenes depicting Ghost Dog's formative experience (the assault by black men years earlier) and his surrender in the high noon shoot out that forms the film's penultimate scene. How does Jarmusch's focus on an ancient Japanese cultural code address the politics of a contemporary black man's life? How does the romance of the samurai way—the individualism, loyalty, honor, and resolute service to a master—express Ghost Dog's condition? The film makes several gestures towards an answer, from the opening meditation on the inevitability of a samurai's death to the scenes in which Ghost Dog commits revenge for his earlier beating and other wrongs, killing most of the Vargo Family as well as a few rednecks in blackface. Along with the flashbacks to the formative moment of his assault, these scenes suggest that it is Ghost Dog's fate to die at the hands of a white man. Within the teleology of the film, we are to understand that the all-important fact that Samurai Way allows him to pick an honorable relationship with that man, to bring meaning to his own death. Ghost Dog explains the sense of the logic of his code, as well as that of the Mafia code to his friend, Raymond: "Me and him, we're from different ancient tribes. Now we're both almost extinct. Sometimes you got to stick with the ancient ways, the old school ways." Here, the old school way means letting his master, Louie, kill him.

The samurai code expressed in *Hagakure* does establish a sense of order in a chaotic world. And in this, there is a powerful juxtaposition with the decrepit Vargo Family, whose code is falling apart and who fail to make any sense of their world. By contrast, Ghost Dog's code offers clear meaning and closure. As Ghost Dog expresses his consent to Louie in the penultimate shoot-out scene, he is serene, surrendering to his realization in death. And yet, it's hard to miss that the code romanticizes violent death as the logical end to Ghost Dog's life. Alain Silver, in describing the samurai figures popularized in 1970s film, writes that they "are estranged from their environment, violence functions as both an existential affirmation of their being and the most direct method for delineating their oppressed relationship to the environment."[21] Ghost Dog's end suggests this conflict. In the vein of African American history, particularly the intense intra-gang warfare of the 1980s and 1990s, Jarmusch's ending for Ghost Dog as a means of attaining selfhood seems either ironic or problematic.

Jarmusch is clearly aware of this sociohistorical backdrop, signaling it through his diverse intertextuality. The books referenced throughout the film all resonate throughout the plot, but perhaps none as powerfully as

W. E. B. Du Bois' *The Souls of Black Folk.* Du Bois' reflections on the doubled condition of black American life indicate a condition that persists nearly a century later:

> The Negro is ... born with a veil, and gifted with second-sight in this American world—a world which yields him no true self-consciousness, but only lets him see himself through the revelation of the other world. It is a peculiar sensation, this double-consciousness, this sense of always looking at one's self through the eyes of others, of measuring one's soul by the tape of a world that looks on in amused contempt and pity. One ever feels his twoness—an American, a Negro; two souls, two thoughts, two unreconciled strivings; two warring ideals in one dark body, whose dogged strength alone keeps it from being torn asunder.[22]

Ghost Dog apparently avoids this fate by stepping out of black American culture and into a different cultural reality, that of feudal Japan. *Hagakure* addresses the danger of doubleness: "It is bad when one thing becomes two. One should not look for anything else in the Way of the Samurai. It is the same for anything that is called a Way. Therefore, it is inconsistent to hear something of the Way of Confucius or the Way of the Buddha, and say that this is the Way of the Samurai. If

"Ghost Dog ... [steps] out of black American culture and into a different cultural reality, that of feudal Japan": facing off against Gangsta and Red (Gano Grills).

one understands things in this manner, he should be able to hear about all Ways and be more and more in accord with his own."[23]

As Yamamoto understands it, this danger is not so much an internalized split as it is a confusion of one philosophy with another. The film suggests that the conflicts inherent to Ghost Dog's blackness are resolved within the logic of his samurai philosophy: he needs only to reject what is not the way of the samurai. Ghost Dog revises his sense of himself within the samurai mythology. Or, rather, he begins to efface his sense of a self-in-the-world via his philosophical path. This adopted identity serves him well when he revisits moments parallel to the assault that Jarmusch presents as his formative experience. As "a revengeful ghost," Ghost Dog acts decisively and without the burden of double consciousness.

Within this context, the film raises questions about ethnicity and mutual social alienation. One might read Ghost Dog's fate as violent death—his only

"Ghost Dog revises his sense of himself within the Samurai mythology": practicing swordsmanship on an inner-city rooftop.

choice being which path he takes to that end. Or, one might understand the samurai code (and, to a limited extent, the other codes of violence) to provide a way of removing oneself from the painful conditions of urban life. Jarmusch quotes *Hagakure*: "It is a good viewpoint to see the world as a dream. When you have a nightmare, wake yourself up and say it was only a dream. It is said that the world we live in is not a bit different from this." The film itself is dreamlike, vague, slowed down, and spare in its landscape. Is this adaptation of Zen Buddhism an escapism for Ghost Dog? Compare him with the young men rapping in the park; they acknowledge him as a powerful and dangerous man. Perhaps he has, as an assassin, simply escaped the sense of limitation that he might otherwise find in mainstream America. Now, when confronted by armed white men (bear hunters and mafiosi), he is ready and quick with his weapon.

Although, as Hagakure instructs, "the end is important in all things," it is crucial that Jarmusch doesn't effect neat closure with Ghost Dog's inevitable end. His death doesn't resolve the questions Jarmusch raises about a black man's code of survival and social conditions in the late 20th century. Others inherit this world. Significantly, Ghost Dog has anointed not the park rappers but two immigrants of the African diaspora as his heirs. Pearline and Raymond function as the next generation of black "Americans" (as Jamaican and Haitian immigrants) learning to survive in this country. As extensions of Ghost Dog, they inherit the challenges of urban life as black people in the 21st century. Ghost Dog bequeaths to each a distinct legacy. Pearline inherits Ghost Dog's doctrine, *Hagakure*, which unlike *The Souls of Black Folk* will offer not just a lifting of the veil of racism (she seems savvy enough already) but will be a proactive means of survival on the streets of her world. One doubts that Pearline will end up like the few lone women we see haunting *Ghost Dog*'s landscape (in fact, the film's web site lists her as a warrior).

Entrepreneurial Raymond, however, inherits the suit in which Ghost Dog "passes" as a black business-man. Although language is his barrier, Raymond understands enough of his adopted country to know what imperils him. The question of whether the costume (the suit) will keep him from getting deported is answered, in part, by Ghost Dog's other gift: the weapons and tools of his trade. As the film closes on Pearline, engrossed in reading *Rashoman*, we can assume that Ghost Dog's adopted code will continue to mutate to fit the complexities of her world.

IV. Fin-de-Siècle Gangsters

> The spirit of an age is something to which one cannot return. . . . [It] gradu-
> ally dissipates due to the world's coming to an end.
>
>   Tsunetomo Yamamoto, *Hagakure* (18th century)

The Sopranos and *Ghost Dog* taken as fin-de-siècle gangster stories depict a logical evolution of their respective narrative expectations and contemporary social conditions. Each narrative foregrounds the importance of a code, but whereas Ghost Dog becomes and succumbs to the warrior role of his code, Tony struggles to bridge the gap between the power of the *Godfather* in a fictional mobster past and his baby-boomer middle-age anxieties. Both contemporary gangster/gangsta narratives reflect social order: the family and class anxieties central to Italian American culture contrasted with the social alienation and disenfranchisement in African American culture. Ghost Dog's isolation and selflessness and Tony's angst are parallel, although inverted. In Tony, the all-powerful "Don" becomes a frustrated baby boomer whose anxiety attacks and unruly family undermine his ability to run the Family organization. The mobster's efficacy and supremacy are gone, along with the Golden Era and social conditions which promoted his imaginary reign.[24] Ghost Dog understands himself as the function of his samurai role. His serenity and single-mindedness proclaim his removal from his everyday world. In the figure of Ghost Dog, the gangsta figure evolves away from trappings of its contemporary characterization, specifically rejecting its victimhood and bravado by giving up his role in society altogether. Rather than what Walton called "a nihilistic embrace of the forces and circumstances against him," Ghost Dog surrenders to these forces in the samurai sense of the term: he becomes *selfless.* This serves as a painfully ironic commentary on the condition of young black men in the United States, today.

These revised gangster narratives register a deep resignation—not so much about the mob/gang as a means of agency, but, rather, hopelessness about individual agency in late-20th-century America. It's not the gangster life, per se, that thwarts Ghost Dog or Tony Soprano. In fact, both experience a certain power and control in their roles as killers. It's in their civilian lives that the codes fail to offer refuge. Accordingly, Ghost Dog all but removes himself from a personal life and Tony struggles with the deep anxiety it causes him. At the close of the gangster's century, both would-be warriors find themselves to be increasingly irrelevant, from "ancient tribes" that are nearly extinct.

Notes

1. Quoted in "Hotheads, Turncoats Putting Philly Mob on Last Broken Legs."
2. The year-long investigation turned up a series of players who were associated with the mob through stock trading: "mobbed up broker-dealers, top-shelf

investment advisers, unscrupulous issuers, unethical lawyers and accountants, and microcap manipulators." "Mafia Spins Stock Market Scam on Web," 10.

3. In his article on Youngstown, Ohio, Grann explores what would be an almost quaint relationship with the mob were it not for the dire economic reality galvanizing this strange alliance: "the community has come to rely on Mobsters who play the same role in civic life that the police and political establishment do in other cities," 31. The flight of job-creating businesses has meant that the community relies on the mob for its economic infrastructure, as well.

4. Beisner, 15. The exportation of gangsta culture as a mode of social interaction and identification reaches beyond even these outposts to surpass national boundaries. Young El Salvadoran refugees and the children of refugees who, in the 1980s, sought refuge from right-wing violence in their home country, learned gang culture and rites in the United States and have become the source of a massive gang culture now that they have been deported. Wallace, 50.

5. David Ruth discusses Capone's desire and efforts to be part of American public life. "Though Al Capone lived in the realm of flesh and blood, for most Americans he existed only as a cultural invention. Foremost among the inventors was Capone himself. By all accounts, he was a man who welcomed the limelight and worked constantly to manipulate public perceptions. This was the concern that lay behind his famous formulation of contradictory labels form him and his most notorious activity—racketeer or businessman, bootlegging or hospitality," 119. Despite his role in inspiring gangster films (*Little Caesar* and *Scarface*), Capone was a social conservative concerned that "these gang movies are making a lot of kids want to be tough guys." Quoted in Mobilio, 73.

6. *Harper's* published part of a transcript from a 1999 trial of the deCavalcante crime family in which New Jersey mafiosi Anthony Totondo, Joseph Sclafani, etc. discuss whether they are inspiration for characters in *The Sopranos*. Rotondo insists that their names are mentioned and that "every show you watch more and more you pick up somebody. Every show." FBI transcript, 26. At least one character, Pussy Bompensiero, is named for an assassinated mobster: Anthony "Little Pussy" Russo.

7. P. 75. Mobilio also notes an inverse encounter of film and fiction when Mickey Rourke and Anthony Quinn attended the trial of John Gotti to research upcoming roles, 73.

8. Elsewhere, I have discussed this dynamic in Ice-T's career. See Walker Fields, 14–16.

9. The story of Puffy Combs and his involvement with Wallace and Shakur illuminates the double-edge of cultivating the gangsta image: Bad Boy (Combs' label) was at war with Shakur's label (Death Row Records) because Shakur thought Combs' orchestrated an assault on him. One theory about the Shakur and Wallace killings is that both came out of their labels' antagonism and their labels' association with Los Angeles gangs. Combs, who faced two felony gun-possession charges, backpedaled, declaiming the gangsta image he carefully crafted. Stevens writes: "In short, Combs must admit that his player persona is nothing more than a role, the fantasy of a little boy from the burbs." Stevens, 169.

On the other end of the spectrum, "O. G." (Original Gangsta) Ice-T claims that the persona is a put-on: "Sometimes I want to become characters, and I can play a drug dealer or drug addict. I can become any person. You know, like in 'Cop Killer' I became a psychopath that went on a rampage. That's not me—I'm not a psychopath that went on a rampage. I make records . . . I drink milk, I play video games, I bounce my little baby on my knee. I'm a normal person. . . . I mean I got a tough side to me but I don't have to walk around and flaunt it. I don't need to do that." Gross, interview.

10. Anthony Walton writes: "Gangsta rap was first created by inner-city blacks for the consumption of young inner city males and—soon after—for the consumption of the mass white suburban audience. In this way, gangsta rap served as a kind of minstrel show for the suburban audience while at the same time giving birth in the inner cities to a culture . . . that is progressively more damaging to the community, and that has turned lethal"; 22. The sales figures following Notorious B.I.G.'s death demonstrate the commercial power of the gangsta lifestyle in popular culture. Christopher Wallace's untimely end became a promotional force in the gangsta mythology of his label, Bad Boy. Puffy Combs' tribute single, "I'll Be Missing You" "dominated the airwaves by mid-May" and Smalls' posthumous *Life After Death* (five million copies sold) went double-platinum. Daly, 166.

11. See Kingpin at http://www.urbangangsta.com. Versace and Chanel have been among those in the fashion industry to lift gangsta style from the street to the runway. Hethorn, 70.

12. Scorsese was quoted in *Rolling Stone* Magazine. George, 34.

13. Millman, 2.

14. Puzo, 291. Contradictions in the Mob's morality are played out in other ways in the Don's strict interdiction of drugs as business even as the novel relies on steamy sex scenes.

15. Cawelti, 66.

16. Puzo, 362–63.

17. Some of the most directly identifiable links—the romanticized emblems of gangland culture that are part of Mafia culture (real and fictional)—originate in the 1930s crime culture and are themselves a mix of social reality and Hollywood fetishization of the gangster. Tupac Shakur, Ice-T, and other gangsta rappers pose with automatic weapons, recalling the tommy guns of Hollywood's gangster films. Hollywood gangstas watch gangster films (Nino Brown watching the 1990s remake of *Scarface* in *New Jack City*). And in *Ghost Dog*, mobsters rap (Sonny Valerio ironically misconstrues rap as gangsta rap and gangsta as samurai when explaining the cultural origin of Ghost Dog's name to his mob boss).

18. This claim to street knowledge has become a hip hop hallmark that N.W.A. made infamous with its opening line on *Straight Outta Compton's* title track: "You are now about to witness the strength of street knowledge."

19. Andrew Ross notes that the edge has been taken off the characterization of the gangsta, a factor that informs all of Jarmusch's gangsta characterizations. "The profile of today's gangsta rapper, scaled down last season to the ultimate, low metabolism vibe of Dr. Dre and Snoop Doggy Dog, evokes an affectless masculinity, conceived under siege, and resonating with a long history of presenting a neutral face as a mask of inscrutability to the white gaze." Ross, 161.

20. Walton, 119.

21. Silver, 38.

22. Du Bois, 3.

23. Yamamoto, 43.

24. In a twist on the theme, Jon Favreau's 2001 mob film, Made, being "made" as a member of the Mafia is rejected in favor of a quiet if unorthodox domestic lifestyle. After a harrowing three-day trial period, Bobby and Ricky choose to raise Bobby's ex-girlfriend's daughter instead of pursuing an invitation to join Max's mob organization. The final scene, in which Ricky and Bobby argue about Chloe's schooling in a Chuck-E-Cheese-esque birthday party scenario, underscores the relief of abandoning the perilous lifestyle of a made man for middle-class fatherhood.

Works Cited

Beisner, Vince. "Boyz on the Rez." *New Republic*, July 10 & 17, 2000, 15–16.

Cawelti, John G. "The Mythology of Crime and Its Formulaic Embodiments." In *Adventure, Mystery, and Romance: Formula Stories as Art and Popular Culture.* Chicago: University of Chicago Press, 1976. 51–79.

Daly, Steven. "The Player King." *Vanity Fair*, August 2000, 130–37, 163–69.

De Stefano, George. "Ungood Fellas." *Nation.* February 7, 2000, 31–33.

Du Bois, W. E. B. *The Souls of Black Folk.* Chicago: A. C. McClurg, 1903.

Favreau, Jon, dir. *Made.* Artisan Entertainment, 2001.

Federal Bureau of Investigation Transcript: "La Drama Nostra." *Harper's*, March 2000, 24–26.

George, Nelson. *Hip Hop America.* New York: Penguin, 1998.

Grann, David. "Crimetown U.S.A.: The City that Fell in Love with the Mob." *New Republic*, July 10 & 17, 2000, 23–31.

Gross, Teri. Interview with Ice-T. *Fresh Air.* 1994.

Hethorn, Janet. "Smooth Criminals." *Icon Magazine*, February 1999, 66–70.

"Hotheads, Turncoats Putting Philly Mob on Last Broken Legs." *Palm Beach Post*, September 19, 1999, 10A.

"Mafia Spins Stock Market Scam on Web." *Sunday Times*, London, June 18, 2000, 10.

Millman, Joyce. "Married . . . With Hit Men." http://www.salon.com/ent/tv/mill/1999/01/11mill.html, accessed August 18, 2006.

Mobilio, Albert. "Made Men of Letters: Our Thing about the Cosa Nostra." *Harper's*, October 1977, 68–78.

Niggaz with Attitude. *Straight Outta Compton.* Hollywood, CA: Priority Records, 1988.

Olmos, Edward James, dir. *Lives in Hazard.* Los Angeles: Olmos Productions, 1993.

Puzo, Mario. *The Godfather.* New York: Putnam, 1969.

Ross, Andrew. "The Gangsta and the Diva." In *Black Male: Representations of Masculinity in Contemporary American Art*, ed. Thelma Golden. New York: Whitney Museum of Art, 1995. 159–66.

Ruth, David E. *Inventing the Public Enemy: The Gangster in American Culture, 1918–1934*. Chicago: University of Chicago Press, 1996.

Scorsese, Martin, dir. *GoodFellas*. Warner Bros., 1990.

Sestier, Valerie S. http://www.northnet.org/americankangdukwon/samurai.html.

Silver, Alain. *The Samurai Film*. Woodstock, N.Y.: Overlook Press, 1977.

Temple, Johnny. "Hip Hop Politics on Campus." *Nation*, May 15, 2000, Vol. 270, No. 19: 16.

Walker Fields, Ingrid. "Entertaining Knowledge: (Popular) Cultural Literacy in the United States." *Oregon Humanities Magazine* (Fall 1999): 12–16.

Wallace, Scott. "You Must Go Home Again: Deported L.A. Gangbangers Take Over El Salvador." *Harper's*, August 2000, Vol. 301, No. 1803: 47–56.

Walton, Anthony. "The Gangsta Myth: What Exactly Has the Outlaw Posture Wrought?" *Oxford American* 21–22: 118–21.

Yamamoto, Tsunetomo. *Hagakure*. Trans. William Scott Wilson. Tokyo & New York: Kodan-Sha International, 1944.

Notes on Contributors

John Baxter is the author of more than forty published books including numerous novels and a number of screenplays both for features (*The Time Guardians*) and documentary films (*After Proust, No Roses for Michael*). His books on the cinema include biographies of Federico Fellini, Luis Buñuel, Stanley Kubrick, Steven Spielberg, George Lucas, Woody Allen, and most recently Robert De Niro. He has worked extensively as an arts journalist and currently lives in Paris.

Sheri Chinen Biesen is a film historian and assistant professor of radio, television, and film studies at Rowan University and author of *Blackout: World War II and the Origins of Film Noir* (Johns Hopkins University Press, 2005). Professor Biesen is the recipient of numerous research honors and has taught cinema history at the University of Texas at Austin, University of California, University of Southern California School of Cinema-Television, and University of Leicester in England. She has contributed to *Film Noir Reader 4, Film and History, Literature/Film Quarterly, Popular Culture Review, Quarterly Review of Film and Video, The Historian, Television,* and *Television History* and edited the *Velvet Light Trap.*

Ronald Bogue is the author of *Deleuze and Guattari* (1989), *Deleuze on Cinema* (2003), *Deleuze on Literature* (2003), *Deleuze on Music, Painting, and the Arts* (2003), and *Deleuze's Wake: Tributes and Tributaries* (2004). He is the editor of *Mimesis, Semiosis and Power* (1991) and co-editor of *The Play of the Self* (1994) and *Violence and Mediation in Contemporary Culture* (1996). He is Distinguished Research Professor and Josiah Meigs Distinguished Teaching Professor in the Comparative Literature Department at the University of Georgia.

Carlos Clarens wrote for *Sight and Sound, Cahiers du cinéma,* and the *Village Voice.* He assisted such directors as Agnes Varda, Robert Bresson, and Francis Ford Coppola and appeared as a actor in *Lion's Love, Goldflocken,* and *The Sorcerer's Apprentice.* Besides *Crime Movies,* he wrote the oft-revised *An Illustrated History of the Horror [and Science Fiction] Film* (1967) and a study of George Cukor. He also taught courses on crime films in New York and was co-owner of Phototeque, a stills service.

Joaquín da Silva lives in Japan. He created and maintains the online site EIGA, which surveys Japanese cinema.

Catherine Don Diego is currently a member of the Ocean County College English Department and formerly taught interdisciplinary arts and humanities at Mohawk Valley Community College. She received her master's degree from Michigan State University and subsequently taught for two years at Central Michigan University. Her most recent publication continues in the crime genre with "Prime-Time Ancient *Controversia* on *Law & Order*," a chapter in *Crime Time-Prime Time-Global Time* (2004). She is completing an essay featuring the works of Giovanni Verga and Leonardo Sciascia on the teaching of modern Sicilian short fiction and developing a course on pre-Code gangster films.

Glenn Erickson is an Emmy-nominated film editor. He also writes articles on films and reviews DVDs under the web alias DVD Savant, and has published a collection, *DVD Savant: A Review Resource Book*. He has contributed to several DVD audio commentaries, and the *Film Noir Reader*s *1* and *4*.

Geoff Fordham is a public policy adviser in the field of urban regeneration and neighborhood renewal. He is also a visiting professor in the faculty of continuing education and community development at Birkbeck College, University of London. His film interests focus on crime in the movies and on the gangster and film noir traditions in particular.

Reynold Humphries is professor of film studies at the University of Lille 3 and author of *Fritz Lang: Genre and Representation in his American Films*, *The American Horror Film: An Introduction*, and *The Hollywood Horror Film, 1931–1941: Madness in a Social Landscape*. He has contributed to *Film Noir Reader 4*, *Docufictions*, and *Monstrous Adaptations*. Articles on film noir, crime, and the Hollywood witch hunts, as well as aspects of the horror film, have appeared in France, America, and the online journal *Kinoeye*, and he is currently working on a book provisionally entitled *Hollywood's Blacklists: Politics and Culture in Context*.

Stuart M. Kaminsky founded and formerly taught at Northwestern University's creative writing program, and was director of Florida State University's Conservatory of Film and Television. His fiction writing has garnered six nominations and one Edgar Award from the Mystery Writers of America. Several novels have been adapted for television and motion pictures, and he has written screenplays and teleplays. In addition to *American Film Genres*, his other books on film include *Basic Filmmaking* (1981); *Writing for Television* (1988); two biographies: *Coop: The Life and Legend of Gary Cooper* (1979) and *Clint Eastwood* (1974); and two director studies: *Don Siegel* (1974) and *John Huston, Maker of Magic* (1978).

Dominique Mainon is a screenwriter and co-author of *The Modern Amazons: Warrior Women on Film* and the forthcoming *Cinema of Obsession: Erotic Fixation and Love Gone Wrong on Film*. She currently lives in Laguna Beach, California. For more information and latest projects, please visit http://www.dominique-mainon.com.

Frank Manchel is Emeritus Professor of English at the University of Vermont, where he was responsible for teaching film history and criticism. The former associate dean of the College of Arts and Sciences, Dr. Manchel was a member of the George F. Peabody Awards Committee for seven years, two of which he served as chair. He has written fifteen books, and numerous articles, including his four-volume work *Film Study: An Analytical Bibliography*.

Colin McArthur, formerly Head of the British Film Institute's Distribution Division, is now a freelance teacher, writer, and graphic artist. He has written extensively on Hollywood cinema, British television, and Scottish culture. His most recent book is *Brigadoon, Braveheart and the Scots: Distortions of Scotland in Hollywood Cinema.*

Andrew Sarris currently writes for the *New York Observer.* Previously he was film reviewer for the *Village Voice* and contributed extensively to *Film Culture,* from which writings his books *The American Cinema: Directors and Directions, 1929–1968* and *Confessions of a Cultist: On the Cinema 1955–1969* were compiled. His other books include the MOMA monograph *The Films of Josef von Sternberg* (1966), *Interviews with Film Directors* (1969), *Primal Screen* (1973), *The John Ford Movie Mystery* (1976), *Politics and Cinema* (1978), and *"You Ain't Heard Nothin' Yet": The American Talking Film, History and Memory, 1927–1949* (2000). He has appeared in numerous documentaries on films and filmmakers.

Paul Schrader wrote *Transcendental Style in Film: Ozu, Bresson, Dreyer* (1972), was the editor of *Cinema* (U.S.), and published reviews and articles in the *Los Angeles Free Press, Film Quarterly,* and *Film Comment.* Since beginning a career as a screenwriter (*Taxi Driver, The Yakuza, Rolling Thunder, Raging Bull*) and going on to direct numerous feature films such as *Blue Collar, Hard Core, American Gigolo, Mishima, Light Sleeper, Affliction,* and the film noir parody *Witch Hunt,* he has been actively involved in such film industry issues as artists' rights and film preservation. His comments on film noir anchored that segment of the PBS series on *American Cinema* and many of his critical writings were reprinted in *Schrader on Schrader* (1990).

Alain Silver co-wrote and co-edited the books listed in the front. His articles have appeared in *Film Comment, Movie, Literature/Film Quarterly, Wide Angle,* the *DGA Quarterly,* the *Los Angeles Times,* the anthology *The Philosophy of Film Noir* (2005), and the online magazines *Images* and *Senses of Cinema.* He co-scripted the features *Kiss Daddy Goodbye* and *Time at the Top* and adapted Dostoevsky's *White Nights* (which he also directed). In addition to independent movies, he has produced soundtrack albums for the Bay Cities and Citadel labels and appeared in commentaries such as those in the Warner Bros. Gangster Collection.

James Ursini is author and editor of the completed volumes listed in the front. He has also contributed articles to various film magazines. He has done DVD commentary, frequently with Alain Silver, on a dozen features including *Out of the Past, The Dark Corner, Nightmare Alley, Lady in the Lake, Kiss of Death,* and *Crossfire.* He has done oral histories and research for the American

Film Institute and has also been associate producer and producer on feature films and documentaries for various school districts and public broadcasting. He has lectured on filmmaking at UCLA and at other colleges in the Los Angeles area where he continues to work as an educator.

Constantine Verevis teaches in the School of English, Communications and Performance Studies at Monash University, Melbourne. He has published in various film books and periodicals such as *Bright Lights Film Journal*, *Film Criticism*, *Framework*, and *Senses of Cinema* and is the author of *Film Remakes* (Edinburgh University Press, 2005).

Ingrid Walker writes about American popular culture, focusing on conspiracy theory, white supremacy, the drug war, and the gangster figure. Her essays have appeared in *The Encyclopedia of American Conspiracy Theories* and *Conspiracy Nation*. A former associate professor of English, she is now assistant director of accreditation at the Higher Learning Commission in Chicago.

Robert Warshow was an essayist on popular culture and film critic for *Commentary* (which he also edited), the *Nation*, and *Partisan Review*. Several years after his death at age 37, nineteen of his essays on America and its art forms and politics were assembled into the book *The Immediate Experience*.

Tricia Welsch teaches at Bowdoin College, where she is chair of the film studies department. Her work has appeared in numerous journals, including *Cinema Journal*, *Film Quarterly*, *The Journal of Popular Film and Television*, *Griffithiana*, and *Film Criticism*, on topics from the use of sound in the films of Jean Renoir and Fritz Lang to Upton Sinclair's collaboration with William Fox, founder of Fox Films. She is currently writing a biography of Gloria Swanson, who is more than ready for her close-up.

Tony Williams is the co-author of *Italian Western: Opera of Violence* (1975) and co-editor of *Vietnam War Films* (1994) and *Jack London's The Sea Wolf: A Screenplay by Robert Rossen* (1998). He is the author of *Jack London: The Movies* (1992); *Hearths of Darkness: The Family in the American Horror Film* (1996); *Larry Cohen: Radical Allegories of an American Filmmaker* (1997); and the forthcoming *Structures of Desire: British Cinema 1949–1955*. His articles have appeared in *Cinema Journal*, *CineAction*, *Wide Angle*, *Jump Cut*, *Asian Cinema*, *Creative Filmmaking*, and several *Film Noir Readers*. He is an associate professor and area head of film studies in the Department of English, Southern Illinois University at Carbondale.

Robin Wood has written numerous books on motion pictures including seminal English-language auteur studies of Alfred Hitchcock, Howard Hawks, Ingmar Bergman, Arthur Penn, and Claude Chabrol. His other books include *Personal Views*, *Sexual Politics and Narrative Film: Hollywood and Beyond*, and *Hollywood from Vietnam to Reagan*. He is the editor with Richard Lippe of *The American Nightmare: Essays on the Horror Film*. He is a former professor of film studies at Queen's College and York University, contributed extensively to *Film Comment*, and remains a founding member of the collective which edits the film journal *CineAction!*